AFTER CRUCIFIXION

AFTER CRUCIFIXION

The Promise of Theology

CRAIG KEEN

CASCADE *Books* • Eugene, Oregon

AFTER CRUCIFIXION
The Promise of Theology

Copyright © 2013 Craig Keen. All rights reserved. Except for brief quotations in critical publications or reviews, no part of this book may be reproduced in any manner without prior written permission from the publisher. Write: Permissions, Wipf and Stock Publishers, 199 W. 8th Ave., Suite 3, Eugene, OR 97401.

Cascade Books
An Imprint of Wipf and Stock Publishers
199 W. 8th Ave., Suite 3
Eugene, OR 97401

www.wipfandstock.com

ISBN 13: 978-1-61097-065-5

Cataloguing-in-Publication data:

Keen, Craig.

    After crucifixion : the promise of theology / Craig Keen.

    xx + 260 pp. ; 23 cm. Includes bibliographical references and index.

    ISBN 13: 978-1-61097-065-5

    1. Jesus Christ—Crucifixion. 2. Theology of the cross. 3. Philosophical theology. I. Title.

BT450 .K43 2013

Manufactured in the U.S.A.

Cover image courtesy of the Franklin D. Roosevelt Presidential Library and Museum, Hyde Park, New York

All Scripture quotations, unless noted otherwise, are from the New Revised Standard Version Bible, copyright 1989. Division of Christian Education of the National Council of the Churches of Christ in the United States of America. Used by permission. All rights reserved.

To my father* and mother:

Jim Keen, who taught me that life is hard and

Corine Keen, who taught me to laugh

---

* My father died on August 16, 2013, as the electronic manuscript of this book lay, typeset, in my email inbox awaiting proofreading. He was ninety-four and died with the same quiet strength with which he'd lived. I miss him. I wish he'd seen this page.

Contents

Preface ix
Acknowledgments xix
Permissions xx

Prelude 1

1. The Root from Which They Spring: Introductions 21

   Interlude 34

2. Where Memory and Hope Converge: Writing the Cross 37

   Interlude 66

3. Working Out the Body and Blood of Christ on the Eighth Day of Creation: Toward a Martyr-Ecclesiology 74

   Interlude 110

4. Thinking the Wounds of the Lamb: To Excess 121

   Interlude 159

5. "The Cup that I Drink You Will Drink; and with the Baptism with Which I Am Baptized, You Will Be Baptized": The Promise Jesus Gives the Gifted, as They Dream of Glory 163

   Interlude 196

6. Teaching the Dead to Praise God: Abiding the Face of Devastation 208

   Postlude 232

   Bibliography 235
   Index 251

Preface

It is truly right and just, our duty and our salvation, always and everywhere to give you thanks, Lord, Holy Father, almighty and eternal God, through Christ our Lord. For the days of his saving Passion and glorious Resurrection are approaching, by which the pride of the ancient foe is vanquished and the mystery of our redemption is celebrated. Through him the host of Angels adores your majesty and rejoices in your presence forever. May our voices, we pray, join with theirs in one chorus of exultant praise, as we acclaim: Holy, holy, holy Lord, God of power and might, heaven and earth are full of your glory. Hosanna in the highest. Blessed is He who comes in the name of the Lord. Hosanna in the highest.

NOT ONLY A WRITER'S pride or her humility may lead her to settle on the conviction that the book she has written is extraordinary. Pride and humility are, of course, complicated phenomena that not uncommonly rub off on the work in which they are complicit. Both do sometimes come in handy in the course of carrying out prolonged and difficult tasks, like writing books. Still, neither is always and everywhere helpful even in this particular line of work, perhaps especially because they contend so bitterly with each other in both happy and unhappy memories and hopes. I am pretty sure that, sometimes consecutively and sometimes concurrently, I am and have been both mortally humble and proud. I confess that, because I do find myself against myself comparing myself to others and find that my level of energy is affected by the way they and I appear to measure up. Consequently, in the writing of this book, I have felt alternately good and bad about a word choice, the turn of a phrase, and the way phrases tumble together to make paragraphs and sections and chapters and then a whole book. Still, I have not set out to write a book that has measured up and even when I have been worried about whether or not it has, I have found that I have written otherwise. In other words, though quite a large number of subjects are discussed

Preface

here—from immigration to education, from the history of metaphysics to the Gospel of Mark, from urban planning to martyrdom, from brain physiology to ecclesiology, from wounded bodies to the forgiveness of sins, from hard work to hard, hard death, from time to resurrection, from theological method to the doctrine of the Trinity, and too much more—this is not a book about certain ideas or practices. This is not actually a book *about* anything (*über etwas*, Bultmann might have said). It is rather a book *of* something (*von etwas*).[1] What I have written, more particularly, is a prayer, a prayer I have prayed precisely in the writing. This is a book that prays and prays in particular that its "speaking voice" would "also be [its] hearing ear."[2] It prays performatively, as an act, as a movement that perhaps without presumption might be called a dance, a perhaps perichoretic one, if the epiclesis of God's good pleasure happens to be answered. It is a dance, though, that calls for a partner. Which means that this is that awkward moment when I stand before you, having crossed the wide well-waxed hardwood floor, and ask with downcast eyes if you would dance with me.

An extraordinary book, however, is not necessarily a good book. I would not claim that this is a good book—or its opposite, for that matter. I don't know how I would even *begin* to make either judgment. It is, it seems to me, simply different, different from ordinary books, and especially those shelved near it in the theology section of university or seminary libraries. Indeed, when asked about what I've been writing, for some time now I have typically reached for a harsher adjective: "I am writing a *weird* introduction to theology," I have said. Now, as anyone who has been to a junior high school dance knows, the surest way to strike out after that long walk across the dance floor from your side to hers is to be labeled by her and especially by her friends as weird. Still, this book, it seems to me, is just that, in part because it does not secure a defensible position, i.e., it will not stand still long enough to stake a claim.[3] Of course, neither does a child's guilty confession or the barely audible moans haunting the aftermath of battle or an exhausted smile in a labor and delivery unit—or a charging bull, for that matter.

On the other extreme, the phrase "introduction to theology" leaves the exact opposite impression. To encounter someone or something weird may at least at times be interesting. Of the items on the long list of academe's

---

1. Bultmann, "Welchen Sinn hat es, von Gott zu reden?"
2. Barth, "Answer to Professor Harnack's Open Letter," 178.
3. Cf. *Oxford English Dictionary*, s.v. "weird, *n.*," "Etymology."

Preface

most perfunctory undertakings, "introduction to theology" has one of the lowest sexiness quotients. Simply utter the phrase and you can feel the room's net hormone level drop. And yet, I would still say, right out in public, that this book is an introduction, i.e., if it is by way of introduction that one person might invite another to dance. *After Crucifixion* is an invitation to you, an invitation to dance, to think, to pray, to hear an extraordinary, weird, uncanny beat and move to it—with me.[4]

At the same time, this is a rigorous text. It is certainly written with hope. It is written toward thanksgiving. And I hope that there will be moments when reading it will in fact have been a prayer of delightful abandon. Still, this book is work. Laboring through it has entailed for me and will likely entail for you, if you take it up, both determination and pain. Life is delightful and it is hard. My task in writing this book has been to be true to life and to those who live it.

This is a book for a wide spectrum of audiences, all of whom I imagine (however naïvely) as *ready* for good work. I have thought as I have written, actually, of my past and present and future students, among whom are undergraduate students, graduate students in professional programs, graduate students in more strictly academic programs, pastors, laborers, university and seminary professors, social workers, artists, drug traffickers, corporate professionals, military professionals, NGO professionals, psychologists, writers, community organizers, musicians, small business owners and employees, pre- and elementary and middle and junior high and senior high school teachers, chaplains, blue-collar workers, medical doctors and nurses and technicians, politicians, farmers, corporation executives, as well as, of course, those unmarked by formal titles; gentle, violent, kind, cruel, forgiving, exacting, faithful, and treacherous people; victims and perpetrators of child abuse, victims and perpetrators of spousal abuse; people with plans, property, and prestige; people adrift, jobless, homeless; people who say "God!" in such a variety of ways that were they to sing that word at once in the same big room, if only for a minute or two, the cacophony might, like a first viewing of Holbein the Younger's *The Body of the Dead Christ in*

---

4. Lash, *Holiness, Speech and Silence*, 63: "George Steiner handles, with impressive honesty, the difficulty—in our supposedly 'post-religious' culture—of giving intelligible expression to the recognition that the possibility of speech is grounded in the possibility of prayer.' . . . If, then, there is a sense in which the fundamental form of speech is prayer, response, *our* words' acknowledgement that all things come into being through the Word that is with God in the beginning, the Word that God is said to be, of what *kind* of prayer are we speaking?"

Preface

the Tomb, "make some people lose their faith."⁵ I have written for them, the same way that I have taught them: by refusing to acknowledge the obvious objection that such a wide spectrum of readers will never be well served by the same demanding, complicated text. I have written imagining a future in which both new, raw, untamed, hungry theologians and decades-long, battle-hardened seasoned professional theologians may come gently vis-à-vis this text, whether because of it or in spite of it, to have been swayed to set sail to the other side, to embark upon a kind of thinking and praying as new, raw, untamed, and hungry as I pray they and I to the end will one day all be remembered as having been.

I have been struck for some time by how we, nurtured as we are by modern Western Civilization,⁶ imagine the locus of thought. Despite the insights of brain research, we still habitually imagine that each of us thinks with her brain, in her head, that elongated sphere suspended on a thin neck between the brilliant, ethereal blue sky far above to which it is drawn, and the thick, heavy torso with its stabilizing limbs held by the force of gravity to the green, brown earth below. The people of ancient Israel imagined otherwise. We think, they believed, with our hearts, that organ in the middle of the chest, in the middle of the body, embraced by lungs alternately filled with sweet, rich air and emptied of it when expended in anticipation of the new breath that may yet come, the heart that pounds out the life-beat of the time that we are given to live together. It seems to me that the Israelites were right. We think from the midst of our bodies, with our bodies, with those social phenomena that are what they are only as they are interrupted and engaged by what they are not. I have written, i.e., for thinking bodies. I have written imagining the sound of words spoken and heard. I have imagined the reading of this book as a moment in which in some unpretentious word-of-mouth underground venue the deep, powerful, resonant percussions of subwoofers roll heavily as a carnal wave across the chest and throat before they become the bass line in a conscious musical thought. I have written for the ears, the chest, the throat, i.e., for a thinking *body*. I suspect that there are sentences in this book that will be better understood if they are read aloud.

---

5. Dostoevsky, *The Idiot*, 238.

6. The words of this phrase are capitalized as a way of acknowledging the presumption of each of them alone and of both together. The phrase is taken as a name, comparable, say, to Church of Scientology or Manifest Destiny or Victor Mature.

Preface

Of course, an academic treatment of any subject is not all song and dance. There are lyrics, too, declarative ones. If a text is not at least in principle vulnerable to a grand or petty professional inquisition as to *what* is said, it is not strictly theological. And as it turns out there is no shortage of *what* in this text, even if the writing has gone through considerable pains to make sure that *what* does not overpower *how*. I have spent an enormous amount of time agonizing over word choices. Writing at once for so many audiences, for so many personal historic trajectories, has called for that. That this is a book awash with puns may be noticed right away. The frequent citation of the etymologies of words signals the extent to which words seldom speak with only one voice here. However, I more often than not let the awkwardness of certain phrases gesture in the direction of the text's multiple concurrent personalities. One of the most important tasks of theological writing, it seems to me, is to write words off themselves. Everything we might say, this declaration as well, is entangled in an overtly or covertly memorial past and a wonderfully or fearfully anticipated future. This book has set out to attend to them, this past and this future, without selling them my soul or yours. Of course, neither have I wished to sell our souls to the curiously durable present upon which I have been trained to presume that even now we rest our weight. Thus the words to come are to be read as moving without nostalgia or expressive spontaneity or the calculative drive of purpose or ataraxic mindfulness. They are to be read as expenditures with neither deep pockets nor favorable investment prospects. They are to be read as invocations and supplications toward an event in which the fruit of the knowledge of good and bad will have been unhanded.

This is a book in six chapters, plus a prelude, a postlude, and a series of interludes. Each of the six chapters is concerned with a different subject matter. The pre-, post-, and interludes that precede, follow, and otherwise interrupt the flow of chapters serve those chapters, in certain unruly ways.

The first chapter claims to be introductory. It in a particular way concerns *me*, as a theologian. It is in that sense "personal." However, I would contend that it is not autobiography. Whatever "self" might even now be thought to have written of and been written into this (theological) life story and the large book in which it is set is, it seems to me, a legendary beast, a kind of abominable snowman, a portent not long to the warm days of an early springtime thaw. This chapter nonetheless tells the reader something of the history from which this discourse is set to task. It makes clear that somebody wrote this book, even if he wrote it by no means as its chief protagonist and author.

Preface

The second chapter is on theological method. Unlike many other treatments of the subject, this one is written on the run. It sets out to say what it says and simultaneously to do what it says, and to do what it says as a kind of outgoing after what this book professes as the way of the cross. It is the task of this chapter to say something of what (and how) "after crucifixion" entails.

The third chapter is an account of work. Its most prominent pun is "liturgy." Of course, I do very much have formal liturgical worship in mind as I write. However, I also write remembering that the work of the people is by no means confined to a formal worship service, but that in fact most of it is performed far outside a certain large designated room in some mappable location with a property value. Adam and Eve work and work hard on our side of the Garden. Punishment or not, their work and ours is to be an expenditure of thanksgiving, every day of every week.

The fourth chapter is an account of bodies. It is also an eschatological venture. It concerns the resurrection of the flesh. The chapter speaks to the question of the finality of death and damnation and it confesses a future in which the whole damned world will have been emptied, the way a large cage might be emptied of a captured pelican, say, were its barred walls, floor, and ceiling suddenly unhinged at their right angles of intersection and cast away.

The fifth chapter concerns martyrdom. More specifically it concerns what a martyr-church might signify. It is chiefly an examination of the hard command of Jesus in Mark 8, his command to "the crowd with his disciples": "If any want to become my followers, let them deny themselves and take up their cross and follow me" (8:34). The question of this chapter is not "Should Christians be willing to become martyrs?" or "Should Christian discipleship always include training in the art of martyrdom?" The question is rather, "How would a local church proceed, if it lived every day with the in-its-bones conviction that it does not have to survive?" That question is thought theologically, of course. There is no programmatic prescription here. Rather there is prayer, prayer that remembers the questions and answers in the temple before the holy, holy, holy One high and lifted up.

The last chapter might have been a chapter on theological education, if I had not become disillusioned with that very enterprise. Disillusion concerning education, of course, is not what one might expect of a longtime university professor who loves his students. I have not grown disillusioned with teaching and learning; it's just that I have given up on "leadership," and especially on leading the ignorant from darkness to light. I am not sure how that kind of exitus is compatible with the good news that the God we are to follow is the God who is with us *irruptively*. The task of learning well before the bread and the wine of the eucharist (the bread and the fish of the wilderness feedings) is the task of learning to live with those, let us say, who have been left behind. Therefore, I speak of teaching and learning in contrast with one of the few most revered educators in the history of the world: Socrates. I speak of teaching and learning toward a liberation that he would have found to be, not outrageous, but pure folly.

Of course, there are also interludes between the chapters of this book, five of them. As the word suggests, they play there. They do hold chapters together, but playfully, while holding them apart. The first is a brief glimpse into the very mundane, very fractured labors of a little local church in inner-city San Diego. The second, too, concerns a gathering of working people in an inner-city neighborhood, South Central Los Angeles, where soil, work, and new life mingled for a while in one of L.A.'s bleakest sectors. The third is a report of the findings of brain physiology, of hard sociobiological research. The fourth is a transcript of a conversation between two of my friends concerning a certain ecclesiological question. The last is a travelogue of a trip I took to England sometime around 1990. Theology, this motley parabolic crew suggests, is not done alone and it is not done well; it is hard work with an uncertain outcome, the work of social bodies, and it is never to be confused with the completion of a circle, the solving of a problem, the closing of a wound, but is rather in the end a gratefully excessive expenditure, a wilderness feeding, a prodigal celebration, a resurrection of the dead, face to face with the faces that we meet, the faces the Crucified faces as he plummets, abased, into the abyss and rises, exalted, with glory.

There is also a prelude to this book and a postlude. The first draft of the prelude—the book's playful overture, really—was delivered at a conference in Granada, Spain, where it was declared (with fanfare and snarky self-confidence) that "metaphysics is the new black!" I thought, "I don't think so." The chapter is written, however, not just as a kind of critique of metaphysics; it is more particularly written otherwise than by the rules of classic metaphysics. It is a story, a story that is frequently interrupted by voices that might have joined with other voices to shout out a history of Western metaphysics. At the time, I titled the essay "After Crucifixion: Unhanding Metaphysics in the Liturgy of the Eucharist." This essay as it

Preface

then stood and under that title is among the essays and addresses collected in the book *The Transgression of the Integrity of God*. The piece here makes the same move it did before, but I pray even more humanely. It confesses what *After Crucifixion* from the beginning is out to confess. I think it and the book's cover are what I most want to say.

The book's postlude is a collection of quoted passages, among which are just a handful of phrases I have written. It does not conclude this book, at least if my prayer is answered that this book will not come to a conclusion, but it does send it off in a certain way, a text that may be madness, but (I pray) not just madness.

There are so many people I want to thank. So many friends have spent their time reading and reacting to one or more of the pieces that follow. I would never have started and certainly would never have finished this book without their encouragement. This is true above all of Elesha, with whom I have spent the last forty-two years. She insisted that I write. She *insisted!* And she kept at me gently, lovingly, kindly, but relentlessly. That I—from deep down in my soul so very uneasy with conclusion—could get a monograph off to a publisher is due above all to her. But it is due to others, too.

Our philosopher daughter, Heather Keen Ross, has spent too many hours reading these chapters and talking through them with me. It is a marvelous gift to have a relationship like that with one's daughter. Our sons, Stefen and Bryan, also have read chapters from this book and have responded encouragingly. I have received critical guidance on brain research from Warren Brown, on current scholarship in the Gospel of Mark from Matt Hauge, on the relevance of my work to the life of the local church from Josh Smith, the priest of the little local church where I am a member. I am so grateful for Charlie Collier's readiness to work with me. He has understood and has been receptive to this book from our earliest conversations. I have gotten encouragement and critical help at various stages of writing from Sam Powell, John Wright, Doug Meeks, Teri Merrick, Donna Techau, Billy Abraham, Ted Jennings, Jack Caputo, and other friends and colleagues too numerous to list.

I do want specifically to mention Nate Kerr, however. He in particular has been my dialogue partner and advocate, since we first met when he was a business major and stumbled into an introduction to philosophy course I was teaching. I could never thank him and Thomas Bridges enough for their gift in compiling and editing *The Transgression of the Integrity of God*. Thomas, too, has in strongly quiet ways supported me in this work, ways to which he will be embarrassed to find me alluding here.

Preface

All the students with whom I have worked have marked all over this text. How could I not smile broadly and wave gratefully to them? This is true also, of course, of my teachers. I would like in particular to thank three of them, the last of whom died just a few years ago: Rob Staples, Paul Bassett, and Ken Grider. It is because of Rob that I am a theologian. It is because of Paul that I hope some day to become a scholar. It is because of Ken that I pray that I may yet learn as a writer to love.

I am grateful also to Azusa Pacific University for giving me time to work by providing me with a sabbatical, a Beverly Hardcastle Stanford Award, room, sky, and sea at Writers' Retreats, a series of Accomplished Scholar Awards, CREV Seminars, and scheduling flexibility. Thanks also to my colleagues who have without complaint taken up the slack left as I have slipped away to research and write.

I would like to draw special attention to Stan Hauerwas. Friendship is a big deal to him, of course. He writes and writes about the importance of friendship. Because he is magnanimous, he has a great number of friends, among whom I am glad to say I am one. In our friendship, however, I have been from him the recipient by far of greater goods, than he from me. I am the beneficiary of his kindness, including his gracious expenditure of time, his time that is so much and so rightly in demand. This book was written and has been published because he has believed in it—from the beginning—beyond anything I could have expected. Stan understood this text immediately and has worked his way through its chapters, responding with a degree of enthusiasm unmatched by anyone outside of my immediate family and closest friends. Thank you, Stan.

Finally, I would like to mention the gift that having a full household has meant for my writing. A few years ago, during a particularly challenging time, Elesha and I opened our house to a handful of friends. We experimented together with a kind of ankle-deep new monasticism. Katrina Alston, Leah Butts (now Rashidyan), Sean Capener, Melanie Dosen, Peter Hawisher (who helped me with the technicalities of writing for Cascade), Tara Roy (now Bishop-Roy), and a number of more temporary houseguests helped us learn how very well the American Dream had smothered our social instincts, and they helped us learn how to live otherwise and especially how to be hospitable. And as we lived together, we talked through ideas at play in this book, and some of them took shape in the days we worked and ate together.

Preface

A little over two years ago our household arrangements had to change, because it was time for Elesha and me to take in my very elderly parents. My mother is ninety, my father ninety-three. However, had our *compañeras y compañeros* not struggled along with us, had they not taught us, the transition to life with my parents would have been much harder, perhaps impossible. As it is and has been, however, life in an extended family—life where we have to lean on each other because we have come to know all the way down that we are not, never have been, and never will be self-reliant or self-sufficient—has risen among us as a beautiful, marvelous, and unmerited gift. We welcome it, throwing open our windows and doors with a joyful yearning to the brisk Wind who bathed the mutilated body of the crucified Jesus with abundant life and gathered the church.

I could never simply lay claim to this book. It is truer that they wrote it—my friends and lovers, my teachers and students, my parents and children, and Elesha, the love of my life—than that I did. In this, too: *Te Deum laudamus*!

It is with joy that I think now back over the faces of all the people named and unnamed in this preface. But I think in particular of the faces of my parents, and I think of them in the roomy, disclosed countenance of the Slaughtered Lamb in whose future theirs, too, will forever vigilantly shine. It is to them that this book is dedicated.

The Feast Day of Ignatius of Antioch, 2012

Acknowledgments

The author would like to thank the following for permission to reprint material from previously published essays.

Thanks to the *Wesleyan Theological Journal*, especially editor Barry Callen, for permission to reprint, with minor changes, the essay "The Root from Which They Spring: Presidential Address," *Wesleyan Theological Journal* 42 (2007) 148–59.

Another, only slightly different, version of this address and an earlier version of the Prelude, under the title "After Crucifixion: Unhanding Metaphysics in the Liturgy of the Eucharist," appear as well in the volume *The Transgression of the Integrity of God: Essays and Addresses*, edited by Thomas J. Bridges and Nathan R. Kerr (Eugene, OR: Cascade, 2012).

Thanks to Eric Severson for permission to reprint portions of the essay "Deferral: A Response to John D. Caputo's *The Weakness of God*," from *I More Than Others: Responses to Evil and Suffering*, edited by Eric Severson (Newcastle on Tyne: Cambridge Scholars, 2010).

Permissions

"Old Coat"
By Elena Mezzetti, Mary Travers, and Noel Paul Stookey
© 1963 (Renewed) Neworld Media Music Publishers (ASCAP).
Reproduced by permission from WB Music Corp.
All Rights Reserved.

"Falling Slowly" (from *Once*)
Words and Music by Glen Hansard and Marketa Irglova
© 2006 The Swell Season Publishing (ASCAP)
Reproduced by permission from WB Music Corp. (ASCAP).
Exclusive Worldwide Print Rights Administered by Alfred Music Publishing Co., Inc. All Rights Reserved

"Iris"
Words and Music by John Rzeznik
© 1998 BMG Platinum Songs and Scrap Metal Music
Reproduced by permission from BMG Rights Management (US) LLC
Reprinted with Permission of Hal Leonard Corporation.
All Rights Reserved.

"Stay Hungry"
By David Byrne and Christopher Frantz
© 1982 WB Music Corp. (ASCAP) and Index Music, Inc. (ASCAP)
Reproduced by permission from WB Music Corp.
All Rights Reserved

"Cosmic Love"
Words and Music by Florence Welch and Isabella Summers
© 2009 Goldzeal LTD. and Universal Music Publishing LTD.
All rights for Goldzeal LTD. in the U.S. and Canada Controlled and Administered by Universal–Songs of Polygram International, INC.
Reproduced by permission from Hal Leonard Corporation.

Prelude[1]

THOSE SEERS WHO KEEP their devices booted and their eyes fixed on global trends tell us that the center of gravity of what they call "Christianity" is shifting, socioeconomically and geographically. If one could survey the bodies assembled as local churches half a century from now, they say, the features that would most recur would not be Euro-pale, mature, male, and healthy, but dark, young, female, and marked by poverty. And so, if you happen to find your way through times and places to a land across which by then little churches will have been abundantly strewn, and you come face to face with one of their faithful, odds are good that her eyes will meet yours in her native Nigeria, say, or Brazil. Churches made up of the noticeably prosperous, classy, Caucasoid progeny of European forebears are expected to have generally declined significantly in number. Of course, even if population flow turns out to yield much more massive changes than expected, not all formal categorical textbook descriptions will need to be altered for all locales. Newer inhabitants may well carry with them patterns of life discarded by their well-established neighbors. Populations to the north of the Rio Grande, e.g., are expected to remain strongly "Christian," but largely because of what will have traveled with more recent immigrants, both the "documented" and the "undocumented," as they carve out living space alongside the grandchildren of the immigrants of another era.[2]

---

1. Mark 2:22: "And no one puts new wine into old wineskins; otherwise, the wine will burst the skins, and the wine is lost, and so are the skins; but one puts new wine into fresh wineskins."

2. Jenkins, *Next Christendom*, 2–3, 90–105; and Jenkins, *New Faces of Christianity*, 8–10. Cf. Senior, "'Beloved Aliens and Exiles,'" 27–28: "Contrary to human wisdom, those who are comfortable in place, fortified with the security of land and possessions and food, are also in danger of delusion about ultimate reality. In the overall landscape of the gospel stories, the rich and powerful are often 'in place'—reclining at table, calculating their harvest, standing comfortably in the front of the sanctuary, or seated on the judgment seat passing judgment on the crimes of others. The poor, on the other hand, are often mobile or rootless: the sick coming from the four corners of the compass seeking

After Crucifixion

And what will have traveled with these newer arrivals? It is tempting to call it "belief." And yet, that word is too easy, too familiar, too casual to be of much help here. It inclines us to gesture presumptively toward a vaguely untouchable inner life of discrete and discretionary private individuals.[3] Certainly, as a devout woman with a history among ecclesial people holds her baby close, as they cross the Pacific or Atlantic Ocean or the Sonoran Desert, powerful memories and hopes carry her.[4] Perhaps these are "beliefs" in some archaic sense of the word.[5] However, to the extent that she *is* savory, to the extent that she *does* believe, she is moved otherwise than by psychic acts that might be graphed on a Divided Line or by electrochemical events some centimeters behind her anterior cranium or by "subjective"[6] impulses racing down tracks laid by habitual association amidst the welter of sense impressions; she is moved otherwise even than by her "*meu bem*," toward whom she travels and for whom she aches.[7] The memories and hopes journeying with her north, say, from Brazil, are not her private property, as if they could be counted among her assets on a credit application. One would speak more faithfully, both of them and of her, were

---

healing; the crowds desperate to hear Jesus, roaming lost and hungry; the leper crouched outside the door of Dives."

3. Cf. Hagan, "Faith for the Journey," 5: "poor and working-class Latin Americans share a long historical tradition of turning to religion for solace and guidance in times of personal crisis, such as illness or job loss. . . . The hundreds of thousands of daily petitions that pilgrims leave at shrines and churches throughout Latin America testify to people's reliance on their church, its saints, and holy images when faced with personal problems or formidable challenges."

4. Ruiz Marrujo, "Gender of Risk," 226, 235: There are "growing numbers of women leaving their homes without documents. Estimates for the northern border [of Mexico] show that women now make up 20 percent of the migratory flows across that border, while data from the southern border reveal even higher rates. . . . [This is] reflected worldwide, where female migrants make up almost 50 percent of the planet's migratory flows."

5. *Oxford English Dictionary*, s.v. "belief, *n*.": "The word shows considerable semantic overlap with the later French loan faith *n*. Especially in theological use, a distinction is frequently made between the two words, *belief* referring either to the intellectual assent to certain propositions or dogmas, or to the acceptance of the existence of God or another god, *faith* involving personal trust and commitment. This lexical distinction is absent from the cognate Germanic languages; in German, for example, *Glaube* covers the senses of both *belief* and *faith*."

6. As opposed to "objective," of course!

7. See Plato, *Republic*, 506–11; Wittgenstein, *Philosophical Investigations*, 127, 127e [427]; and Hume, *Enquiry Concerning Human Understanding*, 27–31 [V].

one to say that she is *in them* rather than that they are in her.⁸ These are the memories and hopes of a work that over disrupted time aligns by hospitable anticipation (even if unevenly) all she is about to think, perform, and speak, one in which she has come to live and move and have whatever goods she carries in the *mochila* on her back and the plastic grocery bag in her hand.⁹ And so if, under the glaring, bare bulb of cross-examination, we determined that her "beliefs" are anything but clear, that she could never articulate them to Socrates' satisfaction and ours, it may only be that we have pressed ourselves upon her too hard, that we have been too swift to make determinations, that in our aggression we have not opened ourselves to her, that we have not loved her.

Were we to love her, we would not too quickly leave her side. We would wait with her.¹⁰ We would lean in toward her as novitiates, probationers. Love asks that much of us. We might walk with her, as she prays. We might attend to the prayers dancing on her lips. In time we might come to suspect that they and she are connected in ways we had not in our haste previously imagined. Even if only briefly, we might now wonder if these prayers were less *borne by her* and much more *have borne her and bear her still*, so far from home.¹¹ Were we to abide with her, we might find that her prayers have marked her, have inscribed a passage across the movements of her hands, back, legs, and face, as one might with one's finger inscribe an elusive message across the dust of the ground.¹² We might in spite of ourselves learn from her how she remembers and hopes still with the assembly of the faithful from whom so many steps have separated her. She may in the heat of the moment join her petition¹³ and re-petition with theirs that

8. Cf. Derrida, *Dissemination*, 56–59, 103–5, 126–30, 168–71.

9. See Groody, *Border of Death, Valley of Life*, 19 and passim.

10. Cf. Berry, "Watch with Me," 77–123.

11. Hagan, "Faith for the Journey," 7–8: "Among the sub sample of 202 departing undocumented migrants, more than three-quarters (78 percent) turned to God to help them with the decision to migrate. Moreover, four out of five members of the sample—women and men, Protestants and Catholics, Central Americans and Mexicans alike—prayed to God, a saint, a religious icon, or sought counsel from trusted local clergy within several days prior to embarking on their journey."

12. Cf. Gen 2:7, 18:27; John 8:6–8. Levinas, "God and Philosophy," 71: "Responsibility for the neighbor is precisely what goes beyond legality and obliges beyond the contract. It comes to me prior to my freedom, from a nonpresent, from an immemorial. Between me and the other there gapes a difference which no unity of transcendental apperception could recover."

13. *American Heritage Dictionary of Indo-European Roots*, 2nd ed., 67: "petition" from the root "pet-, To rush, fly."

this time in this lonely desert, too, will have been honest and true to the work into which she was born, that this time, too, will have been an outcry evoked from her throat, opened by a fair wind that blows without consulting your forecasts or mine.[14]

The prayer in which she and they still touch does not—by definition *cannot*—float intangibly either above them or us. It is situated in a time and place, as are all human works. Though it is indeed marked by the names their mothers and lovers call them, we are more tempted than they to point and call it *theirs*. Even as it happens, this is an event that will not be held fast to be owned. It slips away with deference. It defers indeed *particularly*, across an ugly, broad ditch.[15] It defers to a transient moment, so disposable, so distant, so inapprehensible. It defers to an event so free and so forward that, in spite of ourselves, it comes alongside (*para*) us to make its appearance (*doxa*), all the while no less ranging beyond the horizon line of the most farsighted extrapolative retrospection. That is, the prayer they and she voice defers not to a cause or an idea or an exemplary champion of fair virtue (investment opportunities, kept in mind, to which only a *backhanded* deferral is possible). It defers rather to "one particular thing."[16] It defers beyond our line of sight (of all things) to the trace of an already departed *vagabond*, to a *laborer* (no[,] less), to a dark-skinned *peasant*, a no-count wonder-worker and prophet, to an elusive short life and prolonged death. It defers, i.e., in the mode of witness, even (perhaps especially) when good work cannot use either circumspection or compensation: *em nome de Cristo*.[17]

---

14. See Wolff, *Anthropology of the Old Testament*, 10–25. Cf. Gen 2:7, Ps 104:1, John 3:8.

15. See Lessing, "On the Proof of the Spirit and of Power," 52–55; Kierkegaard [Climacus], *Concluding Unscientific Postscript*, 93–100. Climacus, with some humor, of course, cites Mendelssohn's response to Lessing: "To doubt whether there is not something that not only surpasses all concepts but also lies completely beyond the concept, that I call a leap beyond oneself" (105).

16. Bolaño, *Amulet*, 86.

17. Phan, "Migration in the Patristic Era," 58: "The theology of migration as proposed by the *Letter of Diognetus*, centers . . . on the theology of the migrant's life as *imitatio Christi*. . . . As a migrant, Jesus was a 'marginal Jew,' to use the title of John Meier's multi-volume work on the historical Jesus. His migration carried him over all kinds of borders, both geographical and conventional. . . . Because his multiple border-crossings were a threat to those who occupied the economic, political, and religious centers of power, he was hung upon the cross, between heaven and earth, between the two cosmic borders, a migrant until the end."

Prelude

Thus in *him* (and even saying that little strikes us as excessive, if not unthinkable) the *assembly*, the *liturgical avowal* by which they assemble, and *she* concur. When in loneliness or defeat they cry out, it is *his* outcry they would repeat—articulated in two contrasting, but by no means mutually exclusive, phrases: (1) "My God, my God, why have you forsaken me?" (Mark 15:34) and (2) "Father, into your hands I commend my spirit" (Luke 23:46).[18] They pray in order to pray his prayer—his prayer that opens a way through the stone wall of his tomb—that a way may be opened for them, too, and for all, that in his abased and exalted body *all* things will one day shine.[19] They pray that the logic of this new life—the logic of crucifixion/resurrection—will be given them, that they will be gifted with *metanoia*.[20] There are even immodest moments when they pray that they, too, might join him in his sufferings, i.e., bear witness to his resurrection.[21] That is, they pray toward and through his death and theirs. They pray not to push, not to coerce, but to give thanks, to react well to an action that they could never forestall. There is a yea-saying *preventative*, a *precedent*, an *already*, in the work of these people, like the warm memory of what is yet to occur, arriving before any imperial chess master could collect his thoughts to set up her best defense against it. They work in this way that they and their work may not collapse under their own weight.

When the people gather, they are supported by nothing more solidly weight-bearing than a parable, an icon, a prayer.[22] They are supported by an indeterminate future that they acknowledge as having priority over what they are and have been. Certainly they and the prayers they perform are flesh—"muscles and blood and skin and bones."[23] These are people with a past. They have always left tracks. Nobody has to plant forensic evidence on them in order to charge, convict, and sentence them. The professional staffs of both theoretical and applied sciences turn their attention to them with ease, to manage them, conceptually, programmatically. Philosophers,

18. Cf. Song, *Jesus, the Crucified People*, 228–29.
19. See 2 Cor 5:17; cf. Isaiah 60 and Revelation 21.
20. Cf. Phil 2:5.
21. Cf. Phil 3:8–15.
22. Bevans, "Mission among Migrants, Mission of Migrants," 100: "'The church's finest hours are always at the borderlands of nations and empires, not at their centers.' The body of Christ is the 'Border Christ,' always on the move, never at home in one place, willing to go where needed, wearing the simplest of clothes, carrying no more than needed—but because of this able to enter into every situation."
23. Merle Travis, "Sixteen Tons."

too, attend to them, to their structures and their doctrines, their creeds and their holy books, their "God" and their "Paul." With little disquiet they wrap their minds around their ideas, finding about them nothing seriously anomalous.[24] That, in gathering, these people might have a particularity, a particularity like and secondary to the particularity to which they prayerfully defer, a particularity that would elude all apprehension and exhibition, we are tempted to say, is unthinkable.[25] A truly radically elusive particularity, one that would not stay nailed down, would at best be undetectable. If it proliferated, however, it could only like cancer unmake, only tear down, we think. The masters of good and evil could not hold it in their hands, could not tame it. Its future could not be ours. It would bode "nihilism," we say.[26] It would, if spread, turn every accomplishment into rubbish, into excrement.[27] Such a particular people would travel without[,] a prayer.[28] (As the man—who would, since Soconusco, take neither her dollars nor her sarcastic "Senhor Wilie E. Coiote"—stands watch under a thousand thousand apathetic points of someone else's light in the otherwise heavy, well-woven blackness of an Imperial Sonoran Desert night, the woman who holds her baby close is above all prayer.)[29]

In the face of the prospect of such disaster it is understandable that we would in our anxiety crave a panoptic vision, a world view, which would take in and hold all that we have discerned and might ever discern,[30] a ground for proper action and passion,[31] a foothold off of which we might push to make our way into an otherwise paralyzingly uncertain future in the face of an otherwise inhospitably untamed natural world. Besides, we are people who wonder,[32] we have a longing for rational unity,[33] and we are

24. Agamben, *Time that Remains*, 1: "First and foremost, this seminar proposes to restore Paul's Letters to the status of the fundamental messianic text for the Western tradition."

25. Cf. Milbank, *Word Made Strange*, 152–53, 160, 165.

26. Cf. Gen 3:4–10 and Phil 2:5–11.

27. Cf. Phil 3:8.

28. Cf. Matt 26:36.

29. See Ruiz Marrujo, "Gender of Risk," 229, 231–36.

30. Cf. Kierkegaard [Anti-Climacus], *Sickness Unto Death*, 43–44; Kierkegaard [Climacus], *Concluding Unscientific Postscript*, 122–25; and Blanchot, *Writing of the Disaster*, 2.

31. Cf. Tracy, *Plurality and Ambiguity*, 20–21, 92–93.

32. See Aristotle, *Metaphysics*, 982b.

33. See Kant, *Prolegomena to Any Future Metaphysics*, 89–90 [349–50].

driven by an aesthetic desire for a vision both coherent and adequate to the broad range of our experience or an erotic urge for far-reaching intellectual satisfaction.[34] We are people who desire a grand, integrating vision.[35]

Surely no one could fault the pious for engaging in just this enterprise, specifying in some detail *God's* relation to all the goods (*ousia*) their inquiries have surveyed, goods that come into their hands as their inquiries grow more and more ambitious.[36] Of course, the pious would not wish too quickly to nail God to any vision. They perhaps remember that God is ambiguously related to the act of nailing down. They would want to give God the power to move about freely. Nor would they wish to give God only limited free range.[37] And so, the pious might even dare to say that God is in league with that goodness or truth or beauty and in combat against that evil or falsehood or ugliness they have by rigorous and pious effort come to some degree to determine—*but* they would say this perhaps with downcast eyes, humbly, uncertainly or skeptically or with a knowing, hushed aside that God stands concomitantly in analogical opposition to—even in judgment against—their determinations.[38] (That a displaced young woman, holding a little child, would have no place in their ordered whole could not be definitive, they think.)

In this way—perhaps against our best intentions—we have stumbled into the imposing tradition of the Greeks, those masters of health and unity, of balance and justice, of virtue and well-being, of ethics and ontology. The

---

34. Cf. Whitehead, *Process and Reality*, 219–20.

35. See Dewey, *Common Faith*, 32–33, 50–53.

36. Cf. Luke 15:12: "The younger of them said to his father, 'Father, give me the share of the property [*tēs ousias*] that will belong to me.' So he divided his property [*ton bion*] between them." Marion, *God Without Being*, 95–96: "This question leads us to . . . the parable of the prodigal son, in Luke 15:12–32. This text ineluctably demands our attention, since it offers the only usage in all of the New Testament of the philosophical term par excellence, *ousia* (Luke 15:12–13): 'A man had two sons. And the younger of the two said to his father: "Father, give me the share of *ousia* that is coming to me."' . . . But *ousia* also admits, first of a prephilosophical acceptation that shares with its properly philosophical turn the indication of a present disposability: *ousia* indicates that which, here, and now, remains to be useful for . . . , in short, disposable goods; this trait common to the two acceptations of *ousia*, which Heidegger underscored in his course at Marburg, has to do with the disposability of a 'possession' (*Besitz*) which thus assures a 'power' (*Vermögen*)." See also 97–102.

37. As one might, say, a June bug tied by the leg to a long thread.

38. Thomas Aquinas, *Nature and Grace*, 76 [1.13.5]: "But when we apply the same name [ordinarily applied to a human being] to God . . . it leaves what it signifies uncomprehended, and beyond its power to denote."

Greeks understood as well as any ever have that a people must keep the lines well drawn that mark the difference between "we are" and "we are not."[39] The literature of the Greeks is rich with a paideic vision, cosmic in scope, for the integrity of the body, the soul, and the city-state. Sublimely conceived, the Odysseus of Homer's *Odyssey*,[40] the Socrates of Plato's *Apology*,[41] and the walled *polis* of Plato's *Republic*[42] each rises tall silhouetted against the ethereal sky of a sublimely conceived cosmos, threateningly mature, overtly or covertly beautiful, strong, virile, courageous, daring, wise, complex, well armed, just: whole.[43] To be well adjusted is here to be hale, an inherent harmony properly exercised in controlled agony at one or another battlefield or *palaestra* or *agora*, centered, stalking steadily like a pelican on defensible ground.[44] That there are the ill-adjusted among us simply means, they held, that *therapeia* is to be performed, a *therapeia* in fact that serves not only the patient, but even more the divine that radiates from the temple at the heart both of the city and of the heroic citizen.[45] Indeed we human beings, they held, are here at the center of the cosmos to rise by struggle to become "like

---

39. See Jaeger, *In Search of the Divine Centre*, 256–57. Parmenides, of course, most thoroughly and beautifully sublimates this notion.

40. See especially the last four books of *The Odyssey*: "Odysseus Strings His Bow," "Slaughter in the Hall," "The Great Rooted Bed," and "Peace."

41. The whole of the *Apology* could be cited and much more (certainly including the interchange at the end of the *Symposium* between Socrates and Alcibiades), but this little passage from the *Apology*, 28d–e (33–34) is perhaps illustrative: "This is the truth of the matter, gentlemen of the jury: wherever a man has taken a position that he believes to be best, or has been placed by his commander, there he must I think remain and face danger, without a thought for death or anything else, rather than disgrace. It would have been a dreadful way to behave, gentlemen of the jury, if, at Potidaea, Amphipolis, and Delium, I had, at the risk of death, like anyone else, remained at my post where those you had elected to command had ordered me, and then, when the god ordered me, as I thought and believed, to live the life of a philosopher, to examine myself and others, I had abandoned my post for fear of death or anything else. That would have been a dreadful thing, and then I might truly have justly been brought here for not believing that there are gods, disobeying the oracle, fearing death, and thinking I was wise when I was not." Jaeger, *In Search of the Divine Centre*, 173: "[Socrates'] death is a sort of apotheosis, and he leaves his pupils with calm cheerfulness, like a truly free man. There knowledge is described as the soul's collecting itself—one of the immortal psychological images invented by Plato: it 'concentrates' itself from among the dispersed senses, all pressing outwards to the sensory world, and bends to its own proper inward activity."

42. For example, Plato, *Republic*, 469a–71e.

43. See Jaeger, *In Search of the Divine Centre*, 145–46, 173.

44. Plato, *Symposium* 221b.

45. See Plato, *Timaeus* 90c, and Liddell et al., *Greek-English Lexicon*, 792–93.

the divine, so far as we can."[46] The more we are like the divine, the more we are ourselves, and vice versa. Thus *therapeia* is in the strictest sense a healing act. Who could blame anyone, especially the pious, for praying for such healing? Indeed, who could blame them for conceiving of prayer as such as a salutary act, the deed in itself (whether it is heard by the *Actus Purus* or not) as therapy, as a medicine of the soul?[47]

For the more cerebral Greeks the grandest *therapeia* is what they called *philosophia*, a pursuit of wisdom that—far from fearing or petitioning the gods, e.g., for some undue ephemeral benefaction—aspires and conforms to the surpassing-divine goodness, truth, and beauty the gods, too, serve.[48] Though it is certainly idealized, a kind of monolatrous prayer plays still in the background history of *philosophia*. And yet the gods, idealized though they, too, may be, are honored and trusted to do well the tasks they have been assigned (without the distraction of our entreaties).[49] And *we* are to do well the tasks we have been assigned, to fit no less into this beautiful cosmos that is our native soil and theirs. The end of philosophical *therapeia* is adjustment to the eternally concentric *archai* that order the many, an adjustment that centers the attendant's otherwise disparate faculties and makes him whole.[50] What is truly one, truly whole, is simply self-identical, untouched by what is other than itself: $A \neq \sim A$! It simply *is*. "Integrity" = "identity," "identity" = "being." I *am* insofar as I participate in the integrity that most truly *is*. It is not accidental that the devotion of the Greeks to integrity led them into that discipline that sets out to clarify the foundational meaning of "being." An inquiry into the significance of "being" is thus no idle pastime; it is a quest for *healing*.[51]

---

46. See Plato, *Theatetus* 176b; *Republic* 613a-b; *Phaedrus* 248a, 249c; and *Timaeus* 47c.

47. See Ritschl, *Three Essays*, 244, 255–56. Cf. Tillich, *Systematic Theology*, 1:267; 3:191–93.

48. See Plato, *Laws* 716c–717a; and Jaeger, *In Search of the Divine Centre*, 285–88.

49. Plato, *Laws*, 885b; cf. *Republic*, 364b–365e.

50. Aristotle, *Nicomachean Ethics*, 269 [10.8:1179a]: "For if the gods have any care for human affairs, as they are thought to have, it would be reasonable both that they should delight in that which was best and most akin to them (i.e., reason) and that they should reward those who love and honour this most, as caring for the things that are dear to them and acting both rightly and nobly. And that all these attributes belong most of all to the philosopher is manifest. He, therefore, is the dearest to the gods. And he who is that will presumably be also the happiest; so that in this way too the philosopher will more than any other be happy." See also 16–17 [1.8:1099a–1099b].

51. Members of the church who take on this divinely humane intellectual task are set

Early Greek thinkers were in fact in more than one sense "physicians." They were above all concerned with what they named *physis*, with thinking it and thus serving it. It would be fitting, if anachronistic, to describe at least some of them also as "metaphysicians," but not in the much later sense that discounts *physis*. The prefix "meta-" would not, indeed could not, in their case mean "beyond."[52] *Physis*, which is typically translated into English as "nature," comes from the same root as the English "be."[53] It signifies "what is," what rises by force out of the darkness to make a stand.[54] Beholding *physis* filled Greek thinkers with awe and wonder. There could be nothing higher, deeper, richer, stronger, or purer. Indeed, the Greeks would have found odd any suggestion that there might be something beyond it. In this morning of Western Civilization, *physis* embraced everything without exception, including the earth's rational animals and their gods. Homer and Hesiod, Parmenides and Heraclitus, Plato and Aristotle all agreed:[55] there is by definition only one whole, and it is the task of competent thinkers to show how and why and in that way to adjust to it—to imitate it, insofar as they can—and in turn to lead especially their kind to adjust to it as well.[56] The intelligibility of the cosmos implies, they maintained, that "what is" constitutes a definite totality.[57] *Physis* is one, a beautifully spherical inherence.[58] Here everything *is*. There simply cannot be an outside. If we thought that we had identified an outside, it would by the very act of identification be *inside*; and an outside with no place inside is literally unthinkable.[59]

---

to work. In their aspiration to the Goodness, Truth, and Beauty to whom *they* pray, they must specify—more diligently than did Plato or the Stoics—the way *their* God is to be conceived ontologically. God, they may say—without forsaking Plato or the Stoics—is (a word that may perhaps be used only in passing) "the Supreme Being," "the ground of being," "the cause of being," "being itself"—perhaps even "beyond being" (a less ambiguously ontological assertion than it may seem). It is to this God *who is* that they then pray and in so doing look to obtain integrity themselves.

52. Perhaps it could signify "after," as in "to pursue."

53. Claiborne, *Roots of English*, 9. A "physician" in this sense would be one who served the cause of one's "being," swearing, e.g., to do no harm.

54. I admit that I am thinking of Heidegger's most self-consciously "German" account of *physis* here. See, e.g., Heidegger, *Introduction to Metaphysics*, 14–19, 147–48, 167–72, 188–92, and passim.

55. As would their heirs, Hegel, Whitehead, and Heidegger, by the way.

56. See Plato, *Theatetus* 149a–152c, and *Apology* 29e–30b.

57. Integrity also signifies definiteness.

58. Dupré, *Passage to Modernity*, 21; Parmenides Fragment 8.

59. Cf. Luke 9:58.

Prelude

It is perhaps because the Greeks have taught us so well to wonder, to question, to stay awake (though perhaps a more ancient teaching is responsible) that we may not rest with them in their conclusion. And so, we may find ourselves, against ourselves, asking and asking if perhaps there might be another—uncanny, irrevocably prayerful—way of thinking, a way, say, not out to apprehend, overpower, deport, or naturalize the alien, but rather to defer to her? Might one be of a different mind than that of the founding geniuses of Western Civilization, a mind that opens to what it is not and cannot be? Might there be another way of thinking that would let the outside in without assimilating it? Now, such thinking—if it were possible—would undo "the Man of Reason."[60] It would open wounds through him out into the ground that had hitherto so well supported him, wounds possibly undoing integrity, well-being, wholeness—*physis* itself. The thinker who would think what cannot be thought would undergo a kind of passion.[61] (She shivers in the cold midnight of the Sonoran Desert or faints in the heat of its afternoon. She hides from ICE and even more from Minutemen who would cast her out, with her baby and that strange man. "Pai Nosso, que estás nos Céus, santificado seja o Teu nome. Venha o Teu reino, seja feita a Tua vontade assim na Terra como no Céu. O pão nosso de cada dia nos dá hoje. Perdoa-nos as nossas dívidas assim como nós perdoamos aos nossos devedores e não nos deixes cair em tentação mas livra-nos do mal. Amém.")

---

60. Lloyd, *Man of Reason*, ix, 2, 11–13, 17, 103: "The maleness of the Man of Reason... lies deep in our philosophical tradition.... From the beginnings of philosophical thought, femaleness was symbolically associated with what Reason supposedly left behind—the dark powers of the earth goddess, immersion in unknown forces associated with mysterious female powers.... In Greek thought, femaleness was symbolically associated with the non-rational, the disorderly, the unknowable—with what must be set aside in the cultivation of knowledge. Bacon united matter and form—Nature as female and Nature as knowable. Knowable Nature is presented as female, and the task of science is the exercise of the right kind of male domination over her.... The dominance relation... now holds between mind and Nature as the object of knowledge. Knowledge is itself the domination of Nature.... Both kinds of symbolism—the Greeks' unknowable matter, to be transcended in knowledge, and Bacon's mysterious, but controllable Nature—have played crucial roles in the constitution of the feminine in relation to our ideals of knowledge.... Our ideas and ideals of maleness and femaleness have been formed within structures of dominance—of superiority and inferiority, 'norms' and 'difference,' 'positive' and 'negative,' the 'essential' and the 'complementary.' And the male-female distinction itself has operated not as a straightforwardly descriptive principle of classification, but as an expression of values." Cf. Schüssler Fiorenza, *But She Said*, 171–73.

61. Kierkegaard [Climacus], *Philosophical Fragments*, 37.

After Crucifixion

It was that tradition which does not shrink back from but rather celebrates passion[62] that first gave trouble to Greek thinking, viz., that tradition which not only acknowledges but adores a Creator "who remain[s] outside the cosmos,"[63] who is free in relation to *physis*, to "nature."[64] Perhaps Israel and the church that remembered Israel were less quick to grasp after an integral totality, because its people remembered what it was like to pray, frightened in the imperial desert of Egypt, and heard the declaration, "I

---

62. *Oxford English Dictionary*, s.v. "passion, *n*.": "Originally < classical Latin *passiōn-, passiō* . . . ; subsequently reinforced by Anglo-Norman *passioun, paissiun*, Anglo-Norman and Old French *passiun*, Anglo-Norman and Old French, Middle French *pasion*, Anglo-Norman and Old French, Middle French, French *passion*, Middle French *pascion* suffering of a martyr (second half of the 10th cent.), sufferings of Jesus (end of the 10th cent.), narrative of the sufferings of Jesus (1119), physical suffering (beginning of the 12th cent.), strong emotion, love (beginning of the 13th cent.), fact of being acted upon (1370), enthusiasm, zeal (beginning of the 16th cent.), anger (1553), grammatical passivity (1555), violent love (1572 in plural, *passions*), sense perception (late 16th cent.), person as an object of affection (1671), deep emotion expressed in a literary work (1674) and its etymon classical Latin *passiōn-, passiō* an affection of the mind, emotion, in post-classical Latin also the sufferings of Jesus (Vetus Latina), suffering, affliction (late 2nd cent. in Tertullian), the sufferings of a martyr, martyrdom (early 3rd cent. in Tertullian; frequently from 8th cent. in British sources), sense perception, one of the five senses (early 3rd cent. in Tertullian), ailment, bodily affliction (early 3rd cent. in Tertullian), account of martyrdom (4th cent.), grammatical passivity (4th cent.), quality, attribute (from 9th cent. (frequently from 13th cent.) in British sources), reading of the Passion (from 10th cent. in British sources), the condition of being acted upon (from 12th cent. in British sources) < *pass-* , past participial stem of *patī* to suffer (see patient *adj.* and *n.*) + *-iō* -ion *suffix*1. In Latin chiefly a word of Christian theology, which was also its earliest use in French and English, being very frequent in the earliest Middle English. Compare Old Occitan *passio* violent love (c1200), Old Occitan *passion* suffering, torment, narrative of a saint's suffering (c1070), sufferings of Jesus (c1100; Occitan *passion*), Spanish *pasión* sufferings of Jesus (1228–46 as *passion*, now also in sense 'intense emotion'), Italian *passio* gospel of the Passion (13th cent.), *passion* emotion, suffering (1294), also Middle High German *passie, passiōn* sufferings of Jesus, narrative of the Passion (German *Passion* strong emotion, dedication to a cause, sufferings of Jesus, narrative of the Passion)."

63. Dupré, *Passage to Modernity*, 3; cf. 22, 29, and 126–27.

64. Ibid., 29–30: "An all-inclusive concept of *kosmos* such as the Greeks knew did and could not exist in Israel. The whole of creation manifested Yahweh's power and presence, but it never attained the kind of self-sufficient unity that the Greek *kosmos* possessed. Moreover, the later [teaching of the church] . . . of a world created 'from nothing' [*ex nihilo*] and hence devoid of intrinsic necessity would have conflicted with the divine character of Greek nature." It is worth noting that Dupré does not celebrate this apparent impasse (see his "Introduction," e.g., 7).

Prelude

am the Lord your God," only as the command, "you shall love the alien as yourself," still rang in their ears.[65]

And yet the church has not always remembered Israel well. The church's intellectuals gradually, if unevenly, came to appropriate the synthetic presence of mind of the Gentiles of the northern Mediterranean basin. Doing so was a great and rewarding adventure. Their journey was long and difficult: from Jerusalem to Athens and to Rome,[66] involving "some severe crises."[67] And how could crises not come? Both older and newer champions of *physis* had much to be said in their favor, of course. However, there was only so far the church's gifted children could go toward synthesizing even the most purely idealized essences they and others had distilled from such decidedly uncongenial histories. Ideas never completely shake off the social bodies who gave them life. Before the Edict of Milan, more often than not both the members of the church and those of proper Roman society were struck and shaken by the difference that separated them, e.g., when from opposite sides of an open space,[68] immeasurable in Roman feet, they turned their faces toward each other, a few in the bloody dust of the coliseum floor, many in the wooden or marble coliseum seats above.

Unlike the divine of the physicians of the Greeks (and their heirs), the Creator-God of the Testaments of the church was declared in its baptismal credo first to be "the Father" of the "one Lord Jesus Christ" and only then the "maker of heaven and earth, of all that is, visible and invisible." And the "one Lord Jesus Christ . . . through whom all things were made" is no universal, no centered identity, no bloodless, faceless integrity—but the one "who was crucified under Pontius Pilate." Even when one finds in the texts of the young church what might be called "cosmic symbolism," the cosmos is subsumed under the "one Lord Jesus Christ," not the other way around. Indeed, the church's Holy Scriptures affirm that the whole cosmos was created in, through, by, and for this abased/exalted one. Though freely and without anxiety welcomed into a roomy sanctuary, universality blinks before the broken body of the "one Lord Jesus Christ," lifted up for all to see.[69]

---

65. Lev 19:33–34.

66. This "Prelude" is not best understood as a species of Tertullian's position on this point.

67. Dupré, *Passage to Modernity*, 31.

68. Of course, they oppose each other in very different ways.

69. Dupré, *Passage to Modernity*, 31: "Moreover, if God had definitively revealed himself in the 'man of sorrows,' how could one continue to regard the splendor of the universe as the image of a God who had appeared 'in the form of a slave'?"

Yet the church's sages again and again struggled to find ways of thinking at once both the God at work in the Gospels and the "nature" that has neither work to do nor an outside in which to do it. It struggled to think them at once without forgetting the difference between the things of this world and the things of God. Certainly they recited the Creed of Chalcedon with gusto, forsaking all to follow the incarnate heavenly Logos. Certainly they knew in their bones that God is sharply different from this world. They sang doxologies to that God. And yet . . . it was so very hard to resist the temptation to gather all their thoughts on the way to a profitable vision of a more magnificent, integrated *physis*, one finally with everything inside.

What is impressive is the way this temptation was resisted time and time again in the work of the church's doctors. Thus, though Francis of Assisi was certainly unlikely and exceptional, he was not even among intellectuals without foreshadowing. Yet it is perhaps telling that the revolt he heralded arose above all as he gave himself in naked prayer to the *particular, human* Jesus. That there might be revolution in *this* signals among *these* people the extent to which authorities (even ecclesiastical authorities) tend to pass by particularity—even *that* particularity—in order to get at the stable, integrating principles of which any particularity is by default taken to be an instance—and this, all the while rending a crusty, brown loaf of bread (bread the color of the skin of a tired young mother crossing the Sonoran Imperial Desert) and lifting a cup of deep red wine (wine the color of her thick blood starving for food, water, and air).

(She, sojourner that she is, finds no comfort in nature's appropriation of God.[70] She is not drawn to its physicians and the well-being they hawk. It is out into the open that she calls and steps. A God at home in the presence of "what is" lacks the freedom to turn to "what is not" simultaneously to call her Godward *and* into an open future. That is, the weak, the least, the stranger, the alien finds in *physis* only more of the same hopelessness that has always told her to get back in her place. That liturgy of the eucharist that fills her memory, on the other hand, invites her voice, her deeds, her body to the living God; it lays out before her a path to a holy eschaton[71] that is

---

70. There is comfort for her, however, in Rogers' expropriative understanding of "nature": "Nature, in short, is what the Spirit does with it." Rogers, *After the Spirit*, 151.

71. Note the ancestors of the word *eschaton* (the third numbered item in its language family) in *The American Heritage Dictionary of Indo-European Roots*, 2nd ed., s.v. "eghs.": "eghs Out. (Oldest form *eghs. 1. Variant *eks. a. ex1, ex-, from Latin *ex, ex-*, out of, away from; b. ecto-, ex-, exo-, exoteric, exotic; electuary, lekvar, synecdoche, from Greek *ex, ek*, out of, from. 2. Suffixed (comparative) variant form *eks-tero-*. a. estrange, exterior,

Prelude

coming for her and her little baby, a future free to place in radical crisis, say, an empire's judgment concerning her value for its growth potential.)

Still . . . the liturgy of the eucharist . . . smiles hospitably upon any who would make it their own . . . to consume it. It only asks that in the eating and drinking a reversal take place. Adam is at this wedding banquet to defer to Christ. The bread and the wine of the eucharist are gifts to be given, of course; but *we* who eat and drink are to be consumed by *them*, to be written into their story.[72] The eucharist is hospitable by definition, a good (*eu-*) grace (*charis*). It invites any and all who labor and are heavy-laden to come in and yield themselves, their gathered thoughts and deeds. All that is asked is that those "that are" in eating might be "reduced to nothing" and find fellowship with the elect from among "the things that are not" (1 Cor 1:28). In this they will find fellowship with that particular dark-skinned woodworker who during Holy Week was hanged on a wooden cross in solidarity with "the things that are not." But they will find also that they will have been driven to this end by the life's breath that drove him to the cross and awakened to new life by the gift that awakened him from the dead. Or so the liturgy of the eucharist promises.[73]

The promise is that in a living ecstatic sacrifice of worship a particular child held by his particular mother will have opened toward an eschatologically holy Trinity that in one life history places all claims to ownership under a crisis that crucifies/resurrects every worldly good (and evil), however tightly grasped. Indeed, to say "Trinity" is to say the "outside" of the "eschaton." The Trinity occurs as the unspeakably exalted Father and the unspeakably abased Son are held apart and together by the unspeakably quick Spirit. (Thus the man who stands watch in the night of the Sonoran Desert prays—perhaps only because of his proximity to her[74]—to the Father through the Son in the Spirit, even if he would hardly admit that

---

external, extra-, strange, from Latin *exter*, outward (feminine ablative *exterā*, *extrā*, on the outside); b. further suffixed (superlative) form most (*-mo-*, superlative suffix). 3. Suffixed form **eghs-ko-*, eschatology, from Greek *eskhatos*, outermost, last. 4. Celtic **eks-*, out (or), in compound **eks-di-sedo-*, (see sed-1). 5. samizdat, from Russian *iz*, from, out of, from Balto-Slavic **iz*." Note: whenever an asterisk appears in etymological material, it indicates that the word marked has a strongly attested yet still hypothetical status.

72. See Cavanaugh, *Torture and Eucharist*, 231–32; and Schmemann, *Eucharist*, 110–11.

73. A promise that, far from being a bribe, is taken in only *with* the bread and the wine of the liturgy and the baptism in whose wake they work.

74. Cf. 1 Cor 7:13–14.

such words come and go with his heavy breath.⁷⁵ He leans against a rock still warm from the day's hot sun, and is drawn by the body of the friend of transgressors, who in their memory and hope is lifted up still.⁷⁶ In that prayer in the darkness of the Sonoran Desert he is sent from the Father through the Son in the Spirit into the world that is bent on taking him out, along with the mother and child he had planned by now to have discarded. To him and to this woman and this baby a Mystery gently and lovingly calls out: "The Peace of God is coming and it is coming for you!")

The liturgy of the eucharist is above all prayer.⁷⁷ It is an eating and a working, but an eating not about getting full and a working not about getting paid.⁷⁸ In the liturgy of the eucharist a people eat a very particular performance of the will of the Father. Crucifixion/resurrection is their food and drink whenever they recline or sit upright at a table or lean in

---

75. See LaCugna, *God For Us*, 126–27.

76. Cf. John 12:32. See Nava, "God in the Desert," 71–74.

77. Schmemann, *Eucharist*, 83, 173, 180: "The Great Litany bestows on us, reveals the prayer of the Church, or, still better, *the Church as prayer*, as precisely the 'common task,' in its full cosmic and universal extent. In the church assembly man is called above all to give up, to 'lay aside' his 'cares' for everything that is only *his own*, personal, private, and as it were to 'dissolve' himself and what is his own in the prayer of the Church. . . . What , then, gives this chief, truly 'consummate' prayer of the liturgy its unity, transforms it into that *whole*, in and through which we affirm that this sacrament of sacraments is accomplished? The Church has answered this first and fundamental question literally from the first day of her existence by naming not only this prayer itself but also the entire liturgy with one word. This word is *eucharist, thanksgiving*. . . . The Church lives in thanksgiving; it is the air she breathes. Let us listen and, to the measure of our acceptance of this thanksgiving, we shall grasp, and not by reason alone but with our entire being, that here and only here, only in this knowledge/thanksgiving, occurs our entrance into the sole true—for it is of God—freedom. It is the freedom that the Holy Spirit . . . grants both as our breath, our royal nobility, and as power and perfection, fullness and beauty of life, or better still, *life in abundance*." Italics Schmemann's.

78. Bieler and Schottroff, *Eucharist*, 96, 104, 107, 109: "The economy of grace is about an exchange of gifts in which not accumulation but spending is the primary action, and in which is established an order of gratuitous wasting and not of calculation. . . . Thus the act of thanksgiving is intimately connected with the acknowledgment of God as the giver of life in its very basic physical sense. . . . The appreciation of the givenness of life as it is expressed in this kind of prayer acknowledges the limits to total accumulation and 'thingification' or 'commodification' of human productivity and natural resources. . . . What is given to me is not earned by me; it is not my exclusive possession. The gift rather refers back to the giver and the relationship it constitutes. . . . When we give thanks to God as the giver of life we reject the invisible mechanisms that come with the fetish character of goods." Kierkegaard, *Works of Love*, 321: "Oh, when you think of God, never forget that he does not have the least understanding about money."

cross-legged on bare ground before an open fire, whether there is much or little on their plates, in their bowls, or steaming in their calloused hands.[79] As their throats open to this food and drink, far from centering on itself, their work (*leitourgia*) flies away as a petition that all they do may have been gifted with gratitude and joy (*eucharistia, charis, chara*).[80] To eat and drink the performance of the will of the Father is to pray that we would be inscribed into the particular story of Jesus. It is indeed to hunt and gather, to build and sculpt, to speak and think—all week long. It is to breakfast, dine, and sup. But as written into *this* story, a week's meals and work become free acts of abandon. One carries them ("carries oneself") to that altar at which a gathering of people is taken into the history that on Good Friday is totalized to death and on Easter Sunday is loosed to life. We might call this history, which is simultaneously crucifixion and resurrection, "a living sacrifice."[81]

Thus, every proud discourse, experience, and belief is invited at the ecclesial assembly again and again to be given away. In their prayers the fabric these people weave all week long unravels outward to a world made new, an outside, an *eschaton*, an *eschatos*,[82] that is to liberate what was and is—in the future of the particular body of redemption in whose name they pray. The *telos* of work is here no longer the "goal" of Greek teleology, the stately oak already hidden in the acorn.[83] A new bright, sunless dawn breaks in on and thus dis-closes all 360° of every work-horizon. In time the geometric circle, as such, encloses only dead water. It is as it is spilled that water lives, i.e., that circles, coming to their end, empty what they might have contained, in deferral to the host, the guest,[84] who kindly refuses both the offer to property rights and the threat of eviction. These liturgical prayers declare that there will have been "perfection," "fulfillment," "satisfaction," "abundance," "maturity," "sanctification." Even now, it is said, there is a donation of that eschatological *teleios*. Yet it will have happened only because it will have *come*; "so that no one may boast" (Eph 2:9). It is a

---

79. Cf. John 4:34.
80. See Schmemann, *For the Life of the World*, 25, 37, 55, 87.
81. Cf. Rom 12:1.
82. Jenson, *Triune God*, 67 n. 16.
83. *American Heritage Dictionary of Indo-European Roots*, 2nd ed., s.v. "kwel-1": "Greek telos, 'completion of the cycle,' consummation, perfection, end, result."
84. The host (*Oxford English Dictionary*, s.v. "host, *n*.4") is both host and guest (*Oxford English Dictionary*, s.v. "host, *n*.2").

holy circle, *one* precisely as *many* partake ecstatically[85] in that elusive *Holy Trinity* that will forevermore occur, gratuitously, as a kind of "other-ing," partake *enhypostatically*, not in every respect unlike the glorified mutilated body of Jesus Christ—that is to say, to love in a certain way.[86]

The liturgy of the eucharist is gift. It is given with the particularity of the name Jesus,[87] a name with a baptismal history, a name washed in the coming of the Reign of that Holy Father who opens among and to one after another "little one" of this world and speaks there in the wingbeat of the dove: "this is my beloved child in whom I am well pleased." This corporate work is no healing act, i.e., not as the institution of a closed

---

85. A reader of Kierkegaard may be tempted to write "existentially."

86. Meyendorff, *Christ in Eastern Christian Thought*, 77: "The hypostasis is not the product of nature: it is that in which nature exists, the very principle of its existence. Such a conception of hypostasis . . . implies the existence of a fully human existence, without any limitation, 'enhypostatized' in the Word, who is a divine hypostasis. This conception assumes that God, as personal being, is not totally bound to his own nature; the hypostatic existence is flexible, 'open'; it admits the possibility of divine acts outside of the nature (energies) and implies that God can personally and freely assume a fully human existence while remaining God, whose nature remains completely transcendent." Kierkegaard, *Works of Love*, 182: "Think of an arrow flying, as is said, with the speed of an arrow. Imagine that it for an instant has an impulse to want to dwell on itself, perhaps in order to see how far it has come, or how high it is soaring above the earth, or how its speed compares with the speed of another arrow that is also flying with the speed of an arrow—in that same second the arrow falls to the ground."

87. Barth, *CD* 1/2, 346, 348, 355, 356–57: "The name of Jesus Christ creates the Christian religion. . . . We have to think of [the Christian religion] in the same way as we think of our own existence and that of the world, as a reality which is to be and is created by Jesus Christ yesterday and today and tomorrow. Apart from the act of its creation by the name of Jesus Christ, which like creation generally is a *creatio continua*, and therefore apart from the Creator, it has no reality. . . . There never was a man Jesus as such apart from the eternal reality of the Son of God. . . . The human nature of Jesus Christ has no hypostasis of its own, we are told. It has it only in the Logos. The same is true, therefore, of the earthly-historical life of the Church and the children of God, and therefore of the Christian religion. . . . In a secondary sense we can, of course, explain the necessity of the rise of Christianity in the light of Judaistic development and the political, spiritual and moral circumstances of the Mediterranean world in the Imperial period. But in its reality we can never explain or deduce it from that source. . . . It is this name [of Jesus Christ] which stands in relation to the world of religions, as does the sun to the earth. . . . It means that the Christian religion is snatched from the world of religions and the judgment and sentence pronounced upon it, like a brand from the burning. It is not that some men are vindicated as opposed to others, or one part of humanity as opposed to other parts of the same humanity. It is that God Himself is vindicated as opposed to and on behalf of all men and all humanity."

integrity, a "wholeness." It heals only as sacrifice,[88] standing out prayerfully into the faithfulness of the Holy One who comes to dwell in the work of these people—without ceasing to be holy. It is a healing act in the way that the evocation of Abram from his Chaldean home, never to return, was a healing act, viz., as a journey of promise (Gen 12:1). It is a healing act in the way that the march of Moses into Egypt from the backside of the desert was a healing act, viz., carried by the shout of the unimaginably free God: "Let my people go!" (Ex 5:1; cf. 3:14). It is a healing act in the way that the raising of Lazarus was a healing act, viz., as a call issuing out of the coming Reign of God to "come forth" (John 11:43). It is a healing act in the way that the resurrection of Jesus was a healing act, viz., as the emptying of a tomb by the egress of a body still wounded—gloriously open and inviting (Luke 24:39; John 20:27). It is that healing act that breaks through "what is" from a future never to be cordoned off by the locked arms of a company of guards.

(Let us say that a Brazilian mother and her little baby make their way across the Sonoran Desert, elude the watchful eye of Homeland Security in the Imperial Wildlife Refuge, find kindness among strangers, are given transport across Imperial County and beyond, and at long last find a place to bathe and sleep and eat in South Central Los Angeles. One Sunday morning she, perhaps, makes her way with her baby and the man with the wide face, with broad shoulders and huge hands, who from all appearances could never have begun to finance such a long, long pilgrimage north, to this little church. Let us say that she and they sit just across the aisle from a politically sensitive and intellectually curious man who, because he could, has driven into the neighborhood from across town to attend a vigil at South Central Farm. Let us say that he and they rise together one moment, fall together into one line, walk one after the other toward the front of the church, and together kneel side by side at one altar rail to receive the one crusty bread and drink the one sweet wine. When that bread and then that wine touch their tongues, with what have they been fed? How are they now nourished to live, to respond, to pray?)[89]

---

88. *Oxford English Dictionary*, s.v. "sacrifice, *adj.*1": "Etymology: < Latin *sacrificus*, < *sacri-* , *sacer* sacred (*sacra* neuter plural, sacrifices) + *-ficus* : see –fic *suffix*"; s.v. "-fic, *suffix*": "Repr. Latin *-ficus* '-making, -doing' (< weakened root of *facere* to make, do), forming adjs." "Sacrifice" thus signifies "making sacred or holy."

89. "Is this Brazilian woman an actual, living, flesh-and-blood human being, a woman with a name and address? I mean, do you know this woman, have you met her, have you talked with her? Because if she is and you have—*how dare you tell her story?!*

After Crucifixion

What gives you the right to steal her narrative voice? What gives you the right to objectify her? Frankly, I find it offensive and demeaning that you would presume to represent her here, to commodify her, to force her into this work and force us to become voyeurs with you!" "There is no answer that I—or anyone—could articulate to resolve such questions. Everything would be so much simpler, if I could simply answer that I have made it all up. But something like this, someone like this, something so exceptional, so contrary to the demographics of 'immigration trends,' cannot be made up. If these are my words (and, of course, in a litigious world of property claims and rights, one could argue that case), it is my prayer that, by the time another day of hard work is done, they will have at least stopped being 'mine.' 'Is all this, then, fictive? Is she a symbol of something?' If she is a 'symbol,' she is a non-representational—an iconic—one, or at least this is my prayer. And, if she is 'fictive,' she exceeds fiction, the way every saint, Catherine of Siena, for example, exceeds not only her story, but all the stories of the saints."

1 The Root from Which They Spring

Introductions

> *Take off your old coat and roll up your sleeves,*
> *Life is a hard road to travel, I believe.*[1]

I HAVE BEEN a university teacher for about a third of a century. My area of presumed expertise is theology. Theology is, if it is anything at all, a way of giving attention to God. Simply put, professors of theology profess God. That is why good people send their children off to college to study with theologians, with people like me. And I—professor that I am—do profess God, overtly, loudly, passionately. What is so embarrassing, though, is that I have such a hard time saying what it is that *God* means. You would think that someone laboring in this field for so long would have at least that much nailed down! Yet I must confess that I do not.

The problem is not that I am a closet infidel, hiding behind some plastic mask of public piety (like a candidate running for office). I try very hard to be honest and open, particularly where I am most professional. That is, my comprehension-failure is no secret. In fact I would think nothing would be more evident, as I go on and on in class, than that I *strain* just to get that black hole of a little three-letter word out. But, of course, my task as a professor of theology is not *just* to get that one word out; I am to throw out a whole galaxy of words and ideas and images and passions and practices that are agitated by and drawn into that black hole.

---

1. Stookey et al., "Old Coat."

Of course, speaking of God in this way is hopeless. To say "God" in the field where I labor is surely not to say "a compressed and compressing density, that heaviest, darkest phenomenon of orthodox physics." And though there are speculative physicists and writers of science fiction who think of a black hole as a portal to another, distant point in space-time—and it might not be out of the question to think of one as an exit portal to some altogether different *configuration* of space-time, some new cosmos even—I have for a long time now been unable to speak of God as a way out of this earthy world. Speaking of God seems rather to be a way into it, even if as an alien.

There, I have already said too much. My location is showing. Yet there is nothing surprising about that. Every college sophomore knows that God is tradition-specific. One opens the *OED* to the "G" tab and there one finds a meandering account of the roots of the little English word, roots that draw nutrients from deep inside pagan soil, where perhaps the ordinary usage of God is more happily at home. Provocative phrases about sacrifice and invocation appear in the midst of its history, their subjects and objects mingle, and in it all there is no outbreak into anything particularly transcendent (though transcendence as a universal within this system appears). Everything swims in the warm, immanent amniotic fluid of human consciousness. God as such is contained, subjected to occupational therapy at the merest suggestion of aphasia, and assigned the task to speak well in accordance with reasonable expectations. Thus God says something that is generally true, able to be heard everywhere and by all; a grand linguistic phenomenon, an absolute truth, the chief exemplification of all metaphysical principles, no doubt.

And yet the *OED* is not the only big book. At the "Job" tab, one finds a meandering account of a particularly poor and troubled man, who—sitting on the ash heap, alone but for the company of dogs, aching, burning, and with every new upset tempted to curse God and die—turns his two wide eyes to the open sky and with a passion that rips apart the fabric of space-time and its God cries, "Violence!" (Job 19:7) and as if encountering something new on the far side of the sun, prophesies, "I know my redeemer lives" (Job 19:25; cf. Eccl 1:9). And I read that with him on the ash heap—in a maelstrom so fierce that even Job's immeasurable suffering seems a shadow cast from what is for him yet to come—another poor and lonely man, hanging, dying, gasping for air, opens his throat and cries, "My God, my God, why have you forsaken me?" (Mark 15:34); and when "the curtain of the temple [is] torn in two . . . [as if encountering something new on the far side of death and damnation], Jesus, crying with a load voice, [prophesies], 'Father, into your hands I commend my spirit'" (Luke 23:45–46). It strikes me that there is uttered in these narratives a word that no sequence of letters, however small or large, can contain. And I strain to say this new word when I stand before a classroom full of the children of good people, I strain to say it in such a way that no good person could ever say or hear it. And likely, were I just able to find a really good therapist, I'd put this obsession behind me and get on with my life.

The question for me then is "why, why do I see and hear this way?" Most of my colleagues these past decades have seen and heard differently. They seem much calmer about it all, speaking as they do of the good, the true, and the beautiful and of how God fits so well into a system of values, goals, and ideals, i.e., a worldview; of how the story of Job and of Jesus and of God is a story that resolves questions, not complicates and ruptures them. They have told me that it is all about absolutes and universals and all I seem ever to see and hear are contextualized particulars, the life-stories of people with *particular* faces and voices, of a God with *particularly elusive* faces and voices. Of course, it may just be that I have been beguiled by Protestant nominalism, that I have fallen prey to that most modern of all perversions, postmodernism, that I am a child of my age. Indeed, I suppose this is all true. How could I honestly say anything else, even as I strain to say something else than the banal or high-born talk of my age?

My journey has been a particular one, too, of course. Everyone's is. I don't understand much of it. It is not over, after all. Yet I would venture to say that it is the way I have been given and made time, the way I have come to let time go, the timely way I have begun to be named. Whatever that tiny English pronoun—I—might signify in this case, the thinking and speaking and working attached to it happen here, in this story. And it isn't just my story.[2] I'm not even sure I qualify for a best *supporting* actor nomination.

It is not insignificant that my hard Scots-Irish ancestors[3] cut their way across an ocean and the rivers and forests of a forbidding New World to reach for the promises they'd heard were hidden under the cruel Appalachian Mountains of eighteenth-century Virginia, or the cruel Ozark Mountains of mid-nineteenth-century Arkansas, or the cruel hills of late

---

2. Anymore than this essay is an autobiography.

3. There is some circumstantial evidence that the first "Keen" of my clan was in fact a German mercenary soldier of the Thirty Years' War who settled in New Sweden. He changed his name from Jürgen Schneeweiss to Jürgen Kuhn (from "Snow-White" to the compensatory "Bold"), which over time degenerated eventually to "Urine Keen." Nonetheless, the Scots-Irish predominate in our family.

After Crucifixion

nineteenth-century Oklahoma; that both my parents were raised in abject poverty by single mothers[4] just to the southeast of the official borders of the Great Depression's Dust Bowl; that I am an only child; that I attended nine schools before I went away to college; that I was eighteen in 1968; that in the summer of that year, while reading the book of Acts in the Desert Southwest, I became a pacifist; that the theologians I first threw myself into were Søren Kierkegaard and John Wesley—no theologians at all, the Hollywood Foreign Press would tell us; that I have spent my life among Holiness people; that I still think about the lyrics to Bob Dylan's "A Hard Rain's A-Gonna Fall"; that I am an ordained deacon and not an elder; that I have been married over forty years, have three children and six grandchildren; that my parents, now in their nineties, live with us; that I have had already a long career as a professor in four private, self-consciously evangelical universities; and that I know how to be alone.

Perhaps it is all of that which inclines me on a brisk spring morning—obligated to stay put, though these days I am—to make my way to a tall, broad, clear window and there to dream of the open road.[5] Perhaps it is all of that which inclines me to make my way to an icon—written with bright pigments across a salvaged plank of wood or in the interplay of the black and white on a printer's acid-free rice paper or between the lines and words and along the margins of the credos of saints and sinners or upon the tales of liturgically martyred mothers and fathers or in, with, and under the playful work of the eating and drinking of bread and wine—and there to dream of God.[6]

---

4. My father's father, decades older than my grandmother, his third wife, died in his early seventies in 1926, leaving my six-year-old father and his five siblings, the youngest a babe in arms, to be cared for by their mother. My mother's father was an unchecked alcoholic who neglected and abused his family and was in many ways worse than no father or husband at all.

5. See Cone, *Cross and the Lynching Tree*, 19.

6. Rogers, *After the Spirit*, 98–99:

>   Mary's eyes   beholding Eve
>   and looking down on Adam,   were impelled to tears;
>   but she stays them   and hastens
>   to conquer nature   she who *para phusin* gave birth to Christ
>   her son.
>   Yet her entrails were stirred   in suffering with her parents
>   —a compassionate mother   accorded with the Merciful one
>   So she tells them   —Cease your lamentations,
>   and I will be your ambassador   to him born from me.

And yet a dream of God—*this* God—is no ordinary dream, nor night terror, as Daniel and John the Revelator teach us. It is an *apocalyptic vision*. As such it makes manifest what good people do not want to see, perhaps cannot see. It manifests above all that there is a tomorrow that no yesterday can dictate.[7] But it does so with the ambiguity that accompanies every call to revolution. "The Reign of God is coming," it says, "and it is coming for *you*!" As a member of one of the world's more comfortable socioeconomic classes, I should recoil with horror from this word. "Woe to you rich!" Jesus, the apocalypse of St. Luke, declares (Luke 6:24). And yet, perhaps stupidly, I find myself drawn to the apocalyptic literature of God. It is bewildering, a terrifying mystery story; but somehow fascinating.[8]

Not all mysteries are fascinating, of course, especially if like this one, they are irresolvable. The exact numeric value of pi is a mystery to which is attached neither *tremendum* nor *fascinans*. Those mysteries that most commonly fascinate us are those that we expect with some effort to resolve. They are intellectual challenges—mountains that we set out to conquer, even if only because they are there. They remain fascinating only so long as they simultaneously resist and yield to us. Once they are conquered, we move on to something else. We might wax proudly nostalgic, as we recount the thrills of our victories, but to remember a *former* mystery is not to *face* a mystery.

Those of us who have been struck by this apocalyptic vision of *God* would tell a different story. To be thus God-struck is to face what Kierkegaard's pseudonym, Johannes Climacus, points to, when he tells us that the

---

So Romanos the Melodist, the greatest liturgical poet of the Greek Church, speaks of something *para phusin*.... The Greek preposition *para* is well suited to contain the ambiguities of excess. Its root meaning is spatial: beside, alongside, as in the word "parallel." If the lexicon lists the meaning "against," that is best understood as "*compared against*," as in "paragon," "paradigm," "parable," which indicate no opposition. It would be misleading to indicate contrariety rather than comparison. No one supposes contrast in such words as "paraenesis" or "Paraclete." Even "parasite" is one that "feeds beside," while "paradox" and "paranormal" connote what is beside or in addition to the normal, rather than against it. A "paraphrase" is supposed to say the same thing, not something opposed. Modern coinages such as a "paramedic" and "paralegal" continue the correct understanding of those who work with or alongside, not against others.

7. See Moltmann, *Future of Creation*, 41–48, for the difference between extrapolation and anticipation. Also see Pannenberg, *Theology and the Kingdom of God*, 63, 139–41; and *Basic Questions in Theology*, 2:241–49.

8. I am thinking, of course, of Otto, *Idea of the Holy*.

After Crucifixion

passion of the thinker is to think what cannot be thought.⁹ This apocalyptic God is an irresolvable, engaging mystery that won't let us go, that won't ever let us rest in peace (cf. Ps 139:8 and 1 Pet 3:19). God revealed is God hidden and "how unrestingly active God is in all his creatures, allowing none of them to take a holiday."[10] The engagement of this mystery is absolute. It calls for each of us to stand up to it with her whole heart, soul, mind, and strength, as Wesley never tires of reminding us.[11]

I am a theologian. The work I do is largely academic and intellectual, the work of words. Just about every day I face the challenge of gathering my thoughts before a classroom of students or a blank computer screen. And I have a lot of thoughts, having read too many books and articles, attended too many lectures, attended to too many seminars, spent too many hours—way too many hours—before movie and television screens and loud speakers, and pondered too long the words and deeds of my family and friends and enemies.[12] That means that I have many possessions, intangible though they may be—or at least that's what I hear. The question for me, then, is only a slightly different version of the one that went through the man of Mark 10, the man whom Jesus loved. "You lack one thing, Craig;

---

9. Kierkegaard [Climacus], *Philosophical Fragments*, 37.

10. Luther, *De Servo Arbitrio*, 200–239; the direct quotation is found on 234.

11. Neither Wesley nor Kierkegaard is an escapist mystic, however. They are both children of the earth, practical people who (unlike Luther) love the book of James, who love the way a command of God takes shape in the concrete evenings and mornings of ordinary women and men. Kierkegaard has a better eye for the ambiguity of all human works; Wesley for their definiteness as they become good news particularly for the poor. But the earthy concreteness of the work to which they both give themselves is inspired by a vision of the *New* Earth that we cannot see without the miracle of new eyes (cf. Heb 11:1). Kierkegaard may stress the "cannot" of this miracle and Wesley its "new eyes," but in doing so they both bear witness to the impossible event in which we come to yield to an other who simply will not become our property. Indeed, as we perform the works that bear witness to this other, Kierkegaard and Wesley would have us let go of those works as well, as *formerly* Rich Young Rulers who, without grieving, follow Jesus through the eye of a needle (Mark 10:18–27). To *keep* the works of love, the works we have done, to *hold on* to them as our property, is to be poisoned by them, sickened unto death. See Wesley, *Plain Account*, 112 [25.38.8]; "Repentance of Believers," 352 [III.4]; "Original Sin," 182–85 [III.1–5]; "New Birth," 188–94 [I.1–II.5]; "Good Steward," 296–98 [IV.1–4]; Kierkegaard [Anti-Climacus], *Sickness Unto Death*, 18; Kierkegaard, *Works of Love*, 40–43, 246–63.

12. And found out too many times that I had gotten it all wrong and had to begin again from the beginning. Perhaps that simply shows that even when one has gotten it all wrong, one might still pray. See Barth, *CD* 3/3, 265.

go, sell what you own, and give . . . to the poor, and you will have treasure in heaven; then come, follow me" (Mark 10:21, sort of).

Now, I could look at Jesus' command as an investment opportunity. "Treasure in heaven" sounds like a pretty profitable return. The problem is that when "treasure" gets attached to "heaven," everything gets upended. "Heaven" is, if anything, elusive.[13] "Our Father who art in heaven," says above all that the God whom Jesus teaches us to address will not be laid hold of.[14] "Treasure in heaven" is then a very strange treasure, one I cannot enter into a calculator, one that does not add to my net worth. And so, I'm left, having received the command of Jesus, with an unimaginable promise. It is a heartening promise, *that* I do gather from the passage; but it is one which I cannot objectify enough to covet. I suspect that even Husserl would have had trouble fixing his gaze on such a treasure.[15] I am commanded by Jesus to give up all my property for the sake of a most unsettling impropriety; hardly an alluring proposal. And yet again and again and again the question rings in my ears—"Craig, son of James, do you love me more than these?" (John 21:15–17, sort of). And something stirs in me and I want to say, "Lord, you know everything; you know that I love you" (17).

How do I *not* go away grieving? How do I feed his sheep? I'm a thinker and not a very good one at that. Am I to become more ignorant than I am already? Am I to become thought-poor? Is this a call to some Jungian *sacrificium intellectus*?[16]

How do I *not* go away grieving? Perhaps the answer—like the yes of a child to the voice of her mother calling her name—rises insolubly before the particular mystery precisely of the evocative *gospel*. "When I came to you, brothers and sisters, I did not come proclaiming the mystery of God to you in lofty words or wisdom. For I decided to know nothing among you except Jesus Christ, and him crucified" (1 Cor 2:1–2). The mystery before which I am to give up all my intellectual possessions, Paul is saying, is the crucifixion of Jesus Christ.

---

13. Von Rad, "*ouranos*, Old Testament," 507; Traub, "*ouranos*, New Testament," 520–21, 525.

14. See Gundry, *Matthew*, 106. "Hallowed by thy name" makes a similar point, it seems to me, that we do not name God; God does. This strikes me as an answer to Derrida's account, in *Gift of Death*, 95–115, of the apparent investment logic of obeying the command of God.

15. See Husserl, "Phenomenology," 700; and *Ideas*, 105–7.

16. Jung, *Memories, Dreams, Reflections*, 215.

After Crucifixion

But *this* sacrifice of the intellect—and that is the right, though non-Jungian, phrase—is to be no suicide. The gospel insists that Jesus Christ gives himself to the coming of the "God not of the dead, but of the living" (Mark 12:27), the coming of the *living* God. The gospel insists that Jesus' Holy Father, alive in heaven, is made manifest in *life*. The gospel indeed insists that the forsaken death of the carnal Son makes the Holy Father manifest, but that it does so in the work of the Spirit through the *resurrection* of his dead and damned body. The gospel insists that it is in his *glorified* dead and damned body that *we*, too, are called to move; that it is in that life that we come alive, that we are saved; that there we repeat (derivatively) his life-rhythm of crucifixion/resurrection—through the liturgy of baptism and eucharist—because his body is nothing but the life-rhythm of crucifixion/resurrection.[17] The gospel insists that our evenings and mornings become a kind of dance of death . . . swallowed up in life, that resurrection life is so alive that even death is no contrast to it. It is into this liturgy that Peter and I are called. We are called to Jesus' sheep—standing wide-eyed as they do in this world God so loves—to offer them the *food* that is precisely this body into which we have been incorporated. We hear, Peter and I, and we may yet believe, that to *eat this body* is oddly not for it to be incorporated into us, but for us to be incorporated into *it*—and thus for us to repeat (derivatively) the rhythm of crucifixion/resurrection. It is in this way that we are to *live*, bodies together in one "*living* sacrifice," a thoughtful worship,[18] a "renewing of [the] mind," which defers (Rom 12:1–3), one performed again and again and again, pouring out what is freshly given—as might a spring that gives water only as it is replenished with the gift of unearned rain (John 4:9–14).[19] That, it seems to me, is the mystery of the *gospel*.

As a theologian who would hear and believe, I am indeed to gather my thoughts, but only in order to give them away. Had the Rich Young Ruler not departed grieving, had he indeed followed Jesus, he, too, would

---

17. *Oxford English Dictionary*, s.v. "mystery, *n*.1": "In later Christian use *mysterion* became equivalent to sacrament (in several passages, e.g., Dan 2:18, the Vulgate renders it by *sacramentum*, even when it means only 'secret'; in other passages *mysterium* is used)."

18. The Greek phrase of verse one that the NRSV translates as "spiritual worship" is "logiken latreian." The KJV translates it "reasonable service." Neither translation seems to me to deliver the provocation of the juxtaposition of "logos" and "latreia" here. I do not read this passage the way Sarah Coakley does, however. See her *Sacrifice Regained*, 25–28.

19. Cf. Wesley, "Great Privilege of Those That Are Born of God," especially 434–36 [I.8, II.1] and 442 [III.2–3].

have gathered his property, i.e., in order to dispose of it. But doing so is never dropping the ballast of worldly goods in order to soar into some higher "spiritual" realm, i.e., in order to get out. Following the crucified/resurrected Christ *is* the work of giving away our goods. However, it is performed precisely as an act of plunging into the world, the world hallowed when the carnal body of Christ is glorified in the glorification of the Father on Easter Sunday morning. That is, the glorified *carnality* of the body of Christ calls out to us, Peter and me. "Let the same mind be in you that was in Christ Jesus," Paul writes, "who . . . emptied himself . . . humbled himself and became obedient to the point of death—even death on a cross" (Phil 2:5–8).[20] Therefore, on the day new goods come into our hands, on that day our hands do not become unclean. They are gifted—with a gift that will not become property. And a gift that will not become property is there to be given. To follow Christ is with him perpetually to be emptied (cf. John 4:14).

But how am I, a theologian who has no trouble remembering that he is a human being, to pull this off? "For mortals it is impossible, but not for God; for God all things are possible" (Mark 10:27). Trust in that, one hears. Yet one hears as well that neither can we trust. If we could, trusting would make us haughty (Ephesians 2). It is more than enough that, when we cannot, we do. When we cannot and yet do, we may perhaps learn to give thanks that in spite of ourselves this, too, was possible.[21] The answer to the "how" question, that is, is another "how" question, which may be put in the indicative: It is grace . . . all the way down, just as it is grace all the way up.

To say grace and faith is to say Trinity. God the Father moves out through God the Son in God the Spirit to a world that first and last covets its riches.[22] The Trinity opens to this world from the depths of hell and gathers it into the body broken and left to rot there, the body of Christ in whom the Spirit glorifies the Father. By entering into the body of Christ, the discarded bits of decaying tissue that litter hell are stitched together to make that body's vital organs, they there partake of its glory—the holiness, the love, of the Father—and move in the Spirit into the very world that treated them and him so badly. My calling as a theologian is to do my word-work down this path, too, a body-part of a journeying body, praying without ceasing, in everything giving thanks, rejoicing evermore, moving back and forth from

20. Cf. Wesley, "On Zeal," 308–21.
21. Barth, *Evangelical Theology*, 200.
22. See LaCugna, *God For Us*, 222–23.

this groaning earth to the earth eschatologically redeemed, from the earth eschatologically redeemed to this groaning earth.[23] My calling is to stand before a classroom full of students or to sit before a blank computer screen and in this way to pray, give thanks, and rejoice in the mystery of the gift.

I am to stand on the mound, cleats pressed into the rubber, senses raw and open to the park's batter, runners, and fielders before whom I move, seeing and hearing, almost smelling, tasting, and touching what shifts within and without the strike zone, feeling the weight, density, and contour of the ball in my rosined hand, thought, emotion, imagination agitated, and with everything in me *throw*. Without balking. The Rich Young Ruler, Peter, and I are commanded to disperse our goods to the *poor*. How am I to obey this command without balking, I who profess God before classrooms full of students with the resources to attend expensive private universities?

If I held the opinion that Jesus' attention to the poor in the gospel narratives is to be sublimated into a generic concern for other people ("aren't we *all* poor in some sense?"), then I would have no problem at all. And on any but the heaviest and hardest days I would indeed say that all the students in all my classrooms are given before me by God to be served. However, as it turns out, there are in this present evil age men and women and children whose hunger is *actual* (if the word "actual" might for now be taken to gesture toward such a gnawing absence)—people like my mother and my father were, when they were hungry little children. To be poor is not to have a shortage of cash on hand, a paucity of consumer choices, a slow internet connection, unwieldy student or home loans, or too few toys. The poor are people, not especially good or bad, but more often than not ordinary people, whose life is being sucked out of them day in and day out, e.g., by the forces of what we so calmly describe as globalization. As long as I remember that God emptied the tomb of the crucified Jesus, as long as I remember that God made Adam out of the dust of the earth, as long as I remember that it is the *body* of Christ that is salvation, as long as I remember that the church is constituted by the work of the eating and drinking of the eucharist, as long as I remember that Jesus fed the hungry, as long as I remember that "the whole tenor of scripture" bears witness to God's prevenient grace particularly for the poor—i.e., God's preference for the poor—I cannot reduce them to one more item on a uniform list of those for whom we are to care. As long as I remember, it will follow, as surely as it follows that slaves are not greater than their masters (Matt 10:24–25), that we are to

---

23. Schmemann, *For the Life of the World*, 31–46.

care for the poor in particular and above all. We are to care for the poor in particular and above all, because in the Jewish peasant, Jesus, God cares for them in particular and above all. This God's grace is not an abstract "decision" to forego punishment for those who deserve punishment. This God's grace is God's movement out into the world to save it, i.e., to sanctify it. This grace of God is the Spirit of God, the Spirit that raised Jesus Christ from the dead. The Spirit here is explosive, holy life. She is the wind of a storm, the pounding current of a raging river. And God's grace rushes particularly to the poor.[24] We know that, because she rushed particularly to the poor man Jesus, laid out on a cold slab in a cold tomb. If we pray to enter into that grace, we pray that we will be carried on its current particularly to them, to people with names and faces, dirty, hungry faces, faces I know all too well. That is what I hear in Jesus' call to the Rich Young Ruler, to Peter, and to me.

That, of course, means that they and I are to spend our resources directly for the poor. However, there is in Jesus' command a specific question addressed to me and to people like me, a question that has specifically to do with the word-work of a theologian. Standing face to face with a poor man or woman or child, it seems so bloodless and distracted and insensitive, but I am a theologian and I am compelled to ask it right out loud: what does it signify for me, a theologian, a word-worker, to obey the call of Jesus to give to the poor?

In part it signifies that I am to hope for and remember the poor with my words. I am to give my thoughts away before people who are not hungry for the sake of those who are. I am to teach in the direction of the poor, unhanding my intellectual goods for them, calling my students to unhand their goods, and confessing my own unworthiness to take such words on my lips, praying that I, too, will hear the words I am given to say, that I will hear them and obey. But there is more to the call of Jesus than this. To turn to the poor in obedience to the command of Jesus is not to give them a hand up, to teach them to fish, to give them the business skills to begin the steady climb into the middle class. All that already trembles before the principalities and powers we call capitalism. To turn to the poor in obedience to the command of Jesus does not even require that one be *other than poor*. The poor, too, are called to the poor. And we—rich and poor

24. My friend Donna Techau has told me (in a Facebook conversation, February 2, 2011) that I might also say that the Holy Spirit "is a gentle fresh breeze. She is non-coercive repentance. She brings peaceable joy. She gathers us in her arms and holds us close. She dances lightly across our skin." Rogers notes that "the Spirit blows not only like a hurricane but like a *prevailing* wind" (*After the Spirit*, 198).

alike—are called to stand in solidarity with them—without demanding that they cease being poor. Doing so is a means of grace not only for them, but particularly for us.[25]

Grace comes particularly where calculation has come to an end. And does anyone doubt that standing in solidarity with the poor without demanding that they cease being poor requires an act of trust, of hope, before an incalculable mystery? Not to go away grieving signifies that in the word-work I do I am to take up the task of Isaiah 6 and Mark 4, viz., to be situated like a surd in the pounding, clanging, beating, deafening din of that social-political-economic machine that *makes* people poor. It is to name the beast that devours them and with them to look it in the eye, unafraid. That is, for me to give my goods away to the poor is for me to face the freedom of the God who raised Jesus Christ from the grave, a freedom that does not need sound economic policies, that does not need the system of acquisition, private property, productivity, fixed and circulating capital, investment and return, commodification, supply schedules, derived demand, profit and loss, competition, division of labor, markets, wages, and debt. To give my goods away to the poor is among other things to bear witness to an economy of giving and forgiving, an economy of impropriety, an economy that remembers the hope of the resurrection of the Crucified. That is, to give my goods away to the poor is to live and speak and write before the mystery of God's holy love, a love that comes as an unsettling holiness that will never be a line-item on an asset-management tally sheet.

Trinity, crucifixion/resurrection, church, the poor, i.e., Jesus, who loved the one he calls "Father" with his whole heart, soul, mind, and strength,[26] and because of that would not maintain his personal integrity in the face of his neighbors[27]—this is the mystery I strain so hard to say, when I stand before a classroom full of the children of good people. My task, as a theologian, is to think it and say it again and again and again. That is what *meta-noia* quite literally signifies in particular in my particular case. My task is to think-after, in pursuit of, the way of God into the world, to think-after crucifixion. My task is to take whatever thoughts I can find and let them loose before a classroom or a reader, i.e., in the liturgy of the eucharist, the liturgy in which the broken body and shed blood of Jesus are manna, food that is to be eaten, not stockpiled.

25. Wesley, "On Zeal," 313 [II.5].
26. See Meyendorff, *Christ in Eastern Christian Thought*, 159–60.
27. Ibid., 164.

It may be that one day Alzheimer's Disease will have rotted away all of my thoughts and that there will be effectively nothing there that a professor might give and no professor there to give it. And yet I will not be alone in that place either. Among the wonders of the gospel is that Jesus is there as well—shining with the light of God's glory. Still, as long as I have eyes to see, I am called on each new day to look for the small round things that God has placed on the face of the wilderness where I sojourn, to pick them up and eat them, to hold out in the freedom of grace the works they enliven me to do, and to say right out in public with the plagiarizing Wesley, "I come, Lord, to restore to thee what thou hast given; and I freely relinquish it, to enter again into my own nothingness. For what is the most perfect creature in heaven or earth in thy presence, but a void capable of being filled with thee and by thee; as the air, which is void and dark, is capable of being filled with the light of the sun, who withdraws it every day to restore it the next, there being nothing in the air that either appropriates this light or resists it? O give me the same facility of receiving and restoring thy grace and good works! I say, *thine;* for I acknowledge the root from which they spring is in thee, and not in me."[28]

---

28. Wesley, *Plain Account*, 113 [25.38.8]. These words are a part of a larger passage that Wesley calls "Farther Thoughts on Christian Perfection." That passage ends with an eight-page section that Wesley has adapted from the work of Jean Duvergier. "These 'Reflections'—as can be detected from the style—are not original to Wesley. They trace back, through a series of extracts, to the *Lettres Chrétiennes et Spirituelles* (1645) of Jean Duvergier de Hauranne, Abbé de Saint-Cyran (1581–1643). Wesley's immediate French source was an extract from *Lettres* by Robert Arnauld d'Andilly titled *Instructions chrestiennes* (Paris, 1672). Wesley selected and translated 335 of the 1160 numbered reflections in d'Andilly, titled them 'Christian Instructions, extracted from a late French Author,' and placed them (alongside 'Thoughts on Christian Perfection') among the additional tracts at the end of Vol. IV of *Sermons*, published in 1760 (see Bibliography, No. 131.v). This extract was apparently issued as a separate publication the following year by William Strahan of London. Then in 1763, to provide this conclusion to *Farther Thoughts*, Wesley undertook another round of extracting, reducing his original 335 select reflections to 64, arranging these passages in eight numbered groups with the theme of each group identified by the italicizing of a key word or phrase, and making some further abridgements or revisions of his translations. This final selection from Hauranne's meditations was carried over into the *Plain Account* with little change except for the omission of the first item, and some renumbering of the sections in the edns. of 1785 and 1789. The reflections were omitted from *Plain Account* in *Works* (1773, vol. 24) because the longer extract from Hauranne was included in this same volume, retitled 'Christian Reflections, translated from the French'" (Randy Maddox, Private Correspondence, October 8, 2012). The details of Wesley's editing and use of Duvergier's work will be laid out in Maddox's editorial comments to vol. 13 of *The Works*, to be published in the near future.

Interlude[1]

THE CHURCH OF THE Nazarene in Mid-City is a little urban congregation just off California Highway 15 in San Diego. It is a humble church, a broken church, far from ideal. Between cracked brick walls tagged by turf-contending neighborhood gangs, regret and gratitude, shame and joy, probability and possibility contend. Occasionally, fragmentarily, this little church becomes the address at which something extraordinary occurs, the address at which the throats and hands of ordinary people open (perhaps without purpose or design) to speak and to act and thus to await the consecration of the labyrinth of its hospitable spaces.

Mid-City gathers weekly to worship in five different language groups. Its people variously articulate the good news and feast on the body and blood of Christ. Coordinated with a Lenten calendar, after prolonged catechesis, the church performs yearly baptisms, on Easter Sunday.[2] Particularly on this day a baptizand stands up out of the water as a sign that light still shines in darkness, a sign that these whose destiny it is to assemble as the church have entered, and as the church are repeatedly to enter, into a work that is not their own, a sign that it is *Christ's* work by which the people

---

1. Mark 2:16: "When the scribes of the Pharisees saw that he was eating with sinners and tax-collectors, they said to his disciples, 'Why does he eat with tax-collectors and sinners?'"

2. On Epiphany Sunday, congregants, adults and children, addled or clear-headed, who have not been baptized are invited to take the journey toward baptism. Those who respond are interviewed by their pastor. On Ash Wednesday a sponsor is assigned to provide the baptizand with support and guidance, meeting with her weekly or more often. Although this is a church that ordinarily invites all, baptized or not, to feast on the body and blood of Christ, she is asked to postpone her celebration of the eucharist on subsequent Sundays until she is baptized. Just after the Ministry of the Word each service from Epiphany through Holy Saturday she is invited to stand at a temporary distance from the rest of the assembly to meditate on the catechetical instruction she has received, attending in particular to Genesis 1–3, the Beatitudes, the Lord's Prayer, and the Apostles' Creed. Holy Week services are given to the remembrance of *Christ's* bloody baptism on the cross. Maundy Thursday, Good Friday, and Holy Saturday services call the church to meditation on the abasement of Christ as the pattern of its discipleship. The congregation looks on these days to the baptizand as the icon of all the children of God, lost sheep found on Christ's journey to the cross. Holy Saturday is in particular devoted to explicating the significance of baptism.

of this present evil age are reconciled both to *Christ's* Father and with *this* Father to one another.

When the baptizand is led forward by her sponsor, the whole congregation is invited to celebrate in solidarity with her. They are to remember *their* entry into the work of this Christ. Constituted afresh, the church—embracing and embraced by those wet from the font—comes lightly to hold in its hands the manna it prays it will never presume to stockpile, the food of Christ's work, the work that broke his body and spilled his blood. They come in this way, they are told, to be members of the body of the one who forevermore hangs in solidarity with a world plummeting into the abyss.[3]

Joining this church is joining the poor.[4] Their prayer is that they would travel to where Jesus in the stories they rehearse has already gone, the Jesus into whom they have been baptized. The life of this church is dedicated publicly as a gift—feeding the hungry, clothing the naked, and visiting the imprisoned. Thus the church works to wait upon God's coming, to trust in God's good pleasure, to speak and act without the logic of violence, i.e., to hope. Praying that it might recognize that this is a way of life very different from the way of the principalities and powers, it works to speak and act with a direct and conscious difference from the technologies of violence, including institutions of national military service and social mobility. The church is disciplined—however unevenly—to depend on the grace of God, not the logic of might, status, and resources. The poor of the congregation are among its leaders. Church goods are offered to aid those whose lives have been thrown into turmoil by the competition, technologized efficiency, private property rights, monetized health care, consumerist desire, and work ethic of its neighborhood—the poor themselves sacrificing to others who are poor.

And so, on rainy days and nights the church leaves its doors open for shelter for those without roofs over their heads. Similarly, it leaves time open for prayer requests during its services. It is open to those engaged to be married—advising, guiding, and querying them as close friends do. Those members who have been graced each with a long sacramental marriage provide care for other lovers and beloveds before their promises fail and, breaking apart, one by one slip alone each into a separate despair. That is, in a great variety of ways the church shares a great variety of goods,

---

3. Cf. Barton, "Dislocating and Relocating Holiness," 206; also Cavanaugh, *Torture and Eucharist*, 266–68.

4. Cf. Song, *Jesus, the Crucified People*, 216; and Dostoevsky, *Brothers Karamazov*, 236–37.

face-to-face helping, befriending, and praying through the inevitable and often divisive conflicts that emerge between members of the assembly and between the assembly and those who stay consciously away from it.

And all of this is performed subtly, without pretense or ostentation. Anyone stumbling into one of its services would immediately recognize that there is something both faltering and delightfully extraordinary at play here. The sincerity of this work opens to the flesh as well as the Spirit. Facilities are in disrepair, banter erupts from a homeless congregant off her meds, persons without influence or power fill its pews, the thin walls that frame the sanctuaries let the sounds of drums and the voices that sing to their rhythms mingle with words preached in other languages a few yards away. Everything that takes shape here has the feel of a rough, ad hoc, beginner's improvisational performance. People without homes find that they have cooked meals that have somehow made their way to other, hungry people. There are disagreements and tensions over how to take care of trivial matters (like who is to open the church when it rains or who is to lead the music during a worship service) or weightier ones (like a member who in dealing drugs is gambling with prolonged jail time and jeopardizing the welfare of her children). The church barely keeps afloat financially. There are sewage backups many Sunday mornings. Some of the old friends of the church have grown cold or uncooperative or hostile in part because of occasional eruptions of aggression, inflexibility, and meanness of spirit from those closest to the top on the church's organizational charts and most visible on its raised platforms on Sunday mornings. The Spanish congregation struggles with its leadership; the French congregation is in the midst of a possible split; the new pastor of the Khmer congregation does his job in the wake of his predecessor, who left under a dark cloud of mistrust.

But something beautiful and holy happens, when during prayers one voice after another calls out to a holy Mystery—for the healing of a mother's diseased body or the cessation of a war in a distant country or a change in city housing policy or the spiritual renewal of a friend or a safe home for the abandoned children cared for by the church or for the undocumented workers who continue to flood into the neighborhood. These are prayers entangled in the actions and passions of these people. "This is our prayer," they call out; and the priestly reply joins their words, "Lord, hear our prayer!"

2 Where Memory and Hope Converge
Writing the Cross

> *And games that never amount*
> *To more than they're meant*
> *Will play themselves out*[1]

OURS ARE FAST TIMES. Nothing stands still. The subtle thief of Milton's youth rages now like a bull.[2] Today takes whatever was not nailed down yesterday; tomorrow runs at us with a pry bar. There was a day, we are told, when it wasn't like that. Changes were predictable, foreground adjustments made against a deep, stable background. Foundations were firm. Principles

---

1. Hansard and Irglová, "Falling Slowly."
2. Milton, "How Soon Hath Time," 25–26:

    How soon hath time the suttle theef of youth,
        Stoln on his wing my three and twentieth yeer!
        My hasting dayes flie on with full career,
        But my late spring no bud or blossom shew'th.
    Perhaps my semblance might deceive the truth,
        That I to manhood am arriv'd so near,
        And inward ripenes doth much less appear,
        That som more timely-happy spirits indu'th.
    Yet be it less or more, or soon or slow,
        It shall be still in strictest measure eev'n,
        To that same lot, however mean or high,
    Toward which Time leads me, and the will of Heav'n;
        All is, if I have grace to use it so,
        As ever in my great task Master's eye.

were as they had been from the beginning. There was no question about what was wise or foolish, proper or improper, apt or rash, noble or common; who was free to get married or divorced; who could have children or who was not to be left alone with children; who had a right to kill or was obliged to be killed, a right to be served or was obliged to serve, a right to own or was obliged to be owned; who was a citizen or an illegal, a male or a female; what was right or wrong, real or unreal, meaningful or meaningless. We had eaten the fruit of the tree of the knowledge of good and evil and everything was measurable against a dome of fixed stars.

Not so in our day. Unable to sleep, we rise long before dawn each morning to find that an invisible hand has again wiped more stars from our sky. We tremble before the prospect of a literally disastrous future, one with nothing left to steer by. "Since Copernicus man has been rolling from the center toward X."[3] Maybe so, but we have realized it only of late; too late, we fear. The anxiety exuding from the pores of the leaders of established institutions is thick and acrid. A new ecclesiastical task force seems to be formed weekly to stem the tide of this recklessness. We no longer even know who we are, we say. And so, we huddle together, haul in bus-loads of experts, look each other suspiciously in the eye, do market research, and ache to recover our identity. We want what way down deep *is* still the same and will *remain* the same consistently across time.[4] We know that there must be some essence, some manageable ground upon which we can stand firm. How else could we face the future?

Of course, there are good reasons to be apprehensive. Life can be very dark. If there were any doubt, the wars and famines and unspeakable cruelty of our time have put it to rest. The Holy Scriptures themselves testify to the toil, sweat, pain, and brutality of life this side of the Garden. Indeed the consummate time of the Christian calendar is Holy Week, a time of betrayal, abandonment, unjust arrest and conviction, torture, humiliation, anguish, forsakenness, death, and the unprotested damnation of the innocent: Maundy Thursday, Good Friday, Holy Saturday—dark days, every one. Of course, they are remembered in the bright light of Easter Sunday. But Jesus remains a slaughtered lamb even on that new day.[5]

---

3. Nietzsche, *Will to Power*, 8 (1.5).

4. See *Oxford English Dictionary*, s.v. "identity."

5. That one would not want to believe such a thing is certainly understandable. Everybody wants a clear winner. Many of us are confident that we have one. Many of us are quite proud that our most prominent signature architectural features are "empty." We defend our Christian triumphalism with the gusto of a sports fan. When we find

Where Memory and Hope Converge

All of his days were placed under crisis on his execution day. That day holds his whole life in its fist—and squeezes. It judges that this "good teacher" is and now always will have been the one whose decisive, defining moment is the suffering, death, and damnation of the forsaken (Mark 15:34).[6] All his words and deeds come now to nothing, abysmal nothing. There are for him no more units of time to loosen the packed dust of what is henceforth simply bygone. Holy Saturday is the testimony to that closure.

The following day is, of course, celebrated in all of Christendom as the day when death is defeated. Yet it dawns not as the day when an old order is restored, the day in which the original status quo falls neatly back into place. It is a second, no less insuperable crisis. There is on this day even more reason for the anxious to be anxious than on the previous three. At least on those days the patterns that had always prevailed continue to hold sway. But *everything* changes when the crucified Jesus comes forth. Easter Sunday—and this is the offense of *that day*—says both "yes" to Maundy Thursday, Good Friday, and Holy Saturday . . . *and* "nevertheless." The judgment day of Jesus' last week is itself judged. That the crisis is redemptive does not make it any less shattering. The naked, disfigured *slash mark*

---

ourselves confronted by the news that from Easter morning Jesus is above all the one simultaneously raised *and* crucified, we repeat the words of Thomas, but from the other side: "Unless I see the mark of the nails in his hands, and put my finger in the mark of the nails and my hand in his side, I will not believe" (John 20:25). Unlike Thomas, however, we are not disturbed by the idea that the Crucified has been *raised*. We are disturbed by the idea that the one who has been raised is *still the Crucified*. But in the narratives of the Gospels Jesus' resurrection does not erase his crucifixion. The resurrection reaches farther than that. It is the unmaking of an order in which life and death stare at each other in binary opposition. The resurrection of Jesus is the unsettling of his and every crucifixion. It engulfs them, hallows them, and saturates them with a *new* life. When he is raised, it is the scarred, broken, mortally wounded Jesus who comes forth from the tomb. His story remains the story of loss even as that loss is swallowed up in victory (1 Cor 2:2 and 15:54–57). Cf. Tanner, *Jesus, Humanity, and the Trinity*, 26–30.

6. Cousar, *Theology of the Cross*, 102–8; see Moltmann, *Crucified God*, e.g., 145–53; *Experiment Hope*, 69–84; *Jesus Christ for Today's World*, 30–49; but even more Song, *Jesus, the Crucified People*, 210–33. Despite their best efforts both Moltmann and Song tend to compromise the particularity of Jesus by situating his significance within encompassing and largely undefined concepts such as "justice" and "dignity." Certainly they protest against abstraction and for historical particularity even when the language of universality seems to dilute those protests. That is, despite some distraction they clarify quite well that Jesus is the one who cannot be cut loose from the history of a crucifixion and is as concrete as every flesh-and-blood victim of violence. For a helpful step in the direction of a contrasting vision of justice and liberation that looks to something other than "what is due," see Bell, *Liberation Theology After the End of History*, especially chapters 3 and 4.

between Jew/Greek, male/female, and free/slave (Gal 3:28) is declared on this day to be God with us (John 20:28). It is this one who is as such saturated by Holy Life, who rises to empty his tomb and every tomb. It is the Crucified still hanging dead between thieves who eats bread and fish with Peter at the seashore (John 21) and converses with his disciples on the Emmaus Road (Luke 24:13–32). Light has come to shine in *darkness* (John 1:5), the reach of the love of God has in Christ Jesus exceeded whatever is established as *unreachably* far gone from it (Rom 8:39).[7]

Thursday, Friday, Saturday, and Sunday: *everything* depends on *how* these days face each other and thus come to make one event. Jesus' life as a whole is determined in this week. That is why it is not an overstatement to describe the Gospels as "passion narratives with extended introductions."[8] Each of them is written retrospectively out of the one double turn of events and has Jesus moving toward the one double crisis from the beginning. When their itinerate prophet and contentious miracle worker, Jesus, looks to the future, he sees this impending double end that will have wrapped itself around all his days.

Throughout the Gospel narratives Jesus is always looking to the future. In a certain way like us he is obsessed with it. However, though what he sees will have radically unsettled the present order beyond anything even we have ventured to imagine, he does not fear it. In this he is quite unlike us. All his words and deeds are bursting certainly with a serious, but no less joyful expectation of what will have left nothing as it was. There will be an apocalyptic moment, we read, when the old will have passed away, when not one stone will have been left standing upon another, when the sea will have been swallowed, when the sun will have gone dark, when the stars will have fallen from the sky, when new names will have displaced old ones, when the first will have been last and the last first, and when a new city more spacious than the entire cosmos will have come forevermore to shine with the glory of the Almighty.[9] Though, of course, this is to be read as the future to which all of the world opens, it is also precisely what comes to pass to one very particular first-century Galilean peasant.

---

7. Dunn, "Jesus and Holiness," 190, 192, maintains that the holiness at work in the body of the Jesus of the Gospels was not in danger of being profaned by contact with the impure. Far from withdrawing to a place of safe isolation, he moves outward to touch and thus hallow the impure. When Jesus' crucified corpse is raised from the dead, this reversed infection is worked most dramatically.

8. Kähler, *So-Called Historical Jesus and the Historic Biblical Christ*, 80 n. 11.

9. On the size of the city, see Beale, *Book of Revelation*, 1074.

That is, the localization of the coming of God's Reign in Jesus does not shrink the eschatological field. His crises are particularly but not exclusively his. His story is inseparable from the story of mother and sisters and brothers; of Abraham, Isaac, and Jacob; of Adam and Eve (Luke 3:23–38). From the Gospels' point of view it is not an overstatement to describe every event as having a double role to play in his passion. Every event dies, too— and rises with him (cf. Col 1:15 – 20). All else is to be remembered in him and opened to the comprehensive future that his new body promises. This week is at once his and the world's disaster and new creation, the event that gives notice and hope to the world and birth to the church.

There may be no English word as bent and broken by casual misuse, or drained of blood by idealizing admirers and apologists, or grossly caricatured by huckstering detractors, as *church*.[10] It is a word that has come to say simultaneously too much and too little—so mutually exclusively much that it is hard to tell where to let one's attention fall, so little that it is sometimes hard to tell if it finally says anything very important at all. Even among those who adamantly maintain that my or your place and time are lost without a strong, hopeful, hospitable, humane, and righteous ecclesial body, who work at articulating an ecclesiology faithful to it, who freely rehearse stories of the kindness and goodness of little local churches across a vast field of places and times, who stand up to those finding only villainy at the heart of church history, who hold out hope for the future of the people to whom "church" gestures—even, that is, among those who most gladly send it up for all to see—are men and women who know the dullness of the word, cold in the throat and on the lips, the hollowness of the room as it briefly sounds, echoes, and fades, the memories that float unwelcomed to the surface in the dull gray of color decomposition, the anger, sorrow, hurt, disappointment, aversion, revulsion, confusion, and boredom that accompany the undesired hits of the image search it launches, and the almost autonomic shifting of postures toward the exit when the word is consciously acknowledged. Even, however, after a relatively coherent and significant theological family has by great effort been sifted out of the welter

---

10. There is perhaps no clearer sign of the sad condition of the word than the big blue building in Hollywood whose marquee declares without false advertising that this is the "Church of Scientology."

of uses, what we find is still a complicated word, an old word, a word appraised by commodity brokers as a declining value in a soft market that favors simplicity and currency. We are thus tempted to give up on it and go with something—anything!—else.

And yet there is nothing else, not in this language.[11] Every near substitute fails to mask more than a little of what we are tempted in condescendingly generous moments to describe as its once beautiful, but now decrepit face, its once giving and forgiving, but now acquisitive history, its once eccentric, but now autocentric institutional architecture. Of course, we know that it was never very consistently beautiful, giving and forgiving, or eccentric, anymore than it is now very consistently decrepit, acquisitive, or autocentric. There is in fact no one uniform thing, "The Church," not even in the strictest theological sense of the term. There is only "that church, there," i.e., only particular churches and in the end only particularly little local churches,[12] *catholic* churches because they entail one another. Their past may be settled, but it was complex then, too; no less than the work of little local churches tomorrow will be. Their complex and settled past is no more to be repressed than their complex and indeterminate future is to be foreclosed. To work out the articulation of "church" with grace means slowness of speech, an unpretentiousness of action and passion, a working and waiting that do not presume, but rather let *everything* in. That, of course, means that however much statistical accounts of its measurable institutional patterns are to be minimalized, the church that is faithfully articulated will always have been as visible, tangible, audible, but also as ambiguous and elusive as is every motion of every complex social configuration of humane flesh and blood.

And so, let us say that the ecclesial and ecclesiological tasks are (without self-deceit, despair, or haste) to work and to think "church" with its property sold, its proceeds distributed to the poor, and its future an uncertain journey after the Galilean who walks relentlessly into solidarity with the forsaken (Mark 10:21; 11:13–23). And so, let us say that a little local church is a particular body of people whose prayers are prayed as they learn together to practice (however unevenly) the hard work over long lifetimes of *seeing* the death and rebirth of the world and doing so without removing

---

11. Nor in other languages. Those words that trace their ancestry back to *ekklesia* have had a no less problematic history, as a trip to Spain, France, Italy, or Russia would make clear.

12. *Oxford English Dictionary*, s.v. "little, *adj., n.*, and *adv.*": "probably < the root of Old English *lútan* to bow down . . ."

themselves from it (Heb 11:1). Let us say that it is that gathering of those who pray to know in their bones that the age to come has invaded the present evil age and will not let it be.[13] Let us say that these people sing in their doxologies that the event of the world made new has become an event *pro nobis*,[14] and that they sing it to see it. And so, Saul is blinded, lies three days in darkness, eating and drinking nothing, is touched by a "brother" whom he does not know and would have hauled off to be killed, just days earlier, if given the chance. Saul comes in spite of himself to see, to be baptized, to eat, to grow strong, to linger with the little local Damascus body, to declare in the synagogues that Jesus "is the Son of God" (Acts 9:20), and, far away from the titular heads of the Jerusalem assembly, for three years in the wilderness and then once again in Damascus, to wonder what it all might signify (Gal 1:17–18), i.e., Saul finds in the midst of a little local body of people far from home that his life has come to an end and has begun again.[15] He bears witness: "So if anyone is in Christ, there is a new creation: everything old has passed away; see, everything has become new!" (2 Cor 5:17).[16]

Of course, none of these texts provides a formula for the precipitation of a church. It is not in the least to be assumed that anyone or any household or any village would in this way or in any other way come to be "in Christ." These texts and this "church" are matters of uncoerced possibility[17]—not necessity. What happens in each case could have been otherwise. But when it happens, even if it happens very slowly, Paul tells us, everything changes. To be in Christ is no longer to deny the double crisis of Holy Week, nor to

---

13. Barton, "Dislocating and Relocating Holiness," 209, calls this "an unmaking and remaking of the old . . . [A] dislocating and relocating" of holiness in the life and ministry of Jesus that takes, he says, "a transformation of the imagination" to an apocalyptic extreme even to be perceived.

14. Luther, *Christian Liberty*, 20.

15. The account in the ninth chapter of the book of Acts is a crucifixion/resurrection story: Saul is blinded upon encountering the resurrected Jesus on the Damascus Road, he is laid up for three days in darkness in the house of Judas, he receives the miracle of new vision and is filled by the Holy Spirit on the third day, he arises, and is baptized.

16. Cf. Hays's extensive explication of the "moral vision of the New Testament" in terms of three orienting foci: community, cross, and new creation. Hays, *Moral Vision of the New Testament*, 193–200. It is important to note that within those images he locates the ideas that one might otherwise consider to be central to the texts of the New Testament: love (which "is embodied concretely in the *cross*"), liberation (which "is best understood through the focal image of new creation"), and justice (which "is rightly to be comprehended through the focal image of community") (ibid., 202–5 n. 29).

17. Perhaps "Möglichkeit" is a better term for this.

keep it small. It is to announce and to enact that Christ is the one in whom the history of the whole world is *given*. Paul speaks from the point of view of a body of people who have passed through the waters of Christ's own bloody baptism:

> Do you not know that all of us who have been baptized into Christ Jesus were baptized into his death? Therefore we have been buried with him by baptism into death, so that, just as Christ was raised from the dead by the glory of the Father, so we too might walk in newness of life. For if we have been united with him in a death like his, we will certainly be united with him in a resurrection like his. (Rom 6:3–5)

The people of little local churches in some sense have died, he is saying, and in some sense will be raised from the dead—but even now have a kind of glimmer[18] about them that signals a glory that both is and is not-yet. Their turning through the crucifixion toward the resurrection of Jesus is a turning to see and learn to see the world through the future that happens already—without ceasing to be future—in the Jesus who is the Christ precisely because the Spirit anoints him with the oil of resurrection.[19]

---

18. *Oxford English Dictionary*, s.v. "glimmer, n.1": "A feeble or wavering light; a tremulous play of reflected light, a sheen, shimmer."

19. Cf. Ward, "Displaced Body of Jesus Christ," especially 175–77; and Hauerwas, *Sanctify Them in the Truth*, 80–84, 89–91. Dunn, "Jesus and Holiness," 192, implicitly opens Hauerwas's picture of a holy church, when his account of the outgoing, unthreatened holiness of Christ is extended ecclesiologically. Cavanaugh seems to be making that move explicitly. Cavanaugh, *Torture and Eucharist*, 281. However, not all thinkers associated with Hauerwas are as helpful. John Milbank is perhaps the most prominent example of those who effortlessly dismiss the particularity of Jesus, letting him dissolve into the the historic pattern of the "church" that is imagined as subsidiary to human, especially Western, civilization. Thus he can say that "the name 'Jesus' does not indicate an identifiable 'character,' but is rather the obscure and mysterious hinge which permits shifts from one kind of discourse to another," that "Jesus . . . figures in the New Testament primarily as a new Moses, the founder of a new or renewed law and community," that "there can be . . . an ecclesiological deduction [!] of the incarnation," and further that "the 'deduction' of Christological doctrine from ecclesiology is clearly a 'leading out' which also moves forwards, beyond mere logical consequence, the speculative exodus which is the self-definition of the church." Thus there is no longer a particular Jesus to stand outside the church in judgment. The church becomes the judge of Jesus. Milbank, *Word Made Strange*, 149, 152, 156, 159, 165; cf. Milbank, *Theology and Social Theory*, 387, 398. One is reminded of Adolf von Harnack, the theologian of a century ago, the ghost writer for the German Kaiser who had such a hard time making sense of his former student, the then young Karl Barth. See Harnack's debate with Barth; Harnack, "Fifteen Questions," "An Open Letter," and "Postscript." See Busch, *Karl Barth*, 95.

Where Memory and Hope Converge

To Thomas, the disciple who, though perhaps slow of assent and a little ambivalent, has already announced that, even if it means death, he is ready to go with his rabbi into perilous territory (John 11:16), Jesus declares: "I am the way, the truth, and the life" (John 14:6). Jesus declares this not from the cavernous, acoustically perfect, empty ballroom of eternity, but close to the ground, in the flesh and on the move. Hearing, seeing, attending to this way, truth, and life, not as an abstraction, not as disembodied, not as a lonely core-drilling meditation, but as a pilgrimage of lived time, occurs also close to the ground, in the flesh and on the move. It occurs as a *trial* in hearing, seeing, attending. Indeed, it is a trial in thinking as a kind of journey with an *eschatos*, not a *telos*, a journey of hope, not extrapolation. That is, it is a trial in thoughtfully living moments of short and long duration, moments of deferral, moments entailing other moments, marking out, one by one, generations of a thought expenditure that is unobstructed by the anxiety that one day it may all run dry. The doxological poetry and prose of those women, men, and children who from time to time assemble to follow after the crucified Jesus profess that to see the world anew, to think the world anew, is to think the Spirit's glorification of the mutilated flesh of Jesus of Nazareth not as an *instance* of a *higher* truth, but as *the truth*, particular, wayward, pulsing, warm, and open. As such it violates—genetically—the most compelling justification of responsible thinking to be found in the deep historical tissue of Western Civilization.

It strikes us as beyond indefensible that even thoughtful, vigorously logical interactions between sober persons might occur so particularly and concretely in the crucified, dead, buried, and raised Jesus Christ that they never leave him. Has not all serious thought cut itself loose from such prejudice, such narrow-mindedness? Is the point not first to determine what is universally true and only then find in that "world view" a place for everything—including Jesus Christ and those traveling after him? Other disciplines sharing theology's suffix seem so far removed from death, farther from death on a cross, farther yet from resurrection, and farthest of all from resurrection of one utterly abased. It would seem that theo*logy* must, too, keep its distance.

That it might not, that theology might move to a different rhythm, that theology might never cease casting down its intellectual goods upon the way of an (which is always to say, *this*) irrevocably particular logic, this *logos sarx egeneto* (John 1:14), seems simply and directly to be out of the question. Certainly saints and martyrs tell us all that the logic of the gathering of bodies in Christ is indeed *out of the question*. The task of theology, they say, is always and everywhere to work where all human work is *called into question*, the question that all God's children are here to answer. All holy work works from the question of Holy Week, they tell us all.

Jesus' resurrection is a gift, they say, that enters and exceeds his death. In him the very particularly catholic church,[20] they say, has become a performance of this one double-movement of sacrifice and rebirth, this dance of death ... and life. A theology that does not excuse itself from *this* church would be a theology *in* the event that again and again constitutes *the* (which is always to say, *that*) church, i.e., where the work of Christ is done with and by the ordinary, grateful people who gather to give themselves tangibly to his broken body and shed blood, i.e., to his work.

The word for this task they set out again and again to perform is "liturgy." Liturgy—literally "the work of the people"—is not confined to some customary ritual of a Sunday morning. It is a big word that reaches into every day of every week. Congregational kneeling and singing are liturgical, but so also is getting off a shift or out of bed some minutes or hours earlier, or harvesting a field of grain under a hot sun the mornings and afternoons and under a full moon the evenings of a week that has been marked by this day, or giving birth in a hut as nearby a loaf and a cup are raised for all to see. More precisely, the word for the particular work of those people who are thus in Christ is "eucharist," eucharist as a certain grateful pattern of life

---

20. The word *catholic* need not be taken to be equivalent to "universal." The very first documented usage of the phrase "catholic church" is to be found among the last writings of Ignatius of Antioch in the late first or early second century. "Letter to the Smyrnaeans," 112–16. His declaration that "where Jesus Christ is there is the catholic church" has often been understood precisely as a universalizing move. It does seem, however, that one would expect concreteness and particularity in a letter that declares so forcefully that Jesus was "actually crucified for us in the flesh, under Pontius Pilate and Herod the Tetrarch" (2:1), "that even after the resurrection he was in the flesh" (3:1), that the Smyrnaean congregants were themselves "fitted out with an unshakeable faith, being nailed, as it were, body and soul to the cross of the Lord Jesus Christ" (1:1), that "near the sword [of martyrdom] means near to God ... [t]o be with wild beasts means to be with God ... to share in [Jesus'] passion" (4:2), and that "the eucharist is the flesh of our Savior Jesus Christ" (7:1). Indeed, when he declares the intimate connection between the "catholic church" and Jesus Christ, he is speaking specifically of the tangible eucharist Docetists deny. The role of the "bishop" in the celebration of the eucharist (8:1–2) is quite compatible with the notion that the whole church happens always with concrete particularity, never with the abstraction of universality. Indeed, it may well require it.

nourished by the renewal of the work of Christ. Week after week a tangle of histories moves from and to the social moment in which the women and men and children of this church of friends get up to let in the broken body and shed blood of Christ and by the invocation of the Spirit to throw themselves with him on the mercy of the Father. It is this event that gives to the lives of these people the shape of the cross.[21] It is this event that makes the postures and sounds of the first day of the week and of every day and every time a kind of earthy (though no less spiritual) worship,[22] the food and drink of which are the work of the exaltation of an abased Savior.

> For I received from the Lord what I also handed on to you, that the Lord Jesus on the night when he was betrayed took a loaf of bread, and when he had given thanks, he broke it and said, "This is my body that is for you. Do this in remembrance of me." In the same way he took the cup also, after supper, saying, "This cup is the new covenant in my blood. Do this, as often as you drink it, in remembrance of me." For as often as you eat this bread and drink the cup, you proclaim the Lord's death until he comes. (1 Cor 11:23-26)

This church in this way remembers and hopes.[23] The theological task that does not walk away from this church, then, is not to critique or clarify or

---

21. Cavanaugh, *Torture and Eucharist*, 231-32: "One of the peculiarities of the eucharistic feast is that we become the body of Christ by consuming it. Unlike ordinary food, the body does not become assimilated into our bodies, but vice versa.... The fact that the church is literally changed into Christ is not a cause for triumphalism, however, precisely because our assimilation to the body of Christ means that we then become food for the world, to be broken, given away, and consumed." See also 234-35.

22. Schmemann, *Eucharist*, 242: "The church is not an organization but the new people of God. The church is not a religious cult but a *liturgy*, embracing the entire creation of God." See Wainwright, *For Our Salvation*, 74-78; and *Doxology*, 8-10.

23. The theology that happens here works to remain immersed in the life of the church, rather than stepping away from it in order to compose an independently valid theory or "second-order discourse." This distinguishes it from almost all modern self-consciously theological labor—including even that of such liberation theologians as Gustavo Gutiérrez (*Theology of Liberation*, 5-12, but cf. xxxii-xxxiv, in the introduction to the revised edition, and *On Job*, xi-xix and 15-17), and such liturgical theologians as Saliers (*Worship As Theology*, 15-16) and Jenson (*Triune God*, 11, 18-20). Karl Barth is, as always, more complicated. He can say in 1923 that "the task of theology is the same as that of preaching." Barth, "Fifteen Answers to Professor von Harnack," 167. He can also stress theology's critical function, as if it were a second-order operation. Barth, *CD* 1/1, 79, but see 82. However, Barth even here understands the task of theology to be a relentless inquiry into the *faithfulness* of preaching, an insistence that it give itself to the unmanageable coming of God. This means that theology is itself to live from the urgency of God's coming. Barth, *Evangelical Theology*, 160, 164: "The first and basic act

improve upon eucharistic liturgy. It is rather to dwell in it, the way one might dwell in a cosmos.²⁴

According to a certain liturgical calendar, Easter is the first day, the day the world starts over. But it is also the eighth day, the day that consummates the old order.²⁵ This day of hope for a new life opens to let in what was. The very particular history of Jesus is glorified, but so also are the histories in which his is entangled, the history of the children of Abraham, Isaac, and Jacob first of all. He is not the deletion of the old covenant. He rather embodies a new covenant that exceeds the old, fills it to overflowing (cf. Matt 5:17, Rom 11:24). Adam and Eve are still created on the sixth day and rest on the seventh; but now on the eighth day there is a new Adam, a new Eve. The opening chapter of Genesis announces that the first man and woman were created *in* the image and *after* the likeness of God (1:27). On the eighth day this image is the Christ whom the first man and woman now come to be already in the beginning created to face (2 Cor 3:18, 4:4).²⁶ A theology in Christ remembers and hopes. Memory is for what is hoped; hope is for what is remembered. Adam and Eve still fall, but on the eighth day their fall is situated in the promise of salvation that embraces and surpasses all

---

of theological work is prayer," he says, "true and proper language concerning God will always be a response to God, which overtly or covertly, explicitly or implicitly, thinks and speaks of God exclusively in the second person." Cf. Barth, *Prayer*, 9. Of course, it is one thing to say that theology is prayer and a very different thing in fact to make one's theology a prayer. The trick is to do both at once. Barth pulls off that trick to an extraordinary degree. Though Saliers distinguishes between the imbedded theology of the practice of worship (as that term is ordinarily used) and all secondary reflection upon that practice, say, by the "professional theologian," much of his work suggests a way for the two to be in much more intimate fellowship, neither stepping back to size up an intellectual datum. One of his chapter subtitles is "Gratitude as Knowledge of God" (85). That phrase and much of what he says in that chapter and elsewhere are quite helpful. Comments like this one and others in the footnotes of this book, however, show that it is finally not so easy to give up gossip.

24. Cavanaugh, *Torture and Eucharist*, 206.

25. Schmemann, *Introduction to Liturgical Theology*, 76–80.

26. Cf. Barth, *CD* 3/1, 183–206; and Levinas, "Trace of the Other," 359. For a richer understanding of the icon than Levinas's, one that might in fact allow Levinas's to affirm that human life is iconic, see Marion, *Crossing of the Visible*, 58–65, and the whole of chapter four, *God Without Being*, 16–24; and Ouspensky, *Theology of the Icon*, 154–55, 166.

promises that even in the old order did not leave sin as a hopelessly brute fact. This is not to say that Genesis was in itself all along an account of the coming of Jesus. It is to say that on the eighth day of creation Genesis *becomes* something it was not in itself already.[27]

It is remarkable that the doctors of the church have remembered the doctrine of the fall of Adam and Eve with such energy. Isn't the gospel "good news"? Isn't Jesus sent to save? Shouldn't every Christian thought be positive and hopeful and promising? Doesn't a doctrine of the fall—a doctrine of Godless impotence—leave our future closed? It would seem so. Perhaps it has functioned in theological discourse that way from time to time. Yet the hope of new creation invites us to remember that doctrine differently. We are invited to understand "Godless impotence" as a stuttering toward the word "grace." The hope of a future in Christ is a hope that does not lean on present and available ability, some power-pack of recovery. An act of the properly potential may restore, satisfy, and complete, but it will never break the chain that keeps it tethered to the essentially old. It may be relatively, but it isn't absolutely new.

It is no longer possible to say "fallen" or "captivated by sin" in the same old way in the shadow of Holy Saturday. On Holy Saturday the savior of the world is dead—dead in trespasses and sins (cf. Eph 2:1 and 2 Cor 5:21). For the fallen, as for the Crucified lying dead and still in the tomb, there is no back door of retreat, no dormant power from which to draw.[28] A future is not guaranteed, but may come, if it comes—and how could it come?—only as a gift, as a *novum*.[29] The doctrine of the fall, situated in the liturgy of baptism and eucharist, bears witness to a future that in coming has shifted the old forward beyond itself.[30] It is a doctrine that has significance only as one approaches the altar with thanksgiving, "straining forward to what lies ahead" (Phil 3:13; cf. 12–16). It has its atmosphere in that act; it is not a generic "truth" hovering in intellectual space waiting for the calculative inquirer to make use of it in a meaning-rich frame of reference.[31]

27. Cf. Tanner, *Jesus, Humanity, and the Trinity*, 20.

28. Through his pseudonym, Johannes Climacus, Kierkegaard builds much of his *Postscript* around this notion that in Christian doctrine there is provided no "back door." See, e.g., Kierkegaard [Climacus], *Concluding Unscientific Postscript*, 583–84.

29. Cf. Moltmann, *Coming of God*, 27–29; and *Religion, Revolution, and the Future*, 3–18, 156–57.

30. See Pannenberg, *Theology and the Kingdom of God*, 62–63. For two rather different affirmations of the priority of the future, see Kierkegaard, *Works of Love*, 249, 252; *Postscript*, 307, 357–60, 424; and Cavanaugh, *Torture and Eucharist*, 222–29, 272.

31. That is, I am suggesting that the term *truth* be dislodged vis-à-vis the *mysteriously*

This is how it is as well with the doctrine that human beings have been created in the image of God. The crucified/resurrected Jesus is God's coming. He is God "up close," God "with us." Certainly God is decisively *other*, holy, in this coming. God is the transcendent Father especially in *the Son*.³² And yet God is *here*—a second time, confrontationally. That is to say, in Jesus we confront Emmanuel. Wet from the waters of baptism, the taste of bread and wine on our tongues, we face God's *image*. To be created is in this liturgy of the eighth day to be created in relation to *him*, in pursuit of *him*, created in *this* crucified image, after *this* crucified likeness. It is a serious category mistake to look for evidence of our uniqueness, evidence of the way we differ from other beings in the present order of beings, and from that to explicate Gen 1:27. The image of God is not remembered as something in *us*; we rather are remembered as God's children in *him*. We are *in Christ* in the open liturgy of baptism and eucharist, i.e., in the church.³³

A theology in Christ is performed in the open space where memory and hope converge. It is a life's work, living from the coming of a gift that never becomes anyone's private property, the coming of a gift that never ceases to be a gift.³⁴ Theology thus works to put aside the inertia that resists the new.

---

merciful truth of God and that "God can be called the truth only when 'truth' is understood in the sense of the Greek word *aletheia*. God's being, or truth, is the event of his self-disclosure, his radiance as the Lord of all lords, the hallowing of his name, the coming of his kingdom, the fulfillment of his will in all his work." Barth, *Evangelical Theology*, 9.

32. Schnackenburg, *Jesus in the Gospels*, 314.

33. Cf. McClintock Fulkerson, "Contesting the Gendered Subject," 111–15.

34. Cf. Tanner, *Jesus, Humanity, and the Trinity*, 90–95. Although certainly Tanner affirms the unconditional dynamics of God's grace, dynamics in which we come to participate, and that God's giving or ours in Christ is not an investment itching for a profitable return (84–85), her position seems bound finally to the logic of identity and property. Even while she is speaking of a noncompetitive giving, she maintains that we come to give only "out of our own fullness," in the light of "need," and in such a way that "rights" are implied (69, 89, 94). It is difficult to understand how this position avoids a scheme of the ownership of more or less. For a position that more heartily yields to "the gift," see Marion, *God Without Being*, 95–102, 172–82. For an intentionally contrasting position see John Milbank, who is so committed to the reciprocity of giving that he considers the love of friends higher than the love of enemies. Milbank, *Being Reconciled*, 160; cf. 152–57 and 180–81. For a love that always has the love of God as the "middle term" between the one who loves and her neighbor and therefore has no need of reciprocity,

Where Memory and Hope Converge

It works not to be conformed to the present evil age, but transformed by the renewing of the mind (Rom 12:1-2).

That is, theology does its work hoping in the coming of the Spirit of the Crucified, hoping as the church's stories invite it to hope, that there is yet a future of the crucifixion.[35] Jesus Christ is "God a second time." A liturgical theology is called again and again to enter with the catholic church into *this* image of God. That event of entrance, according to the *epiclesis*, the invocation, of the liturgy of the church, is performed by the Holy Spirit, "God a third time."[36] Without that spiritual work, theology would gaze upon Jesus from the outside, unbelieving. Theology empties its lungs of the breath it has been given every time it speaks.[37] And every time it speaks it cries, "Come, Holy Spirit!" Thus theology waits as it works. It waits for its lungs again to be filled. Without the renewing breath of the Spirit it cannot speak.

---

see Kierkegaard, *Works of Love*, 58,107, 241-42, 260, 349. For a subtle critique of "need," see Levinas, "Trace of the Other," 350-52.

35. The stories of those who would not count themselves among the members of the church remind the church to hope as well. See Raphael's moving account of the women of Auschwitz, "Holiness *in extremis*," 381-401. On the strength of stories to resist the power of ideology, see Cone, *God of the Oppressed*, 93-98. The stories Cone speaks of here may be understood in the light of some comments he makes at the end of the "acknowledgments" section of his book *The Cross and the Lynching Tree*, xi: "my mother and father, Lucy and Charlie Cone, . . . protected my brothers and me from the worst of white supremacy in Arkansas. With an amazing love and wonderful humor, they created a happy home that kept us from hating anybody and instilled in us a belief that we could, with determination, overcome any obstacle placed in our way."

36. Schmemann, *Eucharist*, 213-27; Saliers, *Worship as Theology*, 110-17. When the text above speaks of God "a second time" and "a third time," the point is not that there is some chronological sequence to the event of God's coming, some especially weird and cartoon-like dispensationalism or modalism. God happens as the one event of Father, Son, and Holy Spirit. It is because this one event cuts the way it does that it may be helpful to speak of the "times" of God.

37. Wesley, "Great Privilege of Those That are Born of God," 442 (III.2): "[The] life of God in the soul of a believer . . . immediately and necessarily implies the continual inspiration of God's Holy Spirit: God's breathing into the soul, and the soul's breathing back what it first receives from God; a continual action of God upon the soul, the reaction of the soul upon God; an unceasing presence of God, the loving, pardoning God, manifested to the heart, and perceived by faith; and an unceasing return of love, praise, and prayer, offering up all the thoughts of our hearts, all the words of our tongues, all the works of our hands, all our body, soul, and spirit, to be an holy sacrifice, acceptable unto God in Christ Jesus."

As such, theology is a precarious venture.[38] Its method leads to the cross and from the tomb out into the future coming of Jesus Christ in glory. Since such a method is a peculiarly wayward life and truth—one that is sent to the lost and forsaken, the poor and the sinner, the marginalized and the dying, the crushed and the damned—it is an ecclesial theology with a mission (cf. Luke 7:22).[39] The center of theology is not in itself, just as the center of the church is not in itself.[40] Theology and its church live outside of themselves by faith in God and by love in the neighbor, the one you, I, we see.[41] God is love. To be in God—Father, Son, Holy Spirit—is to write the words of love, to do the works of love.[42]

38. Keen, "*Homo Precarius*," 146–47.

39. I think that Hauerwas has helpfully critiqued certain shame-laden, intemperate middle-class declarations about the mission of the church to the poor. Hauerwas, *After Christendom?*, 46–47. However, see 50–57 for a rather weaker analysis of Gutiérrez, a weakness acknowledged to some degree by Hauerwas in his introduction to the book's second edition (9–10). For Gutiérrez's own acknowledgment of the limits of the category of "justice," see his *On Job*, 87–92. For a more recent and helpful treatment of the notion that God "prefers" the poor, see Groody, *Option for the Poor in Christian Theology*. Gutiérrez, "Option for the Poor," 236: "Ultimately, poverty means *death*" (cf. 241–48). The cross of Christ means that God is with us where the poor are. That does not mean that God fails to love the rich or that there is no way for the rich to make their way to God. It rather means that the way to God for the rich leads to the poor. Yet it is also to be said (but largely because the poor insist on it) that the way to God for the poor as well leads *to the poor*—and that always means the poor *other*.

40. Gutiérrez, *Theology of Liberation*, 118.

41. Luther, *Christian Liberty*, 34; cf. Kierkegaard, *Works of Love*, 154–74.

42. A little more than ten years ago I was asked to teach the doctrine of the Trinity to a group of fifty junior high school students. I was to spend ten minutes each of three successive Sundays—the first morning on the Father, the second on the Son, and finally the third on the Holy Spirit. This was not a task that I would have chosen on my own, and I took it on (with no little trepidation) only because the church asked me to. However, my hosts had ordered our time together thoughtfully. It was understood that each week I would need to keep my comments brief and that the crowd of children would need to be primed by their leaders before I spoke and given room afterwards to process what I had said. I told them those three weeks that when they thought "God the Father" or "God the Son" or "God the Holy Spirit," they were not to think of some "guy" who could be captured in a photograph. The first week I told them that when they thought "the Father," they were to think "mystery." The second week I told them that when they thought "the Son," they were to think "story." The third week I told them that when they thought "the Spirit," they were to think "life." I told them that the Father is not just any mystery, the Son is not just any story, and the Spirit is not just any life. Indeed, this mystery, story, and life occur together in a very particular way that cannot be broken into separate pieces. *This* mystery opens from the crucifixion/resurrection of Jesus in the midst of our world and all of its hells. *This* life drives Jesus to death on a cross and bathes his broken

Where Memory and Hope Converge

Theology is tempted to forget and to despair. When I work hard planning, implementing, and revising, I want it all finished. I want to put it aside, call it a day, curl up and take a much deserved rest. And who deserves rest more than the Christian worker? I mean, you give and you give and you give. Shouldn't you get a little private time to yourself? Isn't there a moment when you've done enough? And certainly theology's day is the eighth day, the day in which it is all finished indeed. Theology is done on the new day of Sabbath rest. There is nothing to be accomplished. It is all *already* accomplished. No theologian is to presume that something more is to be added to the work of Christ. Would it not be the height of presumption to think that anything could be tacked onto what an almighty God has done and is doing?

And yet the theologian *is* to work ... *because* God works. Theological work cooperates with God not as a competitor who grudgingly succumbs

---

body with resurrection. *This* story is the long journey of dust and ashes from the first six days of creation through the exodus of Abraham, his nation of slaves, and a first-century Jewish peasant-prophet to the glorification of the whole world in one very particular event in first-century Palestine. That is, I told them that the doctrine of the Trinity is not some abstraction set aside for the speculations of pale, emaciated, lonely men with too much time on their hands. It is the very blood and breath and future of the world. It is a doctrine for all God's children, red and yellow, black and white, whom Jesus did not forbid, but called into his arms. This life story with mystery all over it does not put an end to all understanding, but gives understanding a future—precisely as it forever eludes resolution. Of course, to speak of the mystery of God to eighth graders or to seasoned theologians is to speak of God's holiness. For example, Rogerson, "What Is Holiness?" 20–21: "the overriding view of the [Second Temple] compilers [of the Old Testament], so far as the holiness of Yahweh was concerned, was that Yahweh was incomparable, sovereign, beyond the unaided comprehension of humankind, unapproachable yet in the midst of his chosen people. . . . [Yahweh's] chief attributes of unfailing love, mercy, and forgiveness mark him off as different from humankind, yet which are intended to transform humanity into what it is unable fully to achieve itself." The phrases "unapproachable yet in the midst" and "intended to transform humanity" lean already in the direction of the doctrine of the Trinity. For the connection between "mystery" and "holiness" in the New Testament, see Dunn, "Jesus and Holiness," 169. Further, LaCugna, *God For Us*, 1: "The doctrine of the Trinity is ultimately a practical doctrine with radical consequences for Christian life. . . . The doctrine of the Trinity, which is the specifically Christian way of speaking about God, summarizes what it means to participate in the life of God through Jesus Christ in the Spirit. The mystery of God is revealed in Christ and the Spirit as the mystery of love, the mystery of persons in communion who embrace death, sin, and all forms of alienation for the sake of life."

to a corporate buy-out.⁴³ Certainly in one sense the task of the church and its theologian *is* to do nothing. We are *commanded* to take up the tool of our own annihilation and follow Christ to the Place of the Skull (Mark 8:34, but also 10:21). We are commanded to *do* crucifixion. The crucifixion that we are called to imitate does not simply befall Christ like a fatal accident (Luke 9:51).⁴⁴ It is precisely a *deed* of nothing—the radicalization of releasing breath, an excessively trusting ex-spiration. But this task is not a desperate closure to the future, a suicide. Though the agony and anxiety of the closing days of Holy Week darken every hue, the coming first day opens the possibility for Jesus to give thanks at his last supper and for his servants to give thanks whenever they remember it. It is not accidental that Jesus' prayer in the Garden of Gethsemane was "nevertheless" (Mark 14:36). One goes to the cross not in some serene mood of "spiritual" detachment, but rather in the birth pangs of one's whole heart and soul and mind and strength, of one's muscles and blood and skin and bones. Even with the foretaste of the Spirit of resurrection, following Jesus always has something of the painful anguish of Gethsemane about it. It is only by the Spirit that raised Jesus Christ from the dead and breathed life into the Adam dust-sculpture of Genesis 2:7 that theology breathes. The Spirit is the hammer blow "nevertheless" that breaks the back of anguish and throws open the promise of a joy that even now violates the laws of gravity. Of course, were it believed that we had the native ability to do theology, were one to write on the basis

---

43. Kierkegaard, *Works of Love*, 362–63: "When one thinks only one thought, one must in connection with this thinking discover self-denial, and it is self-denial that discovers that God is. Precisely this becomes the contradiction in blessedness and terror: to have an omnipotent one as one's co-worker. An omnipotent one cannot be your co-worker, a human being's co-worker, without its signifying that you are able to do nothing at all; and on the other hand, if he is your co-worker, you are able to do everything. The strenuousness is that it is a contradiction or is simultaneous; thus you do not experience the one today and the other tomorrow. Moreover, the strenuousness is that this contradiction is not something you must be aware of once in a while but is something you must be aware of at all times. . . . It is hard enough to work with another human being, but to work together with the Omnipotent One! . . . The difficulty, therefore, is just that I am to work together with him, if not in any other way, then through the continual understanding that I am able to do nothing at all, something that is not understood once and for all. And it is difficult to understand this, to understand it not at the moment when one actually is unable to do anything, when one is sick, in low spirits, but to understand it at the moment when one seemingly is capable of doing everything." See also Kierkegaard, *Judge for Yourself!*, 179–87. Cf. Tanner, *Jesus, Humanity, and the Trinity*, 2–5.

44. The New Testament does not teach a general discipleship—"the imitation of Christ." What it does teach is the imitation of the crucifixion of Christ. See Yoder, *Politics of Jesus*, 125, 131–33; cf. Hays, *Moral Vision*, 452–53.

Where Memory and Hope Converge

of the mastery of a discipline, were theology thought to be a potency to be made actual by skill and good intentions, then it would be exhausting labor. But lifted by the Spirit it is none of that. "Those who wait for the Lord shall renew their strength, they shall mount up with wings like eagles, they shall run and not be weary, they shall walk and not faint" (Isa 40:31).

Certainly we are still "flesh," our time is still embroiled in this present evil age that is not yet the age to come. Unfortunately the testimony of the saints is that we do find ourselves struggling with weariness and some days we do faint. But the saints also tell us that just often enough, waiting for the God who even now is coming, we will have performed a surprising work that breathes a breath of the coming reign of peace. For a time the new order of life will have come. A work of grace that comes to speech in the question "did I just do that?!" is nonetheless a work of grace.

To speak of a church theology is not, however, to speak of a mindless submission to some back slapping fraternity of power brokers. Certainly the life-patterns of a church that is still flesh take on institutional shape—and institutions by their very nature lust for survival and the capital that they calculate will insure it. However, insofar as the church is a faithful gift of the Holy Spirit it will have escaped sociological analysis, breaking elusively through the bonds of institutional inertia, the way a fresh breath breaks from the outside through pursed lips. It is a body gathered by the Spirit whose members differ from, even as they defer to, one another. It is corporate, but not faceless. Indeed the idiosyncracy of each of the persons in this body stands out as she faces her sisters and brothers in Christ. That is, the Spirit works love. The church is a society of those friends who celebrate each other *as* other (Rom 12:3–12). Thus it is to be expected that friendly dissent within the church's multiform mission will characterize the life of these people (Gal 2:11). Indeed a dissent that might in any other order threaten an institution's survivability is here a sign of hope.[45] It signifies the complexity of the way of the cross. Were there not many voices the church would be a deadly monotony.

---

45. Cavanaugh, *Torture and Eucharist*, 270: "The eucharist is . . . an 'event' in the sense of an eschatological performance in time which is not institutionally guaranteed. . . . But the Christian is never able to hold onto that reality as something which can be kept. . . . Paradoxically, it must be given away in order to be realized."

Therefore, as the theologian remembers and hopes, she remembers the church's often differing traditions. The more unbroken the church's fellowship is, the more traditions are remembered. It is the Spirit of God who makes the church alive and calls it to trust that the Reign that occurs already Thursday, Friday, Saturday, and Sunday of Holy Week will have cut through all weeks—that its body parts will have been gathered from all the times that now seem so distant, fragmented, and separate. It is in an ever-widening embrace of anticipation that the theologian's sisters and brothers include the children of all the temporary past, present, and future.

And so, the theologian in a certain sense obeys her old and new friends, as they obey her. She asks them her questions and is asked theirs. She hears their answers and gives them hers. And oddly, as if even the dead still spoke, she does her work in a conversation that transgresses the strictures of broken time.[46] Were her memory rote, were her traditions received without question, were she merely passive, she would blaspheme the Spirit. She will from time to time stand by the energy of God's coming Reign and say not only "yes" to what she has received, but "no" as well. At times she will be heard to say "no" above all—as if she were nothing but a naysayer. But friends say "nay" to friends.[47] And "nay" in the church is always for the sake of God's "yea" (2 Cor 1:18–19). The theologian remembers for the sake of hope.

Nor are traditions only words, as if the point were to grasp and hold some precious linguistic or ritual commodity. The church's traditions open; they are a means of grace, a window of grace, as is every conversation between these friends. It is a give and take, a dance of prayer that moves to the music that washes elusively over them. For a theologian to receive what has been passed on is for her to wait intently for her elders to lead her in prayer and for them to wait for her to lead *them* in prayer. And so,

---

46. Schmemann, *Eucharist*, 43: The eucharist is "the sacrament of the coming of the risen Lord, of our meeting and communion with him 'at his table' in his kingdom." See ibid., 56, 60–61, and Saliers, *Worship as Theology*, 228–29. Cavanaugh, *Torture and Eucharist*, 224–25: "In the eucharist one is a fellow citizen . . . of other members of the body of Christ, past, present, and future. . . . In the eucharist the heavens are opened and the church of all times and places is gathered around the altar. . . . Heaven and earth are united in the eucharistic meal, which anticipates the resurrection not merely of the soul but of a glorified version of the same body which now feasts on earth."

47. No one has more stressed the church as a friendship than Stanley Hauerwas, and no one better exemplifies the naysaying that friendship calls for. See Hauerwas and Pinches, *Christians Among the Virtues*, 70–88; and Hauerwas, *Sanctify Them in the Truth*, 105–21 and 143–56.

traditions include creeds, technical commentaries and speculations, liturgies, stories of the saints, relics, icons, calendars, and songs. The theologian attends to them and asks, "Why did you paint or say or do *that*?" And she asks every way she can find to ask, drawing upon everything else that she has received and every means by which an object of thought has become significant for her.

She thinks. And in a time "between the times" of the age to come and the present evil age she will think with a mind in the Spirit and in the flesh, in life and in death.[48] She will pray the prayer of Abraham (Gen 18:27), but she will nonetheless think.[49] As she thinks, she will draw upon all that she has come to hold by experience, calculation, and meditation. She will remember how she has hypothesized, tested, and verified; how she has moved from premises to conclusions; how she has collected her thoughts by releasing her intellectual habits and opening to an incalculable mystery.[50] In everything she will gather her intellectual goods in order to give them away with the church in eucharistic liturgy. The point is not to gain new property, but to live in the rhythm of the passion of Jesus Christ.

When she first came to find herself among the people of the church, the theologian learned in particular that she is always to remember the Holy Scriptures. In one sense she received these texts with the whole complex of traditions. They, too, came to her from her elders. They are remembered with the very hope as the ancient creeds and icons. Yet there is a difference. The Holy Scriptures are not simply one of many tracks in a music mix. They function in the church with a nonaggressive priority. How and why are unclear. Certainly not all that has come to be included among them is older than everything else that the theologian is to draw from. Her broad intellectual heritage goes back to a time that predates even the oldest scripture. Some of the church's own rituals and texts are older than the

---

48. See Gogarten, "Between the Times," 277–82. The essay is, however, sadly bound to the "period" it claims so movingly to have left behind. The course of Gogarten's later life bears some ambiguous witness to this. Although Levinas speaks too generally (what he says can hardly be applied as such to Barth, even in the 1920s), if we restrict his words in "God and Philosophy," 62, to Gogarten, he is quite right: "The messengers of the religious experience do not conceive another signification of meaning [*signification de sens*, than that of a language made of propositions bearing on a theme, that is, as having a meaning which refers to a disclosure, a manifestation of presence]. The religious 'revelation' is henceforth assimilated to philosophical disclosure—an assimilation that even dialectical theology maintains."

49. Cf. Coakley, *Powers and Submissions*, 34–37.

50. See Heidegger, *Discourse on Thinking*, 53–55.

youngest scriptures. One can find extra-scriptural texts—say, Augustine's *Confessions* or Kierkegaard's *Works of Love*—that are more immediately helpful than certain passages of scripture—say, some of the more obscure portions of the book of Revelation. Its Old Testament is itself ambiguous. Does it include the "Old Testament Apocrypha"? To what extent has it been surpassed by the New? Its New Testament came together only slowly. The first official list that included all New Testament books as authoritative was Athanasius's Easter Letter of the year 367 AD.[51] Even long after that date various New Testament books were disputed.[52]

And yet, when one finds oneself in the church it is to the Holy Scriptures that one is pointed again and again—for example, by Augustine's *Confessions* or Kierkegaard's *Works of Love* or the Nicene Creed or the church's liturgies or the lives of the saints. Indeed, the Scriptures were holy texts from the beginning. Even when what was to be included under that name was anything but settled, it was with them in particular that one was invited to deal. Even now one trusts them, because one trusts with the church.

But again these books are not there to satisfy the lust of the curious. They are not a set of propositions that functions as a guarantor of frozen Platonic truths. They are a means of grace, windows to the Reign of God, impenetrably dense without the Spirit that breathed into the dusty nostrils of Adam and the entombed Jesus Christ.[53] They are prayed liturgically as the truth of a nomadic life.[54] These are the holy texts that by grace are to be performed, read, and in that sense "re-written," not grasped and owned in order to be known and put to good use, the fruit, say, of the Tree of the Knowledge of Good and Evil.[55]

---

51. Kelly, *Early Christian Doctrines*, 60.

52. Metzger, *Canon of the New Testament*, 234–47, 273.

53. Cf. John Wesley's comments on 2 Tim 3:16 in his *Explanatory Notes Upon the New Testament*, 794: "*All scripture is inspired of God*—The Spirit of God not only once inspired those who wrote it, but continually inspires, supernaturally assists, those that read it with earnest prayer. Hence *it is so profitable for doctrine*, for instruction of the ignorant, *for* the *reproof* or conviction of them that are in error or sin, *for* the *correction* or amendment of whatever is amiss, and for instructing or training up the children of God *in* all *righteousness*."

54. See Abraham, *Canon and Criterion in Christian Theology*, xi and especially chapter 1. I do think that Abraham still wrestles with the temptation to grasp after a well-founded epistemology. However, he has very well demonstrated that the means of "knowledge" are not to be confused with the means of grace. Further, were adequate epistemic criteria to be determined, they would still be called upon to be yielded to the gracious God of a martyr church.

55. Though the approach advocated here has the appearance of what is sometimes

An intellectual enterprise of this kind is dangerous, perhaps delusional.[56] It *begins* already imagining an order different from anything visible or calculable or educed by the masters of civilization. It takes seriously an apocalyptic vision that could be relegated easily to a dusty past, a fiction of a primitive people who had no inkling of the chemical processes necessary for the maintenance of life. We have all been trained to think that ends are achieved; they don't come. We have torn down barns and erected elevators that rise to the heavens and we have filled them with seed corn. Our task is to work the fields, to plant, feed, water, and watch the fruit of nature and our labor grow. A faithful little local church imagines itself differently—as a kind of corporate metaphor for an eschatos that no immanent metabolic process can produce. "Thy kingdom *come!*" (Matt 6:10).[57]

Yet after twenty centuries of waiting the eschatos has not come. When questioned about this, the thinking little local church answers that it was not commanded to wait just a little while, but rather simply to wait—and in waiting to act. This must always appear to be sad or foolish or at least immoderate. All those disciplines sharing theology's suffix claim to obtain

---

gathered under the heading "the Wesleyan quadrilateral," and is very much in the spirit of John Wesley, there is at least one important difference. No particular reference has been made above to "*religious* experience." The broader term "experience" is conjoined with "reason" simply to indicate two dimensions of the theologian's acknowledgment of what makes sense, what has significance. There is no doubt that there are religious experiences. However, it is not clear that they are qualitatively different from other experiences. Among human experiences are experiences that may be classified as artistic, or as scientific, or as religious. There is no compelling reason to classify them that way, but it is reasonable to do so. What does seem clear is that none of the subjects of theological attention—not tradition, not reason, not experience, not Scripture—is to be confused with the faith, hope, and love that come from the outside as a gift of the Spirit of Jesus Christ. Religious experiences are to be filled with that gift no less than tradition or reason. Further there is no isolable phenomenon—no "experience"—that is in itself to be identified with this gifting. See Runyon, *New Creation*, 156–60.

56. Cone, *Cross and the Lynching Tree*, 25: "One has to be a little mad, kind of crazy, to find salvation in the cross, victory in defeat, and life in death."

57. Schmemann, *Eucharist*, 39: "[I]n the symbol [that constitutes the church] . . . the empirical (or 'visible') and the spiritual (or 'invisible') are united not *logically* (this 'stands for' that), or *analogically* (this 'illustrates' that), nor yet by *cause and effect* (this is the 'means' or 'generator' of that), but *epiphanically*. One reality *manifests* . . . and communicates the other, but . . . only to the degree to which the symbol itself is a participant in the spiritual reality and is able or called upon to embody it." Cf. Lacoste, *Experience and the Absolute*, 188–91.

a knowledge that is power. Why else go to the trouble? The knowledge of a eucharistic theology in contrast is an emptying: it is a knowledge that might occur in the mind of Christ, "who, though he was in the form of God, did not regard equality with God as something to be [seized], but emptied himself, taking the form of a slave, being born in human likeness. And being found in human form, he humbled himself and became obedient to the point of death—even death on a cross" (Phil 2:5–8). "For I decided to know nothing among you except Jesus Christ, and him crucified" (1 Cor 2:2).

Furthermore a theologian of the church's liturgy has not chosen her life from available options. She has certainly entered upon it having left another, different route; but he has not found his way by good sense and skill and will power. He has stumbled onto it (perhaps decisively, perhaps not; perhaps after long years of struggle, perhaps not) and finds that she cannot take credit for having done so.[58]

How offensive this is to the self-made conservative and liberal caricatures who self-consciously fill the airwaves with the sound of their voices! We have been taught that we are autonomous, rational or intuitive individuals with rights. Every responsible act is to be performed on a grid that provides its justification. Certainly nothing of major proportions is to be done without a good reason—even if that reason be no more than a feeling or a compulsion or a wager or an assertion of will. These things at least we can understand. We push off from hard ground, even if doing so has the appearance of drifting. We know where we came from and we do whatever we can to make sure that we know where we are going, even if we are only going for another rush. When we go into relatively "unknown" territory, we go on our own legs as explorers with compasses and sextants, extending the contour lines of our old maps, carrying the flag of our home country. But to say that we have been laid hold of by an outside force, one to which we have come to be given, one with which we have come to concur with a hope without any ground beneath it, seems the height of irresponsibility. To say that we operate now according to a different rationality, a different justification, one that was not already ours, is not only too much; it is insanity.[59] Haven't we heard of Jim Jones? Or worse, isn't this another instance

---

58. Surely Lindbeck is right in *Nature of Doctrine*, 132, that there are many "logics" by which people come to enter the body of Christ—"noble and ignoble" ones—all of which are finally surrendered to the discipline of that body. Of course, to surrender to the discipline of the church is not to grow deaf to the sound of the voice of the God who calls you by name, nor to become an ecclesiastical functionary.

59. See Lacoste, *Experience and the Absolute*, 178–79.

of the nihilism that so plagues our time and threatens to turn to nothing everything we've fought so hard to achieve? If there were no predictable outcome, if the old sky were wiped clean, if we looked to the birth of a new star, what kind of Magi would recognize it—were it to come—as a sign of anything but the practical irrelevance of anomalies?

But there is a difference between the *metanoia* of the eucharistic theologian and the deluded minds of followers of cult leaders and the evacuated minds of nihilists. The eucharist relativizes every leader. Even the Christ, his Spirit, and the mystery of his Father lead oddly, inimitably. Every human voice comes to the double crisis of crucifixion and resurrection. Even Christ is not followed according to leadership theory (2 Cor 5:16). And when Christ is spoken and heard with new ears, he awakens the body to perform acts that follow no pathfinder, no path, but Christ—even if one friend might for some prolonged time defer to and accompany another. Even in that deferral and accompaniment a good friend will not simply comply.

Theology is the work of a body of people that has been called into being out of nothing (1 Cor 1:28). It does not fear nihilism, for it performs a radical *nihil* with every prayerful "nevertheless." It takes up its cross daily, it expires with every breathed invocation of the Holy Spirit.[60] Yet inasmuch as the Spirit is the gift of resurrection, theology does not remain enclosed in "nothing," as if the point were to be dead. Nor does theology celebrate "nothing" as some happy end of responsibility that makes every act of self-assertion both permissible and desirable.[61] Nor does it look to pass through "nothing" on the way to a glorious mode of existence higher than mere human life.[62] The theology of the cross is with the church a eucharistic act of abandonment of all life—of all being—to the God who is love. It passes through death to life, but only insofar as it is gifted with *God's* category-irrupting life.[63] In Christ all life comes by God's good pleasure, freely, grace-

---

60. Kierkegaard, *For Self-Examination*, 82: "faith is on the other side of death."

61. To that extent such a theologian would agree with Nietzsche's critique of nihilism. See Nietzsche, *Will to Power*, 5–82 [1–134].

62. To that extent such a theologian would disagree with Nietzsche's affirmation of a certain kind of nihilism and the doctrine of the *Übermensch* associated with it. See Nietzsche, *Thus Spoke Zarathustra*, 267, 287, 327.

63. Kierkegaard, *For Self-Examination*, 82: "It is when all confidence in yourself or in human support, and also in God in an immediate way, is extinct, when every probability is extinct, when it is dark as on a dark night—it is indeed death we are describing—then comes the life-giving Spirit and brings faith."

fully. Liberated through the cross of Christ from bondage to the world and liberated by the Spirit of love from quarantine outside the world, the theologian is sent to the world, because the liturgical body of Christ comes forth by the freedom of the God who is love.[64]

The body of Christ is a pattern of tangible, if ambiguous and elusive, practices. What it does can be seen, smelled, tasted, heard, and touched. Yet the one it travels after cannot. In themselves its works are like any others, data available to the circumscriptive scrutiny of the "-ologies" that abound in our institutions of higher learning. The church will listen to their accounts of that scrutiny and will pray that they, too, will enter into the glory of the Sovereign. Yet the church's works are not for the sake of circumscription. Their defining borders are in fact there to be cut open that they might be emptied outward in sacrifice.

But the church's liturgy is at least as thoughtful as the scrutiny of any categorical gaze. Overt acts and subtle thoughts work together. The thinking church is the acting church. Yet so also the acting church is the thinking church.[65] Even the most extreme criticisms, visions, and revisions are called for within the expansive contours of the church. Not to exercise thought as far as it can be exercised is to fail to love God with the whole mind. It would suggest that there are goods not to be gathered and given away to God.

---

64. It is at this point that one might expect an excursion into "theological method" to provide the reader with a proposal for a dependable epistemology. None is to be found here. This is no accident. There is a little passage in Galatians that hints at the reason why: "Formerly, when you did not know God, you were enslaved to beings that by nature are not gods. Now, however, that you have come to know God, or rather to be known by God, how can you turn back again to the weak and beggarly elemental spirits? How can you want to be enslaved to them again?" (4:8–9). It is to the stammering phrase "or rather to be known by God" that this method is most attending. That is, this text is working to think a "knowledge" that is situated not in the apprehending subject, but rather outside the subject in the crucifixion/resurrection—and there not as a commodity that is to be gazed upon, plucked, and consumed, but quite differently as the event of the coming of another, one who wraps around us with a liberty that has no use for idols, conceptual or otherwise. See Marion, *God Without Being*, 22–24, 29–33, and 195–97.

65. Hauerwas, *Sanctify Them in the Truth*, 20: "Once there was no Christian ethics simply because Christians could not distinguish between their beliefs and their behavior. They assumed that their lives exemplified (or at least should exemplify) their doctrines in a manner that made a division between life and doctrine impossible."

Where Memory and Hope Converge

The church rejoices in the entanglement of its destiny in the affairs of the world. Incarnation is anything but indifferent. Indeed in Christ the church moves out into the world, rejoicing in the opposition it meets there. It rejoices, because it remembers that the Father has already gifted the world with the Son. It rejoices as well, because the church and the world have a common future. The church prays that it will be the salt that will have made the world a holy sacrifice to the coming of God's Reign (Matt 5:13; cf. Lev 2:13). That is, the church prays without presumption that it will have been given to the world that the world may thereby have been in a certain sense "enchurched." Evangelism is the work of the Spirit to which the church is to be obedient.[66]

Theology is worldly in this very sense. It thinks the world without imposition, but receptively, hospitably. It is open to the world, because the glorified body of the crucified Christ is not and never will be intact, whole, or closed. Theology's integrity over against the world is undone. Though certainly the theologian will be stubborn, she will not combat with counter-aggression the aggression that will inevitably press in upon her. A church of the baptized has already been crucified and raised and has nothing else to lose or win. Nourished on the broken body and shed blood of Christ, it has nothing to defend. The church theologian will be unapologetic—neither explaining away her difference from the world, nor looking to be excused by it.[67]

Of course, a theology of such a church proceeds very differently from the standard logistics of debate. In fact it is hard even to imagine a serious discussion that is not out to defeat a foe, to show that for every thesis it would assert there is a competing antithesis, for every right it would uphold there is a wrong, for every "A" it would articulate there is a "not-A"—to be

---

66. Kierkegaard, *Works of Love*, 253: "But *lovingly* to hope all things signifies the relationship of the loving one to other people, so in relation to them, hoping for them, he continually holds possibility open with an infinite partiality for the possibility of the good." That passage is in Kierkegaard's amazing chapter, "Love Hopes All Things—and Yet Is Never Put to Shame."

67. Perhaps it is rare that the former differs from the latter. Of course, this is not always *obviously* the case and perhaps it is not *actually* always the case with apologetics. Nonetheless, apologetics seems to remain ill at ease until someone at last accepts its apology.

resisted. Even those inclined to take Matt 5:39 literally set out typically to prove their case by putting down its alternative, the way one would put down a bad dog. Perhaps thinking otherwise takes a *metanoia*, more a re-pensiveness than a re-pentance, that trusts in an outcome that cannot be forced or compelled. "Turning the other cheek" theologically would then have the appearance of thinking backwards from a redemptive future, of opening the language of one's people to a sovereign love that comes as a gift—as all salvation comes, according to the gospel.[68]

Of course, our doctrines tell us (1) that we have been created in *God's* image and (2) that we have fallen into sin—that in ourselves (1) we *cannot* make our way to the love of God and (2) we *will not* to do so. The mode of thought to which these doctrines call us differs greatly from the doctrines that have formed us. How do we acknowledge difference—ours and theirs—without the logistics of violence? Perhaps we do so by remembering that the hope of the world comes as the resurrection of the Crucified comes, as the gift of the eucharist comes, by the Spirit of life and redemption. To live and think and write in this "perhaps" seems to be a precarious venture. No doubt it is. Even when one disagrees, critiques, opposes, excludes, renounces, and anathematizes, one may yet love and hope and embrace the other with one's eyes set on "the day of the Lord" (1 Cor 5:5). The logic of the crucifixion/resurrection, the logic of the eucharist, is the logic of active waiting.[69] It is the logic that works the fields, plants and waters, while looking for the harvest to be given from a mystery beyond our control (1 Cor 3:6–9). It is a logic that lets go of cause and effect.[70]

---

68. It is perhaps a similar logic that leads Barth in his own manner to "think backwards." Already in the first edition of his *Epistle to the Romans* he referred to theology as "ein Denken von Gott aus," a thinking outward from God, what he also later calls "Nach-denken," a thinking vis-à-vis the way of *God* into the world. McCormack, *Karl Barth's Critically Realistic Dialectical Theology*, 129–30, 425. One's thought is given to what is other, elusive and itself the free guarantor of a moment of particular theological significance. This is also the import of Barth's use of the word *analogy*, which in *Evangelical Theology*, 17, he puns as a reply (*ana*) to the Word of God (*Logos*).

69. See Wesley, "Means of Grace," especially 383–84 (II.7–III.1); cf. "On Zeal," 312–15, 320–21 (II.1–11, III.12).

70. Yoder, *Politics of Jesus*, 240: "And might it be, if we could be freed from the compulsiveness of the vision of ourselves as the guardians of history, that we could receive again the gift of being able to see ourselves as participants in the loving nature of God as revealed in Christ? Perhaps the songs of the earliest church might restore this to us if the apostolic argument cannot."

Where Memory and Hope Converge

The method of this theology goes after the truth and life that cut a path to the mystery of the crucifixion and resurrection of Jesus Christ (John 14:6).[71] Theology will pursue that path only if it lives by the Spirit of the liturgy of the eucharist. It is theology's service to the church and the world (whose salt it is) to have constantly on its lips the breath and the name of the one whose double end the eucharist hopes to remember. The church has been with some consistency from the beginning a discipline of thought and action that has proceeded according to two parallel patterns: (1) that God the Father goes out through the Son in the Spirit to the world and (2) that we worldly creatures are to pray in the Spirit through the Son to the Father.[72] The coming of God calls the theology of the church to walk this path of righteousness. The theology of the church prays that it might not be conformed to the training of the world, but transformed by the renewing of the mind (Rom 12:1–2), knowing that it, too, is to be judged by the Lamb of God.

---

71. Meta + hodos = "in pursuit of the way," perhaps mindful of where the way in fact moves. *Oxford English Dictionary*, s.v. "method," and "meta- *prefix*."

72. LaCugna, *God For Us*, 117–27; Pelikan, *Christian Tradition*, 1:217; Margerie, *Christian Trinity in History*, 50; Kelly, *Early Christian Doctrines*, 264. Cf. Lossky, *In the Image and Likeness of God*, 93–95.

Interlude[1]

IN THE MID-1980S a rectangle of derelict property lay between East 41st Street on the south, East Martin Luther King Jr. Boulevard on the north, South Alameda Street on the east, and Long Beach Avenue on the west—fourteen acres in South Central Los Angeles.[2] The businesses that once stood there were gone; pieces of foundation concrete littered the ground beside discarded appliances, furniture, and tires, piles of rags, broken glass, the other rubbish that collects in abandoned lots in crowded cities, and the vermin that hide and multiply there—especially in the most neglected quarters.[3] The city needed a place to build an incinerator, and its leaders chose to throw it up in this gray neighborhood of warehouses, factories, and the homes of poor, powerless people. And so, in 1986, the space was expropriated by eminent domain for a little under $5 million from nine companies, the largest of which had owned just over three-fourths of it.[4]

The people living nearby wanted anything but an incinerator in their backyard. After years of protests and the shock of the riots of 1992, the city changed its plans. By a complicated process those fourteen acres were made available in 1994 to the Los Angeles Regional Foodbank, which was housed directly across Alameda from them. The foodbank in turn offered the land to its neighbors. They responded. Marginalized, largely propertyless people walked from the houses and apartments where they had slept too little after

---

1. Mark 4:26–29: "He [Jesus] also said, 'The kingdom of God is as if someone would scatter seed on the ground, and would sleep and rise night and day, and the seed would sprout and grow, he does not know how. The earth produces of itself, first the stalk, then the head, then the full grain in the head. But when the grain is ripe, at once he goes in with his sickle, because the harvest has come.'"

2. Long Beach Avenue points north like an arrow at Los Angeles City Hall.

3. For the history of South Central Los Angeles Farm, see Hayasaki, "Seeds of Dissension Linger"; Hernandez and Zahniser, "Seeds of Secrecy"; Hernandez, "Brown Day in L.A."; Hernandez, "Bushel of Complaints"; Hoffmann, "History of the South Central Farm"; Marroquin, "Deputies Evict Farmers"; Hecht, "Twilight in the Corn"; Hopkins, "End for South Central Farm?"; Hopkins, "Last Gasp in Fight for Farm"; Norrell, "Navajo Says Evictions of Farmers from Urban Farm Sends a Message"; Boehm, "Theater: Cornerstone Mobilizes the Troupe"; Hetherman, "Attorney: City Sold South Central Farm at Major Loss for Taxpayers"; Llanos, "Judge Rules on Urban Garden"; Parker, "Huntington Housing Ex-Farm's Trees."

4. See Hecht, "Future at War with the Past."

working too long, methodically cleared the land, and covered it thickly with fertile soil they carted in and raked smooth. A decade later those fourteen acres of earth stretched out as a well-tended, green and brown patchwork quilt garden: ancestors' seeds bedded in rows as straight as the hoe handles strong hands had held to draw them. Blessed by an endless growing season without frost or flood, nutritional and medicinal plants at any given moment quietly stirred, ripening—some not yet breaking through the soil to the abundant sunlight above, some standing taller than the children, women, and men who gave them time, sweat, and the compost and water they carried to them in buckets. Families gathered to work side by side, breathing air cleaned by the leaves of stalks rooted in new earth and rising to redeem the brown-gray city sky, children running down paths between garden plots, playing, dancing, making the mischief and art children make, their mothers, fathers, and grandparents with dirty boots, knees, and hands working, sometimes laughing, sometimes troubled, usually simply on task. Corn, potatoes, chiles, cilantro, cactus, onions, tomatoes, tomatillos, agave, yams, sugar cane, beans, alfalfa, mallow, chamomile, purslane, quintoniles, and more grew in rows (or beside them). Plots were dotted with avocado, walnut, banana, guava, and other fruit and nut trees. In all, there thrived between 100 and 150 species of nutritional and medicinal plants.[5] Of course, there would be nothing particularly startling in all of this were these parcels situated in farm country, someplace far from South Central L.A. But *in* South Central L.A., blighted property in a blighted neighborhood came to life. Off the beaten path of city development, a parable of hope blossomed into a heavy fabric of work and stories.

Divided into plots, cared for by over 350 "documented" and "undocumented" families, largely of Mexican and Mesoamerican descent, the South Central Los Angeles Farm, as it came to be called, grew to be perhaps the largest urban garden in the nation. The discipline that gave rise to "the Farm" was also homegrown. The people who worked this land organized it into eight sections, each of which elected a council member, the council itself electing a president. The Farm council oversaw the land, kept plots tended, collected a little money for the water the foodbank made available, and got out of the way of people who had long before learned from their

---

5. Peña and Tezozomoc, "Preliminary List of Botanical Species Grown at South Central Community Garden"; Peña, "Farmers Feeding Families"; Peña, "Putting Knowledge in Its Place."

After Crucifixion

parents and grandparents who learned from their parents and grandparents how to care for the earth and its bounty.[6]

In 2001 a partner of the company that had owned the largest portion of the property the city acquired in 1986 insisted that, when plans to build an incinerator were abandoned, he by law had had the right to buy back the land.[7] The city at first denied his claim, but in 2003, in a session closed to public scrutiny, it agreed to the sale. He once more acquired the land for approximately $250,000 more than the city had paid for it seventeen years earlier.[8] Since that time advocates for South Central Farm have battled with its new owner, who at last agreed to sell it to the farmers (minus two and a half acres or so) for over $16 million, an outrageous and seemingly impossible sum, particularly for these people. When charitable nonprofit organizations added millions to the dollars a grassroots effort had brought in and, beyond all expectations, met the asking price, the owner refused to accept it, claiming to have been the subject of public insults and character assassination.[9] On the morning following Independence Day, in 2006, the

---

6. Juarez, Personal Interview.

7. This was on the eve of the opening of "the Alameda Corridor," i.e., just as property along Alameda Avenue was becoming once more very valuable. "The Alameda Corridor" runs immediately across the street from South Central Farm. It is hard to believe that anyone would have wanted to spend good "development" money for the Farm, when it fell into the hands of South Central L.A. residents just after the 1992 riots. See the Alameda Corridor Transportation Authority "Fact Sheet": "The Alameda Corridor is a 20-mile-long rail cargo expressway linking the ports of Long Beach and Los Angeles to the transcontinental rail network near downtown Los Angeles. It is a series of bridges, underpasses, overpasses and street improvements that separate freight trains from street traffic and passenger trains, facilitating a more efficient transportation network. The project's centerpiece is the Mid-Corridor Trench, which will carry freight trains in an open trench that is 10 miles long, 33 feet deep and 50 feet wide between State Route 91 in Carson and 25th Street in Los Angeles. Construction began in April 1997. Operations began in April 2002."

8. Adjusting for inflation, the 2003 purchase price was equivalent to over $3,000,000 *less* than what the city paid for it in 1986, i.e., in 2003 dollars.

9. The charge was specifically that Farm supporters had engaged in anti-Semitic rhetoric. Although it is true that hate-groups are found among all large populations, there is no evidence of anti-Semitism at any official Farm Web site. Indeed, Lila Garrett's account ("Who Owns the Farm?") makes the developer's accusation seem to be a red herring: "We sat down in Mr. Horowitz's comfortable office and introduced ourselves. Our all Jewish committee of six was clearly progressive, so Horowitz also quickly identified himself as a conservative. He spoke bitterly about the farmers, although when pressed he could not come up with who called him an anti-Semitic name. When we asked if he had accepted the farmers' apology he nodded, I thought reluctantly, but then added he wouldn't sell them the land if they gave him a hundred million dollars. His bitterness was

Interlude

Los Angeles Sheriff's Department cleared the way for a crew that over the next two days systematically bulldozed the fruit of over a decade of the sweat and pain and care of hundreds of the people of this land. Seven years later the acres lay untended. A perimeter fence locked the farmers out, the seeds of their ravaged gardens stirring and sending out green shoots, which the city from time to time mowed down, leaving brown earth and stubble beneath the dust their tractors threw up. Supporters of the Farm continue to fight at City Hall constant attempts by developers to turn those acres into sterile, high trafficked retail warehouses.

Rufina Juarez and Tezozomoc are two of the elected representatives of the Farm. They are the children and grandchildren of Mexican farmers, but it was at South Central Farm that they came as adult bodies to remember what it means to work the soil among people who work the soil. They came to see and smell and hear and feel and taste differently. They came to hope differently, the way family farmers hope before a field newly planted with seed as the rain clouds of early spring gather. They spoke of this particular fourteen acres of earth less than a month after bulldozers raped it:[10]

---

palpable. And we couldn't really figure out the root cause of it until he suddenly burst out: 'These immigrants, they come over here, they think they own the place' . . . And behold, immigrant bashing filled the room and we spent an uneasy hour being regaled with it. In the end of our attempt to stem the tide of violence and anger in our community, we realized that our meeting with Mr. Horowitz had fallen on deaf ears. He proudly announced that he was a hero to his conservative friends. When we asked if he was concerned about the ripple effect of his accusations of anti-Semitism, he said, 'No.' As long as he was true to himself, that's what mattered."

10. Written of the eviction of weeks earlier, which damaged, but did not devastate, the Farm, the following account takes on special poignancy after the farm's unrestrained razing in the shadow of "Independence Day": "The plants cry out. *Hay tristeza en las milpas y el campo.* The people or *gente* are unable to retrieve their seeds from all over Mesoamerica brought to L.A. by the diaspora of indigenous peoples forced to migrate. This includes Sara Haskie Mendoza's wedding corn—heirloom Navajo corn—struck down in a violent assault against a community's medicine. As a Diné elder once instructed us, taking care of the land is traditional medicine. Denise Andrade finds it hard to tell the story. Not because she can't. Quite the contrary. She finds it hard to look at the plants, the crops and the *yerbas*. Many are strewn about from the *tormenta* that has cut through the 14-acre urban farm here with the forced and violent eviction of 350 farmers from their plots. Here, Denise does not [initially] speak of the police violence against those that resisted. Instead she states: 'The earth was raped.' Her words are not hyperbole. Amid the largest urban community farm in the nation, the crops are yanked out. Others are stepped upon, thrashed, crushed and lifeless. If you pause, you can still hear the screams. Yet, not all the plants are down. They continue to plea. They stand here as witnesses. She asks Alberto Tlatoa to come along . . . to tell the story . . . and in short order, this 19-year-old speaks of dignity and sets the

After Crucifixion

Tezo: My father . . . was one of the original organizers [of South Central Farm] . . . so he spent a lot of years with the community here. . . . [He worked a plot at the Farm] for five or six years, [until] . . . he contracted leukemia and he became very ill. . . . After that he had a couple of strokes and . . . went to a convalescent [facility] where he needs 24/7 care. . . . One of his bedside requests was for somebody to take care of his plot. . . . Out of all things to concern him that was his greatest concern. . . . And so, [about eight years ago I started taking care of his plot and] I kept coming. . . .

This [pointing through the perimeter fence at the bulldozed wreckage of a section of the Farm] is the dividing line. It would go all the way up to the banana trees. . . . This was part of the legacy [my father] left. He taught a lot of people how to do things right [weeping], how to grow food correctly, how to plant. A lot of people respected him, because of his honesty. . . . We had . . . these agave plants, they were very important, and then I had a lot of sugar cane; [pointing] there's some of it . . . and the little banana tree. This is the first year it's given bananas. And it's pretty sad, you know. There was a pomegranate tree over there that he had left and there was a whole row of cactus that we used to eat from. On this side [pointing] . . . right there in the middle, right there, there was a guava tree. That was the last thing, the only real thing that I think my father left me [weeping]. The first day of bulldozing it survived, but the second day they came by and they tore it all down. . . .

[The Farm] was organized like the *ejido* system in Mexico, the kind of representational government we're used to. . . . [My dad was one of the elected leaders] and that was one of the reasons people kind of looked to me, when things came down. They looked at me as representing the same historical situation and that was one of the reasons they elected me to represent the community. And, you know, we fought hard, we fought pretty hard, and I'm so close to this that I cannot tell if it made a difference [laughs and weeps]. To me this represented a direct connection to my father [weeps more strongly]. . . .

For me the *land* has always been associated with my grandfather. When we were kids, my father had to come north to make a living, so we were basically left with my grandfather [weeping], who is still alive, who's still a farmer in an *ejido*, or communal landholding. . . . For me the farm [in Mexico], it was a special place. It was rough and it was hard, but I had a lot of good times. I worked hard; when you're a kid you work hard. . . . When I grew

---

record straight: 'We are farmers, not gardeners. We are *campesinos*.'" Gonzales, "We Are Farmers, Not Gardeners."

Interlude

up ... [where] we lived ... there was no road ... you had to pack mule all the way in there, which was like eight hours. . . . And what we loved to do was ... go down ... the River de San Juan ... and you would just go down the ravines and they were full of guava trees and all day long you would take off and just go picking guavas just straight out of the wild. . . . And so to me [weeping] the bulldozing of the guava trees was [weeping strongly], was breaking the whole connection [his voice trails off] and [in its place is left] a feeling of numbness. . . .

And it's tough, you know, [weeping] because now you understand how much a little piece of dirt means to the people. It's kind of symbolic of a lot of things, like the struggle of doing for yourselves [weeping].

I'm going to have to stop; this is way too hard for me. . . . I haven't been able to process it, I haven't been able to breathe, I've been busy fighting. So, you know, this stuff catches up with you. . . .[11]

Rufina: The last thing I planted was corn ... [from my paternal] grandmother's side [of our family]. . . . My uncle still works [their] land [in Mexico]; . . . and my father, my mother, and my sister, we planted that corn and it was growing real beautiful, but they killed it and that's just wrong. . . .

[There were] a lot of children [at the Farm], [children at] every parcel—except I think there was one couple that didn't have nobody and maybe the Russian gentleman that was with us and the Cambodian lady [but they probably didn't have family]—everybody else ... , every single parcel, had children—maybe that their nieces would come, grandchildren would come, somebody would come. . . . You would get to know everybody's children after a while. They'd be running around down the walkways, the aisles [between plots]. . . .

This place was opened every day from sunrise to sunset. . . . When we started organizing more ... we would ask people, "Well, okay, it's the Fourth of July, should we close down?" They were like, "No! We have no other place to go to!" [We'd ask,] "You know, it's going to be Thanksgiving, do you guys ... ?" "No!" "Well, what about New Year's Eve?" And then they said, "No, let's open and close early!" Why? Because you have no other place to go! . . . This is their only place, this is *the* place. They didn't want to be stuck

---

11. Tezozomoc, Personal Interview.

in their apartment, probably sharing rent with other families; they needed a space....

We had the best meals, the best times, the best music.... And underneath ... the walnut tree we would have the services, the Christian service, the Catholic service.... [At] one of the [worship services] ... we introduced two crosses, one for the north and one for the south. A farmer made them out of wood, real plain. And then we would rotate them, because there was mass once a month and then you would take care of that cross, take it to your house for prayer and worship and then you would bring it [to the next service] and then that person would bring some food, because that's the tradition: eat with everybody. And then another family would take it.... We would do a yearly feast [in June], the Abundance Feast.... We would have the dancers come in and we would have prayers all night. We would start up with a mass and feed people and then do the offerings ... then take a rest and then have breakfast and then dance. And then in the evening [we would] invite everyone to come and eat.... In Mexico the Abundance [Feast] ... [is] a real old tradition of giving thanks [at the end of the growing season] ... for the abundance of what [the land] gave you. ... People would do an altar and it was real pretty, decorated with ... flowers, people would bring the most beautiful flowers they had.... That is, I think, what makes up a community: how you pray, how you play, where you live, where you eat....

[At the Farm] faces were happy, because they were working the land and growing a plant and cleaning and weeding, like they were so much at peace with themselves. In the middle of all this bad violence, in the middle of this concrete and contamination, there was this little, little peace ... like they were really one with, well, the Creator, one with the Creator. And I think if you look at all the special moments, [they] were when the trees were moving because there was a light breeze, the birds were singing, the kids were running, the sun was up, you could smell if there had been watering of the land, and the people of the community ... were just greeting everyone, like, ... "Buenos días!"

And the other part is the sharing. You'd say, "Those are beautiful zucchinis!" And then [they would reply], "Have some!" And I said, "No, no, no!" And they'd say, "No, please!" And then you'd say, "Well, then, you have some [of my things]." ... Or you would walk by and greet somebody and they'd say, "Come in, come into my little parcel!" And they'd be heating up a tortilla and they would offer you whatever they had.

Interlude

> I think [the one time I most felt] "well, I've done something in life!" is when I saw some of the young children marching for the first time [protesting in support of the Farm] and that's when I knew... I did something good.... And if nothing else happens, that was so important for those children and people who... have been real quiet, submissive, [who] worked all their lives, all because they needed to do that for their children—and to see them, the elders and more important the children, I knew that that's it, that those children will never, ever be afraid to stand up!¹²

---

12. Juarez, interview. Rufina is President of the South Central Farmers of Los Angeles. It should not be thought that the forces that sent the bulldozers to raze the Farm simply broke the backs of its supporters. Since that time the Farm's leaders have continued to meet. For a while they worked a piece of land near Fresno, California, over two hundred miles away, carrying produce into Los Angeles for sale. More recently, they have worked land near Bakersfield, still over a hundred miles away. Rufina gave a report on the Farm at the 6th session of the United Nations Permanent Forum on Indigenous Issues, May 18, 2007. As of the summer of 2008, plans are becoming increasingly concrete to build a warehouse at 41st and Alameda. See Chawkins, "A New Setting for Their Plots"; "United Nations Permanent Forum on Indigenous Issues"; "South Central Farmers' Report"; "Request Full CEQA EIR Process."

3   Working Out the Body and Blood of Christ on the Eighth Day of Creation

Toward a Martyr-Ecclesiology

> *When everything's made to be broken*
> *I just want you to know who I am*[1]

IT TAKES A CERTAIN audacity to bring children into the world. The world is not an easy place, not even for those prosperous and well-adjusted families whom we come to know too rarely and for too short a time. Indeed, finding one's way through this world can be quite an ordeal. The pain of childbirth is not the mother's alone. Therefore, when, the afternoon following the hour he first consciously witnesses a baptism, a little boy turns to his mother and asks, "Why did they pour water over that baby today?" she has been called upon to say more than her son can bear, more than she herself can say. She has been called upon to tell him the story of Jesus and his place in it. In her faltering reply to the child she loves more than her own life, she will inevitably tell him how much *Jesus* loved children; she may even tell him that he was crucified for children as well as for adults; but saying much more than that will strike her as premature, as unsuitable for one so young, and even the little she does say may cause some disquiet in her own mind, when she later ponders how she might have answered him better. "Was I baptized?" he will ask. "Yes, you were baptized, too, when you were very small."

1. Rzeznik, "Iris."

Working Out the Body and Blood of Christ on the Eighth Day of Creation

How does a mother or father tell any child that we who have brought her into the world—we who have promised to love and shelter her, to feed and nurture her, to give her all that we have—have in fact given her away to be inscribed into the most shocking and disturbing of stories, a story that itself is an indictment against the whole world?

> But truly it must be a strange human being, or rather an inhuman brute, who would not involuntarily drop his gaze and stand almost like a poor sinner the moment he is going to tell a child this for the first time, a child who has never heard a word about this and of course has never suspected any such thing. At that moment, the adult stands there as an accuser who accuses himself and the whole human race.[2]

Not even the prosperous and well adjusted have the resources to take in and mollify the story of Jesus, though they have often tried. Of course, it is no tragedy. At its open end is resurrection. And yet *this* resurrection is not the stuff of comedy, not even in the most formal sense of that term.[3] Easter Sunday follows Good Friday. Yet the Jesus who "stands up" on Easter Sunday has not gotten over being crucified. He stands up on the far side of tragedy. What do we hope for as we tell a child, even in the most "age appropriate" manner, what she has been baptized into? Having told her, how do we then pray for her? How do we counsel her to approach the time that lies ahead of her? Do we dare pray that she will repeat, however differently, the passion of Jesus? Even without burdening her with *that*, her life no doubt would be hard. How could a mother, without a perverse, pathological abuse of a child's unquestioning trust, pray for her to come to *Jesus'* end? How could she teach her little boy that his baptism means that he will suffer as Jesus suffered? Even the ghost of an image of such pedagogy would send a shudder through any but the most aberrant. And yet to baptize a child *is* to give him to be inscribed into the story of Jesus, a story that even in all of its heaviness is declared already in the words of the baptismal liturgy to be the only unqualifiedly good news.

It is indeed good news. The story of Jesus is the story of a light that shines to the far side of darkness. It is the story of a life that ceases to be threatened by death, because it has outbid it. It is the story of a life free to undo competition, a life whose abundance makes useless both the claim to

---

2. Kierkegaard [Anti-Climacus], *Practice in Christianity*, 175–76.

3. His story's conclusion is by no means "prosperous, pleasant, and desirable," in any ordinary sense of those terms. *Oxford English Dictionary*, s.v. "comedy."

"mine" and to "yours." It is the story of an excessive love given freely both to friends and to enemies. It is the story of the forgiveness even of great debt, of the emptying of prisons, of the feeding of the hungry, of the renewal of the strength of atrophied legs and blind eyes, of the coming of peace, of the awakening of a righteousness that will not be defiled by contact even with what is most unclean. It is the story of a sanctity that comes to dwell among even the vilest of criminals, humbly and invitingly. And it is the story set inseparably in the context of the kind of grueling life that the great majority of the human race lives, has lived, and will live for as long as we can imagine. That is, it is good news only where news, more often than not, is bad.

The mother and father who give their child to be baptized will hope and pray that the redemption of the resurrection will so saturate her that when times come that would tempt her to despair, she will face them with trust. But they would also pray—if they understood baptism a certain way—that her life would become redemptive, i.e., cruciform, that she would "suffer approximately as he suffered in this world."[4]

To baptize a little girl is to send her down the path that leads to resurrection, but only through crucifixion. Although it is not possible to predict the way she might be described in a case study after she has spent years and other countable resources on this path, one might imagine a now young woman some difficult evening writing:

> After a weary day of preparing the land for a [community] garden last April, I put down a shovel and lifted my gaze along the two-story cement walls that enclosed our little open plot of land. My eyes eventually reached the sky, and I was met with an amazing sense of renewal. I felt as if God was saying, "I am inviting you to take part in an act of creation."
>
> My tired mind and plans for the garden were suddenly unimportant. Whether I was the one working on it, whether the beds

---

4. "So what effect do you think this story would evoke in the child? . . . [Gradually], as the child went and thought about this story, he would become more and more passionate . . . —for the child would have firmly resolved that when he grew up he would slay all those ungodly people who had treated this loving person in that way; . . . childishly forgetting that it was over eighteen hundred years since those people lived. . . . Then, when the child had become older and mature, he would not have forgotten his childhood impression, but he understood it differently. He no longer wished to strike, because, he said, then I am not like him, the abased one, who did not strike, not even when he was struck. No, now he wished only one thing, to suffer approximately as he suffered in this world, which philosophers have always called the best but which nevertheless . . . crucifies love and shouts, 'Long live Barabbas.'" Kierkegaard, *Practice in Christianity*, 177–78.

were [bordered by] stone or wood, even whether we planted a Japanese maple or a dogwood—these things clearly did not matter. What I understood from God was: "I am doing something to redeem creation in this place. It is far more vast than you can imagine, yet you are invited to help as best you can." . . .

As I turned from the sky, the abandoned factory across H Street loomed in my peripheral vision. . . . From when I first came to Kensington, I'd felt the factory's ominous presence over our neighborhood. It was all I could see from my room, the sun sank behind it hours before darkness fell. . . . [At] the moment, it stood abandoned—a monument in opposition to new creation. . . .

On June 20th, early in the morning, our senses were overwhelmed first by the smell of smoke, and soon followed by an intense heat, crackling, and [glaring] light coming from within the H Street factory. . . . I started shaking. We grabbed what we could as we left the house, stopping to pray as hundreds of our friends and neighbors poured into the streets. By the end of the day, more than a city block and nine homes had been consumed, including ours. The garden-to-be served as a gap between the row homes that day, stopping the flames from spreading around the corner to affect even more of our neighbors. . . . The building smoldered for days. My mind raced for nights, acknowledging miracles and mourning over what might have been spared or lost. Just a few feet from our home, the dogwood tree we'd planted had somehow survived. I was personally spared more than I can fathom, and don't know what to make of this. Nearly a month has passed, yet I am still numb and amazed that no one was hurt. . . . My role is still to trust and continue caring, and I dare to pray that God's vast redemption of Creation will rise from the ashes. . . .

Recently, I have been reminded that we must empty ourselves so that God can fill us. If we fill our lives—there is no room for God to act. I have only the best intentions in what I do, and yet I consistently take on too much—or try to do things by myself—and somehow end up both drained and over-filled at the same time.

The solitude of which I speak is not for the purpose of remaining alone in nothingness. Rather, it is a space and time created for becoming still enough to enter into communion . . . [with] God. Without this space, we lose sight of how completely God loves us, and thus—we can't know how to love each other as perfectly as we are loved.[5]

---

5. Walz, "Redeeming Creation." Jesce Walz was at that time a twenty-five-year-old member of The Simple Way, a "new monastic" missional community in a particularly impoverished corner of Kensington, a neglected North Philadelphia neighborhood. Cf. www.thesimpleway.org.

After Crucifixion

It is having been baptized into the extraordinary history of Jesus, having come to the strange thoughtfulness—the *metanoia*—that baptism entails, that we may begin to slip out of the grasp of "natural consciousness" to see the task of life with a particularly uncanny difference, to see the whole world immersed in baptismal waters. Surely it would take a *metanoia* to walk into a village of peasants bent and broken by the relentless demands of day labor and remember even with idiosyncratic joy that it was to such peasants that Jesus said, "Come unto me . . ." (Matt 11:28). A room full of comfortable people presuming to have put poverty behind them[6] is a collection of counterfeit servants of the master who never got over being poor.

Human beings work.[7] Their lungs open, they climb to their feet, not quite falling, they walk; sometimes they run. They thrust their rough hands into the earth that in rising to meet them tempts them to believe it gives them support. They cut a path through the world that in surrounding them tempts them to believe it gives them room. They walk furrowed fields, they carry what they've gathered in their skirts, and at the end of a good day they eat.[8] Human beings work and work is hard.[9] Though in weary moments we dream of a time when work was or will be effortless—like an overflowing spring—we touch that dream only fleetingly, say, when we give ourselves to tasks with exhilarating abandon.[10] Yet on any ordinary day,

---

6. Perhaps by "redemption and lift."

7. This and similar pronouncements do not claim to be self-evident, nor do they stand in competition or league with more familiar one-liners that aim to grasp a purported "essence" of human life (such as "*homo sapiens*" or "*homo faber*"). Unlike those formulae, the pronouncements here are not universalizing conceptions at all. Though they do ask that the reader think widely, they do so by pointing to particular human beings who live particularly exacting lives and ask the reader not to forget them—indeed, they ask that these be remembered above all.

8. Those familiar with Heidegger's "The Origin of the Work of Art" will recognize my borrowing his imagery. See Heidegger, *Poetry, Language, Thought*, 32–34. Of course, Heidegger's position is not thereby being affirmed.

9. The *Oxford English Dictionary* follows the etymology of the word *work* (s.v. "work, v.") to an ancestor that signifies "to feel pain." Cf. s.v. "labour, labor, n.": "ad. L. *labōrem* labour, toil, distress, trouble."

10. I imagine Tom Joad: "Tom hefted the pick. 'Jumping Jesus! If she don't feel good!'" Steinbeck, *Grapes of Wrath*, 308. I also imagine the chain gang sitting on their shovels at the end of an extraordinary day of hard labor, shaken, bewildered, and elated: "Dragline: 'Where'd the road go?' Luke: 'That's it. That's the end.' Koko: 'But there's still daylight left.'

Working Out the Body and Blood of Christ on the Eighth Day of Creation

when with freshly washed hands we sit on our heels to eat, what we have known has been hard. Certainly, it is ambiguously so. Even on an especially painful day labor comes not only with distress, but also with joy—there are contraction and dilation, pushing and crowning, breathless silence and the death-defying, piercing cry of new life. And when new life comes warmly into her arms, she holds it close and it suckles at her breast.

It would be a strangely abstract fantasy were we seriously to imagine a future without work or food. Even while lying in her death-bed a worker dreams of a new day, perhaps before a feast table with the fruit of her labor bountifully spread for her children and grandchildren, for her brothers and sisters, for her mother and father, and for her, too, and the man to whom she has again and again turned in invitation. Life is a work and a feast that cease only under the cold weight of death. Feuerbach was right that we are what we eat.[11] Marx was right that we are what we do.[12]

Work constitutes no private property; its goods are not mine because my individual, sweaty intentionality is mixed with it.[13] Certainly the stories of our covetousness, of our grasping for the "product" of labor, what tumbles off a factory conveyor belt onto a half-off retail display table, stories of our fixation on belongings as the end of our human resources management, stories of our laying hold of goods and making them "mine," are no less plentiful than dark. Nonetheless all that we do is a moment in the unendingly fluid, open, long march of work. It is only in the postponement of indolent, disengaged neutrality that privacy and propriety make any appeal to us.[14] Work was there before your diaphragm tightened to receive your first gasp; work will be there long after it softens to release your last sigh. It is no more yours than mine. Indeed it is not "ours," some asset of a corporation desperate to operate in the black. It is rather a commission that comes to us, the way we together are sent to be fruitful and multiply

---

Dragline (checking the sun): 'Bout two hours left.' Loudmouth Steve: 'What do we do now?' Luke (smiling): 'Nothin.' Dragline [laughing]: 'Oh, Luke, you wild beautiful thing! You crazy handful of nothin'!'" *Cool Hand Luke*. But I imagine especially John 4:14, to which these parables awkwardly point.

11. For brief accounts of the context of Feuerbach's famous words, see Kamenka, *Philosophy of Ludwig Feuerbach*, 30, and Höffding, *History of Modern Philosophy*, 281.

12. See, e.g., Marx, "Theses on Feuerbach"; and Marx and Engels, *German Ideology*, 42.

13. That is, the economic tradition that includes Marx has not been adequately mindful of a certain *charisma* of work.

14. Solitude is not to be confused with privacy, nor with "solitariness."

and fill the earth, to cast our shadows on the earth's seeds, green plants, and grazing wildlife; the way we are to move toward the interval of silence when the work week is full, the day we overtly and particularly wait upon that mystery we too casually call "God" (Gen 1:28—2:3).[15]

We are textile workers, together weaving the fibers that rise uncompelled into the world from the earth. We are gleaners, filling fabric bags with grain left for us at the edges of fields, grain we will grind and mix and knead and bake. We are vine-dressers, tending rows of vines gnarled with age, collecting and gently crushing clusters of their fruit, and pouring new wine into fresh wineskins. We are poets, who ply our craft from memory, scratching out new songs of lament, petition, thanksgiving, praise,[16] and intercession. We are dancers moving to the breath- and blood-rhythms of lungs and hearts. What we gather, bake, and pour, we eat and drink, gracefully singing and dancing our long, unfinished story. Work is food and food is work—each undulating into the other in an expenditure that holds out what it is doing, has done, and will have done, as a child might to an approaching parent—that is to say, righteously.

Work is charismatic.[17] *What* we are given to work upon precedes us, a gift sent our way the first five days of creation, the days when the Spirit hovered

---

15. Since we and the wildlife over which we are to have "dominion" are said in this passage to be given seeds and green plants to eat, whatever "dominion" might be taken here to signify, it doesn't include the shedding of blood.

16. Pannenberg's early explorations into doxology may have led to a very different theology had he not spent his time looking for the "theological implications" hiding in the work of nontheological disciples. See his very helpful essay, "Analogy and Doxology," in *Basic Questions in Theology*, 211–38; e.g., 218–19, 221: "Thus, talk about God rooted in adoration does indeed intend to speak about God's eternal reality by analogical transfer of meaning, but it does not intend to accomplish this as an analogue, but rather by opening itself unreservedly to the infinity of God. . . . In the very act of adoration, our words, since they are transferred to God, become equivocal in relationship to their ordinary meaning, no matter how well founded and free from arbitrary derivation this use of words may be. . . . The concept of meditation points to an understanding of God which does not allow him to be comprehended in concepts . . . but is utterly turned toward God in the act of adoration."

17. It might be helpful to note explicitly here that I am particularly in this paragraph thinking of Heidegger's phrase "*Sein zu*." Heidegger uses this phrase, of course, in his significantly pagan nonsubstantialist ontology. It functions in part as a critique of the traditional Western notion that beings are relatively independent and circumscribable,

Working Out the Body and Blood of Christ on the Eighth Day of Creation

over the face of the waters, before our dust first stirred. *That* we are given to work is a gift of the sixth day of creation, the day the Spirit is breathed into our nostrils and we rise to our feet. The work that we are given to *do* is a gift released on the seventh day of creation, the day that belies our "productivity" and invites us to remember whose Spirit opens the way before us (cf. Deut 5:14–15 and 1 Cor 3:6). In doing and waiting we are given to live for creation's eighth day, the day the Spirit will have been poured upon all flesh and all work will have shone—and even now on occasion and in anticipation shines—with a liberative glory full of grace and truth.[18] The "was," "am," "are," and "will have been" of these days are the passion of giving.[19] Work is the way we give ourselves away, the way we are given to be stretched out, the way we are given to take time.

A worker's time, however, cannot be held for long. As with all gifts that do not collapse into property, it comes newly into our hands only to get away again. Indeed we don't so much take it as surrender to it, as to a

---

items centered in themselves. For Heidegger there is no being that is not also a kind of entailment of the totality of beings, as an event of gathering, a happening-together. To think "a being" is thus to think of its relation to the larger happening of *being*. That is, "a being" is always a "being-to," a movement out into what is both different from it and (from another point of view) precisely what it is (in the way, say, that words entail each other). This is seen perhaps most significantly in *Being and Time*, when Heidegger speaks of *Dasein* (which may be taken here to be the way a human occurs) as "being toward death" (*Sein zu Tode*). Here, along the way of life, a human being is a relation to all that is happening, all that has happened, and all that will happen—and it is that as it struggles through life in anticipation of its own coming death, that moment when its particular instance of being will have ended and thus become all that it will ever be, i.e., a totality. See, e.g., Heidegger, *Being and Time*, 219–46. What I wish to suggest here is the *theological* point that a human life, though indeed living-*to*, is a living simultaneously to others and to God, who concurrently elude all totalizing. "Living to" here becomes the gift of love from and to the Father—and with the Father to the neighbor (Mark 12:28–31).

18. "[You] see . . . it is not your present Sabbaths that are acceptable [unto Me] . . . but the Sabbath which I have made, in . . . which, when I have set all things at rest, I will make the beginning of the eighth day which is the beginning of another world. Wherefore also we keep the eighth day for rejoicing, in the which also Jesus rose from the dead, and having been manifested ascended into the heavens." Ep. Barn. 15:8–9. Cf. Acts 2:15–18 and John 1:14.

19. There are no hard-and-fast rules for determining when a particular occurrence is to be judged to have been providential. However, to point to a providence that has not been conflated with fate is to acknowledge that a charisma has been at play, one that "provides." "Give us this day our daily bread," we pray. In praying this prayer we abandon the hypothesis that we are trapped. But what does it signify that today, just before noon and just after finishing lunch, I opened the fortune cookie tossed randomly on my tray to find that its slip of paper read, "Time is precious, but truth is more precious than time"?

promise. Time is as it happens, the trace of a not-yet, a coming *new* time which unsettles constancy. Admittedly, it is not obviously so. Indeed the distilled wisdom of the great thinkers of record begs to differ. Every "principle of correct thinking" ascertains at most a restorative future which, held fast by the old, rests in changeless peace.[20] The image of a truly new day may well seem a fantasy. Even if *this* and *that* have gone, we recall, their matter/energy and the "laws" that hold them continue unabated. ("Scoffers [come] ... saying 'Where is the promise of his coming? For ever since our ancestors died, all things continue as they were from the beginning of creation!'" [2 Pet 3:3–4].)[21]

The persistent widow imagines differently.[22] She imagines a time that is patient and kind even as it delivers its unsettlingly ambiguous pronouncement, "I am coming for *you!*" (Cf. 2 Pet 3:8–9). Her time forecasts an "outside" that surprises and wounds our property, prying open our bolted doors and windows, breaking into our houses like a thief in the night. Already—as if in anticipation of an impending fire storm—in every day of hard labor, however partially and fragmentarily, it comes (cf. 2 Cor 5:17). Our stockpiles of goods open to a disaster, word of which not every ear hears as good news.[23] Or so she tells us. She looks us in the eye and without speaking asks, "Don't you feel the ground shaking; don't you feel

---

20. I take the phrase "principle of correct thinking" from my copy of Copi and Cohen, *Introduction to Logic*, xix. Could one even begin to think the ascendancy of anything but the fixed constancy of "sameness," if all thought comes down to the venerated Principle of Identity, A = A?

21. Cf. Augustine, e.g., *City of God* 12.13–14.

22. I think not only of the widow who is often given this title, the widow who would not leave her unjust judge in peace (Luke 18: 1–8), but even more of the other Lukan widows: the eighty-four-year-old prophet, Anna, a widow since the seventh year of her marriage, who met the eight-day-old Jesus in the temple ("she never left the temple but worshiped there with fasting and prayer night and day") when he was carried by his parents to be circumcised (Luke 2:36–37); the widow whose only son was raised by Jesus from the dead during his funeral procession (7:12–13); and the widow who "out of her poverty ... put in [the temple treasury] all she had to live on" (21:2–3).

23. Blanchot's "disaster" is only a parable of what I am saying here. For example: "The disaster: break with the star, break with every form of totality, never denying, however, the dialectical necessity of a fulfillment; the disaster: prophecy which announces nothing but the refusal of the prophetic as simply an event to come, but which nonetheless opens, nonetheless discovers the patience of vigilant language. The disaster, touch of the powerless infinite: it does not come to pass under a sidereal sky, but here—a here in excess of all presence. Here: where, then? '*Voice of no one once more.*'" Blanchot, *Writing of the Disaster*, 75.

the heat of the approaching new day?" Before her gaze it is a cold man even among unjust judges who does not swallow hard. In unguarded moments we wonder, contrary to our better nature (like children), could it be in *some* (horrifying?) sense that in our time "the heavens *will* pass away with a loud noise, and the elements *will* be dissolved with fire, and the earth and everything that is done on it *will* be disclosed" (2 Pet 3:10)? We ask, because her gaze *is* already an apocalyptic question, a question that points at you and me from an outside beyond our grasp.[24]

"Why is there something rather than nothing?" Leibniz asks and Heidegger echoes.[25] Indeed anything *we* might ask of an impending time in one way or another repeats the question that has already arrived with the very breath out of which our words are shaped.[26] *Everything* depends on *how* we repeat it, how we lean into it.[27] How do we live, when we remember that whatever we hold in our hands (as well as our hands themselves) will crumble one day into the dust from which it has come? ("Since all these things are to be dissolved in this way, what sort of people ought you to be in leading lives of holiness and godliness, waiting for and hastening the coming of the day of God, because of which the heavens will be set ablaze and dissolved, and the elements will melt with fire?" [2 Pet 3:11–12].) Do we dare to answer through the sweat of our labor: "in accordance with his promise, we wait for new heavens and a new earth, where righteousness is at home" (13)?

Thus the time of waiting is to be no mere passivity. We are in no sense masters over time, but it does not happen without us. We make time. It is no less a gift that we do than a deed we receive. When all our work ceases, our time is up. Without work we are dead (cf. Jas 2:26). We work with the widow, however, not to acquire time, but to give it away—to the holy one who is "to come" and with the holy one to one another (cf. Rev 4:8). Each

---

24. *American Heritage Dictionary of Indo-European Roots*, 2nd ed., s.v. "eghs."

25. Leibniz, "Principles of Nature and Grace, Based on Reason," 4 [7]; Heidegger, *Introduction to Metaphysics*, 1.

26. Cf. the notion that God is *die Fraglichkeit* of the world in Ebeling, *Word and Faith*, 347–53, and *God and Word*, 31–32. Though Ebeling's vision is quite different from the one I am voicing, in his own way Ebeling points the reader to the engaging and unsettling mystery of God.

27. *Oxford English Dictionary*, s.v. "obey," "ob-": "classical Latin *oboedīre* (also *odēdīre*) to listen, pay attention, obey, submit to < *ob-* + *audīre* to hear. . . . In combination classical Latin *ob* has the following senses . . .: In the direction of, towards; facing, in front of; as classical Latin *obvertere* to turn towards, *oboedīre* to listen to."

moment in this way arrives and in arriving gets away.[28] Inspiration precedes expiration and may by God's good charismatic pleasure follow it. That is how with the widow we dare to wait—even to the far, silent side of the cold metallic knell that in lingering tempts us even now to put an end to all waiting.

> We do not live to ourselves, and we do not die to ourselves. If we live, we live to the Lord, and if we die, we die to the Lord; so then, whether we live or whether we die, we are the Lord's. For to this end Christ died and lived again, so that he might be Lord of both the dead and the living. (Rom 14:7–9)

Thus together we are given to live and move and unhand our being, i.e., we are given to pray. Led by an unlikely teacher, himself fresh from prayer, we turn our thinking bodies toward the mystery from which breath comes, acknowledging that we have no control over who or what this mystery comes to be. We remember all we have done, all that our ancestors have done and would have their children do, all that we yet plan to do, and we call upon the mystery to gather it all into a city of restless peace and righteousness.[29] We pray for this city to come freely—as freely as the cool dawn that breaks a long, hot summer—manifestly, out of hiding, here among these fists full of dust and ashes. And looking out into an open future we pray in the day when inertia drags us down and we ask that it nonetheless be a good day of food and work. We pray that our closure to the future, our self-exaltation or self-abasement, our possessive grasping after what is to come, and our clinging love for what was and is, that it all will be purged from our bodies precisely as we in good faith give up what we have a right to claim from others as ours (cf. Luke 11:1–4). We pray that our day will trace a line down the path of righteousness (cf. Ps 5:8; Isa 40:3; Mark 1:1–4).

Wet from the waters of baptism in the Spirit who drove Jesus to the cross and raised him from the dead (cf. Mark 1:8; 1 Cor 12:13; Rom 6:3), we are little tempted by the notion that the path of righteousness could ever be hewn out of the forests and tangled brush of the wilderness or discovered amidst dangers and hardships by the intrepid pioneers of civilization. In

---

28. Cf. Pannenberg, "Appearance as the Arrival of the Future," in *Theology and the Kingdom of God*, e.g., 136–41; Ware, *Orthodox Way*, 53–54.

29. I might modify the opening of Augustine's *Confessions* in this way: "You have made us for yourself and our hearts are at rest till they become restless in you." There are times when I think that he would not mind.

that moment we know that it comes to us. We are led into it, graced by it—from the outside. The path of righteousness opens before us in the precarious moment that is neither simply present nor simply future. Admittedly, we step into it with some deliberation, *telos* in hand. Yet in coming this path unhinges teleology. Stepping into it calls for a postscriptive, eschatological, and grateful "nevertheless" (cf. Matt 26:39).[30] The captains of industry who ride the raging bull of economic expansion, blinded by the whirlwind of dust their busyness stirs up, may presume to be masters of their own fate and the fate of the world, bringing history to its end, but the day of the giver of all gifts bears down on that property upon which the unrighteous stake their claims. The future comes to them as a crisis that will have hauled them as defendants before the bench upon which sit the poor evicted from South Central L.A. Farm (cf. Luke 6:20, 24; 1 Cor 6:2; Rom 14:10).

The Gospels tell the story of the way Jesus' faithfulness to the coming of the Reign of God took him into the darkness. It is because readers of the Gospels have been bold to think this "end" that without committing the fallacy of hasty generalization they sometimes hear themselves saying that among us all there is *none* righteous. It is not by inductive reasoning that they declare the whole human race to have his blood on its hands, to be "sinners." The doctrine of sin[31] has emerged rather by the simple fact that this Emmanuel is ultimately to be found among the lost, the damned, those consigned to hell.[32] He is a mission into that perditious field.[33] One might even go so far as to say that to meet him is always to meet him there.[34]

---

30. Cf. Barth, *Evangelical Theology*, 109–20.

31. The doctrine of sin is not to be confused with a doctrine of *guilt*. See Kierkegaard [Climacus], *Postscript*, 525–31, 572, 583–86.

32. Cf. Luther's understanding of the alien work of Spirit. For example: "It is by living—no, rather it is by dying and being damned that a theologian is made, not by understanding, reading, or speculating." W.A. 5.163.28 (*Operationes in Psalmos*, 1519–1521), cited and translated by Gerrish, "'To the Unknown God,'" 269.

33. This is not to say that the incarnation is to be located within a doctrine of sin, as if the former were nothing but a solution to the latter. What is to be said is that the incarnation is God's liberative solidarity with us, we who in making a pact with death, in throwing ourselves into a desperately competitive death-dealing, have blasphemed the Holy Spirit.

34. "I the chief of sinners am, but Jesus died for me" and "the best thing of all is that God is with us" are phrases that meet each other provocatively in the decline and death

Of course, no one simply believes such things. One must be nurtured into them, e.g., as one comes with the church to celebrate his broken body and shed blood. It is in that prolonged moment when the church professes that God is with us above all on the cross that it calls upon the Spirit to open our ears to a tradition of grace that does not shrink back from saying the most extreme things:

> All . . . are under the power of sin, as it is written: "There is no one who is righteous, not even one; there is no one who has understanding, there is no one who seeks God. All have turned aside, together they have become worthless; there is no one who shows kindness, there is not even one." "Their throats are opened graves; they use their tongues to deceive." "The venom of vipers is under their lips." "Their mouths are full of cursing and bitterness." "Their feet are swift to shed blood; ruin and misery are in their paths, and the way of peace they have not known." "There is no fear of God before their eyes." (Rom 3: 9–18)[35]

There is no shortage of narratives in the traditions that are gathered in this passage that approve of its claim. Within a certain confessional imagination it is more than understandable that the "they" of those stories quickly becomes "we." Here *we* are the ones who close our hearts and throats and hands to the Spirit's future, to the coming of the holy God (cf.

---

of John Wesley. See Elizabeth Ritchie's account of Wesley's last words in Heitzenrater, *Elusive Mr. Wesley*, 2:145–50; and to contextualize it, see Rack, *Reasonable Enthusiast*, 526–34. Of course, Wesley is one of history's most vigorous advocates of the doctrine of sanctification. He was quite troubled by Luther's doctrine that the justified is *simil iustus et peccator*, at once righteous and a sinner.

35. It is sometimes suggested that the universality of sin is empirically obvious. See Niebuhr, *Man's Nature and His Communities*, 24. Certainly, as far as anybody can tell there has not ever been a time when we failed to inflict misery on one another. However, the sweeping extent of Paul's words cannot ever be "verified." Not only will even the most careful scrutiny never be able to set aside the possibility that among all the perpetrators of injustice there is some relatively small number who do "good"—and that continually—but even more so sin is not just any destructive act; it is an act performed precisely *coram Deo* as a "strong" or "weak" despair in the face of the future coming of the God who is love. God is the "third term" without whom there is neither righteousness nor sin. Kierkegaard [Anti-Climacus], *Sickness Unto Death*, 13–14, 79–82; Kierkegaard, *Works of Love*, 38, 40–43, 58, 107, 130, 252–56. How one is related to God may be known by one's "fruits" (Matt 7:15–16, a passage actually about "false prophets"), but human fruits are even more ambiguous than apples and peaches that may be deceptively clear-skinned or spotted. Believing the exhaustive concreteness of sin as Paul lays it out takes entry into the sociality of discourse and practices he exemplifies—the sociality that is always on the way from and to the crucified/resurrected Jesus.

Gen 3:4–5), building to shake our fists at the sky (cf. Gen 11:4). Before the merciful God who elects the poor, the slave, the orphan, those who labor and are heavy laden—*we* murder (cf. Gen 4:8); *we* close our doors to wayfarers (cf. Gen 19:8–9); *we* sell our sisters and brothers into slavery (cf. Gen 37:28); *we* multiply the pain of those already broken by hard labor (cf. Exod 1:8–11); *we* pursue our own good, perched above the poor while life is drained out of them;[36] *we* ignore the motherless and fatherless, the friendless, the strange (cf. Malachi 3:5); *we* survive, thrive, compete, and amass by trampling others underfoot (cf. Isa 59:7). The face of the destitute fades from view, because we have turned our backs to it or because we look through it to a greater good or because the glitter of something we more desire distracts us from it. Time and time again we anxiously meet an alien body of people, shrink back from its unpredictability, rise only to intern it, and with violence and delusion "secure" *our* homeland.[37] In the fantasy of good and evil, food and work inscribe a closed circle. And so, we feed workers just enough to keep them on schedule. Without the prospect of a new day, the pain of their labor soon eclipses delivery, new life threatens to be stillborn, and a barren yesterday increasingly holds sway over tomorrow (cf. Exod 1:8–14).

---

36. Cf. Job 24:1–12: "Why are times not kept by the Almighty, and why do those who know him never see his days? The wicked remove landmarks; they seize flocks and pasture them. They drive away the donkey of the orphan; they take the widow's ox for a pledge. They thrust the needy off the road; the poor of the earth all hide themselves. Like wild asses in the desert they go out to their toil, scavenging in the wasteland food for their young. They reap in a field not their own and they glean in the vineyard of the wicked. They lie all night naked, without clothing, and have no covering in the cold. They are wet with the rain of the mountains, and cling to the rock for want of shelter. There are those who snatch the orphan child from the breast, and take as a pledge the infant of the poor. They go about naked, without clothing; though hungry, they carry the sheaves; between their terraces they press out oil; they tread the wine presses, but suffer thirst. From the city the dying groan, and the throat of the wounded cries for help; yet God pays no attention to their prayer." Jas 2:6: "But you have dishonored the poor. Is it not the rich who oppress you? Is it not they who drag you into court?"

37. I think of the Japanese-American internment camps of World War II. The precedent for these "camps" is the "Indian reservation." Their descendent in the current "immigration crisis" with its border enforcement and ICE agents is the spatially ambiguous field of the "undocumented," who have been in their own way systematically "disappeared." Certainly the most obvious and horrifyingly extreme example in the living memory of the rise of European civilization is the Nazi concentration camp. However, the internment of Hebrew slaves in Egypt provides a paradigm by which these and other phenomena become particularly theologically significant.

But, of course, it is also to be said that "they" do oppress "us." "We" are also the betrayed—the poor: the widow, the orphan, and the stranger.[38] In fact "we" are the poor in greater numbers, not uncommonly poor because we have been faithful to the call of the God of Jesus Christ.[39] In this sense, the suffering bear witness to their Lord; they are "martyrs" (cf. Rev 12:11). And though there is a certain blessedness to that mode of life and death, it is no less an appalling injustice. Even if one with good reason says that persecution for the sake of righteousness is in the tradition of persecuted prophets and that the path of righteousness will lead one into the jaws of the beast (cf. Matt 5: 12 and 1 Thes 2:14–15), it is only because death not only will have been, but already has been swallowed up in victory that the murder of "the least of these" is not completely unholy (cf. Matt 25:40 and 1 Cor 15:54–58). The blood of Abel still cries to God from the earth (cf. Gen 4:9–10).

In the end, however, "*we*" oppress "*us*." We betray and deny—we are betrayed and denied by—our sisters and brothers, our friends, the ones with whom we journey through this wilderness. The whirlwind of righteous crisis bears down on us—not abstractly, but with the concreteness of a face-to-face encounter (cf. 2 Sam 12:7, 9). Before the crisis of the coming of the holy one, even the upright fail to stand.[40]

---

38. The word *poor* is the bigger term, since it signifyies the one whose life is being drained away. See Gutiérrez, "Option for the Poor," 241–42.

39. Cf. Ps 44:22: "Because of you we are being killed all day long, and accounted as sheep for the slaughter." But see how this verse works in Rom 8:35–36: "Who will separate us from the love of Christ? Will hardship, or distress, or persecution, or famine, or nakedness, or peril, or sword? As it is written, 'For your sake we are being killed all day long; we are accounted as sheep to be slaughtered.'" Hauerwas makes this point well in his *After Christendom*, 46–47. When the prosperous have kept the poor hidden, it is easy to seduce the shielded into thinking that faithfulness to God yields a measurable "blessing." Most of the world knows better. In some parts of the world it is even pretty clear to all that the servants of the crucified do not receive in this world a rosier fate than their master (Matt 10:22–25). In no case, however, are "the poor" to be romanticized. Dreadfully, but not uncommonly, a single woman or (more often) a single man is both oppressed and oppressor at once (as "civil wars" bear witness).

40. Isa 6:1–5: "In the year that King Uzziah died, I saw the Lord sitting on a throne, high and lofty; and the hem of his robe filled the temple. Seraphs were in attendance above him; each had six wings: with two they covered their faces, and with two they covered their feet, and with two they flew. And one called to another and said: 'Holy, holy, holy is the Lord of hosts; the whole earth is full of his glory.' The pivots on the thresholds shook at the voices of those who called, and the house filled with smoke. And I said: 'Woe is me! I am lost, for I am a man of unclean lips, and I live among a people of unclean lips; yet my eyes have seen the King, the Lord of hosts!'" John 20:27–28: "Then he said to

As if blatant treachery were not enough, there is another, more insidious betrayal, faceless and all but nameless. We stutter and say "the Satan" (Job 1–2) or "principalities and powers" (Eph 6:12). Without warning and from out of nowhere anyone might be thrown down by drought, fire, flood, earthquake, famine, disease—afflicted, broken, disinherited, forsaken, no less prey to despair than anyone.[41] Even if from all appearances some one of us had lived in righteousness receiving to give, when he is by some disaster left alone to rot, he is tempted to imagine that some retributive justice were getting even with him for what he had unwittingly done. When a day is lived under the weight of a heavy, invisible hand, it might seem that it is a vengeful God who wears the torturer's mask.

It is among the greatest of mysteries that smothered by the dark shadow of great loss the throat of the sufferer does not simply and inevitably close. In fact, improbable as it is, it may open not only to receive again one last wisp of a breath, but to fill lungs painfully near to bursting in order to release a cry, a cry that tears through earth, heaven, and the "God" of retribution—to the holy one free to save.[42] "I cry out 'Violence!'" (Job 19:7).[43] And whether it is the apparently blind violence of storm or shifting land mass, or the designer violence of an economics of competitive profit, there is a word to be heard: "Listen! The wages of the laborers who mowed your fields . . . cry out, and the cries of the harvesters have reached the ears of the Lord of hosts" (Jas 5:4, cf. verse 11 and Ex 3:9). It seems so unwarranted, when a body—disintegrating to the dust and ashes out of which it was shaped—rises into the firestorm and lets the words spill from her lips: "I know that my Redeemer lives" (Job 19:25).[44]

Thomas, 'Put your finger here and see my hands. Reach out your hand and put it in my side. Do not doubt but believe.' Thomas answered him, 'My Lord and my God!'" Mark 4:11–12: "And he said to them, 'To you has been given the secret of the kingdom of God, but for those outside, everything comes in parables; in order that "they may indeed look, but not perceive, and may indeed listen, but not understand; so that they may not turn again and be forgiven."'"

41. Job 2:9: "Then his wife said to him, 'Do you still persist in your integrity? Curse God, and die.'"

42. See Gutíerrez, *On Job*, 63–66.

43. Cf. Lola before the roulette table in *Run Lola Run*.

44. It is the testimony of the fellowship of the cross that the outcry of hope from one under the shadow of despair is uttered already with the breath of the Spirit that raised the crucified Jesus from the hell into which his body was dumped. In saying this, a "universal truth" is not represented. It is not that only a fool would deny this. These words are spoken because the light of the eighth day of his holy week shines back upon

After Crucifixion

The Jesus Christ of the Gospels is *this* Word, too. He is the Word that above all stands out of an open and parched throat—as death, sin, and hell sink in their claws—and says, "Father, into your hand I commend my spirit" (Luke 23:46). He is the one in solidarity with all those under the cold, crushing weight of despair. Even when they cannot speak, he speaks for them. Even when they cannot move, he calls them to himself, lifted up as he is, and in calling them breathes the breath of life into their lungs. Further and above all, he calls them to make his journey theirs. He calls them to be liberated, not only for their own good, but to move—givingly, lovingly—into solidarity with other sufferers: the hungry to feed the hungry, the imprisoned to visit the imprisoned, the naked to clothe the naked; but also the full to become hungry with the hungry, the free to become imprisoned with the imprisoned, the clothed to become naked with the naked.[45]

Thus Jesus calls them into a life in which intercessory petition opens to thanksgiving and thanksgiving opens to praise. When, by the violence of disregard, life is made harder, when the fruit of one's labor is seized and trampled underfoot, when the land that would have yielded food and medicine is paved over and bigger barns thrown up in its place, when the interlacing paths of richly variegated, storied work are bulldozed into an abstract waste land, the sin is not that the property that certain people had a right to keep has been taken away from them. The closing of South Central Farm is not to be decried because a developer ripped off the stuff of some poor people. It is to be decried, because their praise has been foreclosed. What they and we are given to do is work to the glory of God. Certainly, the women, men, and children rarely had praising God on their minds, when they set out for the Farm some Saturday morning. Nonetheless, it

---

their speakers from what was then only a hope for which there was no good reason. He who breaks bread at the wayside along the road to Emmaus (Luke 24) breaks bread with them, too. He calls to them, too. And though he brings peace to them, it is the peace of a life of love that moves to stand in solidarity with all those whose backs break on every lonely mountain of injustice. He says to them, too, "feed my lambs" (John 21:15). And when those words strike home, a body is gathered that is sent with him into the pit of hell where "we" oppress "us."

45. This has nothing to do with the abstractions "the beauty of a tragic life" and "salvation through suffering." There is nothing beautiful about tragedy. Suffering does not save—not in the abstract. To "love your neighbor as yourself" is to love your flesh-and-blood neighbor with your flesh and blood. Even though that means that you will bear your neighbor's suffering with her, that is not all that will come your way. Further, even in bearing your neighbor's suffering your task is to perform the coming of a certain peace, joy, feast, and laughter that take promising shape precisely in the giving of the concrete love celebrated here and there, say, on any given Sunday morning.

is precisely by the labor they and we were and are given to do that God is praised. When workers are locked out of a day of good work, the offering that they would have made is undone. It is the offense against God that makes the rape of South Central L.A. Farm more than a guilt-laden deed and crime, that makes it a sin.

In the stories that arise among the people whose memories of him are still warm, Jesus is no disembodied spirit hovering in sweet bliss above the birth pangs and sweat of our days and nights.[46] He, too, pounds out his life as a worker. He, too, labors and eats, one of us. He works wood; he attends to his mother, brothers, and sisters; he stands with friends vis-à-vis their enemies; he obeys the law of his people; he pays taxes to the foreign military power that holds his people captive; he washes feet as a common servant; he teaches and preaches; he attends to the sick; he rejoices and weeps; he fights the temptation to despair; he is arrested and dragged away at night; he is locked down on death row; he is publicly shamed and tortured; and he agonizes alone through a brutal execution, abject, his body as cut, broken, and humiliated as was South Central Farm on July 5, 2006. He acts and is acted upon. Yet he performs it all in a particular way—playing fast and loose with the institutions to which he so freely and inexplicably subordinates himself.[47] That there were terrorists in his inner circle is a reminder that we'd best not too quickly align him with an order against which he did not rise up in arms.[48] Indeed he was hunted down as an enemy of the state and put to death according to the logic of national and international

---

46. That is, even early Gnostics have calcified memories of Jesus—a sad irony.

47. Mark 3:33–25: "'Who are my mother and my brothers?' And looking at those who sat around him, he said, 'Here are my mother and my brothers! Whoever does the will of God is my brother and sister and mother.'" Matt 5:43–44: "You have heard that it was said, 'You shall love your neighbor and hate your enemy.' But I say to you, Love your enemies and pray for those who persecute you." Matt 22:21: "Give therefore to the emperor the things that are the emperor's, and to God the things that are God's" (a command that does not reduce the scope of the sovereignty of God). Of his woodworking, one need only think of the instrument of execution upon which he breathes his last breath.

48. On this matter of "terrorists," admittedly a hyperbole, see Yoder, *Politics of Jesus*, 39, 56–58.

security. And for good reason; he embodied way more than "the transvaluation of all the ancient values"[49] that sent him to the gallows.

What is most striking about his worker's life, however, is that his hard days and nights have about them such an unprecedented prayerfulness. Prayer is not a part of his work day, say, a "quiet time" in its early morning. *All* his work is performed as a prayer.[50] He hungers and thirsts and eats and drinks and cuts and planes with us, but what enlivens him is the work he has been sent above all to do, the work of his Father that, as the Father's Son, he is to "complete" (cf. John 4:34 and John 5:19). He attends to this work with abandon, throwing his life out into his Father's imminent Reign. Prayer is all over him. Indeed his life is consumed by prayer—and consummated. His life is a journey of prayer that more and more lets loose of the good that he has done and would do. As he approaches his last week, what he "is" becomes in the gospel stories more and more translucent to the light of the Father. When finally he sets his face on Jerusalem, he sets out to be utterly effaced.[51] His journey throws open his body—like a hinged triptych—and, though a dispassionate observer could hardly have expected it, from that space the face of the hope and mystery of the world shines. To see him baptized in his own blood is in the Spirit to see his Father (cf. John 14:9, 26, John 16:13–14, and John 20:28).

The technical theological term for Jesus' work is "atonement." All theological textbooks tell us that the holy God and we are reconciled in the work of Jesus. In doing so, they follow Paul (see 2 Cor 5:18–19). "Atonement" is a familiar, all too familiar, term. Familiarity breeds thoughtlessness. Here in particular everything depends on how and among whom this atonement is to be understood. Indeed the fellowship of the cross is precisely a way—a bodily way—of understanding the atonement.[52]

Atonement in the fellowship of the cross is in fact a tensive term. It does not collapse difference into "sameness." To bear witness to it is to acknowledge that we were and are and will forever have been radically

---

49. See Nietzsche, *Twilight of the Idols*, 32.

50. Cf. 1 Thess 5:16–18: "Rejoice always, pray without ceasing, give thanks in all circumstances; for this is the will of God in Christ Jesus for you." Of course, Jesus certainly prayed in more obvious ways, as when he slipped off to pray alone (e.g., Matt 26:36).

51. It is this that gives narratival significance to the doctrine of the enhypostaton, that the human, all too human Jesus is a person only *in* the person of the eternal Son of God. That is, that he has *in himself* no personhood.

52. I am thinking of the phrase "the Way" as it is used in Acts 9:2 as a designation of the church.

Working Out the Body and Blood of Christ on the Eighth Day of Creation

different from the reconciling God.[53] Nonetheless, through the history of Jesus, we and God are "at-one."[54] Through him the holy one is here, where we are.[55] His is the event of a decidedly non-Platonic "participation." He is the open place where all that God is participates in all that we are that all that we are may participate in all that God is. That is the doctrine. Jesus bridges nothing, but he does so give away whatever might obstruct the coming of his Father that "the whole fullness" of that Holy One is pleased to dwell in him "bodily" (Col 2:9). Indeed he gives away to such an extent that he "is" a give-away, a sacrifice, an audacious emptiness. The "kenosis hymn" is a worker's tale that stands in contrast to the story of the idle Adam and Eve who, though they were in the image of God, regarded equality with God as their property right:[56]

> Let the same mind be in you that was in Christ Jesus, who, though he was in the form of God, did not regard equality with God as something to be exploited, but emptied himself, taking the form of a slave, being born in human likeness. And being found in human form, he humbled himself and became obedient to the point of death— even death on a cross. (Phil 2:5–8)[57]

---

53. In the light of the sanctification worked by the coming of the Son, that radical difference shifts in significance from the past to the present to the open-ended future perfect tense.

54. This seems like a bad pun, but the word actually does come precisely from that etymology. See *Oxford English Dictionary*, s.v. "atonement."

55. And where are we? Cf. Cone, *Cross and the Lynching Tree*, 26: "The cross places God in the midst of crucified people, in the midst of people who are hung, shot, burned, and tortured. Seeing himself as a man crucified like Jesus, Isaiah Fountain (January 23, 1920) insisted that 'he be executed wearing a purple robe and crown, to analogize his innocence to that of Jesus Christ.' Before he was lynched in Oxford, Mississippi (1899), Steve Allen testified to his 'peace with God,' saying that 'Jesus died on the Roman cross for me; through his mercy all my sins are forgiven. I am anchored in Christ.' With that testimony, 'he went to his death without a tremor.' Before Charles Johnston, a black minister, was hanged in Swainbora [Swainsboro], Georgia, 'he preached his own funeral sermon, inducing the crowd to sing, kneel, raise their hands, and pray along with him.'" See Cone, *Cross and the Lynching Tree*, 18.

56. Gen 3:4–6: "But the serpent said to the woman, 'You will not die; for God knows that when you eat of it your eyes will be opened, and you will be like God, knowing good and evil.' So when the woman saw that the tree was good for food, and that it was a delight to the eyes, and that the tree was to be desired to make one wise, she took of its fruit and ate; and she also gave some to her husband, who was with her, and he ate."

57. See Dunn, *Christology in the Making*, 114–19.

After Crucifixion

His emptiness is nonetheless filled, the Definition of Chalcedon tells us, but by the Holy One, the one apart—by the "divine nature" that as such is other than his "human nature." Jesus is thus filled by the one who is free not only to be without us, but also to be with us and is with us in Jesus' unobstructed surrender, in Jesus' work that, as sacrifice, "makes holy."[58] What he does and what is done to him—his whole life history—is in this way the manifestation of holiness. That is, the long path his thirty-three years cut through earth and world is the glorification of God.[59] And yet it is precisely the end to which his openness to the coming of his Father takes him that makes this a most unexpected glorification.

The work of Jesus is particularly among the unclean, those who could not be contacted with impunity, those whose bodies by definition would defile anyone contacting them, including anyone otherwise holy. Jesus is always among them: the poor; the sick, the maimed, the diseased; Gentiles, questionable women and men, the demon possessed; sinners. Leaving behind the stable equilibrium of one after another "here and now," Jesus crosses over to them. He touches them and is touched by them. He eats and works with them—and is undefiled. He loves them and he takes them in—and is uninfected. Rather they are infected by him. Without Jesus' falling prey to profanation, his embrace hallows them.[60] He is the event of the coming of that holiness which crosses the great divide, the one who rises up in invitation to those who labor and are heavy laden. To come to him is to come to a body that is anything but intact. In touching them he throws his integrity aside. As if Good Friday were a knife that already cut him as he walked the long roads of Palestine, he opens.[61] "Eat my flesh and drink my blood!" he says (John 6:53). His body—nourished with the doing of the will of the Father who sent him—his body—a worker's body that does the work of justifying justice—his body—lifted up in a spectacle of shame for all to see—his body—broken, cut, dying, dead, and damned—his body is *food*. It

---

58. *Oxford English Dictionary*, s.v. "sacrifice, *n.*": "ad. L. *sacrificus*, f. *sacri-*, *sacer* sacred . . . + *-ficus*"; "-fic, *suffix*": "repr. L. *-ficus* '-making, -doing.'" It is not that his union with God is the effect of his sacrificial life as its cause. Rather he is as the perfect sacrifice the place where the whole fullness of deity freely dwells. The concurrence of these events constitutes the significance of two-nature Christology. (Does it need to be said as well that the use of the word *surrender* above has nothing to do with Appomattox Court House?)

59. Gammie, *Holiness in Israel*, 54, 98, 176, 197.

60. Dunn, "Jesus and Holiness, 190.

61. Cf. Marion, *God Without Being*, 24.

draws all people to itself. Taking him in is in his work to be consumed—and consummated. Taking him in is with him to be sent to those who hunger and thirst. Taking him in is with him to present ourselves a living sacrifice (Rom 12:1), to give ourselves with him to be food, the food without which there is no life at all. Taking him in is with him to pray.

In this way, among these people, the atoning work of Jesus comes to carry on its shoulders the significance of all work. His work will not yield to the allure of a disembodied universality, say, in order to determine *in general* what makes for a good day's work. *His work*, when it is finished (John 19:30), comes in all its *particularity* and concreteness to determine what makes for a good day's work—and an evil one. But he unhands "good" and "evil" in his work. He lets them come and go, as the Father wills. His only concern is that he faithfully walk the path of righteousness—a path the Spirit drives him into the wilderness of temptation to blaze and finally in the bright evacuative light of glory to become.

It is the glory of his particular, abased and exalted body that shines like a searchlight in the eyes of the investors of this unrighteous world as they squint to turn a profit by grinding the faces of those whom the march of progress is destined to forget. His is the work of justice that *coram Deo* refuses to yield to pain, but bends and breaks outward into an improbable future, a future precisely for those whom pain has bent and broken and left in a past without promise. He is the one who comes as judge and advocate at the dark end of a long day. Despite their mastery of the mechanics of cause and effect, the sacred and secular cities that pursued him to death—that beat and cut him, bled and smothered him, and threw his cold and lifeless body into the ditch—came at last to have shattered against his tender flesh. The testimony of the saints is that they shatter still. To follow him is with him to work his unlikely righteousness. To follow him is forever to be entangled in the social fabric of labor, never abstracting from the calloused hands, straining backs, and dirty faces especially of the least of his sisters and brothers, not even to rise into the ether of a "truth" that is by its own definition greater than both they and his crucified/resurrected body. In him in particular the evicted poor are first.

Work and workers are as concrete as are muscles and bones. As much as Augustine found the opening of the Gospel of John in the books of the

Platonists,[62] it is there perhaps only if some Aramean wandering through the streets of fourth-century Tagaste, Carthage, and Milan happened to drop it there.[63] The Word becomes flesh for all, but with a hard particularity that somebody could trip over.[64] Of course, the Word *becomes* flesh. Incarnation happens as contingently as any grace and joy. The fleshy Word is not a pale reflection of a "higher reality," an exemplar of some metaphysical *ratio*. No doubt the Word is the liberative site of the in-breaking of what is unrestrictedly other, and so, free, say, in relation to space and time. However, the Word is free above all to *be* spacious and timely, to give room precisely by coming close enough to hold close and be held close by those whom propriety decrees are not to be touched.[65]

This Word engages the concrete "You!"—the flesh and blood sister, daughter, lover, mother, and friend: the woman or the man with a face. And even if it takes an apocalyptic storyteller to say it, that broken body who breathed his last on one particular Friday and, though dead and damned, came to be bathed in the new life of resurrection on one particular Sunday—this body has come to address even those who long before gave their days and nights to the fresh coming of God.[66] Though what this Word evokes has an eerily similar vocabulary and syntax to the punch line of

62. Augustine *Confessions* 7.9

63. Ibid. 5.13–6.4, cf. 1.11–12, 3.1–12.

64. John 1:14: "And the Word became flesh and lived among us, and we have seen his glory, the glory as of a father's only son, full of grace and truth." Heb 10:19–22: "Therefore, my friends, since we have confidence to enter the sanctuary by the blood of Jesus, by the new and living way that he opened for us through the curtain (that is, through his flesh), and since we have a great priest over the house of God, let us approach with a true heart in full assurance of faith, with our hearts sprinkled clean from an evil conscience and our bodies washed with pure water." Acts 17:30–31: "While God has overlooked the times of human ignorance, now he commands all people everywhere to repent, because he has fixed a day on which he will have the world judged in righteousness by a man whom he has appointed, and of this he has given assurance to all by raising him from the dead." 1 Cor 1:23: "we proclaim Christ crucified, a stumbling block . . ."

65. By the way, the beginning of the Gospel of John reads rather differently, when it is juxtaposed with its ending an ending that confronts the reader with the singularity of the human being, Jesus. For example, first (once more) John 20:27–28: "Then he said to Thomas, 'Put your finger here and see my hands. Reach out your hand and put it in my side. Do not doubt but believe.' Thomas answered him, 'My Lord and my God!'" And only then John 1:1–2, 14: "In the beginning was the Word, and the Word was with God, and the Word was God. He was in the beginning with God. . . . And the Word became flesh and lived among us, and we have seen his glory, the glory as of a father's only son, full of grace and truth."

66. Cf. John 8:56–58 and Matt 17:2–3.

Descartes' second meditation, it even more strongly says the humane "I am."⁶⁷ The worker, the point of intersection of line after line of work, is named and turned loose by the Word, i.e., no less than is the dead brother of Mary and Martha: "Lazarus, come forth!" (John 11:43).⁶⁸ Were ontology not so loaded with overweight baggage, one might say that the Word gives one to "be." And yet what one is particularly given to "be" is a martyr, a bodily witness to the crucifixion/resurrection of Jesus Christ. The work of the martyr who testifies to *him* is kenotic, a work of emptying.

It is because the call of this Word is the call to perform the work of kenosis that the pattern of life that it gives cannot without radical qualification be called "virtuous."⁶⁹ The Greeks are the ones who first taught us of virtue. Already in their early paradigmatic texts the word figures large. There one who is virtuous is one who has become whole, who is well-adjusted, above all a man of integrity. Odysseus is among the most powerful early images of virtue. He is wealthy, noble, handsome, strong, cunning, skillful, resilient, the lover of beautiful and elegant women, a decorated war hero, and the last man standing in a triumphant bloodbath of revenge, prevailing against all odds, even in the face of the wrath of the gods; in short, virile.⁷⁰ He stands on his own two feet and no one can throw him down.⁷¹

When a modified paradigm of virtue appears in the fourth century with Socrates, Odyssean virility is sublimated, but not significantly altered. There are obvious differences. Socrates is ugly, a pug-nosed old man with a pelican-body; the husband of an odd and forgettable woman; content to be short on cash; seldom found outside the thick walls of Athens; and an apparently idle conversationalist. Yet he is, if anything, an even more impermeable man of integrity and authenticity. To his loving student, Plato,

---

67. There is an "unsaying" in this "I am," too. See Gen 22:1–2 (cf. 12:4); 22:10–11; Exod 3:4; Isa 6:8; Luke 1:35–38. For the phrase "I am," see Descartes, *Meditations on First Philosophy*, 17; and Levinas, "God and Philosophy," 68–69, 75.

68. See Kierkegaard, *Sickness Unto Death*, 7–9.

69. Bauernfeind, "*aretē*," 460: "To understand the few passages where *aretē* is used in the NT it is important that . . . the LXX use [of the word] is purely tentative and that there is no real place for *aretē* = virtue in the translation of the OT. For a world in which man constantly saw himself morally responsible before a holy God the Greek concept of virtue could not finally fulfill its apparent promise. Though not irreligious, it was far too anthropocentric and this-worldly in orientation. What both the OT and NT attest is not human achievements or merits but the acts of God."

70. *Oxford English Dictionary*, s.v. "virtue, n.": "ad. L. *virtūt-*, *virtus* manliness, valour, worth, etc., f. *vir* man." Cf. Bauernfeind, "*aretē*," 457–60.

71. Jaeger, *Archaic Greece*, 20–26.

it is not his body or his social standing or his observable actions that make him that. His virtue, his wholeness, resides in his soul. And there nobody can touch him. All the way to his placid end, he shows his self-sufficiency, his wisdom, his courage, and his aloofness, all of which serve especially his extended Athenian family by example.[72]

When the Word that is the crucified/resurrected Jesus calls one of us by name and sets her free, it is among other things from integrity and authenticity that she is liberated. What strikes the Greeks as the end of all human life is in Christ so much *skubalon*.

> Yet whatever gains I had, these I have come to regard as loss because of Christ. More than that, I regard everything as loss because of the surpassing value of knowing Christ Jesus my Lord. For his sake I have suffered the loss of all things, and I regard them as rubbish [*skubala*, excrement], in order that I may gain Christ and be found in him, not having a righteousness of my own that comes from the law, but one that comes through faith in Christ, the righteousness from God based on faith. I want to know Christ and

---

72. Jaeger, *In Search of the Divine Centre*, 46: "It was Socrates' summons to men to 'care for their souls' that really turned the mind of Greece towards a new way of life. From this time onwards, a dominant part of philosophy and ethics was played by the concept of life . . . as a clear and comprehensible unity, a deliberately shaped life-pattern. This innovation was caused by the way Socrates lived; he played the part of a model for the new *bios*, the life based on spiritual values. And his pupils realized that the greatest strength of his paideia came from the change he had introduced into the old educational concept of the heroic Example which is a pattern for other lives to follow. He made himself the embodiment of the ideal of life which he preached." See Pickstock, *After Writing*, 201–2. Cushman, *Therapeia*, 296: "Plato was inspired by the figure of Socrates . . . he was 'the figure of man "equilibrated" and "assimilated" to virtue's self perfectly' so far as that is possible to humankind. . . . Moreover, the wise man was the happy man, blessed in the integrity and self-agreement of his own *psuchē*. Plato also discerned in Socrates one who was sufficient to himself. Socrates was the true *autocratēs* . . . because he ruled over himself." Virtue is applied by the Greeks not only to the individual. A city-state is also to be virtuous. Its justice is its wholeness, its balance, its harmony, and its power—encircled by a thick and strong city wall. Just as an authentic, virtuous soul has its power in itself, so also does a virtuous *polis*. It stands on its own feet, a strong rational animal, beautiful, good, and swift in enforcing the justice that keeps its scales balanced. The wisdom, courage, and temperance of its classes attune it to an unchanging standard of order, to the energy that feeds resolve, and to the self-control that keeps the passions in check. It is self-sustaining, rich in native resources; its center of gravity is fixed, its doors locked on the inside, its army standing in readiness. No foreign army can touch it. No insurrection could arise from within. It is a city with (dreadful) integrity and authenticity.

the power of his resurrection and the sharing of his sufferings by becoming like him in his death. (Phil 3:7–10)[73]

Paul lets go of everything that might distinguish him, every medal of valor, every mark of a noble ancestry, every achievement, every quality of soul. His eyes are set on a criminal's despicable execution, a deed he gives himself to imitate, seeing in that execution the personal irruption of the future of the invisible holy God (cf. Heb 11:1). Since it is in the crucifixion of Jesus that God is glorified, Paul works to be crucified with him. This view of life could only strike the Greeks as absurd (see 1 Cor 1:22–23).

Nonetheless the language of virtue comes already in the childhood of the church to be taken up in its prayers. Perhaps that move is forgivable, even inevitable, and quite possibly helpful. However much we have come to enter into the glory of God's coming Reign, we still live among a people of unclean lips—and their language is ours. And yet, servants of the master who hallowed the unclean might yet by the Spirit of resurrection work a miracle, even with the most deadly term. And though the shift was more often than not rather awkward, as this word has been lifted up, it has undergone a *metanoia*. In the prayers of the church thanks is given not so much that *I* or *we* have been made whole, but that *between* our way of life and the way of God's life into the world there is now an alignment, our works have been set right, woven together, opened Godward, and in that sense cured of their mortal sickness.[74] Indeed an "authentic," i.e., self-sufficient,[75] individual would be thought in this new discourse to be anything but virtuous. Rather the language of "virtue" is in these prayers unsettled, de-centered, outworked, by the irruption of an other without whom no prayer may happen at all.[76] And so, unlike the Greeks who think of virtue as an immanent,

---

73. Verse 11 is quite important to this passage ("if somehow I may attain the resurrection from the dead"). I have left it off only to moderate a triumphalism that leads one to ignore every sacrifice that precedes mention of the coming resurrection—a move that may already have been made by the reader of verse 10. It is important to remember both that resurrection is not the effect of the cause of an admirable life, and that the resurrected body of Christ—in which all resurrection is to occur—has not gotten "well." It is forevermore scarred by the crucifixion.

74. For the multivalency of the etymology of "*therapeia*," see Liddell et al., *Greek-English Lexicon*, 792–93.

75. See *Oxford English Dictionary*, s.v. "authentic, *adj.* and *n.*"

76. Wesley, *Plain Account*, 107–8 [25.38.2–3]: "To abandon all, to strip one's self of all, in order to seek and to follow Jesus Christ naked to Bethlehem, where He was born; naked to the hall where He was scourged; and naked to Calvary, where He died on the cross, is so great a mercy, that neither the thing, nor the knowledge of it, is given to any,

internal balance that is ex-pressed (still immanently) as temperance, courage, and wisdom, the church prays for the *gift* of the virtue of faith, hope, love, humility, hospitality—and of prayer itself.[77] The language of virtue is the language of "sanctification," i.e., a free, open, vital movement into the

---

but through faith in the Son of God. . . . True humility is a kind of self-annihilation, and this is the centre of all virtues."

77. Mantzaridis, *Deification of Man*, 88: "For, though it would be correct to say that the practice of virtue encourages likeness to God and prepares the way for the believer's union with Him, it is mistaken and dangerous to aver . . . that prayer actualizes this union. . . . Man's union with God and his deification are not the result of human activity but a gift of divine grace. Divine grace secretly performs man's deification, while virtue simply renders him capable of receiving deification. Prayer as a human activity is classed as a virtue, and is not sufficient by itself to bring about man's union with God or his deification" (cf. ibid., 91). (Perhaps the capacity virtue renders is also a gift.) That prayer could be thought to be a virtue is bewildering only until it is remembered that here a virtue is not so much what is *in us* as *that in which* we are given to live. Further, even when the language of the Greeks is used (e.g., when a saint is said to be "wise"), everything has become different. Here wisdom is a gift that never ceases to be a gift, one for which God alone is to be praised. Similarly, to pray for prayer is already to acknowledge that every prayer is a gift that arrives before we could ever collect ourselves to pursue it. The technical term for this fore-giveness is "prevenient grace." Pickstock, *After Writing*, 196–97: "[The] one who calls upon God is one to whom God in turn speaks, thereby situating the unidentified worshipping 'I' with which the rite opens, not only within a shifting place, but also within a relational place, in an I-Thou relationship with the ultimate Thou. In the case of apostrophic address to God, the calling 'I' does not occupy a prior or more primitive subject-position, because God alone makes the cry both possible and audible, such that to call upon God is always already to have entered into Him." Bondi, *To Pray and to Love*, 16, 27: "Christians . . . stood out from the rest of their culture by their unusual love for each other in their communities. This love . . . was a way of being together, a way of prayer, and a way of living in the world, rooted in their experience and understanding of the God who had come to them in the resurrected Jesus. . . . Indeed Christian love, Christian prayer, and Christian virtue were so interwoven that the individual elements are hard for us to separate in their early writings. . . . There is no 'holy' life that calls us to renounce parts of ourselves as unworthy. If we are to pray, we are to love, and for both love and prayer all of ourselves with nothing left out is needed." For some of the ways Wisdom literature informs the New Testament account of Jesus, see de Jonge, *Christology in Context*, 194–99.

coming of God.[78] To be virtuous is to be named and liberated by the Word made flesh.[79]

As hard as the earliest pioneers of Western Civilization pushed for authenticity, we, their modern children, far outstrip them. Even when we try with all of our might to think our way to the sociality of bodily life, we remain stuck in the vision of a purely formal erotic lure to fulfillment, one that breaks into some purported "solitariness."[80] In prayer everything comes differently. The Word that names and liberates is as tangibly particular as any worker, and, as a worker, is no in-dividual, but a body of social

---

78. There is so much in Cushman's work that is helpful. His thinking of human virtue in terms of worship as sacrifice is especially helpful. See his essay, "Worship as Acknowledgment." And so, according to Isaiah, he writes, "worship was to become the giving up of oneself, . . . the entailment of the whole man, . . . assimilation of the whole life to the likeness of Him who is magnified" (190). More broadly worship is "the penitential commitment of the whole life . . . at once abased and exalted by an overpowering awareness of the divine Holiness, . . . entire consent to God's sovereignty [and thus] consent to his gracious intention toward the creatures and, among the creatures, other men" (191–92). It "is simply life that, in entire trustfulness, is given back into the hands of Him who gave it" (193). "Whatever more the Eucharist may have come to signify, it signified to the early Church the Lord's own invitation, indeed command, to participate with him in his 'full, perfect, and sufficient sacrifice.' . . . The true worshiper is, first, Jesus Christ himself, and true worship is attained for those who, 'crucified with Christ,' walk in newness of life. This is life in which God's dominion is regnant. It is life in which autonomy is no longer reserved, and in which the stewardship of all of life is acknowledged" (197). However, the ontology into which this understanding of worship is lodged may well distract from active worship. In the end Cushman maintains that worship is the fulfillment of an inherent *conatus*, i.e., fulfilled by the free exercise "of responsible dependency . . . the overcoming of alienation and the establishment of community through consent to Being, first to the Being of God, and, through Him, consent to the being and inherent worth of the creatures" (181, cf. 360 n. 1). Worship for Cushman is acknowledging an unmanageable "*moira*, fate, or *nemesis*, or call it *logos*" manifested in the "apparent configuration of things and events" (181–82). It is hard to understand how worship is sacrifice of the whole of life, if one holds back a being-reserve, even if the impulses of the dominant traditions of the West tempt us to hold onto it with both hands. The ghost of Pelagius may yet haunt Cushman's work.

79. Although there is no question that the work of MacIntyre shifts the weight of the theory of virtue off of the individual or collective subject and makes it quite helpfully a social, historical, lived, and open tradition (and thus the evocatively ambiguous phrase "after virtue"), it yet lacks a certain decentering ecstasy. MacIntyre's virtuous traditional community does indeed step out into *future* possibilities, yet it pushes off *from* what is extant. See, e.g., *After Virtue*, 218–23. For a very fine account of the way Greek virtue has been critiqued even as the term has come to be used in historic theological discourse, see Hauerwas and Pinches, *Christians Among the Virtues*.

80. I am thinking of Whitehead and in particular his *Religion in the Making*, 16.

entanglements. The Word lays into, receives, and releases the stuff of this world quite differently than the relative novelty of romantic "creativity." The one who names me and sets me free is my brother and yours, the one who cuts, plains, drills, and hammers at your side, the one locked with me in the box, the one who cannot be held fast for long. This Word is an event of hope, a body that opens to and out of the space and time of every day of hard labor. And he is contingent, might have been otherwise, might not have been at all, as vulnerable as a newborn infant.

When one considers how easy it is to kill a child, it is quite a lot to declare in the strong sense that a "virgin shall conceive and bear a son, and they shall name him Emmanuel" (Matt 1:23). And in quiet moments of honesty we know that the precariousness of the child remains in the adult. "God with us" is God's solidarity with us, taking on the pain of sinful flesh, of injustice, torture, humiliation, death, and damnation—and being overcome by none of it.[81] It is God become flesh, living among us, whose glory we see, "full of grace and truth" (John 1:14).

There is a particularly striking mystery at work in the affirmation that it is God's *glory* that we see in this transient Jesus. It is not finally simply for us that the Redeemer comes, as if our plight forced God's hand. The God who cannot but fight for us is a false redeemer, a company doctor in a company town, a function of our world, to be explained in and by its structures. The Redeemer "whose glory we see" is a stranger in our house—and that by definition.[82] "Glory" is precisely the manifestation of holiness. It is the strangeness of the absolutely other dwelling *here*, among us. To be befriended by this one is to be touched by that strangeness. Indeed his coming is liberative precisely because he and what is manifested in him are other than we and ours are.[83] That he is at once one of us *and* other means that in him the doors and windows of human life already open to what it is not. In him human life breathes. The work he does is worked out into what this world must always perceive as an abyss, that is, not perceive at all. And yet he is the redeemer of this world. The future he embodies is the future of this

---

81. John 1:5: "The light shines in the darkness, and the darkness did not overcome it."

82. Schnackenburg, *Jesus in the Gospels*, 314–16.

83. Barth, *CD* 3/2, 159, 166: "This creature . . . exists in this movement from another to itself and itself to this other—a movement which, since God the Creator is this Other, it is quite impossible to describe as a movement within itself. . . . To be summoned is to be called out of oneself and beyond oneself. Because it is God who speaks here, what is said has the right and power to enable the creature to transcend itself."

Working Out the Body and Blood of Christ on the Eighth Day of Creation

world. Just as he—body, soul, and spirit—is glorified, so also all those with whom he stands in solidarity are touched by glory and have glorification as their future. The future of this world is this world made new.

This worker's story pairs *two* commandments, however. That God was pleased to dwell in him, that his whole history was raised from the dead and exalted at the right hand of the Father, is not a private adventure, one which perhaps we can admire and imitate from afar. It already touches my history and yours, for the heart, soul, mind, and strength of this one not only open Godward, but open also to his brothers and sisters, to you and me (Mark 12:28–31). Indeed, we are indistinguishable from his "self." For God to be glorified in him is for the radical difference of God to enter not only into him, but concurrently into those into whose lives his has worked, even those whose last breath is "no" to God's mercy.

The church, let us say, is a body of workers whose paths meet in the breaking of that bread they are invited to call the body of Christ. The degree to which a random sampling of these workers has been aroused by his call to remember him may not be perceptible even by them; but it is because in a certain broken way he is remembered among them that we may quietly say that they come together to be grafted into his work. Their coming together, whether they perceive it or not, thus signifies (signified even before they thought to leave their homes) that they have come in order to "present [their] bodies as a living sacrifice," one which even by the miracle of God's sacramental grace would at best repeat his (Rom 12:1). As unwise as it might be to expect to be able to measure it on any given Sunday, they are the ones who, insofar as they have in a certain broken way abandoned the demand for reciprocity, have come to be precarious friends, come by the gift of the Spirit to "love one another with mutual affection" (10).[84] Perhaps we may be forgiven the boldness of imagining that on some days they actually are the ones who in *giving* to one another—in a certain way deferring to one another without the profit logic of economic investment—are delightfully surprised that they have come to *receive* from one another as well. As circumstantial as no doubt the evidence is that it has taken recognizable shape in some local neighborhood, perhaps these *are* the ones who, as

---

84. The King James Version translates this phrase as "be kindly affectioned one to another with brotherly love."

"*many*, [have come to be] *one body* in Christ, and individually ... members one of another" (5–7). Before a whole world of those who shake their heads in disbelief, perhaps they have come this one week by the miracle of sacramental grace to "bless those who persecute [them], bless and ... not curse them" (14). Perhaps already they have come not to "repay anyone evil with evil" (17), no longer to avenge themselves, but to leave the determination of good and evil in the hands of the inscrutable mystery of the Father of the crucified Jesus (19). They are told unambiguously by the terms of their passports: "if your enemies are hungry, feed them; if they are thirsty, give them something to drink" (20).[85] Perhaps they have come today to bear witness that to their surprise they have this week traveled in this very manner. In other words, this church is that body of workers—in themselves no more altruistic than anyone—who again and again assemble to enter into the body of the Christ who with abandon, they have heard, gave himself to his neighbors, whomever they were, as he gave himself with abandon to the coming of his holy Father. It is the Spirit he breathed in the upper room upon his by no means altruistic followers, they have heard, who may yet make it so, as these people, caring for and yielding to be disciplined by one another, rub shoulders as they move in and out of huts, shops, rice paddies, coffee plantations, and more solemnly dedicated sanctuaries.

The technical term for the work these people gather to do is "the liturgy of the eucharist."[86] The eucharist is that text in which their work is inscribed.

> For I received from the Lord what I also handed on to you, that the Lord Jesus on the night when he was betrayed took a loaf of bread, and when he had given thanks, he broke it and said, "This is my

---

85. Of course, Paul *exhorts* the Roman congregation to do these things. Thus it cannot be assumed that they are already doing them. He exhorts them almost certainly because they are not doing them—at least not consistently. Nonetheless, Paul is declaring that this mode of life is precisely the one to which the church is called, without which the church is not faithful to its calling. It is for such work, whether they acknowledge it or not, that they assemble, that "they come."

86. Schmemann, *For the Life of the World*, 25: "[Originally the Greek word *leitourgia*] meant an action by which a group of people become something corporately which they had not been as a mere collection of individuals—a whole greater than the sum of its parts. It meant also a function or 'ministry' of a man or of a group on behalf of and in the interest of the whole community. Thus the *leitourgia* of ancient Israel was the corporate work of a chosen few to prepare the world for the coming of the messiah. And in this very act of preparation they became what they were called to be, the Israel of God, the chosen instrument of His purpose."

Working Out the Body and Blood of Christ on the Eighth Day of Creation

body that is for you. Do this in remembrance of me." In the same way he took the cup also, after supper, saying, "This cup is the new covenant in my blood. Do this, as often as you drink it, in remembrance of me." For as often as you eat this bread and drink the cup, you proclaim the Lord's death until he comes. (1 Cor 11:23-26)

The liturgy of the eucharist is the way holy week in this church is particularly to be remembered. That is, the end and new beginning of the history of Jesus is remembered by *performing* Jesus' crucifixion/resurrection. Doing the work of Jesus entails a by no means ordinary vision of the world and our place in it.[87] The liturgy of the eucharist signifies that in Christ each chop of a hoe, each turn of a bolt, each ten-finger run across a keyboard, and each molding of a cool compress to the forehead of the dying, i.e., all the gestures by which the peace is passed, together make an imitation of the work of the Lamb whose food was doing the will of his Father (John 4:34).

The liturgy of the eucharist, however, need not be the esoteric ritual of a secret society walled off from the rest of the world.[88] It need not be the organizing center of institutional self-identity. It need not be a religious sleight of hand fixated on arcane items nestled in plates and cups out of which no one will ever have had a meal. It may rather be as fluid as the hard work of people together in a certain broken manner imitating the passion of the master than whom they are not greater.[89] Nor need it be a one day affair. Particular days almost certainly will figure importantly here. It is unlikely that even revisions of this liturgy will ever for long simply level the days of the week. Yet the day of greatest importance for this work, even when it is most institutionally canned, is the day that remembers and repeats the work of the day of holy week that the words of institution acknowledge has gathered and renewed every day.

The time working people have lived is in a certain broken manner gathered together in this work. All week they move—lunch under their arms, tools in their hands—from and to the celebration that does not get over Easter Sunday. Christ is raised on *that* day, not on the sabbath, not on the last day of the week, but on a new day that exceeds the old order of a

---

87. See Cavanaugh, *Torture and Eucharist*, 8-18, 31, 57, 65-71, 206-7, 222-52, 267-68, 271-81.

88. It seems to me that the Wesleyan tradition has been wise to invite all to an "open table," even if it has sometimes confused hospitality with careless "tolerance" or claustrophobic "inclusion."

89. See Yoder, *Politics of Jesus*, 51.

seven day cycle. One might say that resurrection joy irrupts as the dawning of an unprecedented first day, a first day that will not stand in competition with the old order, but penetrates it, saturates it, and folds it into the new, the way a baker might fold flour into what will have been batter. Thus this *new* first day in its relation to the old is also the eighth day.[90] And this is the day of the celebration of the eucharist, the day in which a particular working class enters into the apocalyptic coming of God.

God's future Reign is here the redemption of time. It is the gathering of all the hard days and nights of work in the glorification of the holy God. Therefore, as we enter that coming apocalyptic event in a certain broken manner in the celebration of the eucharist, the works of days and hands enter into it, too. This need not be an ethereal shadow play. It may be as actual as the crop that is threatened in every growing season by drought, flood, disease, pestilence, and fire; but also as actual as "the *hypostasis* of things hoped for" (Heb 11:1). In the eucharist our praxis enters God's peace and is sent back into the world, alive with the freedom of God's coming glory.[91]

It is in the liturgy of the eucharist, let us say, that we come to what we are created for: to gather the fruit of the earth and to offer it in adoration to its creator.[92] The church need not have a sacred function standing in opposition to the profane. That line of separation in fact is transgressed in the resurrection of the crucified Jesus. The eucharistic liturgy is an assembly of people who carry the "world" with them wherever they go.[93] Admittedly, in one sense they may be said to assemble on Sunday in order to *asc*end in prayer with their goods to the God who *trans*cends all of creation. Yet even then in a certain broken manner they pray for the coming of a fullness of time in which all that will have occurred will have come to be glorified in God's embrace.[94] The world as it stands is in such a prayer taken to the world

---

90. Schmemann, *Introduction to Liturgical Theology*, 77–78: "The eighth day is the day beyond the cycle outlined by the week and punctuated by the Sabbath—this is the first day of the New Aeon, the figure of the time of the Messiah.... This eighth day (coming after and standing outside the week) is also, therefore, the first day, the beginning of the world which has been saved and restored."

91. Schmemann, *Eucharist*, 40: "We can therefore say that the symbol [of the eucharist] reveals the world, mankind, and all creation as the 'matter' of a single, all-embracing sacrament."

92. See Schmemann, *For the Life of the World*, 3, 11.

93. Saliers, *Worship as Theology*, 25–31.

94. Schmemann, *Eucharist*, 218: "The liturgy is served on earth, and this means in the time and space of 'this world.' But if it is served on earth, *it is accomplished in heaven, in the new time of the new creation*, in the time of the Holy Spirit." See 213, 222, 225, and *For the Life of the World*, 42; cf. 16 and the Lord's Prayer.

Working Out the Body and Blood of Christ on the Eighth Day of Creation

as it is redeemed. The two meet in the glorified crucified Son of God—the deified destroyed human temple of God—the pivot upon which the whole liturgical procession turns.[95]

> Then I looked, and I heard the voice of many angels surrounding the throne and the living creatures and the elders; they numbered myriads of myriads and thousands of thousands, singing with full voice, "Worthy is the Lamb that was slaughtered to receive power and wealth and wisdom and might and honor and glory and blessing!" Then I heard every creature in heaven and on earth and under the earth and in the sea, and all that is in them, singing, "To the one seated on the throne and to the Lamb be blessing and honor and glory and might forever and ever!" And the four living creatures said, "Amen!" And the elders fell down and worshiped. (Rev 5:11–14)

Such a eucharistic liturgy begins before those who will gather get out of bed in their homes, before they retired the night before.[96] It continues as they trace out tangled lines of movement to the place of assembly, lines that eddy before the performative site of the parabolic exaltation of a mutilated body to the end of sacramental Mystery. There is no fixation here on what is laid out on a plate or contained in a cup, nor is this food disregarded as a mere "representation."[97] By the Spirit it is the whole liturgy, embracing as it does the works of every day, that is the eating and drinking of the body and blood of Christ: food, life.[98]

It is because such a liturgy is the work of the redemption of the whole of time, of every week and day, that departure from the assembly does not bring the eucharist to a conclusion. One leaves the coming new creation precisely to get to work in the world as it is.[99] Those who gathered are sent

---

95. If Christ is the pivot, the Spirit (to put it overly simply) is the turning. Thus every liturgical move already leans toward the coming of the Spirit to whom the prayer of epiclesis cries out in appeal. There is indeed no epiclesis without the prevenience of the Spirit.

96. Schmemann, *For the Life of the World*, 27.

97. The bread and wine, the words of the liturgy declare, are the broken body and shed blood of Christ.

98. Schmemann, *Eucharist*, 226: "The purpose of the eucharist lies not in the change of the bread and wine, but in our partaking of Christ, who has become our food, our life, the manifestation of the church as the body of Christ." Cf. 11, 49–50.

99. Schmemann, *For the Life of the World*, 64–65: "We are always *between* morning and evening, *between* Sunday and Sunday, *between* Easter and Easter, *between* the two comings of Christ. . . . God revealed and offers us eternal Life and not eternal rest.

into the days to come to carry both the wounds and the liberative glory of Christ in their bodies. They do so not by marketing a solution to some speculative question. They offer rather a gift, a gift that can never become someone's private property.[100] That is, what such a church is sent to offer is Christ, the food of the world. It offers that food as a mode of life into which to enter. It is in this sense that the church's mission occurs within the pure gift of the living God—a gift that in coming brings joy, not satiety, journey, not arrival.[101] It is because the church is the body of Christ that it is sent where life is threatened, taken, and undone, to offer itself as food, as the bread of heaven, i.e., in the way the Christ of the passion narratives is offered. The church is sent to work, not as a Gnostic physician tending to non-material souls, but as a tangible body that provides to be metabolized what it might have kept as its own.

On a given Sunday, when with freshly washed hands the people of the church sit on their heels to eat, what they have known has been hard. Certainly, it is ambiguously so. Even on an especially painful day labor comes not only with distress, but also with joy—there are contraction and dilation, pushing and crowning, breathless silence and the death-defying, piercing cry of new life. And when new life comes warmly into her arms, she holds it close and it suckles at her breast.

Of course, the church does not float above this world's brutality. Its people are threatened and undone no less often than people anywhere. People who have been starved, beaten, run out of their villages, and robbed even of the fruit of their wombs have every right simply to roll over and die or to lash out in explosive rage or by heroic effort simply to get on with their lives. It is a sacramental miracle, when they turn instead in a new manner to give themselves away—not out of weakness or submission or cowardice, but by an uncanny and shocking audacity that may yet elude that tempest that would throw us all into the sea. And with the one who feeds the hungry and will not be their hero-king there might be a little body

---

And God revealed this eternal Life in the midst of time.... [Every] day, every minute resounds now with the victorious affirmation: 'Behold, I make all things new. I am the alpha and omega, the beginning and the end . . .' (Rev. 21:5–6)." See *Eucharist*, 244–45.

100. See Schmemann, *For the Life of the World*, 47.
101. See Catherine of Siena, *Prayers*, Prayer 10.

Working Out the Body and Blood of Christ on the Eighth Day of Creation

of people who bear witness with their bodies to the coming of a new and just city. That kind of freedom, the freedom to give your very breast milk, when all you have, when the little one who would have been your baby, has been ripped out of your hands, cannot be forced, not even when without her gift the stranger stretched out on the dirty floor, with breath enough only to whisper, would perish.[102]

---

102. Steinbeck, *Grapes of Wrath*, 472–73: "Suddenly the boy cried, 'He's dyin', I tell you! He's starvin' to death, I tell you.' 'Hush,' said Ma. She looked at Pa and Uncle John standing helplessly gazing at the sick man. She looked at Rose of Sharon huddled in the comfort. Ma's eyes passed Rose of Sharon's eyes, and then came back to them. And the two women looked deep into each other. The girl's breath came short and gasping. She said, 'Yes.' . . . Ma leaned forward and with her palm she brushed the tousled hair back from her daughter's forehead, and she kissed her on the forehead. Ma got up quickly. 'Come on, you fellas,' she called. 'You come out to the tool shed.' . . . She herded them through the door, drew the boy with her; and she closed the squeaking door. For a minute Rose of Sharon sat still in the whispering barn. Then she hoisted her tired body up and drew the comfort about her. She moved slowly to the corner and stood looking down at the wasted face, into the wide, frightened eyes. Then slowly she lay down beside him. He shook his head slowly from side to side. Rose of Sharon loosened one side of the blanket and bared her breast. 'You got to,' she said. She squirmed closer and pulled his head close. 'There!' she said. 'There.' Her hand moved behind his head and supported it. Her fingers moved gently in his hair. She looked up and across the barn, and her lips came together and smiled mysteriously."

Interlude[1]

The newborn infant is a bundle of raw sensory receptors. For nine months the fetus is swathed and insulated in its mother's amniotic fluid. Though there are sensory stimuli in utero, they are dampened. The newborn is ill-prepared for the sudden inundation of stimuli at birth. Suddenly it is literally propelled into an environment full of new and intense sensations of touch, sound, taste, sight, smell, cold, heat, and pain. The infant screams in response to this first flood of stimuli. But when placed on its mother's belly, hearing her familiar (if previously muffled) voice, and feeling her loving touch, perhaps even smelling her familiar scent, the newborn is quickly soothed.[2]

THE BODY REMEMBERS. WHEN the percussion of trauma—say, a rape or the haphazard bloodletting of some agency of homeland security—puts her down, she may in good time rise to her feet, dust herself off, straighten her torn clothes, and clock back into daily life, but she will not forget.[3] She

---

1. Mark 14:22–23: "While they were eating, he took a loaf of bread, and after blessing it he broke it, gave it to them, and said, 'Take; this is my body.' Then he took a cup, and after giving thanks he gave it to them, and all of them drank from it."

2. Rothschild, *Body Remembers*, 23.

3. Ibid., 6–7: "The currently accepted definition [entails] . . . that PTSD can develop in an individual in response to three types of events: (1) incidents that are, or are perceived as, threatening to one's own life or bodily integrity; (2) being a witness to acts of violence to others; or (3) hearing of violence to or the unexpected or violent death of close associates. Events that could qualify as traumatic for both adults and children . . . include combat, sexual and physical assault, being held hostage or imprisoned, terrorism, torture, natural and man made disasters, accidents, and receiving a diagnosis of a life-threatening illness. In addition . . . PTSD can develop in children who have experienced sexual molestation, even if this is not life-threatening." Astur et al., "Hippocampus Function Predicts Severity of Post-Traumatic Stress Disorder," 234: "PTSD is often characterized by intrusive thoughts of the traumatic event, sleeplessness, hypersensitivity, and chronic stress. Despite these stark symptoms, PTSD is greatly under-diagnosed and has lifetime prevalence rates of approximately 13% for women [sic] and 6% for women in the US. Moreover, it is estimated that 60% of men and 50% of women are exposed to a traumatic event that might potentially lead to PTSD; hence, this is an issue that is pertinent to the majority of people. Due to the debilitating nature of symptoms, PTSD causes substantial amounts of medical illness, unemployment, and homelessness." The term *disorder* is, of course, relative. There are those who carry with them the wounds of trauma but who nonetheless manage to cope without signaling either themselves or

will not forget, not even when the rabid beast that shook her in its jaws, withdrawing, refuses to refract light, its growl inaudible in the darkness at the edge of oblivion. She will not forget, not even when every effort evokes from her lips hardly a directly intelligible account of what for her has now ceased to be "that day." Horror does not always have a folder in which it might be filed and managed: coordinates on a *Thomas Guide*, a box on a wall calendar, a line in an attorney's brief. Indeed, when an arrested terror is roused, it may well grow to loom so threateningly that it will not yield even to be pre-understood with a beginning, middle, and end, with a vocabulary and syntax. Though such terror is "speechless," it will not quickly detach itself from the traumatized body. Indeed, it is because of the way it clings to the traumatized body that it perdures . . . speechlessly.[4]

The body remembers. When memory is "complete" and broadly articulable, it draws both from directly engaging and from more subtly complex systems: the former, "declarative," system associated with the intricate patterns of reverberating electrical activity that is spread over much of the cerebral cortex and runs through the medial temporal lobe; the latter, "non-declarative," system with processes at play in the deeper recesses of the brain.[5] "Declarative memories" are memories perhaps in the most

---

others that something is seriously amiss. See Bremner et al., "Neurobiology of Posttraumatic Stress Disorder," 125–26, 129; and Isaac et al., "Is Posttraumatic Stress Disorder Associated with Specific Deficits in Episodic Memory?" 939–52.

4. While retaining an indefinite memory of the emotions of a trauma and its largely unsorted reactions to the complexities of the event, the body of one suffering from PTSD literally does not know what to do with them. See Kandel et al., *Essentials of Neural Science and Behavior*, 656, 666; and Kandel, *In Search of Memory*, 344–45; cf. 343.

5. Kandel, *In Search of Memory*, 132, 279–80: "What we usually think of as conscious memory we now call . . . explicit (or declarative) memory. It is the conscious recall of people, places, objects, facts, and events. . . . Unconscious memory we now call implicit (or procedural) memory. It underlies habituation, sensitization, and classical conditioning, as well as perceptual and motor skills such as riding a bicycle or serving a tennis ball. . . . Implicit memory is not a single memory system but a collection of processes involving several different brain systems that lie deep within the cerebral cortex. . . . Implicit memory often has an automatic quality. It is recalled directly through performance, without any conscious effort or even awareness that we are drawing on memory. Although experiences change perceptual and motor abilities, those experiences are virtually inaccessible to conscious recollection. . . . When we speak, we do not consider where in the sentence to place the noun or verb. We do it automatically, unconsciously. . . . Implicit memory is responsible not only for simple perceptual and motor skills but also, in principle, for the pirouettes of Margot Fonteyn, the trumpeting of Wynton Marsalis, the accurate ground strokes of Andre Agassi, and the leg movements of an adolescent riding a bicycle. Implicit memory guides us through well-established routines that are

ordinary sense of the term. They comprise, first, what comes to my mind or yours concerning those particular lived times and places of that history that we habitually describe as "mine" and as "past," and, second, that "knowledge" that you and I may freely and consciously access and discuss with each other at will, knowledge which has lost contact with the times and places that once perhaps gave it birth, and which we treat as "general." The former are described as "episodic" or "narrative" or "autobiographical," the latter as "semantic." Non-declarative memories are much more opaque and may not at first seem like memories at all. They are unconscious and under normal conditions function in unobtrusive coordination with declarative memories. And so, "emotional" and "motor" memories are both non-declarative.[6] Motor memories are those skills we come ordinarily to exercise without deliberation, such as during a daily bicycle ride or while balancing a checkbook. Emotional memories are subtle, though not always benign, processes in which certain mental or environmental cues elicit emotions of varying degrees of intensity, while often the events that first gave rise to them remain unconscious. Thus a young soldier on leave may find an inexplicable elation stirring in her, when on a bright Saturday morning, she wakes in her boyfriend's tiny apartment to hear and smell through open windows the frying of bacon and eggs from the apartment next door; or may with the deep, rolling percussion of a nocturnal thunderclap leap from his side in a panic, her heart racing, thrust her hand out to grasp her weapon, and then feel oddly relieved when she brushes against her boots which to his dismay she has wisely kept beside her in bed.[7]

And so, if some lazy late November afternoon your whole bodily vitality is well-engaged with the world and the clusters of gray matter—upheld by bone and muscle just behind your face and above your throat—are

---

not consciously controlled." For a fuller outline of the difference between declarative and nondeclarative memory, see Anderson, *Cognitive Psychology and Its Implications*, 234-41. See also Bremner et al., "Neurobiology of Posttraumatic Stress Disorder," 119-22, 124-25.

6. "Semantic priming," the automatic activation of a chain of ideas or semantic associations triggered by a verbal, mental, environmental, or emotional cue, is also nondeclarative, as are certain other processes.

7. Tyson, "Woman Gains Silver Star—and Removal from Combat": "Military officers in the field and independent experts have said it is both infeasible and contrary to the Army's own warfighting doctrine to prevent women from serving in proximity to—or together with—all-male combat units in today's war zones. They contend that if the goal of the policy is to protect women from capture or bodily harm, it cannot be done in the scramble of conflicts such as those in the Middle East."

Interlude

managing both kinds of memory well, you might find your attention, drifting to another time and place, recollecting the warmth of the dining room and the grumbling of your stomach as you took your seat, the color pattern of the table cloth and of the cranberries, collards, and dressing on your plate, the way a bone deflected the knife as you carved the turkey, the way you laughed at your brother's jokes, the gratitude that seemed not only to fill you, but the room itself, and the way it all seemed to rectify an otherwise empty holiday.[8]

When memories break, however, *we* break.[9] The ordeals that shatter or suppress declarative memories leave literally unthinkable non-declarative ones to be thrust about like the debris of ships run aground and wrecked in heavy surf. We will not walk steadily on our feet until we open to the whole hulking beast that hurt us and give it room in our history both to act and be acted upon.[10] By letting it in, non-declarative "encoded sensations, emotions, and behaviors" are given a "context," even if a still painful one, and become cogently significant. This is the work *words* do, words that take on the moments that mark the body and thus draw them into an intelligible tale.[11] Through the gift of language the wounded come "to think and

---

8. Rothschild, *Body Remembers Casebook*, 31: "Basically, the acronym SIBAM stand for . . . : sensation (S), images (I), behaviors/movements (B), affects/emotions (A), and meanings/cognitive understanding (M)."

9. Ibid.: "[T]hose still troubled by traumatic incidents are likely to have one or more of these [SIBAM] elements dissociated from their memories of those incidents—that is, disconnected from the other elements and from consciousness. The goal of trauma therapy . . . is to integrate all aspects of a traumatic experience, bring them to consciousness, and create a cohesive narrative."

10. One of the many tragedies of life is that, try as we (and those who love us) might, there are "hulking beasts" that we do not ever open to this side of our last dark night.

11. See Rothschild, *Body Remembers*, 30, 160; cf. Kandel, *In Search of Memory*, 281. But see in particular Gibbs, *Embodiment and Cognitive Science*. Gibbs (9) stresses that, although meaning certainly entails the brain, it is also to be acknowledged that (1) the brain is an abstraction when considered without the whole human body of which it is a part, and (2) the whole human body is an abstraction when considered without the "physical, cultural world" of which it is a part. For example: "People's subjective, felt experiences of their bodies in action provide part of the fundamental grounding for language and thought. Cognition is what occurs when the body engages the physical, cultural world and must be studied in terms of the dynamical interactions between people and the environment. Human language and thought emerge from recurring patterns of embodied activity that constrain ongoing intelligent behavior. We must not assume cognition to be purely internal, symbolic, computational, and disembodied, but seek out the gross and detailed ways that language and thought are inextricably shaped by embodied action."

feel concurrently—that is, to be able to sense their sensations, emotions, and behaviors while formulating coherent conclusions about the relationship between those and the images and thoughts that accompany them."[12]

Though the language by which we come concurrently to "think and feel" is nobody's private property, as if a well-grounded autonomous individual were ever in a position to do with it whatever she wished, it is not forced on us. Indeed we speak freely.[13] Language comes and goes with our breath. Its textures—intricate, momentary, delicate—run through us like waves through a salt-marsh. If the words printed on a page or vibrating in an ear canal were merely deficient instances of a deep or overarching detail-discarding changeless *logos*, discourse—coming and going the way it does—could only beguile us.[14] Yet if at least from time to time it does not, if language steps up (let us say) righteous and earthy, how are we to *think* it, what are we to *say* of it? It is surely not enough to imagine it as software loaded onto the organic CPUs encased in our skulls, updated periodically by faceless software retailers; or the conventions by which the otherwise shocking improprieties of our subterranean brutish drives are managed; or the ex-pression of the deep creativity of the human spirit; or the imposition of labels on the items we have independently inventoried. Language has about it something at once unmanageably historic, gritty, corporeal, open, reserved, social, particular, outgoing, patient, surprising, evanescent, promising, and ancestral. There is to that discourse a timely speaker or writer both remembers and makes . . . as much "outside" as there is "inside," as much "you" and "we" and "they" as there is "I," as much "that" and "when" and "how" as there is "what," as much "toward" as there is "from," as much "who" as there is "why," as much "not yet" and "no longer" as there is "still," as much "body" as there is "mind."[15] Discourse runs through everything we do. It is in our clothes, hair, gait, posture; the angles of our jaws, the curves of our backs, and the tautness of the muscles around our eyes. It is this language—the language we may see, touch, hear, heft, and carry—that from time to time invites and evokes trust and courage from the broken.

---

12. Rothschild, *Body Remembers*, 160–61; cf. *Body Remembers Casebook*, 199.

13. This is not to say "by free will," a notion devised to protect freedom but that finally ensnares, captures, and displays it like a sedated wild animal we may at our leisure visit in a zoo.

14. Perhaps they do seduce us, but not to sin—not if "the way, the truth, and the life" never gets over incarnation.

15. Cf. Gibbs, *Embodiment and Cognitive Science*, 12.

Interlude

Of course, language entails "concepts," just as reaping grain with a sickle entails grasping tufts of its stalks.[16] Yet a concept need not be as definite and stable as we have been trained to believe. One might, in fact, imagine it as a kind of experiment, an improvisation, an emergency shelter, a climber's handhold, rather than a fixed and permanent unit of thought or meaning or order in a human or higher mind.[17] Even the loftiest concept—e.g., "truth" or "goodness" or "beauty"—may in fact simply *occur* on the way to something else, as a groping for a set of metaphors to do what could not be done otherwise.[18] A concept is thus already a language act, a multiform phenomena-collection, not seated in long-term memory, but always already on task in "working memory."[19] It steps into the light, let us say, imaginatively, non-propositionally, as a way of tending "bodily perception and movement," cutting across the broad spectrum of the body's activity and receptivity: "at once visual, auditory, kinesthetic, and tactile."[20] It may thus be said to be an "experiential gestalt"—constantly shifting in

---

16. *Oxford English Dictionary*, s.v. "conceive, v.": "Nearly all the senses found in Fr. and Eng. were already developed in L., where the primary notion was app. 'to take effectively, take to oneself, take in and hold.'"

17. Gibbs, *Embodiment and Cognitive Science*, 86, 88: "These observations suggest that concepts are temporary constructions in working memory, based on embodied simulations, and not stable structures stored in long-term memory. . . . Concepts arise as on-the-fly simulations of events. In standard categorization tasks, for example, people first simulate referents of the concept perceptually and then scan their simulations to produce the required information."

18. It may be, as Lakoff and Johnson maintain, that though perhaps there are "nonmetaphorical concepts," they are of quite limited use, particularly as one is thinking of what may be called "subjective experience." Lakoff and Johnson, *Philosophy in the Flesh*, 58–59, 77–78, 88, 128. "If we consciously make the enormous effort to separate out metaphorical from nonmetaphorical thought, we probably can do some very minimal and unsophisticated nonmetaphorical reasoning. But almost no one ever does this" (ibid., 59).

19. Gibbs, *Embodiment and Cognitive Science*, 122: "Metaphor is fundamental to conceptual processing. Abstract concepts are partly created from the metaphorical mapping of embodied source domains onto various target domains. In fact, abstract concepts would not exist in the ways that they do in ordinary cognition without body-based metaphor. Metaphor is not a way of accessing previously articulated abstract knowledge, but is inherent in the creation and maintenance of abstract construals in different situations. This position suggests, then, that human conceptual processing is deeply grounded in embodied metaphor, especially in regard to abstract understandings of experience." Cf. ibid., 144.

20. Ibid., 89–91; cf. 120.

a variety of directions, a "complex interplay of brain, body, and world."²¹ And perhaps it is this "complex interplay" that is most to be stressed. The boundary lines Western Civilization's nation-builders may want to assign to "concepts" to set them off from "words" and "deeds" are too quickly drawn and are nonetheless powerless to hold these nomads in place. As concepts and words and deeds emerge, they are neither simply "mental" nor simply "physical," simply "private" nor simply "public." They occur together, as somebody—brain and bone—confronts and is confronted by an *outside*, a very concrete "world" that is never *simply* outside. They are points of occurrent, fleeting, shifting "stability," on the way elsewhere.²² To think silently or right out loud is already to be outside working in a field or on a stage, handing off or being handed a shovel or wrench or page of sheet music, engaged.²³ Which of them is the cause and which is the effect is not so easy to tell.²⁴ What is easy to tell, however, is that the work of language is

---

21. Ibid., 96, 114. Lakoff and Johnson, *Philosophy in the Flesh*, 497: "Concepts arise from, and are understood through, the body, the brain, and experience in the world. Concepts get their meaning through embodiment, especially via perceptual and motor capacities. . . . . Abstract concepts arise via metaphorical projections from more directly embodied concepts (e.g., perceptual and motor concepts)."

22. Gibbs, *Embodiment and Cognitive Science*, 115.

23. Ibid., 157: "Traditional views of higher-order cognition as computational processing on symbolic representations fail to capture the importance of embodiment in human thought. People's previous and current embodied actions serve as the grounding for various aspects of imagination, memory, and reasoning. On-line embodied processes emphasize overt sensorimotor activity to assist with cognitive tasks that interact with the immediate world. Off-line embodiment occurs when sensorimotor processes run covertly to assist with the representation and manipulation of information in the temporary absence of task relevant input or output. Both of these aspects of embodiment work to create an embodied model of mind that is not internal to people's heads, but is distributed as a 'cognitive web' across brains, bodies, and world. This distributed, embodied view of cognition offers a vision of human thought that is far less internally computational and far more bodily extended into the real world of action than is traditionally understood in cognitive science. . . . [T]here is an ever-growing literature to support a view of imagery, memory, and reasoning as intimately tied to bodily activity, such that higher-order cognitive process are situated, embedded, and embodied." Cf. 147. Lakoff and Johnson, *Philosophy in the Flesh*, 78: "Meaning has to do with the ways in which we function meaningfully in the world and make sense of it via bodily and imaginative structures." Cf. Dewey, *Reconstruction in Philosophy*, 156–57.

24. Gibbs, *Embodiment and Cognitive Science*, 281: "Each of the parts continuously affects, along a different time scale, the overall behavior of the system to the point that its independent contribution cannot be sorted out from the behavior of the whole. Most important, the performance of cognitive systems emerges from coordinated activity among interdependent sensorimotor ensembles. These strongly nonlinear, qualitative

the work of bodies—bodies with brains, but also with hands, throats, and shoulders; with lovers, mothers, children, enemies, and friends.

Language decenters privacy, propriety, autonomy, and individuality. It opens me, disrupts and disturbs my identity, and introduces me to those I simply could never have met without it. Certainly, language also provides us with the means and opportunity for yielding to the allure of the fantasies of integrity and authenticity. "*I* speak and write after all!" "Every proper sentence has a *subject* after all!" And yet, we succumb to these temptations only when we forget that language comes always as a gift that will have been at play long before we presumed to make use of it. Language is larger than I am, larger than you are. It is "in us" only on the way through.[25] Thus it is we who are in *it*—"in language" the way somebody might be "in trouble" or "in transit" or "in love." And though language occurs between persons who face each other, the inertial restraints of serial time fail to hold it in place. Discourse has the audacity to reply toward a future that has not quite arrived, *your* future that is expected just beyond the brief pause at the end of the string of words *I* am now uttering.[26] Language moves between those who—far from being fixed in a sterile presence—anticipate each other, persons both awaited and sought in the open time of hope.[27]

Human beings are hunters, gatherers, and priests. They collect what comes into their hands, whether by sagaciously deliberate pursuit or by chance, and they carry it home to eat, drink, carve, weave, wear, or understand. They track, meet, sight, and place their shots; they clear, plough, plant, tend, and harvest. And once goods lie spread across the ground their hands have smoothed and covered, they offer them over the course of hours, days, months, and years in the oblatory fires of hard work—a ritual sacrifice freely given with a clear eye to an uncertain future.

---

transformations show the impossibility of reducing cognitive performance to singularly causal neural assembles, or even singularly causal component oscillations. This self-organizing gestalt allows fluid continuity between action and perception, and organism and environment."

25. This, too, is an aspect not of "the right," but of "the gift" of freedom of speech.

26. Or in this case writing.

27. I speak to you, because you have first spoken to me, even if under threat of perjury, you could only deny it. To be human is to be an invitation with an RSVP. Further I speak to you in anticipation of a future in which you will have heard and replied—a time which in the manageable present of my speech is not yet. Thus it is disappointing when, in the silence after a particularly apt comment during a lively late-night conversation, it becomes suddenly clear that your friend, stretched out on the hard floor in the room's dim, smoky light, has fallen asleep.

Thus we speak and write. The cadence of every line of every chapter and verse makes a priestly ritual as well, a rhythm by which the collected fruit for which language has labored is released. Even the most hardened hunters, gatherers, and priests are song writers and story tellers, though perhaps they would want no one to find it out. Poetry and narrative are not exceptional cases of some symbolic system of facts and representations, decorative or entertaining diversions from serious, adult work. They rather situate all speaking and writing. When half awake a child first touches her tiny bare feet to the cold, hard floor beside her grandmother's iron bed and makes her first near-sentence, she has already for some time been both writing and being written into a story that is by no means only hers.[28] Stories are told of characters that are named as they entail and are entailed by a cast of characters. They are worked out by a *poiesis* that makes what was not and thus unmakes what was. Even a cosmos secured by an impermeably totalizing metaphysical calculus fails to detain and intern us—because it, too, has a literature catalogued in the libraries of cities built by the poetry and stories of hunters, gatherers, and priests. The language of a society of deterministic astrophysicists is given to the very indefinite future as is the language of a band of wandering Arameans. Because something unheard of is approaching from just beyond the consonant or vowel anyone at any moment is working through, tellers of the human tale are free not only to call for retreat or hostility, but also for a by no means naïve peacemaking that walks out into a battlefield-world bearing gifts neither to be lost nor gained in the giving.

Bodies work; they remember and hope; they speak and write—but they are never alone. Flesh and blood, they entail and are entailed by each other. When they meet, the surfaces we purport to outline on spring-loaded or tomographic two-dimensional anatomical charts are breeched with ease—perhaps by the touch of a lover, the gaze of a stranger, or the whispered deception of an interrogator. Whether we want to or not, we let each other in.[29] Bodies are social and historical. Certainly social bodies are different from each other, a difference not in every respect unlike the difference between one person and another. Certainly they say not only "yes," but also "no" to each other, sometimes with the bloody violence of militant ex-

28. This continues to be the case even if decades later her obituary recounts her many accomplishments as a defender of an all-consuming economy repulsed by story and song.

29. You got in before I thought to lock the gate. It was you who turned to lock it; but by then it was too late.

Interlude

or in-clusion. Yet even the social bodies locked for generations in mutually genocidal brutality get into each other and one history is inscribed across another.

Words gesture. No ghostly essences fallen to earth (wrapped temporarily in animal skins) words are bodies at work, as are childbirth, barn-raising, and fly-fishing. Words contact us, sometimes most forcefully when performed without overtly discernable speech or script. A nursing home resident's smile, the public hanging of Mussolini, a key pressed into a hand, the downthrow of the Twin Towers, John Paul's prison visit with Mehmet Ali Ağca—all these are words.

Words never simply inform. They carry us into each other even when we'd much prefer to be left alone. And yet there is a great difference between the way a young man's bodily integrity is transgressed by the caresses of his lover at the last sunset of his short, hard life and the way it is by an empire's field tested data extraction techniques. And there are more than one way a fratricidal military class suckled by wolves on Palatine Hill may turn to the Passover children of refugee mothers. It is one thing to be baptized into a foreign Galilean body and thereby engrafted into the history of the body of that people; it is another thing entirely to mutilate it on the way to execution.

Language, taken up on the lips, heard in the ears, read by the eyes or the finger tips, and played out with physiological changes, may invite us, however ambiguously, to imagine a future particularly for bodies. There have always been human beings who have lacked the luxury to forget the uncertainty of work and food, who have known that a simple open wound or broken bone may over time come at the cost both of one's own life and of the lives of those for whom one has provided. They have not had to be told of the importance of work and food. As humbling as it might be for some of us to entertain the hypothesis, let us say that we, in ourselves but dust and ashes, have been provoked to live, perhaps by an elusive, excessive, unsettling non-proprietarily charitable donation. Let us say that as bodies on this earth we take each step, breath, and bite as children vulnerable to collapse, asphyxiation, and starvation. Let us say that as bodies we carry the dense, dry, dark earth out of which we have been sculpted. And yet, let us say as well that the body is not to be mistaken for the body-*shaped* quantum of necrotic tissue laid out on an autopsy table or grinning alluringly on a glossy magazine page. Let us imagine that as long as we heed without covetousness the promise of another step, breath, or bite, there is a future

After Crucifixion

for these mortal bodies that mortality alone cannot circumscribe—even if it takes a certain soulful giddiness in this way deliberately to stay hungry.[30]

---

30. Cf. Bell, *Liberation Theology After the End of History*, e.g., 192–95.

4 Thinking the Wounds of the Lamb of God

To Excess

> *Stay hungry, stay hungry, stay hungry.*
> *Here's that rhythm again.*
> *Here's my shoulder blade.*
> *Here's the sound I made.*
> *Here's the picture I saved.*
> *Here I am.*[1]

BODIES SLIP THROUGH THE fingers at the working end of the long arm of the law. Classificatory schemas never quite lay hold either of the concrete sociality of bodies or of their particularity. Bodies happen—as "that one" and "that one" and "that one" (*hiin Enkelte*).[2] A body stands out, perhaps especially so by contrast to well established ideals. "That" body may look (for those with eyes to see) much more like a young, delicate, ill-formed bean shoot, little more than a root breaking through dry ground, trampled underfoot, than those beautiful heroes and other stars of stage, screen, and

---

1. Byrne and Frantz, "Stay Hungry."
2. See Eller, *Kierkegaard and Radical Discipleship*, 101–18, 137–38, 178–79, 194–95, 201–12, 342–52. "But whether consciously or not, S. K. was constructing one of his characteristic dialectics— . . . *Den Enkelte*, apart from the *Gemeinde*, contracts a sickness in his God-relationship, becomes melancholy and/or vain. The *Gemeinde*, if it loses sight of *den Enkelte*, also loses its *Gemeinschaft* and degenerates into a crowd. Although he failed to emphasize it as he might have, S. K's most basic premise was not '*den Enkelte* before God' but actually '*Enkelter* in *Gemeinschaft* before God'" (352).

historical novels, the ones who seize our attention: majestic oaks, rooted deeply in moist, fertile soil, holding the earth in place, heavy limbs reaching to the sky, cleaning and enriching the air with each leafy breath, the standard of greatness. "That one" may stand out "despised and rejected by others; a man of suffering and acquainted with infirmity; and as one from whom others hide their faces," one we, too, perhaps hold "of no account" (Isa 53:1–3). It may in fact be because we don't know what to do with her that she stands out. He may have no place to lay his head in our good, true, and beautiful world. She may be a migrant worker wandering from place to place. We always notice strangers, outsiders, aliens, especially if they do not speak our language or speak it with heavy accents we must strain to understand. We notice them in particular if they won't duck their heads and avert their eyes. It is hard to be a stranger, all the more where one's ancestors lived and worked, to breathe the dust stirred by legions of ambassadors propagating an empire's *pax* and *iustitia* by a force that "in the end, after some necessary adjustment, is a *bonus*, really," for the subjected.

"I cry out 'Violence!'" is the prayer of subjugation.[3] Untamed, chafing under the yoke, it may take on apocalyptic overtones. Long-sufferingly persistent and resilient, the prayers of the subjected, spoken and written with unrestrained, uppity verbosity, may with satisfaction strike the critic as having the traits of a literary genre. It is not unreasonable, of course, that they are catalogued under the heading, "apocalyptic literature." Even the casual twenty-first-century use of the word *apocalyptic* signals something of the wound that tears through these prayers. However, the "literature" this category aims to manage will not yield easily to categorization. Eschatology, especially apocalyptic eschatology, remains an outside of not good use, indeed an affront to civilization and its management teams. Yet let us say that the clay thrown to make the patterns of speech and life not only of the Apocalypse of John, but of the little house churches which gave it room and a hearing, and of the felled peasant they called "Lord," to whom they sang "as to a god,"[4] may without great hermeneutical strain or abuse be called—in more than one sense—"apocalyptic."[5]

3. Collins, *Apocalyptic Imagination*, 38. Collins uses the word *distress* and describes the ones that give rise to apocalypses to be "of various kinds."

4. Pelikan, *Christian Tradition*, 1:173: "The oldest surviving pagan report about the church described Christians as gathering before sunrise and 'singing a hymn to Christ as though to [a] god.' The oldest surviving liturgical prayer of the church was a prayer addressed to Christ: 'Our Lord, come!'"

5. Beale, *Book of Revelation*, 37: "Commentators now generally acknowledge that

Thinking the Wounds of the Lamb of God

"Apocalyptic was the mother of all Christian theology," Ernst Käsemann once wrote.[6] Having such a mother, however, can leave a mark on a child. Even as a young adult yields to be assimilated into a more polite, level-headed, healthy world, deeply ingrained, not always conscious memories of tales told at a wild woman's breast would not so easily be shaken—tales of sorrow, torment, death, destruction, and the audacious promise of a future on the far side of revolution, a new world pulsing with light and life; long-standing institutions for centuries anchored in stone dashed to the ground in a grand, sweeping disaster; angels and demons striving with each other tooth and claw in the rubble now strewn across continents devoid now of the high and mighty; in the end the face of a victorious royal mediator shining with the glory of God, standing tall as the smoke and dust clear in the light of the new dawn of the Reign of God.[7]

It is no surprise, then, that a dramatic tension agitates the earliest church's apocalyptic hopes. The future it prophesies is beautiful, but it, too, comes only where the blackened debris of a starless night too long smolders.

John has utilized the three genres of apocalyptic, prophecy, and epistle in composing the book." Cf. Bauckham, *Theology of the Book of Revelation*, 1–17. Collins, *Apocalyptic Imagination*, 282–83: "The language of apocalypses is not descriptive, referential, newspaper language, but . . . symbolic attempts to penetrate the darkness, which provide[s] ways of imagining the unknown, not factual knowledge. The value of these imaginative ventures cannot be assessed by a correspondence theory of truth, but only by evaluating the actions and attitudes which they supported. . . . Apocalyptic language . . . has a pragmatic aspect. . . . Accordingly, apocalyptic language is *commissive* in character: it commits us to a view of the world for the sake of the actions and attitudes that are entailed. . . . The apocalyptic literature does not lend itself easily to the ontological and objectivist concerns of systematic theology. It is far more congenial to the pragmatic tendency of liberation theology, which is not engaged in the pursuit of objective truth but in the dynamics of motivation and the exercise of political power. . . . The apocalyptic revolution is a revolution in the imagination. It entails a challenge to view the world in a way that is radically different from the common perception. The revolutionary potential of such imagination should not be underestimated, as it can foster dissatisfaction with the present and generate visions of what might be. The legacy of the apocalypses includes a powerful rhetoric for denouncing the deficiencies of this world. It also includes the conviction that the world as now constituted is not the end. Most of all, it entails an appreciation of the great resource that lies in the human imagination to construct a symbolic world where the integrity of values can be maintained in the face of social and political powerlessness and even of the threat of death." One might, however, imagine as well a "systematic theology" that is not stuck in "ontological and objectivist concerns."

6. Käsemann, *New Testament Questions of Today*, 102.

7. Collins, *Apocalyptic Imagination*, 12–13. Collins would accept this description (which is drawn from his account of Klaus Koch's work on apocalyptic literature) only for "historical apocalypses."

After Crucifixion

Its texts tell of baleful "principalities and powers" advancing across once green plains with an eye to fill the earth with a Sabbath-less, acquisitive practical wisdom; their legions guarding and enlarging the precincts of temples erected on land promised to the poor slave-children of immigrants and other strangers, temples from which shine the elegantly graven images of an empire's grand fixations. Ambassadors of occluded legality rise up in these tales to put away or assimilate competitors, say, the God Abraham, Moses, Samuel, Isaiah, Mary, and Jesus would not put away or assimilate. Desire and terror radiate from them like heat from newly forged iron. They demonstrate their potency in the clear light of midday, in the marketplace and along public highways, through acts both of raw and of refined violence, of artful allure and unmistakable threat. It is as if a boundary were being drawn through heaven and earth at the cutting edge of armies that advance to make the world safe for buying and selling.

The church's apocalyptic prayers were not pure fantasy. In the face of the powers that held its world in check, pure fantasy or some other tension-decompression technique, some distractive dream world, some opiate, could certainly come in handy. Surely a propertyless, sparsely populated collection of powerless little house churches and renegade village assemblies could only comply, even if, on their own time, their members might quietly withdraw, perhaps into a serenely detached, sublimated "spirituality," not without precedent among Hellenistic "religions" and "philosophies." Yet a surprising number of them would not. The liturgical prayers of those little churches and village assemblies resisted both compliance and withdrawal.

Among the least submissive of its apocalyptic doctrines is the one that seems to us (who have been so well pacified by its alternatives) most escapist: "the resurrection of the dead," of the *flesh* that otherwise would simply putrefy beneath the feet of increasingly oblivious passersby.[8] Indeed the bloody crucifixion of Jesus is such a revolutionary story, precisely because it tells of his wounded flesh, his dead body, viz., that it was not left to rot on Easter Sunday, but immersed in a "life" quite different from the life that comes and goes, the life analyzed by biochemists and insurance companies. It is the upending resurrection of Jesus that makes the slaughtered Lamb the Lion of the Tribe of Judah, the Root of David, as well, i.e., without ceasing to be the slaughtered Lamb (Rev 5:5–6). It is the story of Jesus' flesh

---

8. Although Thornton Wilder's *Our Town* has the dead growing more and more oblivious to the living, rather than the other way around, the result is the same, even if Wilder does it for the sake of a kind of (naturalistic) "living." See in particular the third act.

that calls for little churches and village assemblies to walk into the coming future, i.e., on hard ground, even if it is the future and not the ground that supports them. Without picking or being drawn into a fight, the children of the Lamb would not recoil from that stench of battlefield violence the principalities and powers breathe and exude in this present evil age. Still, they would look through that haze to the eyes of peace that abide by no means voyeuristically. Thus they bear witness to a future which armies of empire builders can neither make nor unmake. They bear witness to the flesh of Jesus, his regard for what was not-yet-seen, what was seen as not-yet. Martyrdom is not suicide. Still, "if you are to be taken captive, into captivity you go" (Rev 13:10), for thereby you "persevere," thereby you "conquer."

Of course, the poor and distressed people of little house churches and village assemblies yearned for integrity of body, soul, and spirit no less than we do. There is no shame in yearning for integrity. Jesus, the slaughtered Lamb, the Lion of the Tribe of Judah, was remembered as a healer, i.e., as one who made the wounded whole. And yet, there is a word in the forgiveness and resurrection of Jesus that will not be held fast by integrity. He is no more "whole" on Easter Sunday than he was on Good Friday. Rather, his wounds come to be the capacious house of that glory that by good authority was not to be found in weakness, such as his, and never to be found in death and damnation, such as his. That is, his crucified body rises as this word become flesh: to the very end to live a short or long life unhealed, with a mutilated body, soul, or spirit, is no impediment, not to the Spirit who raised the mutilated body of "that one" Jewish peasant from the tomb of dereliction.[9] This word was "good news" to those for whom good news was in short supply.[10]

---

9. Wright, *Resurrection of the Son of God*, 227: "Paul's initial appeal to the Philippian Christians . . . is that they will live worthy of the gospel in their public, even civic, life (1:27). . . . They will, of course, meet opposition, and face persecution, as they are already doing. But their cheerful refusal to be cowed will be a sign to their opponents that . . . those who belong to the Messiah, Jesus, are assured of *soteria*, . . . a deeper 'salvation' which nothing in the imperial system can either rival or harm. . . . [This salvation consists] in rescue from death, not by avoiding it, nor by regarding it as an irrelevant transition to a better life, but by the overcoming of death in bodily resurrection (3:20–21)."

10. Cf. Coakley, *Powers and Submissions*, 166.

After Crucifixion

Good news was in short supply for first-century Jewish peasants. Even before Roman occupation life was crushingly difficult for them. But with the coming of the armies of the Republic—and with them an imperial confidence in a Stoic *status natura*—life became for them all the more "short, brutish, and nasty." Work was forced hard labor; disease was rampant; legal practice was the implementation of investment and career strategies; starvation was an inescapable, insistent threat.

When hunger is among the countless controlled consumerist choices that we make over the course of a busy week decorated with food options—perhaps in order to take a fasting blood sugar or in fixated obeisance to a televisual phantasm or to decrease the risk of debilitating disease or to tantalize a lover or to sit out a little longer the dance of death—we are tempted to forget that *we* are the *bodies* who hunger. When antibiotics are readily available, when we have easy access to doctors and hospitals, when there are generous prescription provisions in our health insurance plans, when life expectancy charts promise us longevity, when childbirth is increasingly private and decreasingly dangerous, we are tempted to forget that *we* are the *bodies* who with the ineluctability of "it is finished!" will die. When by training we come to presume that the coercive agencies that enforce the imaginary borders that define a nation, neighborhood, home, and person also save us from incursions of foreign armies, marauding terrorists, predatory capitalists, and illegals, we are tempted to forget that *we* are the *bodies* whom no military heroes will ever "protect and serve" out of their vulnerability to violence and proximity to strangers. When we have lived lives of social, political, economic, ethnic, gender, or domestic privilege, when we have been trained to imagine that we are the very image of a God who is the very image of us, we are tempted to forget that *we* are the *bodies* upon whom a crowd of principalities and powers bears down strategically on every negotiable field to surprise, secure, seize, defeat, restrain, and exploit.

The vast majority of the children, men, and women who will have continued to draw breath (or will have breathed their last), as your eyes pass over the spot of ink at the end of this sentence, will not have wrestled seriously or often with such temptations.[11] Stooping to rescue for spring

---

11. Cf. Berquist, *Controlling Corporeality*, 1: "The literature Jews call the Tanakh and Christians call the Old Testament or the Hebrew Bible obsesses about bodies. The obsession comes to the forefront of the texts in many ways: priests need to see the skin of worshippers to judge whether or not they have diseases; God creates human bodies as the pinnacle of all creation using nothing more than clay and spit for the first one and a rib for the second; and people pray for wombs to be opened, for warriors to run without

Thinking the Wounds of the Lamb of God

planting the few ancestral seeds spared by a flashflood in a land without supply stores; leaning forward cross-legged and wide-eyed beside a pallet at the break of a smoggy urban dawn as a little girl delirious all night with fever grows still, opens her eyes, and whispers; rising slowly, badly cut and broken after a headlong fall down a dry, rocky hillside, a determined two day's walk on good legs from anything resembling medical care; exhaustedly laughing beside a midwife in a dirty hut, a tiny baby wrapped in rags and calmed, his weight nestled upon a warm belly now grown soft just after the twenty-first hour of labor; holding a wad of discolored bandage while making out the movements in the twilit room after a prolonged infection of both badly injured eyes; waking with a start to the shouts of mercenaries, machetes and rifles raised, descending on a little village—all this and more resolve before it could arise any controversy over "embodiment," even if ideological scripts echoing in our memories and theirs would indignantly beg to differ.[12]

The body will not bow out of life—especially in a world hard on bodies, a world, say, of small peasant villages of half a hundred people each, scratching out a living, tending little flocks of sheep or goats, doing some

---

fainting, or for enemies' babies to be dashed against rocks. The text takes the reader on a tour of all human bodily existence, with exquisite descriptions of events from childbirth to death, and yet the Hebrew Bible can also recount pregnancies and births one after another in stultifying genealogical progression, or mention in passing the deaths of thousands as if national decimation was banal. From God's first touch of humans at creation, through the narratives of ancestral priests and kings whose regulations governed bodily practices, through the prophets and poets whose speech celebrates embodied life, the Hebrew Bible centers on the human body."

12. Even after a few cities were built, the vast majority of Israelites lived painfully difficult lives in and about the rural villages of Israel's dry, rocky hills. Berquist, *Controlling Corporeality*, 112–13, 115: "The labor itself was back-breaking; it took a substantial toll on each person within early Israel. The most frequent causes of death in early Israel would have been accident, plague, and starvation, especially for men. Malnutrition would have been widespread throughout most of early Israel's history, and most people would have experienced multiple periods of severe undernutrition during their lifetimes. . . . The hillside was rocky, so that any person who slipped and fell ran a high risk of an injury such as a broken bone. Whether there was merely a scrape, a laceration, or a compound fracture after such a fall, the break in the skin would leave the person at risk of infection. Without sophisticated modern health care, an infection could well prove fatal, or could be serious enough to lead to other illness or permanent damage. . . . For women, the leading cause of death was complications arising from pregnancy and childbirth." Women unable to bear children would have lived longer. Of course, in a controlled courtroom, under metaphysical cross-examination, bodies might be convicted, by a jury of their peers, of being merely accidental encasements of untouchable immortal souls. Even if its testimony remains unheeded, however, the body remembers otherwise.

farming, gathering wild nuts, grains, tubers, and berries, living hand-to-mouth—with too little left over to trade.[13] In such a world those who can, work every available hour, mindful of the death members of the household in irregular intervals will before long fail to avert. Very small children, the elderly, the sick, and the injured do what little they can—or simply abide.

The epics empires tell (about themselves) tend to disregard the stories of those who have negligible front-loaded imperial potency.[14] Empires cast for themselves visions of a virile ancestry, long- and aristocratically well-lived. Their noble imagination is not hospitable to peasant populations liable to be dead by the twenty-fifth year of hard life, whose "elders" are lucky to make age thirty.[15] Acknowledged or not, however, once we were all strangers, slaves, brutalized peasants, motherless children, short-lived in the land of Egypt—or might have been.[16] We have all been and will again one day be as helpless as the babies human households celebrate, pray for, and mourn. Our memories and hopes rely on helplessness, especially on babies, who grant to a household and its traditions a kind of conditional immortality.[17] It is because babies are born and are raised to their childbearing years that we don't simply fade away. Even in the most sterile, technology- and expertise-saturated medical center, every day a newborn emerges from a birth canal is as momentous as it is ephemeral. Its heavy delicacy keeps it from floating to those strata of the moneyed West where people can buy their way to an anxious, oddly self-promoted, sporadic imperviousness to significant times of joy and danger. Those who spend their days and nights too closely together to hide from their flesh—working beside each other on a common land all day, sleeping on mats beside each other in a common room all night—do not have to be told of the weightiness of an approaching childbirth. And yet, when every young daughter or son in a poor village is more likely to be dead than alive at the end of the coming year, everything

---

13. Ibid., 112.

14. Cf. *The Odyssey*.

15. Berquist, *Controlling Corporeality*, 63, 114: "Rural life would have been the experience of at least ninety percent of the people throughout the period represented by the Hebrew Bible.... Their rural culture involved such hard living that the age of twenty would have begun one's elder years.... Life expectancy and life cycles for rural persons would have stayed mostly constant for Israelites from 1300 or 1200 BCE to at least 600 BCE."

16. In some cases, of course, that last phrase is unnecessary.

17. That is much of the reason for the horror of God's command to Abraham to slaughter his son, Isaac. The journey to the mountain in Moriah was a martyr's journey.

depends on early and frequent pregnancies. When the lucky members of a household have two dozen years on this earth, it might be just barely possible for parents to raise more than one of their children to puberty.[18]

A body cut or broken open by injury or childbirth—a body with compromised integrity—is weakened, often imperiled. The bodies we care for, we protect. We struggle variously in our various ages and places to keep them safe from rupture. It is because they are important to us that we make their boundaries clear and address and correct whatever compromises them, keeping the outside from breaking inside. And so, we make distinctions between what and under what conditions they and we may and may not contact. As these distinctions intensify and formalize, touching the wrong person or thing may well be taken to constitute a kind of breach of security calling for quick repair. Thus one is perhaps only in the most prescription-laden manner to touch a corpse or a diseased body or even a body differently gendered or the body of one or another species. However normal or healthy it may seem to persons naturalized elsewhere, even an oozing or seeping of fluids might be taken to call a body's integrity into question.[19]

Once the boundaries of a body are surveyed and hedged in, guards are posted at points of entry. Since particular bodies are incorporated in more complex wholes, the transgression of one entails other transgressions as well. Just as a cut in one's skin is a portal through which infectious agents might enter, so also an insecure national or more local border could well endanger a larger national or familial body.[20] There is in this way an "inside" to the household or nation, as well as an "outside." Their boundaries are no less vigilantly to be protected.[21] As a small nation, for example,

---

18. Berquist, *Controlling Corporeality*, 114: "In many cases [in ancient Israel], a fourteen-year-old man would marry a fourteen-year-old woman, who would die in childbirth when they were both twenty. The man might then marry another fifteen-year-old woman, and they would have another set of children before they both died five years later. This might leave two or three or four children as orphans, to be raised by distant relatives. Some of the children would never have known their parents, but only the community that raised them. Almost no one would know their grandparents."

19. Ibid., 19.

20. Ibid., 20–22.

21. Ibid., 44: "In early Israel . . . the focus was upon the household. . . . The family is like a body. It needed integrity, wholeness, and productive functioning to survive. . . . Each family had to work hard to survive, and their struggles were crucial to the survival of each individual. . . . For Israel, especially in its earlier times and in its rural locations, family and body were almost coextensive." By the time Israel's monarchy was instituted

imagines itself as a weak and vulnerable person facing larger, aggressive neighbors,[22] its identity comes to be delineated by a darker line. Other nations, from which it would thus consider itself antagonistically excluded, would by confrontational proximity mark it off quite clearly as a distinct and separate unity, its vulnerability to invasion intensifying its difference and hardening its borders.

However, precisely because a social body is a network of connections between particular bodies that are never entirely closed, outsiders cannot be kept simply out.[23] Bodies are permeable; others get in.[24] Try as they might, the task for those whose duty it is to keep the body safe is not the impossible one of eliminating, but at best minimizing and controlling boundary crossings so that patterns of interaction will be managed and possible disruptive contact avoided.

the nation took on a much more important role. Not only the household, but the nation, too, came more and more to be understood as a social body. Further, the king came to be imagined as the embodiment of the nation. David's violation of Bathsheba's body and of Uriah's household had serious, larger negative consequences. By tearing open those integrities, the integrity of the kingdom itself was undone. Berquist, *Controlling Corporeality*, 49–50.

22. Ibid., 43: "Just as the whole body was important to Israel, so was the whole society. Israel's ideology reflected its self-identity as a marginal and minority group within a hostile world." Cf. 44–45.

23. Exclusive national identity grew in importance as Israel found itself awash with Hellenistic configurations of power after the conquests of Alexander the Great. Ezra, Nehemiah, Proverbs, Sirach, and the Wisdom of Solomon work to make Israel's difference from other nations as inviolable as possible. See Berquist, *Controlling Corporeality*, chs. 5 and 7.

24. Ibid., 135–36: "Bodies and households are constantly growing. Although the body appears to have integrity and solidity, it is a permanently permeable structure. Through the lungs, the body takes in air and exchanges oxygen with carbon dioxide. Through digestion, the body intakes food and gains nourishment that energizes further activity. The body's cells die and are flushed away, and are rebuilt with new molecules constructed from what the body takes in from its environment. After the transmission of semen from man to woman across the limits of the body's boundaries, pregnancy allows the growth of a new body and the formation of a new generation; the birth of that new body also requires the transgression of bodily integrity. Likewise, the inviolable household protects itself from outsiders but brings in women from outside in order to keep itself alive, and to move itself into the next generation by bringing new members into its midst through procreation."

There is no "social body" in the abstract. We would do well to use the phrase in proximity with one or another large or small historic gathering of households. When we habitually sort particular flesh and blood human beings into broader and more useful categories, it is easy to forget them, to forget that they work and eat alongside each other on the land their and others' ancestors cared for or despoiled. Artfully formulaic stories routinely garner good box office receipts, but formulaic stories "[try] so hard to forget one particular thing that [they end] up forgetting everything else."[25] As hard as we try, nobody lives formulaically. The question from which we so often heartlessly shrink is how to remember "one particular thing," how to speak of a people not with a timeless essence, but with place and time, a transient season, footsteps, perhaps left across a wilderness on the backside of a promise given but never had.

Let us once more say that as bodies on this earth we take each step, breath, and bite as children vulnerable to collapse, asphyxiation, and starvation; that as bodies we carry the dense, dry, dark earth out of which we have been sculpted; that as long as we heed without covetousness the promise of another step, breath, or bite, there is a future for these mortal bodies that mortality alone cannot circumscribe. Let us speak, as we have been speaking all along, of the ancient Hebrews, a loose, if sometimes resolute, gathering of households, a precarious "nation" of peasants and priests, one of the least likely ancient "nations" to be remembered millennia later in the era of the border obsessed nation-state. Let us speak, i.e., of Jesus of Nazareth, called "rabbi" and "Messiah," in whose Hebrew body the ancient Hebrews are remembered.

> In ancient Israel, the priesthood formed one of the key social institutions for managing and maintaining the human body. Through religious practices, the priests instructed Israelites in matters of nutrition, promulgated a legal code that regulated sexual behavior, adjudicated between disputes involving bodily injuries, inspected the body for disease and abnormality, and assessed the economic value of the body. In these ways and more, priests paid attention to the bodies of individuals in an effort to maintain their health and wholeness, and at the same time the priesthood formed an important part of Israelite society that served to maintain the

---

25. Bolaño, *Amulet*, 86.

social body of the people. The priesthood kept people whole, at individual, household, and social levels.[26]

Even those ancient Israelite laws that may seem to be impractical and arbitrary, empty abstractions simply to be memorized and thoughtlessly "obeyed," were written as prescriptions for well-being.[27] The work of the priests of ancient Israel (when time on earth was "short and miserable") was among other things a kind of triage and emergency medicine for the welfare of a people who did not have to slow its pace to remember that it was bodies all the way down.[28]

It would be a poor reading of their holy texts, however, were one to imagine these ancient priests as health care professionals, their backs turned to the sky all day long as they diagnose and bind up the afflicted. Whatever critical-historical reconstructions might make them out to be, in their holy texts they are . . . priests. They attend to the God by whose power and mercy they and their people have been granted a future. Priests care for the people, because *God* cares for the people and has *commanded them* to concur. Yet the God of these texts is far from innocuous. God is a *dangerous* caregiver, unpredictable, immodestly different both from all other gods and from the chosen themselves—demanding non-calculative, even non-representational obedience:

---

26. Berquist, *Controlling Corporeality*, 165–66. For the significance of the phallus for "wholeness," see 35–37. The following text shows how much a variation from normative masculine "wholeness" is thought to obstruct one's access to the holy God: "The Lord spoke to Moses, saying: Speak to Aaron and say: No one of your offspring throughout their generations who has a blemish may approach to offer the food of his God. For no one who has a blemish shall draw near, one who is blind or lame, or one who has a mutilated face or a limb too long, or one who has a broken foot or a broken hand, or a hunchback, or a dwarf, or a man with a blemish in his eyes or an itching disease or scabs or crushed testicles. No descendant of Aaron the priest who has a blemish shall come near to offer the Lord's offerings by fire; since he has a blemish, he shall not come near to offer the food of his God. He may eat the food of his God, of the most holy as well as of the holy. But he shall not come near the curtain or approach the altar, because he has a blemish, that he may not profane my sanctuaries; for I am the Lord; I sanctify them" (Lev 21:16–23). See Hentrich, "Masculinity and Disability in the Bible," 82–84.

27. This is not to deny that law became from time to time quite ideological. The critique of the prophets makes it clear that it did.

28. Their law was spoken by the throat and tongue, heard by the ear, eaten by the mouth, taken into the belly, and to be written on the heart, after all. Further, priests had among their tasks the ritual securing of the order of the cosmos and of the alignment of the people with it. Their work was done in this world. Berquist, *Controlling Corporeality*, 167–73.

> You shall not make for yourself an idol, whether in the form of anything that is in heaven above, or that is on the earth beneath, or that is in the water under the earth. You shall not bow down to them or worship them; for I the Lord your God am a jealous God, punishing children for the iniquity of parents, to the third and fourth generation of those who reject me, but showing steadfast love to the thousandth generation of those who love me and keep my commandments.... Hear, O Israel: The Lord is our God, the Lord alone. You shall love the Lord your God with all your heart, and with all your soul, and with all your might. (Deut 5:8-10, 6:4-5)[29]

The God whom they serve cannot be contained either in laws or in the means by which laws are put to work.[30] And so, even as they adhere most tightly to a prescribed course of obedience to the dictates of God, the priests lead the people in the performance of an imagination that moves through and beyond the identity- and integrity-forming opposition between inside and outside, whole and broken, kindred and stranger, male and female, is and is not.[31] The imagination they perform, however detailed its script, defers to a mystery before whom they and (through them) the entire world are to bow in hope and thanksgiving, to whom all words, thoughts, and deeds are to yield in parabolic doxology.[32]

The strictness of the demand placed upon priests in particular has everything to do with the difference between the ways even of the faithful and the ways of the holy God. Their work places them in fact in quite serious peril.[33] Priests are the point of least insulated contact with God and

---

29. This is such a provocative text! God, of course, appears so unfair, so cruel, punishing those not yet born for their parents' and grandparents' violations of some law. And yet everything gets thrown into uncertainty when it is realized how very elusive God is here. This text asks us to wonder . . . to consider what it might be to love—and to love with everything—a God who cannot be represented.

30. That this breaks through precisely as the law is being laid down is particularly provocative.

31. Cf. Brueggemann, *Theology of the Old Testament*, 195: "The sacrificial system of ancient Israel attests both to the generous availability of Yahweh to Israel and the ominous, unapproachable holiness of Yahweh. The sacrificial system mediates between availability and holiness.... [This] attestation on Israel's part has contemporary pertinence in the practice of faith that must push behind moral resolution to the enigmatic, where Yahweh's holiness is faced in all of its ominous, generous, enigmatic reality."

32. Even rage. Thus the book of Job.

33. For example: "Now Aaron's sons, Nadab and Abihu, each took his censer, put fire in it, and laid incense on it; and they offered unholy fire before the Lord, such as he had

God will not be managed. Israel has been freely created as a people by this God—not as a payment for goods received, but as a gift. The rain, sun, earth, and growth that yield grain in their fields, nuts and berries on hillsides, pasture land for flocks and wild game come by God's good gratuitous pleasure, even if daily life is both uncertain and painful.[34] Israel knows its neighbors' gods and priests to be attached to a symbolic logic of wealth and of political and military might. Their images of silver and gold signify the coercive, acquisitive power kings and armies have at their disposal and the means by which they unleash it. The God of Israel, on the other hand—free in relation to "graven images"—*gives*. Israel is to live vis-à-vis *this* God and thus differently than their neighbors—to sacrifice, to release, to love—even if doing so disrupts the constructs that maintain the security of its households.[35]

The unmitigated holiness of the God who never stops freely creating these people, the ungeneralizable particularity of God and therefore of God's chosen, keeps them moving. Although God is indeed understood to have a restoring shalom in store for the children of Abraham, to be concerned to reinstate their integrity when it is ruptured,[36] the radical differ-

---

not commanded them. And fire came out from the presence of the Lord and consumed them, and they died before the Lord. Then Moses said to Aaron, 'This is what the Lord meant when he said, "Through those who are near me I will show myself holy, and before all the people I will be glorified."' And Aaron was silent" (Lev 10:1–3).

34. Or precisely because it was.

35. Belo, *Materialist Reading of the Gospel of Mark*, 51, 52: "In contrast to such *signifiers* [of silver and gold], the absence of *images* of Yahweh and the remembrance of the story of his strength show the preponderance in Israel of the principle of *gift*. . . . 'Listen, Israel: Yahweh our God is the one Yahweh. You shall *love* Yahweh your God with all your heart, with all your soul, with all your strength' (Deut. 6:4–5). To *love* is to *give*; in the terminology of Bataille, to love is to consume and to lose. To steal and kill, on the other hand, is to be in *debt*, or, in Bataille's terminology, to be cursed and destroyed."

36. Wholeness is perhaps more ambiguous than it might at first seem. Olyan, *Disability in the Hebrew Bible*, 79: "Although utopian texts function to exalt Yhwh through his saving and transformative acts, they also tend to stigmatize disabled persons in a number of ways: by eliminating their disabilities entirely in the envisioned utopia, suggesting that disabilities have no place in a model world; by suggesting that disabled persons require Yhwh's special intervention to mitigate the marginalizing effects of their disabilities, thereby allowing their inclusion; by making devaluing comparisons (e.g., of disabled persons to a desert); by the deployment of stigmatizing binary discourses (e.g., that of shame); and by associating disabled persons with other stigmatized and marginalized groups (e.g., the poor, the afflicted) and with undesirable traits and conditions to be left behind in the ideal future in some cases, to be perpetuated in others (e.g., weakness, vulnerability, immobility, dependence, feminization [of males], and divine rejection)."

ence between God and every creature means that it is never enough for them to have Abraham as their father. As long as Israel wrestles with God, its identity will not harden, its center of gravity will not settle down in itself, i.e., it will in a certain sense be blessed with a limp. It remains the people who had been homeless, Passover children who even in the Promised Land perform the memory of homelessness. And though it is in no sense a kind of principle by which uniformity of narrative is guaranteed, the particular hospitality to which the people are summoned promises that their bodies/body will not remain intact. God specially elects ruptured bodies at crucial moments in Israel's stories just often enough to prevent the pursuit of happiness from becoming an *archē* upon which everything settles.

It is always a mistake to describe the leaders of ancient Israel as "heroes"[37] in any straightforward way, as if they were men of inherent power and ability.[38] It is not any of them or the nation as such and in itself which has the potency to make a better world, which has been invested with the seeds, fertile soil, and atmosphere for "flourishing." When Abraham's children love the God who loves them, the nation's boundaries yield to a not yet determined future, like a body opening to a lover who will neither fill nor sadden[39] her, like a body opening to give birth to a child who will neither leave nor forsake her. Tamar, Rahab, Ruth, and Bathsheba are not simply random characters in a collection of patriarchal hero legends.[40] They are—in a precise, but forgotten sense—accidental dissidents. They are where the surface of the national body opens.[41] Four women remembered,

37. *Oxford English Dictionary*, s.v. "hero, *n*.": "A name given (as in Homer) to men of superhuman strength, courage, or ability, favoured by the gods; at a later time regarded as intermediate between gods and men, and immortal. The later notion included men of renown supposed to be deified on account of great and noble deeds, for which they were also venerated generally or locally; also demigods, said to be the offspring of a god or goddess and a human being; the two classes being to a great extent coincident."

38. Hentrich, "Masculinity and Disability in the Bible," 77: "Contrary to its original meaning . . . the alleged hero in the Hebrew Bible is often described as somewhat 'unheroic,' almost too human. The reason is that the power and might of the [*gibbor*] does not lie within the hero himself, but is rooted entirely in YHWH who lets the hero partake in it. . . . One example of such an anti-hero is Moses himself. When called upon by YHWH to guide the Israelites out of Egypt, he refers to his stuttering and slow speech as reasons why he would not be qualified for the job of hero (Exod 4:10). Nevertheless, YHWH insists that he rely on God's power to succeed in his task."

39. *Oxford English Dictionary*, s.v. "sad, *adj.*, *n.*, and *adv.*": "Sadden" is from "the same Indo-European base as classical Latin *sat*, *satis* enough, *satur* satisfied, full."

40. Cf. Matt 1.

41. Women always problematize and complicate ideologies of seamless familial and national borders. Some do so more than others.

among countless forgotten women, four women whose guarded doorways open to a stranger. It is to a "not-yet" that they give themselves when they bear their children, to a perhaps distant future of a distant child who will have lived and died long after they and everyone they know have returned to dust. "Israel" is unmade and made in them—in the abandoned woman who seduces her dead husband's father; the harlot who betrays her people to spies; the poor alien, childless widow attached to a poor alien, childless widow; the wife who succumbs to the seductions of the man who murders her husband—i.e., "Israel" is the mother of a child nestled in a little basket sealed with bitumen and pitch, released into the waters of the great river, the child in whom one day there will be no more male and female, native or foreigner, slave or free. "Israel" is this anointed child, too.

> Abraham was the father of Isaac, and Isaac the father of Jacob, and Jacob the father of Judah and his brothers, and Judah the father of Perez and Zerah by Tamar, and . . . Salmon the father of Boaz by Rahab, and Boaz the father of Obed by Ruth, and Obed the father of Jesse, and Jesse the father of King David. And David was the father of Solomon by the wife of Uriah . . . and Jacob the father of Joseph the husband of Mary, of whom Jesus was born, who is called the Messiah. (Matt 1:2–3, 5–6, 16)

The difficulty of life in early Israel did not diminish for most people living in the region by the time the New Testament was written.[42] Power structures were more clearly defined. The ruling class effectively owned all the land under its authority.[43] Except for a very few merchants, the inhabitants of villages lived in poverty, many little better than slaves. By far the largest number of them were peasants, people bought and sold, like farm animals, with the land they were compelled to work, often literally to death.[44] In ad-

---

42. Riley, *River of God*, 173, 175, 178: "Most people then lived but one or two droughts or crop failures away from severe hunger and even starvation. Even without the dubious reliability of nature, the depredations of tax farmers, bandits, and military campaigns had devastating effects on food supplies. . . . In Palestine during the two and a half centuries from Alexander the Great to the advent of Roman rule (63 B.C.E.), there were nearly two hundred military campaigns. Until the reign of Augustus, the Romans were continuously at war for nearly two centuries."

43. Herzog, *Parables as Subversive Speech*, 59, 61.

44. Ibid., 63–64: "[The] goal of the aristocracy was to push exploitation to the limit

dition to peasants there were "the unclean and the degraded" whose work forced them to engage in activities or make contact with materials others regarded as "offensive or unclean." Now untouchable, too, they were excluded from the rest of the population. "[They] were people with nothing left to sell but their bodies or their animal energies, and they 'were forced to accept occupations which quickly destroyed them.'"[45] And then there were "the expendables." In times of great economic distress it was not uncommon for households to abandon some or all of their children to claw out their own survival any way they could. These children hired themselves out as day laborers or begged on the street. In desperation, they easily turned to crime, joining bands of thieves, living hopelessly until they were hunted down and killed.[46]

Whatever else we might insist that the little three-letter word means, "God" resounds particularly well when—from under the heel of the beast, pressed down as beasts always are by the weight of their provisions for a negotiable future—prayers for salvation tear out of the bellies and throats of "expendables": "God, Creator of Israel and of the world, rain fire down from heaven!" "God, Creator of Israel and of the world, save your people!"[47]

As long as there is time, it may be that there is the prospect of miraculous intervention for those who are not otherwise long for this world. And miracles do happen. The lame walk, the mute speak, slaves are set free, and slumdogs become millionaires—however rarely. Such miracles do not annihilate those they benefit. They change them, certainly; but not from "are" to "are not" or "are not" to "are." The slumdog-become-millionaire is an unfinished story. His early chapters are there to be read, adding bounce in fact to the steps of his celebratory dance—and of hers and theirs. His last

---

in order to maximize their yield. . . . At times the burden of tribute was so great that it entailed the deaths of the older and more infirm members of peasant households."

45. Ibid., 65.

46. Ibid., 65–66: "The presence of expendables was the inevitable outcome of a system driven by unbridled greed. As the elites squeezed the dwindling resources of their peasant base, they forced households to exile their children into the most degrading and lethal form of poverty. For the expendables, life was brutal and brief; characteristically, they lasted no more than five to seven years after entering this class, but [the numbers of this class] . . . were constantly being replenished from the classes of peasants, artisans, merchants, and the unclean and degraded immediately above it." One might think of the chief protagonists of the film *Slumdog Millionaire*.

47. See Rev 19:1 and 20:9; cf. Isa 43.

chapters are yet to be written.[48] "Once I was blind, but now I see!" Yet what *will* I see?

Not everyone who could use it, however, is miraculously healed. Indeed, what would healing signify to one whose time is up? How is one to be made whole, when "it is finished"? When there is no more slack, when every attempt at resuscitation has long since failed, when the pronouncement "I am" comes at last no longer to be premature, when there are no more new days, weeks, or years for plot twists or punch lines, how is one who has died, e.g., mutilated, to be made whole again—without being turned into somebody else, a story with a different plot and characters? Not only that. Though as long as a human body draws breath, great changes may indeed occur, it may also be unkind in some cases blatantly to hold out the prospect of *too* great a change among even the living. Before he dies, a certain man may spend decades disfigured or poor or paralyzed or emotionally scrambled or intellectually deficient or unable to look in a mirror without debilitating shame—or his children may. For what does he hope, when he cannot hope to be made—or for them to be made—whole?

And what is it to be made "whole"? Who is in charge of that determination, and to what end?[49] How does "relapse" or "recurrence" figure in the history of healing—or "rehabilitation," "assimilation," "opportunity," and "promotion"? It is one thing for a paralytic to take up his bed and walk through a world in which paralytics don't last long and in the meantime drain scarce resources from their already imperiled households. It is another thing for the paralytic to rise and walk through a dreamscape of lonely, by no means autonomous or flawless human beings—who pretend that some day they will be and in the meantime will not countenance anyone

48. The punch line of *Slumdog Millionaire* may or may not be "it is written." At the very least, however, the story puts its weight on that line and it swells to significance by the story's "end." It is tempting for freedom-loving Westerners to roll their eyes and mutter "fatalism!" And technically, I suppose, it is that. However, this is not a fatalistic tale in the way we ordinarily use that term. Otherwise, there could not be dancing as the end credits roll. In any case, what is written is yet to be read and reading is always a kind of rewriting.

49. Betcher, *Spirit and the Politics of Disablement*, 6–7: "Because this politics of representing certain others as disabled often pulls the shades over conscience by cloaking 'the weak and helpless' in pity and consequently inflecting the subject's actions as obviously benevolent, it has been easy to ignore the fact that the representation of disablement has been and continues to be a template for the colonizing interests of empire and must be considered a form of 'anti-conquest rhetoric.' Disablement, too, belongs among the gallery of representations that imperial forces use to rationalize as innocent, even compassionate, their own imperial interests and colonizing actions."

pretending otherwise. In a well-heeled, "benevolent" world in which to be paralyzed (or blind or lame) is not often to have been given a death sentence, envisioning "healing" comes easily to focus its gaze where "dignity," "social mobility," "satisfaction," "fitness," and "esteem" mean more than "life," "work," "food," "kindness," or "hospitality." It is difficult within the purview of self-consciously mainstream America for "the blind [to] receive their sight, the lame [to] walk, the lepers [to be] cleansed, the deaf [to] hear, the dead [to be] raised, the poor [to] have good news brought to them" and concurrently for "the oppressed [to] go free."[50] A miraculous healing is a spectacular event. The principalities and powers of this world have a place for spectacles and great skill at harnessing the potency spectacles generate. Slumdog Millionaires become celebrities—and hit the Talk Show Circuit.[51]

In the meantime amputees, burn victims, the blind, or those suffering from PTSD are imagined by aspirants to media ideality as occupying their time in a kind of combination doctor's office waiting room and Reality Show set. Will they be voted off the island? Will he be "The Biggest Loser"? Will her skin grafts take? Will he effectively re-narrate his traumatic past? Will they find funding for nice, life-like prostheses? We are nurtured in a world of investment and return, profit and loss, pay-scales, benefits-packages, and retirement funds, i.e., disinfected net worth. *Of course*, "dignity" strikes us as more "valuable" than and thus preferable, say, to forgiveness or sacrifice or the patience once characterized as "long-suffering." We are nurtured in a world that aspires to be populated by free-standing well-adjusted individuals, a world that has been so beguiled by its aspirations that it has systematically blocked the paths by which human bodies may fall laughing or weeping into one another's arms. *Of course*, failure first to take care of one's able telegenic self strikes us as pathological—as pathological as sparing the cost of access to the Halls of Power, the weight of whose towers of nervous functionaries compresses the bedrock upon which great cities languish in a Promethean nightmare. Perhaps it *is* pathological—and perhaps there is more hope in pathology than we are likely to admit in a midday conversation.

---

50. See Luke 7:17–23 and 4:16–21.

51. Cf. Betcher, *Spirit and the Politics of Disablement*, ix: "When Christianity mistakes its own ancient analytic of world brokenness as having something still to do with me and my body, treating my body as if it were defective and needed to be made whole, it substitutes the standards of Fitness World™ for the visitation of passion, which would unhinge us from the values of 'the society of the spectacle' (Debord)."

After Crucifixion

And yet since long before the spoken word of Plato came to hold the Western world captive, integrity—wholeness, well-being, soundness, balance, symmetry, unity, identity—has been taken for beauty itself. We know intuitively that integrity is of all things most to be desired, indeed what is always already desired in all things. "If an artist were to paint a bloody wound admirably, the sight of the wound would strike me, but it would not be art."[52] And what mania would or even could stir in us a yearning for the pathetic—the diseased, the corrupt, the anomalous, the defective, the insane, the weak, the deficient, the sick, the dying, the grotesque, the misshapen, the misbegotten, the misfit, the mutilated, the poor, the barren, the dishonored? It would be as scandalous as yearning for—as being ecstatically agape before—crucifixion . . . as if before a new star in the night sky.[53]

Life is hard, even for those who go to pains to prove it otherwise. For some there never has been ease of transit across fields of labor, and never will be. When you are an alien or the rhythms of your extraordinary anatomy or physiology have been systematically excluded from the design and construction of the paths that cut between and through villages and cities, obstacles to safe passage are randomly thrown up and absurdly reshuffled.[54] When in a strange land you are private property, a work animal—and also blind, lame, or in late pregnancy—and then are told with great authority that God, the particular God who set your ancestors free from Egyptian bondage, is coming to turn *you* loose, to set *you* out to cross the great, untamed, open expanse to the Promised Land, you will not know how to take such news in. What kind of voice prophesies deliverance without the imposition of ability? Some people simply cannot overcome some things. What happens, though, when "insurmountable" seems to have lost its authority?

> For thus says the Lord: Sing aloud with gladness for Jacob, and raise shouts for the chief of the nations; proclaim, give praise, and

---

52. Tolstoy, *What Is Art?*, 105.

53. See *Oxford English Dictionary*, s.v. "yearn, v.1" and "yere, v.": "Etymology: . . . With Germanic *ger-* . . . to long, desire, have pleasure, are probably allied . . . *cháris* favour, grace." Schmemann, *Eucharist*, 137–38: "In [love] each person mysteriously obtains the power to 'yearn [*epipothéō*] . . . with the affection [*splágchnon*] of Christ Jesus' (Phil. 1:8) and to be witness to and bearer of this love in the world." "Agape" above, of course, is an English/Greek pun.

54. Cf. Krieger and Morrison, "People Are Strange."

> say, "Save, O Lord, your people, the remnant of Israel." See, I am going to bring them from the land of the north, and gather them from the farthest parts of the earth, among them the blind and the lame, those with child and those in labor, together; a great company, they shall return here. With weeping they shall come, and with consolations I will lead them back, I will let them walk by brooks of water, in a straight path in which they shall not stumble; for I have become a father to Israel, and Ephraim is my firstborn. (Jer 31:7–9)[55]

When in a strange, inhospitable land which functions by the force of a presumed normality to which you do not conform—yourself an anomaly, an enemy of the people or cruelly maimed—you are told with great authority that God, the particular God of the anomalous, is coming to admit you to the temple, you who by law cannot be admitted to the temple, you will not know how to take such news in. What kind of voice prophesies deliverance to those who may not be delivered? Some people simply may not do some things. What happens, though, when "impermissible" seems to have lost its authority?

> Thus says the Lord: Maintain justice, and do what is right, for soon my salvation will come, and my deliverance be revealed. Happy is the mortal who does this, the one who holds it fast, who keeps the sabbath, not profaning it, and refrains from doing any evil. Do not let the foreigner joined to the Lord say, "The Lord will surely separate me from his people"; and do not let the eunuch say, "I am just a dry tree." For thus says the Lord: To the eunuchs who keep my sabbaths, who choose the things that please me and hold fast my covenant, I will give, in my house and within my walls, a monument and a name better than sons and daughters; I will give them an everlasting name that shall not be cut off. And the foreigners who join themselves to the Lord, to minister to him, to love the name of the Lord, and to be his servants, all who keep the sabbath, and do not profane it, and hold fast my covenant— these I will bring to my holy mountain, and make them joyful in my house of prayer; their burnt offerings and their sacrifices will be accepted on my altar; for my house shall be called a house of prayer for all peoples. Thus says the Lord God, who gathers the

---

55. Olyan, *Disability in the Hebrew Bible*, 82, 84: "In this text, there is no radical transformation of the blind, the lame, and the others who travel with difficulty; rather, through Yhwh's initiative, even they are to be included among the returnees. . . . It is their situation and status that are transformed, allowing them to perform acts that were evidently impossible before Yhwh's intervention."

outcasts of Israel, I will gather others to them besides those already gathered. (Isa 56:1–8)[56]

When in an unwelcoming, impregnable land which functions by the force of a virtue to which you cannot conform—yourself an open wound, the point of entry for adversaries and aliens—you are told with great authority that God, the particular God of the vulnerable, is coming to exalt you, you who by definition cannot be exalted, you will not know how to take such news in. What kind of voice prophesies a future to and for those who have no future? Some people simply cannot do some things. What happens, though, when "impossible" seems to have lost its authority?

Hope stands at the door, *dieser unheimlichste aller Gäste*,[57] no place to lay his head, a gift not to be owned . . . and knocks. To open to him, to dine with him ("this is my body"), is with him—walls and roof blown away behind (Luke 9:57–62)—"to witness," as he witnessed (Rev 11:7–11). Hope spreads, like a beam of sunlight across a vast, darkened room from a crack high above its cold stone floor.[58] Hope exceeds.[59] Hope aches not for

---

56. Ibid., 85: The text "does not envision the normalization of the eunuch through the efforts by Yhwh to mitigate any marginalizing effects of his physical disability. . . . Rather, it is the cultic proscription of the eunuch, based on a broad reading of Deuteronomy 23:2, that is to be eliminated in the future utopia, allowing the eunuch to participate fully in the rites of Yhwh's temple, even if he cannot sire children. . . . In short, the text rejects any stigma . . . as wholly illegitimate and unwarranted." Brueggemann, *Theology of the Old Testament*, 524–25: "Yahweh, belatedly, appears here to accept Israel's enemies as legitimate candidates for membership in the covenant. . . . [The] move beyond judgment and nullification toward new national possibility is rooted in Yahweh's freedom, freedom to restore an enemy. . . . There is also . . . a predilection toward forgiveness, restoration, and rehabilitation, propelled by an old and enduring positive concern and not undercut even by resistance and rebellion." Cf. Mark 11:15–17 where Jesus "cleanses" the temple while appealing to this passage.

57. This is the way Nietzsche speaks of nihilism, of course. Nietzsche, *Der Wille Zur Macht*, 7. The adjective *unheimlichste* is reasonably translated as "uncanniest"; the whole sentence (*Der Nihilismus steht vor der Tür: woher kommt uns dieser unheimlichste aller Gäste?*) as "Nihilism stands at the door: whence comes this uncanniest of all guests?" Nietzsche, *Will to Power*, 7. *Unheimlichste* is a derivative of *Heim*, the German relative of the English "home." The negative prefix indicates that here before the door stands the guest who is most un-at-home. The English "uncanny," a word the *Oxford English Dictionary* finds to have been used first in the seventeenth century, derives from the English "can." Thus it signifies that which undoes ability, know-how. *Oxford English Dictionary*, s.v. "uncanny," "un-1," "canny." The suggestion above is that hope is uncannier yet, *unheimlicher noch*.

58. Perhaps between panes of stained glass into Chartres Cathedral.

59. I remember the stone image at Chartres of Christ with a bird superimposed

a healer, but a caregiver, not health, wholeness, integrity, but a cure—sanctity, justice, splendor, ecstasy, righteousness. It is despair that would lock every window, draw every curtain; i.e., close every circle. Hope is the joyful wound of the eschatos, not the meeting of the need for a telos.

When in the Lukan narrative the peasant girl Mary hears the voice of the angel Gabriel before her door and then receives the Holy Spirit through it, when she trembles under the shadow of God at the open end of a momentous history, she is not the first to be called upon to give herself to the dangerous coming of God:

> After these things God tested Abraham. He said to him, "Abraham!" And he said, "Here I am." He said, "Take your son, your only son Isaac, whom you love, and go to the land of Moriah, and offer him there as a burnt-offering on one of the mountains that I shall show you." (Gen 22:1–2)
>
> Then Abraham reached out his hand and took the knife to kill his son. But the angel of the Lord called to him from heaven, and said, "Abraham, Abraham!" And he said, "Here I am." He said, "Do not lay your hand on the boy or do anything to him; for now I know that you fear God, since you have not withheld your son, your only son, from me." (Gen 22:10–12)[60]
>
> When the Lord saw that he had turned aside to see, God called to him out of the bush, "Moses, Moses!" And he said, "Here I am." Then he said, "Come no closer! Remove the sandals from your feet, for the place on which you are standing is holy ground." He said further, "I am the God of your father, the God of Abraham, the God of Isaac, and the God of Jacob." And Moses hid his face, for he was afraid to look at God. Then the Lord said, "I have observed the misery of my people who are in Egypt; I have heard their cry on account of their taskmasters. Indeed, I know their sufferings .

---

across his forehead, human beings before him. The English caption of the postcard bearing this image (available, by the way, in the cathedral's gift shop) is "God creating man while thinking of birds." On the failure of the notion of extrapolation to point to hope, cf. Moltmann, *Future of Creation*, 41–58.

60. Though one may question the reading of this text by Kierkegaard's pseudonym, Johannes de silentio, surely he is right that as devastating as a loving father's obeying God's command to sacrifice his one and only beloved child of promise, the command at the last minute to restrain the force of the act of sacrifice in full swing would in the absence of an incalculable marvel be more devastating still. Kierkegaard [de silentio], *Fear and Trembling*, 34–36.

> ... So come, I will send you to Pharaoh to bring my people, the Israelites, out of Egypt." (Ex 3:4–7, 10)

> Samuel was lying down in the temple of the Lord, where the ark of God was. Then the Lord called, "Samuel! Samuel!" and he said, "Here I am!" and ran to Eli. ... The Lord called again, "Samuel!" Samuel got up and went to Eli, and said, "Here I am, for you called me." ... The Lord called Samuel again, a third time. And he got up and went to Eli, and said, "Here I am, for you called me." Then Eli perceived that the Lord was calling the boy. ... Now the Lord came and stood there, calling as before, "Samuel! Samuel!" And Samuel said, "Speak, for your servant is listening." Then the Lord said to Samuel, "See, I am about to do something in Israel that will make both ears of anyone who hears of it tingle." (1 Samuel 3:3–11)[61]

> And one [seraph] called to another and said: "Holy, holy, holy is the Lord of hosts; the whole earth is full of his glory." The pivots on the thresholds [of the temple] shook at the voices of those who called, and the house filled with smoke. And I said: "Woe is me! I am lost, for I am a man of unclean lips, and I live among a people of unclean lips; yet my eyes have seen the King, the Lord of hosts!" Then one of the seraphs flew to me, holding a live coal that had been taken from the altar with a pair of tongs. The seraph touched my mouth with it and said: "Now that this has touched your lips, your guilt has departed and your sin is blotted out." Then I heard the voice of the Lord saying, "Whom shall I send, and who will go for us?" And I said, "Here am I; send me!" And he said, "Go and say to this people: 'Keep listening, but do not comprehend; keep looking, but do not understand.'" (Isa 6:3–9)

The voices of Abraham, Moses, Samuel, and Isaiah rise precariously to meet the Holy One, the Creator of Israel and of the world. It is not surprising to find that there is terror in their voices.[62] Nonetheless they respond faithfully: Abraham, silently leading his beloved son, his only guarantee of immortality, to the mountain in Moriah, his premeditated filicide halted in midcourse; Moses, an exile on the cusp of the paradigmatic event of the history of God's people, setting his face toward the Egypt from which he had fled; Samuel, a ward of the temple, yet to be the last of Israel's judges

---

61. Of course, Samuel utters his "here I am" thinking it is Eli who is speaking to him. His words to God are "speak, for your servant is listening." Nonetheless his rising from his bed and offering himself to Eli accords with his response to God once he understands who in fact is calling to him. Mary's "here am I" seems to parallel Samuel's in particular.

62. What is surprising is that it is not in Abraham's voice.

and the first of its major prophets, yet to be the instrument of God by whom Saul and David are granted authority, speaking even through his child's lips the devastating word of God; Isaiah, the slag burned out of everything in him that might yield speech, prophesying an impossible liberation of a people as faithless as he himself had been—all of them turn their living bodies to the future with hope: "Here am I!" Yet it is a peasant girl who has been called upon to be *Theotokos*, the mother of the child who will have been the capaciousness in whom the Most High is pleased to dwell; the peasant girl who not only speaks God's word, but bears it.[63] She more even than Abraham, Moses, Samuel, and Isaiah shows that the "here I am!" is no disembodied soulish "willingness," but a soulful, righteous upstanding of everything about a human being that eats, works, and prays.

> The angel said to her, "Do not be afraid, Mary, for you have found favor with God. And now, you will conceive in your womb and bear a son, and you will name him Jesus. He will be great, and will be called the Son of the Most High, and the Lord God will give to him the throne of his ancestor David. He will reign over the house of Jacob for ever, and of his kingdom there will be no end." Mary said to the angel, "How can this be, since I am a virgin?" The angel said to her, "The Holy Spirit will come upon you, and the power of the Most High will overshadow you; therefore the child to be born will be holy; he will be called Son of God.... For nothing will be impossible with God." Then Mary said, "Here am I, the servant of the Lord; let it be with me according to your word."[64] (Luke 1:30–35, 37–38)

63. And so, perhaps Mary is better understood as a new Samuel, rather than as a new Hannah. Elizabeth may be the better parallel with Hannah. See 1 Samuel 1 and Luke 1:5–17. This is not to deny the parallels between the Song of Hannah (1 Sam 2:1–10) and the Magnificat of Mary (Luke 1:46–55). The Definition of Chalcedon (451), of course, affirms that Mary is *Theotokos* "according to [Jesus Christ's] humanness [*kata tēn anthrōpotēta*]."

64. The Greek rendered in the NRSV as "Here am I, the servant of the Lord" (*idou hē doulē kuriou*) may also be translated, e.g., as "Behold, the bondslave of the Lord!" (NASB). The translation hinges on the significance in this passage and elsewhere of *idou*. The translation exemplified by the NRSV suggests a connection between this passage and certain extraordinarily important Old Testament narratives concerning the human response to the call of God in which an identical translation is often used. It is significant that the LXX has *idou egō* for what is in the NRSV translated as "here I am" (or "here am I") in Gen 22:1, 11; 1 Sam 3:4, 6, and 8; and Isa 6:8. Although Exod 3:4 has *ti estin* instead, the import of Moses' response to "the Lord" seems very much to accord with the others (and so, it too is translated as "here I am" in the NRSV). Litwak, *Echoes of Scripture in Luke-Acts*, 101: "Mary's question and Gabriel's response are comparable conceptually to

After Crucifixion

The earthiness of "womb," "virgin," "conceive," "overshadow," and "bear," the earthiness of peasants, of the girls who by the gravest of hardships will too soon become women, the earthiness of everything about this moment of the irruption of God into a first-century world of fetuses, pregnancies, blood, amniotic fluid, placentas, infant mortality, and the mortal danger of bearing children signals the earthiness of God's word. The life of God enters the body of this Mary and what grows just below her heart and lungs, to be pushed through her birth canal nine months later, is the coming of "the glory of the Lord":

> ". . . and all people shall see it together, for the mouth of the Lord has spoken." A voice says, "Cry out!" And I said, "What shall I cry?" All people are grass, their constancy is like the flower of the field. The grass withers, the flower fades; but the word of our God will stand forever. (Isa 40:5, 6, 8; cf. Luke 1:7; 3:3–6)

And yet this word stands henceforth on the two feet of a human, all too human, first-century Jewish peasant body.[65]

Jesus is pictured as a peasant among peasants in the Gospels, an itinerant preacher and wonder worker who carries constantly on his lips and hands the declaration that the Reign of God is coming, coming in particular for peasants, the unclean, and expendables. He does indeed make the sick, blind, lame, and paralyzed "whole." He does indeed raise the dead. But he does more than that, too. If it is recalled that first-century Galileans are bodies all the way down and that "sin" is an oppression, Jesus' work under that rough hewn skylight does more than restore integrity:

> And when they could not bring him to Jesus because of the crowd, they removed the roof above him; and after having dug through it, they let down the mat on which the paralytic lay. When Jesus saw their faith, he said to the paralytic, "Son, your sins are forgiven." (Mark 2:4–5)

In this moment Jesus' words embrace the paralytic and, with his friends and all the richly textured entanglements of his lifetime, lift him into the light of what is to come. Without making him whole or shaving away what might be presumed to be "inessential" to him, Jesus' words make

---

God's conversation with Moses in Exod. 3–4. . . . Luke uses intertextual echoes through framing in discourse to identify Mary, in historiographical terms, as continuing the line of heroes from Israel's past, like Moses." I am not convinced that the word *hero* is flexible enough to be applied helpfully to the people on this list, including Moses.

65. See Rogers, *After the Spirit*, 105, 109.

Thinking the Wounds of the Lamb of God

in this room an unqualified and unrestrained "Yes!" Far from "loving the sinner and hating the sin," he forgives. As every sinner in quiet moments of clarity knows, if you hate my sin, you hate me. Jesus, on the other hand, is confident that the Reign of God is of children, paralytics, and sinners. But this sin in the midst of which the paralytic is forgiven is no defect of character, no addiction, no failure of will, no deep longing for illicit pleasure—i.e., it is not what we associate with people with too many resources and too much time on their hands. The sin that afflicts the paralytic is a fist that closes around and crushes the life out of him, a fist that closes around and crushes the life out of fourteen-year-old mothers with new babies to feed, laborers who will be dead by 25, bandits who rush headlong into an unforgiving retributive system that knows how to deal with dogs who steal in order to live. Of course, those who beg and steal and use themselves up in hard labor are not "good" people. They are simply people—people who have no reason to expect a way out, who have no reason to expect more than a short and miserable life. Do they cry out for magic? No. Magic has been co-opted by the powers, too, the powers that weigh them down. Do they cry out for resurrection? Yes, that is what they cry out for, as do we, and it is good news to hear that the God who raised the friend of tax collectors and expendables from the dead has heard their cry, and ours.

It is hard to say what "resurrection" *is*. *Anastasis*, to stand up to, to stand anew, to stand toward—*that* is easy to plug into a sentence, if we are given free rein. Yet how is the word used when Jesus says to Martha, "I am the resurrection and the life. Those who believe in me, even though they die, will live" (John 11:25)? What does Jesus perform, when, though *he* dies, *he* lives? How is "resurrection" used as it informs Jesus' words to Mary, "Do not hold on to me, because I have not yet ascended to the Father" (20:17); later to a group of his disciples (just before releasing the breath of holy life on them), "Peace be with you" (19–22, 26); then to Thomas, "Put your finger here and see my hands. Reach out your hand and put it in my side. Do not doubt but believe" (27); and finally when Jesus sits with Peter on the seashore eating bread and fish and commands him to feed his lambs and sheep? What kind of thanksgiving meal is this?[66] How is Peter to

---

66. Brown, *Gospel According to John*, 2:1099–1100: "There are good arguments for finding eucharistic symbolism in the meal of John xxi. . . . [In] all the Gospels the account of the multiplication meal [of the loaves and fish] has been conformed to the account of the actions of Jesus at the Last Supper, with the result that a connection was made between the multiplication meal and the Eucharist. . . . We doubt, then, that a meal so similar to the multiplication meal could be described in John xxi without reminding the

147

feed lambs and sheep, with what bread and fish? Jesus says to Peter, "Very truly . . . you will stretch out your hands, and someone else will fasten a belt around you and take you where you do not wish to go" (21:18); and, "Follow me" (19). Is it by stretching out one's hands a certain way that one both follows Jesus and feeds his sheep and lambs? The resurrected Jesus remains in John's gospel quite obviously still the crucified Jesus. Does the resurrection of Jesus not put an end to crucifixion? Could it be that he does not suffer in order to keep us from suffering, but rather suffers in order to show us the way to and through precisely the very suffering he journeyed to and through? Could it be that when you give your body—your life, your work, your time, your hunger—as food for the hungry of the world that the ones whose "strategies for a better world" keep the hungry hungry will be glad to bring your sacrifice to fulfillment? Is this what resurrection life is? What kind of existence, what kind of ecstasy, what kind of *anastasis*, is such a resurrection? It has flesh and blood about it; soil, too—not of a Master Race, but of peasants, the unclean, and expendables. When it is remembered that we are bodies, it is easy to remember that to love is to feed and to feed is to stretch out your hands a certain way. Cruciform, nothing hidden, nothing grasped, Peter perhaps turns to everyone he meets, looks her in the eye, looks into the coming of the Reign of God and says with the quiet hospitality of a young peasant girl, "here I am!"[67]

The recorded memories of the human race have about them no shortage of rapacity. The tales we tell of our noble history, of the brave revolutions we have fought against tyrannies, of the great justice we have done by our civil and world wars, and of the thrashings we continue to give our enemies on battlefields all over the globe—these and other tales of victory weave for our children a vision of a future gained by agony (though, of course, discretion demands that we leave unsaid the soliloquial, "better theirs than ours!").

Johannine community of the Eucharist. Moreover, [there is a] resemblance between the meal in John xxi and the meal that Luke xxiv 30–31, 35 describes in the account of appearance of Jesus to the two disciples on the road to Emmaus . . . [which] is often taken as eucharistic teaching meant to instruct the community that they too could find the risen Jesus in their eucharistic breaking of the bread. . . . Certainly, in primitive iconography, meals of bread and fish (rather than bread and wine) were the standard pictorial symbols of the Eucharist."

67. Cf. Acts 3:1–10.

"Our homeland is secured," we say, "only when our forces pose a realistic threat at our borders." "The best that can be achieved," we say, "is an uneasy peace enforced, when challenged, by swift, retributive or preemptive force." This is the future we foretell. Though we would never want to leave the impression on our children that we are the rapacious ones—"*we* defend our children against the rapacity of *our enemies* after all!"—in the telling it becomes harder and harder to make out which is which (our children will ask, "are they the ones who torture or are we?").

That a different future might be told is hardly thinkable in the world we have been trained to imagine. And yet a different future *is* told:

> And I heard a loud voice from the throne saying, "See, the home of God is among mortals. He will dwell with them as their God; they will be his peoples, and God himself will be with them; he will wipe every tear from their eyes. Death will be no more; mourning and crying and pain will be no more, for the first things have passed away." . . . Then one of the seven angels . . . came and said to me, "Come, I will show you the bride, the wife of the Lamb." And in the [Spirit][68] he carried me away to a great, high mountain and showed me the holy city Jerusalem coming down out of heaven from God. . . . I saw no temple in the city, for its temple is the Lord God the Almighty and the Lamb. And the city has no need of sun or moon to shine on it, for the glory of God is its light, and its lamp is the Lamb. The nations will walk by its light, and the kings of the earth will bring their glory into it. Its gates will never be shut by day—and there will be no night there. (Rev 21:3–4, 9–10, 22–26)[69]

That there is a passage such as this among the best remembered volumes of world literature might remind us, if nothing else, that there are alternatives to our customary expectations. The calculative way we make forecasts could never yield this picture. A hope that does, gives us pause. If just for a moment, we may find ourselves imagining social, political, economic bodies interacting without anxiety. It's a good moment. Perhaps, however, we should keep ourselves in much more guarded realism and reply immediately, if politely, that this future is simply too different from ours. Frankly, once we have come back to earth, it is hard even to read it with adult seriousness. It strikes us as fantasy literature. We could no doubt find in it certain "morals" or encoded "life lessons." But to take it

---

68. See Bauckham, *Theology of the Book of Revelation*, 116.

69. Ibid., 135: "In the beginning God had planted a garden for humanity to live in (Gen 2:8). In the end he will give them a city."

more seriously than that could only interrupt everything we are about: our habits of mind, the way we manage our past and extrapolate our future. It is difficult to say what it would take for it to enter into our ordinary way of carrying ourselves into a day. It strikes us simply as too much, as promising more than it can keep. Still, as odd as it is, there is nothing naïve about this text. As tender as its images are, one would do well to forego the supposition that they are drawn as if this world were not hard. Their larger story is in fact a violent tale of persecution and judgment. To read it is in fact to be transported down a charred road into a bleak and ugly land—sinister, bloody, and terrifying.[70]

The story takes violence so seriously and pictures it so graphically that it would be quite understandable were its reader, unable for a time to wake from this nightmare, to dream of imploring the mountains of the story's landscape to lift their skirts to hide her under their rocky weight (Luke 23:30). Certainly it is a story of redemption. However, "redemption" here stands up out of the uncompromising finality of total loss. Victory comes here not *instead of* defeat, but *in* defeat.[71] The redeemer toward whom this tale leans, the one who shines brilliantly near the story's glorious end, the one who battles for the persecuted, is from its beginning a slaughtered lamb (Rev 5:6, 13:8).[72] It is a tale *of martyrs*, who wait, despite all evidence, for a *coming* redemption.[73]

---

70. Cf. McCarthy, *The Road*.

71. Bauckham, *Theology of the Book of Revelation*, 90: "The point is not that the beast and the Christians each win some victories; rather, the same event—the martyrdom of Christians—is described both as the beast's victory over them and of their victory over the beast."

72. Beale, *Book of Revelation*, 351: Rev 5:6 "is crucial to understanding how 'the Lion from the tribe of Judah, the root of David, overcame.' There is no doubt that v 6 portrays Jesus as resurrected and that the resurrection is essential to his overcoming. He conquered death by being raised from the dead. But the present victorious effect of the Lamb's overcoming resides not only in the fact that the Lamb continues to 'stand' but also in the fact that it continues to exist as a *slaughtered* Lamb, the perfect participle *esphagmēnon* ('having been slain') expresses an abiding condition as a result of the past act of being slain (like perfect tense 'crucified' in 1 Cor. 2:2)." It might be added that the Lamb is still slaughtered from the foundations of the world, even if 13:8 is to be translated as the NRSV has it.

73. Bauckham, *Theology of the Book of Revelation*, 38, 72: "Though there had been martyrdoms [in the technical sense] (2:13; 6:9-10; 16:6; 17:6), it is clear from the seven messages to the churches that persecution was only sporadic and local. But John sees that the nature of Roman power is such that, if Christians are faithful witnesses to God, then they must suffer the inevitable clash between Rome's divine pretensions and their witness

Of course, this different kind of "realism" blocks our access to the text from the other side. Contrary to our initial expectations, reading forward to chapter 21 from chapter 1 uncovers a story *so* harsh that one might wonder now what kind of poet would write it. "Surely only a sadist," we think, "would so vividly picture the blood of those crushed in a wine press rising to the bridles of horses!"[74] But there is no sadism here. The story's end is even in its beginning the promise of a reign of peace that will put all destruction behind it, perhaps even destruction as a means to that end.[75] "Surely only a pathetic heart filled with Nietzschean *ressentiment*," we think, "would so exalt the lowly and humiliate the mighty!" But there is no *ressentiment* here. Those for whom the poet most writes are certainly small and weak, slaves of negligible value to the empire that holds them in its grip.[76] Their persecutors are self-consciously noble and strong.[77] But the slaves of this story, whom armies and investors have such anxious trouble pacifying, do not cower in fear, pining for the brutal intervention of a comic book champion. They rather expect for themselves the very end that was met by their "Lord." They are counseled to set their minds on it, that on the day when their

---

to the true God. . . . The word 'witness' (*martys*) does not yet, in Revelation, carry the technical Christian meaning of 'martyr' (one who bears witness by dying for the faith). . . . But it is strongly implied that faithful witness will incur opposition and lead to death." Cf. 92–93.

74. See Beale, *Book of Revelation*, 780–84, for an account of the difficulty of interpreting Rev 14:18–20. Although he finds this to be an account of God's judgment of the unrighteous, he acknowledges the (he thinks unconvincing) reading that it points to the blood of martyrs.

75. For both Revelation's hope for the redemption of all people and its acknowledgment of the judgment and destruction that would follow their continued hard-heartedness, see Bauckham, *Theology of the Book of Revelation*, 84–88, 94–104.

76. I am thinking of Nietzsche's critique of the church as "a slave religion" that "transvalued" or "revalued" heroic ancient "values." Cf. Nietzsche, *Will to Power*, 115, 127, 242. Members of churches in the first century were by no means all literally slaves. Indeed, among the circumstances of the writing of the book of Revelation seems to be their "compromise with trade guilds and their patron deities." Beale, *Book of Revelation*, 30.

77. Their persecutors are the imperial enforcers of a divine *élan* that has from all appearances made their *civitas terrena* great. And yet they, the mighty, are threatened by little house churches, by the refusal of women to perform empty acts of devotion to and mouth empty phrases in praise of the genius of Caesar, by nonviolent adherents to the *religio* of a backwater people who themselves have disavowed them. These enforcers are no *Übermenschen*. They are functionaries, field office managers, who are more likely to be afraid of their superiors than serenely buoyed by Stoic *apatheia* and adherence to a cosmic *ratio*.

enemies come, they will simply go with them (Rev 13:9-10).[78] Awaiting the nations is not the pay-back justice of a heavenly bully. Indeed, the story is so boundlessly convivial that its hope is that even these very nations, too, will thrust their bloody hands into the waters of life and, washed clean, pass through open gates into the holy city.

This storyteller is the friend of those who are easy to kill (cf. Mark 10:15), those without an advocate among the mighty.[79] As far as their eyes can see, there is no reason at all to hope. They have worked the soil and tended their flocks and sat watch through the night over their babies' bodies trembling and burning with fever. They would not long for a "liberation" devoid of hands, backs, faces, earth, and sky. They would only recognize news as good that announced a future of bread and wine, of sisters and brothers, of strength and good work—i.e., precisely of what again and again is taken from them. Yet in this story they are invited to expect what the most connected and resourceful army of efficiency experts could by no means ever produce (Isa 43:19, Rev 21:5).[80] Its main character, the slaughtered Lamb, is not only the one who fights for them; "he has himself experienced their lot."[81] He is "the Lion of the Tribe of Judah," indeed, but only as

---

78. Bauckham, *Theology of the Book of Revelation*, 38: "[I]t is a serious mistake to suppose that Revelation opposes the Roman Empire solely because of its persecution of Christians. Rather Revelation advances a thorough-going prophetic critique of the system of Roman power. It is a critique which makes Revelation the most powerful piece of political resistance literature from the period of the early Empire." Cf. Beale, *Book of Revelation*, 28-33.

79. Bauckham, *Theology of the Book of Revelation*, 39: "There is therefore a sense in which Revelation takes a view from the 'underside of history,' from the perspective of the victims of Rome's power and glory. It takes this perspective because, if they are faithful in their witness to the true God, their opposition to Rome's oppression and their dissociation of themselves from Rome's evil will make them victims of Rome in solidarity with the other victims of Rome."

80. What Wright says of Philippians 2 is not to be said of the views of Paul alone. N. T. Wright, *Resurrection of the Son of God*, 231-32: "There is no need [according to Paul] to escape from the created order; the Messiah is its lord. Nor is there any need to escape from earth to heaven; instead, the Messiah will come from heaven to earth, to rescue his people not by snatching them away from earth but by transforming their bodies.... Though ... Philo too was capable of serious and sustained political critique of Rome ..., for him the goal of the process was always to escape from the present world order entirely.... For Paul there is much more sense of confrontation. The return of Jesus from heaven to earth, the *parousia*, was formulated ... in conscious opposition to the *parousia* of Caesar.... God's plan for the world is thus, in Paul's mind, the reality of which Caesar's dream of world domination is the parody." Cf. 348-56.

81. Collins, *Apocalyptic Imagination*, 274; cf. 22, 38, 41-42.

Thinking the Wounds of the Lamb of God

"the Lamb," who before Pilate was dumb, only as *one of* the weak, the poor, the lost, the forgotten (Rev 5, Mark 15:5, Acts 8:32).

These Lamb texts are written in the language simultaneously of mystery and of politics. The reader would be wise to learn this language, if she is to read them well, imagine with them a future that does not grow out of the past, but which comes freely to it. These texts tell of their world's *personae non gratae*, citizens of a *polis* different from Rome or Washington, DC, a *polis* advancing toward us from a future beyond the reach of our longest-range arms.[82] They tell of a power and sovereignty utterly unlike that of the nations of this world. The true hope of the world has no ground *in* the world, they say. The world cannot make or unmake the future that is coming, nor can it give it to or take it away from anyone. That is the prerogative alone of the one who is coming. Though for their violation of the weak, judgment will have come down hard on the strong, they ultimately pose no threat. Despite all their gesticulating to the contrary, they do not have power over life and death, though it may take a certain bifocal vision to recognize it. Thus these texts speak, more specifically, of a politics of bodily witness which declines the heritage of fear even when threatened with death. They speak of a politics, i.e., of martyrdom:

> Then I heard a loud voice in heaven, proclaiming, "Now have come the salvation and the power and the kingdom of our God and the authority of his Messiah, for the accuser of our comrades has been thrown down, who accuses them day and night before our God. But they have conquered him by the blood of the Lamb and by the word of their testimony [*martyrios*], for they did not cling to life even in the face of death." (Rev 12:10–11)[83]

> Let anyone who has an ear listen: If you are to be taken captive, into captivity you go; if you kill with the sword, with the sword you must be killed. Here is a call for the endurance and faith of the saints. (Rev 13:9–10)

These Lamb texts are not sedative. They call their hearers to rise up, to "testify" in a very particular way. They point to the Messiah who set his face

---

82. Bauckham, *Theology of the Book of Revelation*, 43, 44: "No writer of Scripture . . . [is] more aware of this difference [between earthly power and the power of God] than John [the Revelator]. . . . Absolute power, by definition, belongs only to God, and it is precisely the recognition of God's absolute power that relativizes all human power."

83. Ibid., 75: "The whole verse [11] requires that the reference to 'the blood of the Lamb' is not purely to Christ's death but to the deaths of the Christian martyrs, who, following Christ's example, bear witness even at the cost of their lives." Cf. 79.

on Jerusalem (Luke 9:51). They call their hearers to a testimony that sets *its* face no less on Rome, the city of military and economic supremacy. They call their hearers to *perform* the good news. They are texts that give a name to salvation, the name of a peasant across whose resurrected body the word, "crucified," is chiseled, a salvation into whom the elect enter with a baptism that on the darkest days of trial they are given especially with their bodies to remember and thus to work and to speak.[84] The one who is coming to save, they say, is "the infinite mystery" whom we remember, whom we work, and whom we speak by letting our memories, works, and speech go—apophatically in a certain sense—out into his coming.[85] In a world where with our mothers' milk we are trained to contend for good and (against) evil by the dictates of authenticity, excellence, identity, and integrity,[86] it is dangerous

---

84. Beale, *Book of Revelation* 353: "What best explains this predominance of 'Lamb' [in the book of Revelation] and its use in place of other titles? The most plausible explanation is that John is attempting to emphasize that it was in an ironic manner that Jesus began to fulfill the OT prophecies of the Messiah's kingdom. Wherever the OT predicts the Messiah's final victory and reign, John's readers are to realize that these goals can begin to be achieved only by the suffering of the cross.... [B]elievers should remember that Christ also suffered at the hands of the world but triumphed over it. His destiny is to be theirs, if they persevere. This is why the saints are described as 'those who follow the Lamb wherever he goes' and in 14:4-5 are even likened to the lamb of Isa. 53:7-9. This identification is enhanced by the use of *spházo* ('slaughter') for the suffering of the saints and of the Lamb.... In the light of how believers overcome according to the letters, we can say that Christ himself overcame by maintaining his loyalty to the Father through suffering and finally death (cf. 1:5)." Cf. chapter 12, "The War of the Lamb," in Yoder's *Politics of Jesus*, especially 237-38: "We thus do not adequately understand what the church was praising in the work of Christ ... if we think of the cross as a peculiarly efficacious technique (probably effective only in certain circumstances) for getting one's way. The key to the ultimate relevance and to the triumph of the good is not any calculation at all, paradoxical or otherwise, of efficacy, but rather simple obedience.... The cross is not a recipe for resurrection. Suffering is not a tool to make people come around, nor a good in itself. But the kind of faithfulness that is willing to accept evident defeat rather than complicity with evil is ... aligned with the ultimate triumph of the Lamb."

85. Bauckham, *Theology of the Book of Revelation*, 45. As the suffix "*-phasis*" and related terms come in this essay to open to a great many phenomena beyond narrow "speech," one might remember the variety of ways that *prayer* (which we ordinarily associate with "narrow 'speech'") comes to take shape. For example, Miller, *They Cried to the Lord*, 50: "in ancient times as much or more than in the present, dimensions of prayer were expressed with the body and in acts, movements, and gestures as well as with words. Affective and symbolic aspects of the activity of prayer contribute to the wholeness of the 'act.'"

86. *Oxford English Dictionary*, s.v. "authentic, *adj.* and *n.*": "f. *authentía* 'original authority,' and *authéntes* 'one who does a thing himself, a principal, a master, an autocrat,' f. *auto-* self + *-hentes* ... -worker"; s.v. "excel, *v.*": "ad. F. *excelle-r*, ad. L. *excelĕre* to rise

Thinking the Wounds of the Lamb of God

to bear witness to a slaughtered lamb. A witness to a slaughtered lamb may do well to expect its oddly apophatic discourse to be met with strong disapproval.[87] It is not hard to imagine such a person being so stigmatized by disapproval that the two—witness and stigmata—come to be inseparably linked. Martyrdom, we might say, is *apophasis* that bleeds.[88]

This is by no means "apophasis" in the rigidly propositional sense, i.e., "negative" as opposed to "positive theology."[89] It is apophatic less properly, less acquisitively, more kenotically. It does not disregard kataphasis, i.e., what is "said," the discourse that gathers speech. Indeed, without the "said" of gathered speech this apophasis would have no move to make. And yet the "said" is regarded not with the proprietary eyes that would keep it safe,

---

above others, be eminent, f. *ex-* ['out,' 'forth,' 'thoroughly'] + **cellĕre* to rise high, tower, a vb. found only in compds., whose root appears in the *adj. celsus* lofty"; s.v. "identity": "ad. F. *identité* (Oresme, 14th c.), ad. late L. *identitās* (Martianus Capella, *c* 425), peculiarly formed from *ident(i)-*, for L. *idem* 'same' + *-tās*, *-tātem*: [denoting quality or condition]; s.v. "integrity" and "integer, *adj.* and *n.*": "a. L. *integer* untouched, intact, entire, f. *in-* [negation or privation] + *tag-*, *teg-*, root of *tangĕre* to touch." Cf. Col 2:20-23: "If with Christ you died to the elemental spirits of the universe, why do you live as if you still belonged to the world? Why do you submit to regulations, 'Do not handle, Do not taste, Do not touch'? All these regulations refer to things that perish with use; they are simply human commands and teachings. These have indeed an appearance of wisdom in promoting self-imposed piety, humility, and severe treatment of the body, but they are of no value in checking self-indulgence [the flesh, *tēs sarkos*]."

87. Cf. Young, *In Procession Before the World*, 2, 39, and passim.

88. Bauckham, *Theology of the Book of Revelation*, 92-93: "Does John [the Revelator] expect that, in the impending conflict with the power of the Roman Empire, all faithful Christians will suffer martyrdom? He certainly writes as though he did.... The message of the book is that if Christians are faithful to their calling to bear witness to the truth against the claims of the beast, they will provoke a conflict with the beast so critical as to be a struggle to the death . . . [that requires] that every faithful Christian be prepared to die."

89. It is not at all uncommon to find "apophatic theology" to be defined the way it is in Douglas et al., *Concise Dictionary of the Christian Tradition*, s.v. "Apophatic Theology": "A way to the knowledge of God that proceeds by negations, by saying what God is not.... It is the opposite of cataphatic theology, which proceeds by positive, rational propositions about God." Lash, it seems to me, has a much better understanding in his *Holiness, Speech and Silence*, 17: "There are not now, nor have there ever been, two theologies: one 'positive,' the other 'negative.' The negative way, the '*via negativa*,' is simply the endless and endlessly demanding *disciplining* of language and imagination which we need. Newman put it rather well.... 'We can only set right one error of expression by another. By this method of antagonism we steady our minds, not so as to reach their object, but to point them in the right direction . . . by saying and unsaying, to a positive result.'"

as it is, and bearing interest.⁹⁰ Rather it is regarded with eyes that quietly welcome the sojourner—however undocumented, however alien—who might slip across heavily guarded borders into the sovereign nation-state, the sojourner "possibility." The "said" is regarded in order to give it away to the stranger. This is the work a rich young ruler might do, were he to gather his goods in a certain way to let them go (Luke 18:18–27). It moves away (*apo-*) from speech the way work might move away from the belly that had been filled with bread. It moves away from speech the way the epiclesis—itself a gift of the Spirit it invokes—moves away from the lungs that had been filled with air. It moves otherwise than on the tracks of the vector logic of chemical reactions, the pushing motions of muscles, the yielding of resistant flaps of tissue, and the enhancement of the quality of sound in the resonance chambers of the skull and the empty spaces beyond it.⁹¹ The question is no more "what powers proper to a speaking subject can produce such speech?" than it is "what substance proper to a nutritious meal could produce such work?" The question is: "to whom are work and speech given?" Or to put it differently: "to whom do work and speech answer?"⁹² And since the come-back to this question is "the transcendent mystery of [a] God" not to be confused with "the mystification of [the] finite,"⁹³ there is no fluent transition from work and speech to the outcome to and for whom they are given. These are a work and a speech that no investment strategy will carry to their particular end—an end which remains not only an "X," but even more an "ex-" in relation to all that we have been trained to call "prior." And yet, this is an "ex-" that *comes*, an irruptive *eschaton* of yea-saying, an eschaton of redemption, an eschatos of "resurrection," i.e., of life.⁹⁴ "The slaughtered Lamb" is "the Lion of the Tribe of Judah." The witnesses to the Lion/Lamb, the Lamb/Lion, witness precisely by a work and speech that have abandoned control over their outcome.

Witness to the slaughtered Lamb occurs neither by a kind of acquiescence to brute force nor by some physiologically autonomic response in kind. It occurs neither by a monologue of opaque propositions nor by an assault of intractable logic or rhetoric. Incompliant and unashamed, a

---

90. "The eyes that fix you in a formulated phrase." Eliot, "Love Song of J. Alfred Prufrock," 5.

91. Certainly such an account is easily enough had and need not be simply discarded.

92. Cf. Levinas, "God and Philosophy," 74–75.

93. Bauckham, *Theology of the Book of Revelation*, 45.

94. *American Heritage Dictionary of Indo-European Roots*, 2nd ed., s.v. "eghs."

witness *speaks*, she announces good news, she opens her deed, but also her suggestive interpretation of it, that her crime not be too quickly stamped "SOLVED" and archived away. Noncompetitive and hospitable, a witness *works*, he gives his life, he opens not only his discourse, but also his overt performance of it, that his uppity talk not be too quickly brushed aside as the ex-pression of a psychological, religious, or philosophical pathology, some sad world-denying credulity, curved in upon itself, as credulity so often is. When by God's good pleasure it is to the slaughtered Lamb that a gentle soul bears witness, her work and speech trace a soft line of motion within the current of the eucharistic liturgy of his body. The Lamb/Lion, the Lion/Lamb, is the one whose devastation, whose death, whose crucifixion, whose headlong plummet into the abyss, marks no barrier, no contradiction to the life that is to come. The future of the witness is the future of the slaughtered Lamb. Although there are no doubt forces operating within the binary opposition, "life or death," i.e., forces with the power to consign any number of corpses to their graves, the witness to the slaughtered Lamb witnesses precisely to a life that has slipped through the fingers of binary opposition. The word for such an extraordinary life is "resurrection." To witness to the slaughtered Lamb is to have learned to see in the death dealing of the principalities and powers a kind of charade, a kind of delusion, a kind of useless, desperate resistance to the Spirit of the coming New Jerusalem of peace. In anticipation of the coming of the Holy God, the one all things are created to praise (cf. Rom 8:22–25),[95] the slaughtered Lamb carries in his scarred and glorified body the hope of the resurrection of all who with him have fallen.[96]

Though elusively "not-yet" among goods subject to seizure, resurrection comes as a "may" to cut through the necessity that would bar

---

95. Beale, *Book of Revelation* 331–32.

96. Wright, *Resurrection of the Son of God*, 201. "The real problem [for the Sadducees, who rejected the doctrine of resurrection] was that resurrection was from the beginning a revolutionary doctrine. For Dan 12, resurrection belief went with dogged resistance and martyrdom. For Isaiah and Ezekiel, it was about YHWH restoring the fortunes of [YHWH's] people. It had to do with the coming new age, when the life-giving god would act once more to turn everything upside down. . . . It was the sort of belief that encouraged young hotheads to attack Roman symbols placed on the Temple, and that, indeed, led the first-century Jews into the most disastrous war they had experienced. . . . People who believe that their god is about to make a new world, and that those who die in loyalty to [their god] in the meantime will rise again to share gloriously in it, are far more likely to lose respect for a wealthy aristocracy than people who think that this life, this world, and this age are the only ones there ever will be" (138).

the redemption-to-come from entry into the action and passion of that bodily work and speech that without regret journey close to the ground. In a newly dawning day, no post to hold in the mortal combat between "can" and "cannot," a work of peace may yet be done with neither presumption nor desperation.[97] Standing up before an in-finitely[98] opening future, one may shake off the violence of "must" and "must not" for a love that "believes all things—and yet is never deceived," "hopes all things—and yet is never put to shame."[99]

---

97. See Barth, *Evangelical Theology*, 200.
98. Cf. Levinas, "God and Philosophy," 63, 66–67.
99. These are chapter titles of Kierkegaard's *Works of Love*.

Interlude[1]

Sent Wednesday May 3rd, 2006, at 9:33 p.m.:[2]

Nate: I would say that the church is what happens when our histories are ex-propriated, and borne along solely by the historicity of Jesus of Nazareth. I would say that what it means to be "in Christ" is precisely to have one's own history dispossessed by the history of *this* one, and so given over to all that God's free grace makes of us as the history of the resurrected one. The church happens as our histories are taken up by the apocalyptic historicity of Jesus.

George: Nathan, as a lowly Bible thumper, I always need help with "theologese." Allow me to ask a stupid question—sincere, but stupid. What does this mean in more prosaic English? How do I explain this to my Sunday School class? How does one live this?

Nate: Allow me, if you will, in response to your questions, to share the story of Chuck and Molly. Stories take time. They take time to tell. They take time to write. They take time to read. And this, of course, because they take time to live.

I met Chuck and Molly when I was called to my first pastoral position at a relatively small church in a very affluent Chicago suburb. My role was to be associate minister of education, and to serve, of all people, with my father, who was (and still is) the senior pastor. I don't actually remember much about the two years I spent in that role; but while I was there, Chuck and Molly's story forever changed my life.

Chuck and Molly were in their mid-fifties. Chuck was baptized Catholic (which simply meant that he was the descendent of a Polish Christian family that immigrated to Chicago). I had learned through my father that Chuck had just a few years earlier held a seat on the Chicago Board of Trade, and was known as one of the most savvy and successful businessmen in the city. Molly, Chuck's wife, was in a wheelchair, and was severely debilitated, both mentally and physically. Molly was one of those people you looked at and just couldn't help but know that she had been

---

1. Mark 4:9: "And he said, 'Let anyone with ears to hear listen!'"
2. This conversation took place on the listserv "Wesleyans in Theological Dialogue." Both my friends George Lyons and Nate Kerr have given me permission to provide it here.

After Crucifixion

a beautiful, energetic, and passionate woman. She had been in a tragic automobile accident that changed all that, so it seemed, just five years earlier.

What struck me at first about this couple was Chuck: Chuck seemed to be one of those people who never really want to be at church, always somewhat critical, and negatively opinionated. I could not have been more wrong.

Chuck did always want to be at church, but why he wanted to be there was by no means for the sake of his own personal "happiness." But I'm getting ahead of myself. I noticed also that there was not a single Sunday in which Chuck was not present in Sunday School and Worship with Molly. And he was there! Committed. You knew he had to be—just watching him take 15–30 minutes sometimes getting Molly out of the car, sometimes with her fighting him. And they lived in Oak Park, which is about 45 minutes from the church, where they had moved after Molly's accident from their high-rise in the loop. I wanted to get to know Chuck, and so one Sunday I asked if he would allow me to come visit with him and Molly in their home. The next evening I arrived at their home for dinner. Early in the evening, as dinner was winding down, and as we were clearing dishes, I asked Chuck what brought him and Molly to this church.

Chuck began speaking and did not stop for four hours, except to take what were apparently regular breaks to attend to Molly, and eventually put her to bed. I listened intently. I don't remember saying much the whole evening. Chuck told me about how prior to her accident Molly had attended Uptown Baptist Church, a prominent mission in Chicago begun by a man named Jim Queen back in the 60s. Molly was also a social worker and counselor in the Chicago Public School system, a job she certainly did not have to take, as Chuck provided more than enough for her not to have to work. Chuck was entirely uninterested in church, and never attended Uptown with Molly, preferring to golf 36 holes every Sunday morning and afternoon instead. Every day before going in to her job at the public school, Molly would wake up early, make the trek to Uptown, where she would help prepare meals at the shelter there. Chuck stressed this, repeatedly: "Every day!" he said. Once, Chuck said he asked Molly why she did this. Her reply—and I can still remember his words clearly; you knew they were ingrained in his memory, the way he said them—was this: "Because that's where I see Jesus. It's the only way I know how to make sense of the fact that we live the life that we do, seemingly with the ability to make of it whatever we want, and yet I still go to church on Sunday

Interlude

and say the Lord's Prayer." This of course made no sense to Chuck; Chuck had the life he wanted; his life meant something; he had the life that generations of family members before him had wanted but were unable to achieve.

But, Chuck said, with Molly's accident, all of that changed—over night; but in one sense, over a long, slow, and painful period of time. He did what he could do for Molly, getting the best hospice care, giving up his job at the Board of Trade and many of his luxuries to make her comfortable and share his life with her. But the problem, Chuck said, was that he didn't any longer know how to make sense of this unfinished life of Molly's. He began to wonder about Molly's oft-repeated statements regarding those people she served in the shelter; statements like: "Only Jesus makes sense of their lives. And somehow, I can tell they know that better than I do." All he knew is that Molly would tell him that only Jesus could make sense of her life; and Chuck had no idea of how to honor this other than to take her to church. So about a year after the accident, Chuck called up the pastor of Uptown Baptist and asked for recommendations of where to take Molly to church. The pastor recommended First Baptist Church of Clarendon Hills, which had been a church-plant mission in the suburbs that originated from Uptown itself. Chuck had Molly at church the next week, and when I was there in 1999–2000, had not missed a Sunday since.

But here is the really remarkable aspect of the story. Chuck began to tell me how this weekly trek to church changed his own life. He said that getting Molly up and ready on a Sunday was such a lengthy and touchy ordeal, that he literally had to orient his entire weekly schedule around getting Molly to church on Sunday. He had to make sure that certain steps were being taken throughout the week, beginning with Sunday evening and Monday morning, to make sure that Molly would be healthy enough and alert enough to "get out" and make the trip every week. Sleep schedules, eating schedules, hospice schedules, Chuck's work schedules all had to change for this one weekly trip back and forth to the suburbs. As Chuck said it, half-chuckling: "The irony is, having never gone to church with Molly a single day before her accident, I am now *always* on my way to church. *Everything* I do throughout the week is now about going to church with her." Chuck began taking Molly to church as a matter of attending to her, as a matter of doing what he knew that she would want, giving her over to Jesus to make sense of her life. And now "church" for Chuck is all about attending to Molly. He became a member of First Baptist, because, as he put it: "In taking Molly to Church, Jesus' prayer [the Lord's Prayer, he meant] finally made sense to me."

I asked Chuck for permission to tell his story to the church, a story which people thought they knew, but actually did not know the half of. As members of the church began to hear more about Chuck and Molly's story, they naturally began more and more to look for ways in which they could "help Chuck out." It started with the usual ecclesial "niceties," like the making of meals on occasion, and led eventually to a schedule in which persons in the church would "relieve" Chuck, allowing him some free time of his own. When first confronted with this possibility, Chuck said: "What I'd really like is if someone could come and stay with Molly during the dinner hour every now and then. Because I'd like to go serve meals at that Uptown shelter like Molly used to do." To this day, three evenings a week, Chuck drives downtown to serve the people of Uptown Baptist Church mission, while a member of his "home" church visits with and attends to Molly.

This is a remarkable story in itself, as a story about Chuck. But this has now become the story of the church. Molly changed that church. That church, since 2000, has come more and more to live *for* persons like Molly. Just as Chuck spends his week getting Molly to worship on Sunday, so that he can "offer her up to Jesus Christ," the members of that church come to worship on Sundays looking to be sent out, to offer their lives up, for people like Chuck and Molly. On Sundays, in worship, these people seek to have their lives broken, they really do seek for their gathering for worship to be a sacrifice of praise. They are learning, day by day, what it means that they worship a broken history that is raised. They are learning, day by day, that such worship only makes sense as broken lives and histories are lived in such a way that they testify to the fact that with Christ's death and resurrection, these histories too have been put to death and raised to the promise of new life. They are learning, day by day, to seek ways to tie their own life as a church to such broken histories, and to live these broken histories as histories of resurrection. They are learning, slowly, that going to church on Sunday means caring for the needs of persons like Molly during the week; indeed, to have their weekly schedules entirely rearranged by the needs of persons like Molly. And as this small church is learning all of this, slowly, and falteringly, in fits and halts, amidst all the politics and egoisms that come along with learning to be a corporate people, the miracle of the Body of Christ is happening.

5 "The Cup that I Drink You Will Drink; and with the Baptism with Which I Am Baptized, You Will Be Baptized"

The Promise Jesus Gives the Gifted, as They Dream of Glory[1]

> *Wade in the water,*
> *Wade in the water, children,*
> *Wade in the water,*
> *God's a-going to trouble the water*[2]

THE GOSPEL OF MARK—a discourse deeply rooted in the rich soil of the illiterate peasant performance-culture of first-century Palestine,[3] but more

---

1. I will write, therefore, of a performance. Not of a letter, but of a gospel, the first gospel, if ordinal time, and most of the speculations which have ventured into it, are to be believed. I will write, therefore, of Mark, this initial gospel which it apparently has been necessary to insinuate, here and there, into the performance of the tale *incarnation*; and to do so in the course of a speaking on speaking, and also of a speaking within speaking whose different trajectories thereby find themselves, at certain very determined points, intersecting with a kind of gross rhetorical mistake, a lapse in the discipline and law that regulate speaking and keep it seemly. And I must state here and now that today's discourse will be less a justification of, and even less an apology for, this silent lapse in speech, than a kind of insistent intensification of its play. Cf. (of course) Derrida, "Différance," in *Margins of Philosophy*, 3.

2. "Wade in the Water," 8–9, microfilm. Cf. Dylan, "Rainy Day Women #12 & 35."

3. Wire, *Case for Mark Composed in Performance*, 3: "The current estimate of literacy in Roman Palestine is three percent."

recently affordably displayed in gold-leaf-stamped genuine leather binding—is a *written* text.[4] It was not always so and it has always been possible, since it was first inscribed, that at some point it might cease to be. It is easy to imagine a world in fact without this little book.[5] It is just as easy to imagine a world in which the glad tidings it would broadcast came instead to be utterly dissolved in the strong, rolling currents of a civilization's widening stream, to become perhaps a casually appropriable rumor disambiguated by backslapping auditors' domesticating voices. Yet the Gospel of Mark is *written*—and in such a way that it resists (sometimes manifestly) being put to such good use. It may even instead be read with the slowness of a certain non-proprietary wandering eye, its characters and spaces, its lines and margins rising to evade the entropy of idle talk. It may be found to induce a reader to raise her head, listen, make eye contact, and get off herself.[6] It may be found to evade the more brazenly formidable warrant and arrest, prosecution and conviction, imprisonment and rehabilitation of the blind

---

4. For Mark as written, see Waetjen, *Reordering of Power*, 2–3. But: "What kind of contact the original addressees had with [the text of Mark] is difficult to determine. Given their socio-economic identity as rural peasants and artisans who very likely were illiterate, the text may have been read publically; and entry into its story world was made by hearing rather than seeing" (2). For Mark as even more significantly performed, see Wire, *Case for Mark Composed in Performance*; Shiell, *Delivering from Memory*; and Horsley, *Hearing the Whole Story*. Wire, *Case for Mark Composed in Performance*, 3: "As a physiological reality produced by a human voice and received by a human ear, the sound has a force among humans beyond whatever it is signifying. . . . A spoken statement is always social, always in context, whereas writing can be composed elsewhere and be read alone." Horsley, *Hearing the Whole Story*, 62, 73: "In contrast to the silent, solitary reading in modern print culture . . . recitation of a story . . . was usually a communal experience of a group in the ancient Mediterranean world. . . . Recitation or performance of oral-derived texts was a relational, interactive event. . . . In contrast to modern readers, who read to gather information, hearers of oral performance participate in the narrative. . . . Hearers do not listen to take away new information, but together with the performer experience the performed narrative." Shiell, *Delivering from Memory*, 1: "In the ancient world, a performance affected an audience. Most performers expected the audience to pay attention and participate in the persuasive process. . . . By repeatedly meeting together and listening to performances, their lives were shaped by the experience. They expected one another to live up to their standard, and they retold the story to each other and to people outside the group. During the performance, they interrupted the speech with questions and dialogue and debated during and after the speech about the topics. The process bonded them and continued the cycle of early transmission of and response to the stories."

5. Is it a book?

6. Wire, *Case for Mark Composed in Performance*, 177: "when we read we . . . seek a conversation."

"*The Cup That I Drink You Will Drink . . .*"

gavel-justice of one or another monarchical world view. Unbeholden to decorum and fashion, it would thus trace a subtle, undulating path even across the stubs of a harvested papyrus field, as if this holy tale were holy writ all along, written, perhaps, in the air through the dust stirred from the hard ground by the swift movements of women in lively performance.[7] In its time a strange mode of discourse, Mark does its work not by nailing down antecedent oral traditions and red-letter Jeffersonian anthologies, but by unleashing them.[8] Its action/adventures throw open what otherwise stand closed: the sky (1:10), the house (2:4),[9] terms of endearment (8:31), a peasant body (14:22), the Temple (15:38), and the tomb of a malefactor (16:4). The Gospel of Mark is *written* to *rend*.[10]

The Gospel of Mark is nonetheless *written* because it was *enacted*, empathetically seen and heard; and in order to *be* enacted, to *be* empathetically seen and heard, e.g., by a small body largely of ordinary, illiterate peasants no longer warmly welcomed on cold nights around the fire pits of the kith of their now bygone lives.[11] We might imagine working people, laborers, sitting cross-legged just after sunset in a little out of the ordinary village assembly or on the floor of an open space in somebody else's house,[12] tired and bruised after another seven day stretch of hard labor, listening afresh to "the beginning of the good news of Jesus Christ, the Son of God" (1:1) that Mark oddly repeats, leaning in as it opens in a wasteland not unlike the one

---

7. See ibid., 182–84.

8. See ibid., 3–6.

9. Certainly Jesus is shown to be hospitable in one house after another, but perhaps his hospitality in this passage takes place especially in the house of the dead?

10. Wire, *Case for Mark Composed in Performance*: "The scribe [of Mark] writes from inside the community tradition . . . and continues the practice of composition in performance, but with a reed and ink as mouth. This person is constrained in the same way as previous performers to move the traditional audience to renewed commitment in their present context." See 56–59. Cf. Myers, *Binding the Strong Man*, 414.

11. See Waetjen, *Reordering of Power*, 5–13.

12. Myers, *Binding the Strong Man*, 151: In the Gospel of Mark "the 'household' (*oikia, oikos*, synonymous with livelihood, 10:29f.; 12:40) . . . is portrayed as a 'safe' site for the discipleship community (6:10). There Jesus dines with the outcast (2:15; 14:3) and attends to the crowds (1:32f.; 3:20); it is the locus for private instruction (7:17; 9:33; 10:10) and healing (1:29–31; 5:38; 7:24). . . . [T]he *oikos*, the basic Hellenistic social unity, was adopted and modified by early Christians, becoming the alternative social site of resistance to the alienation of the dominant culture surrounding them." Cf. 421–23. See also Waetjen, *Reordering of Power*, 4–5.

across which Hebrew slaves (they have been told) sojourned for forty years. Jesus, they hear, has gone there to be baptized by John.

As the account of his descent into the River Jordan and his ascent out of it fills their eyes and ears, their thoughts and dreams, they would be reminded of the baptisms they had witnessed and of the stories they told or had been told of their own baptisms (cf. Mark 10:38).[13] They would perhaps recall hearing that it was in that way that their now bygone lives were washed away, the way that they entered into Jesus' crucifixion and resurrection (cf. Rom 6:3–5).[14] Already in the Gospel's opening shout there is a forecast of its end.[15]

Taken up into the event by the strong voice and dancing body of their storyteller, they see and hear Jesus stand like an island out of the water and the Spirit descend *into* him, as if he were the dry dust into which breath is breathed in Genesis's second creation account,[16] "like a dove," as if he were the dry earth that emerged, when the waters of the great flood receded.[17] "And a voice came from heaven, 'You are my Son, the Beloved; with you I am well pleased'" (Mark 1:11). Straightaway the Spirit, like the strong wind that dried the Sea before the Hebrew children, drives him farther into the wilderness, where he is tempted by the one who would by no means follow him, but who nonetheless fails to block his way.[18]

---

13. Hovey, *To Share in the Body*, 26: "The surging waters of the baptismal do not only cleanse, they kill; they do not only wash the body, they destroy it."

14. I am thinking especially of Paul's phrase in v. 3, "Do you not know . . . ?" Of course, some particular assembly might at the time have held to a view very different than the one Paul would spell out in detail, e.g., as washing.

15. Waetjen, *Reordering of Power*, 68–69: "Surrendering himself to John's baptism, Jesus . . . drowned; he died eschatologically; he embraced the reality of his death before his physical expiration. . . . All of the debts that had been incurred . . . have been canceled: to his parents for feeding, clothing, and sheltering him; to his friends for their love, encouragement, and support; to his society for educating and civilizing him; and to the government for its maintenance of law and order. . . . As a result, he has become wholly unobliged!" Cf. 73–74.

16. Mark 1:10: "And just as he was coming up out of the water, he saw the heavens torn apart and the Spirit descending like a dove [into, *eis*] him."

17. Waetjen, *Reordering of Power*, 70: "The narrator's metaphor of the dove-like descent of the Spirit may allude to the symbolism of the new creation which the image of the dove conveys as the bearer of a freshly picked olive leaf, a sign to Noah and his family at the subsiding of the great flood of a new beginning." Perhaps not Ararat, but another mountain, the one upon which Jerusalem sits, would one day be cast into the Sea also to be baptized (11:23; cf. vs. 30).

18. Ibid., 74: "Immediately after his baptism Jesus is driven *into* the wilderness by the

"The Cup That I Drink You Will Drink..."

When John is disappeared by the security forces of his occupied country, the Son gets up and throws himself headlong into a work even more unsettling than the Baptist's, the work, Jesus will soon say, of plundering the strong man's house (3:27). He marches into towns where people work to eat and eat to work. There with urgency he cries out: "The time is fulfilled, and the kingdom of God has come near; repent, and believe in the good news!" (Mark 1:14). He is sent to carry and deliver this by no means universally uplifting message.[19] As hard as is its edge, he proclaims it almost against himself with compassion (e.g., 1:37–44). He teaches in synagogues, the domain particularly of the Scribes.[20] He refuses the compliments of the "unclean spirit" he meets there; indeed, he evicts it from the synagogue—with a shocking authority that demonstrates how unlike the Scribes he is (1:22–27). As if the words of his mouth were spoken with an authority more about him than their thought-content, he finds himself not only declaring the coming of God's Reign, but—contrary to his plans—gesturing obliquely toward it (cf. 5:30; 6:56). He heals the sick and the demon possessed, silencing those who would presume to determine who he is (1:23–27, 34). And alone in the deep darkness before the first vague light of dawn, while others search for him, he prays (1:35–37).

He is so mobbed by the afflicted who have heard of his power to heal that he cannot get out the words he is to proclaim. He tries to slip away to a place where he can find room to preach, but he is intercepted by a leper and out of pity[21] presses his hands on the man's ruptured skin, the marks of transgression on the boundary of his body, and heals him, too. Once more,

---

very Spirit that descended into him. The wilderness is a reality of chaos and formlessness, and it is symbolic of the anarchy he now confronts as a result of his experience of nothingness and his entry into a reordering of power. For him the old order of reality, with its first principles and absolutes, its myths and the structures they constitute, its redemptive process and the rules governing the use of power, has been abolished." "Satan" signifies, of course, "ad-versary," "one who op-poses."

19. It is good news for those who day in and day out hear little more than bad news.

20. See Waetjen, *Reordering of Power*, 8–9; Myers, *Binding the Strong Man*, 142.

21. Or anger. Myers, *Binding the Strong Man*, 153–54: "Jesus' anger, then, is directed against the symbolic order of purity of which the man is a victim. The system subjects the physically ailing to a double oppression: not only are they second-class citizens in Israel, but they must make special payment as well.... In this story, both cleansing and judgment have drawn nigh." The anger, if that is what it is, may however be due to Jesus' commitment to a much more extreme Reign of God that carries with its coming much more than healing. He heals, he makes whole, but the Reign of God is coming with such an abundance of life that being broken or blind or lame is no obstacle to it.

when word gets out about what he has done, desperate crowds rush to him for care. It is as if the whole world were broken, maimed, sick, possessed, and dying. And when he boldly casts out a man's sins (2:5–12), he performs in a far more radical way the good news he carries.[22]

It would not surprise those hearing this tale read aloud in a little village assembly or in somebody else's house that, whether he is at home or not, Jesus contacts lepers or is found eating with sinners and other misfits or that he violates Sabbath regulations, though it shocks those in the story who are spiritually and politically well-heeled and adjusted (1:29–31, 41–44; 2:1–17, 23–28; 3:1–6; cf. 3:31–35; 7:1–5).[23] There is thus in the opening of Mark a signal that sinners and misfits in particular hear: Jesus bears the news of the coming of God's Reign with his body; it is in his breath, in his guts, in his bones, in his hands. It is news he performs by proclamation, exorcism, and healing; by casting out sins and dipping bread and fingertips into the very bowls as ill-formed, unwashed people who do not have to be convinced that they are in trouble. "God is coming for *you*!" That is his work, a work that, far from being plugged into any extant order, rather rises in insurrection against it. He is an audacious wonder worker with an audacious voice. "Who then is this, that even the wind and the sea obey him?" (4:41). Not just any ears even begin to take in such a word (4:9–13, but also 22; 8:18): not the ears of unclean spirits, who fear and would manage it (e.g., 3:11), not the ears of Scribes, Pharisees, or Herodians (cf. 3:6),[24] only the ears of those audacious enough to stand up into it (e.g., 2:12).[25] "Little girl, get up!" (5:41).

Jesus walks by the Sea to collect disciples (1:16–20; 2:13–14).[26] Again by the Sea, pressed by the crowds, he has his disciples keep a boat at hand in case the afflicted press in too hard (3:7–9). Once more by the Sea, still more broken and desperate people push against him and his disciples. This time Jesus lifts his feet off of solid ground, boards a little boat, and pushes out

---

22. That by Jesus' word the paralyzed man rises, takes up his mat, and leaves this house is perhaps a testimony to the coming resurrection of those who have been lowered by four pallbearers into the house of the dead.

23. See Myers, *Binding the Strong Man*, 117, 152–61.

24. See ibid., 162.

25. It might be worth remembering at this point that the Greek word for "resurrection," *anastasis*, literally signifies "to stand up." "Insurrection" signifies "to stand into."

26. Myers, *Binding the Strong Man*, 190: "Mark is the first writer to refer to the inland, freshwater lake (*limne*) as a 'sea' (*thalassa*), in order to invoke images [of the exodus from Egyptian bondage] from the Hebrew scriptures."

onto the waters of the Sea (4:1). There, for the first time in Mark, Jesus—rocking, nothing steady under him but the vague threat of drowning—begins to teach in *parables*. "Listen!" he says (4:2–3). And in his first parable, Jesus tells of how rare it is that sown seed takes root in good soil and bears fruit, as rare as it is that a parable is understood. He teaches by throwing his word to the side (para-ble). He throws it on the beaten path, too, and on ground in which rock is embedded and exposed or thorns are rooted and poised to take hold and spread. But Jesus' word thrown to the side falls, too, upon ears that hear. It is to the side where, without "know how," what is "hidden" is "disclosed," what is "secret" comes "to light" (4:22–23, 27). For everyone else, those who would roll on down tracks laid straight across the backs of long dead navvies: "They may indeed look, but not perceive, and may indeed listen, but not understand; so that they may not turn again and be forgiven" (4:11–12).[27]

Further describing this alternative, parabolic trajectory, Jesus and his disciples make their very first trip together across the Sea. "Let us go to the other side," Jesus says to them (4:35). As happened long before to the prophet sent to Nineveh, that Gentile city to which God showed compassion, a storm so violent arises that it threatens to capsize the vessel. Like Jonah, Jesus (perhaps also already as good as dead, however differently) sleeps through the tumult.[28] When awakened, he rebukes his disciples and the wind, and "to the sea," he says, "'Peace! Be still!'" (4:36–41).

Landing among the Gerasenes, i.e., impossibly far into Gentile territory, he encounters another man tormented by an "unclean spirit." This time it is not in contrast to the Scribes that he works (he is no longer in Galilee and he is not yet in Judea). This time he works in contrast to a (Roman) "Legion." The unclean spirits, as before, want to identify him, to nail

---

27. Of course, Mark has Jesus quote Isaiah 6 here, that passage in which before the "holy, holy, holy" God Isaiah stands to declare "here am I, send me!"

28. Jonah's fleeing from the presence of God is simultaneously his fleeing to death. The poem from the belly of the great fish is an account of death. "The waters closed in over me; the deep surrounded me; weeds were wrapped around my head at the roots of the mountains. I went down to the land whose bars closed upon me forever . . ." (Jonah 2:5–6a). That it ends with the declaration that God has delivered him from the sea is a kind doxology of proto-resurrection: "yet you brought up my life from the Pit, O Lord my God" (6b). That Jonah slept in the hold of the ship as waves threatened to break it apart is also an allusion to the death to which he was fleeing. The difference in the case of Jesus, of course, is that it is precisely because he does not flee from the presence of God, it is precisely because he travels where God travels, that he, too, is as good as dead.

him down. In response Jesus casts them out of the man and into swine who charge into the Sea and are drowned like Pharaoh's army (5:1–13).[29]

On his return by boat to the Galilean side of the Sea, in the midst once more of a mob of desperate people, he finds himself before two who are particularly so, each bowing at his feet: one an upper class righteous man of means, the father of a terribly sick child on the verge of death, the other a destitute woman, perpetually unclean, perpetually untouchable, with no father to plead her case. He finds himself also before two daughters, one the twelve-year-old daughter by birth of the privileged leader of the synagogue, a child who has died before Jesus arrives at her bedside, the other, as he hurries to the first, interrupts and delays him, the twelve-year-afflicted fatherless woman, whom Jesus heals without design and freely declares before one and all to be *his*: "Daughter, your faith has made you well" (5:34). Though he and both daughters—while they are still unclean—*touch*, they do not infect him with their highly communicable impurity, but in anticipation of what is to come, they are infected[30] by his "power," a power unlike the force that had held them in its fist and would have crushed the life out of them (5:21–43).

Thus Mark, the good news of the coming of the Messiah, *begins*. The tale it proceeds to tell is not exactly what Judeans and Galileans had been led to expect, but initially there are about it signs that this Jesus *is* indeed the One. Mark *ends*, however, quite differently, uncannily, with an "(e)x" of an end, really. Jesus has been executed by Rome in the most humiliating manner. His dead and mutilated body has been consigned to a tomb. When women come to pay their respects to their dead leader and friend, they find his grave evacuated. A young man sitting in the tomb orders them to report to the disciples what they had found and to follow Jesus into Galilee. The very last verse of the Gospel, however, is without resolution: "So they went out and fled from the tomb, for terror and amazement had seized them; and they said nothing to anyone, for they were afraid" (16:8).

---

29. Myers, *Binding the Strong Man*, 191: "In 5:9 Jesus wrests from this powerful demonic horde its name: Legion. A Latinism, this term had only one meaning in Mark's social world: a division of Roman soldiers. Alerted by this clue, we discover that the rest of the story is filled with *military* imagery."

30. *Oxford English Dictionary*, s.v. "Infect, *v.*": "Latin *infect-* , participial stem of *inficĕre* to dip in, stain, taint, impregnate, spoil, etc., < *in-* (in- *prefix*2) + *facere* to make, do, put."

"*The Cup That I Drink You Will Drink . . .*"

Of course, none of us rests easily with an irresolute text. We like our theater to have satisfying last acts. We like our feasts to leave us sated. We like our final punctuation marks to be final. It is no wonder that this gospel's ultimate unseemly gash would come to be sutured, indeed, its profile surgically enhanced. And yet Mark's sixteenth verse 8 may be heard to resound with earlier (or are they later?) moments in the gospel when conclusion is averted. The wound that rips across the sky already in its first chapter—"And just as he was coming up out of the water, he saw the heavens torn apart and the Spirit descending like a dove upon him. And a voice came from heaven, 'You are my Son, the Beloved; with you I am well pleased'" (1:10–11)—is the very wound that rips through the curtain of the Temple when the worst is done to this Beloved Son on Golgotha: "Then Jesus gave a loud cry and breathed his last. And the curtain of the temple was torn in two, from top to bottom" (15:37–38).[31] Jesus adamantly enjoins both the demons that oppose him and the grateful to whom he has given new life to refrain from naming him, from pressing on his work an opaque categorical nomination, from closing the wound that rips through him. His miraculous feedings of the five thousand (6:1–52) and the four thousand (8:1–26) occur not in the walled, secure *polis*, home of the well-nourished, well-housed, and well-respected ruling elite; nor in the productive *chora* around the city, agricultural land directly and indirectly from which the goods of the city's aristocracy come; but in the *erēmos*, the wilderness, the nonproductive, empty land, the resourceless, barren, dangerous land,[32] land out of the dark caves and pits of which might at any moment emerge those murderers and thieves who for a little while survive by preying like hyenas on wayfarers, murderers and thieves who are desperate children abandoned by their desperate parents, nobodies whom enforcers of the peace hunt down and kill, the scum among whom Mark's Jesus is explicitly counted on Good Friday.

But it is midway through Mark that a vague red glow at the horizon appears to signal the dawning of a very different day and to make manifest that the noble *vision* of a noble victory to the Messiah's noble struggle is rather a *blindness*, a visual conversion disorder, a refusal in fact to turn and open the eyes to a new sun. "Then he began to teach them that the Son of

---

31. Each passage uses a form of the word *schizo* in its account of this tearing.
32. Liddell et al., *Greek-English Lexicon*, s.v. "*polis*," "*chora*," "*erēmos*." Of the last of these three words in particular: "desolate, lonely, solitary, . . . freq. of poor, friendless persons . . . void or destitute of, . . . bereft of, . . . wanting, without, . . . free from, . . . of a vessel, empty." See Hock, "Why New Testament Scholars Should Read Ancient Novels," 124.

Man must undergo great suffering, and be rejected by the elders, the chief priests, and the scribes, and be killed, and after three days rise again. He said all this quite openly" (8:31–32a).

The gap between these phrases and the ones immediately to follow is never wide enough on the printed page; nor does the printed page alert us adequately to an abrupt change of the tale's pace or decibel level. It takes a certain imagination to recognize the way Jesus and his disciples lean into each other during this interchange. When he hears Jesus prophesy, Peter pulls him off the road, bears down on him face to face, and refuses the end to which Jesus has just said he will come—an end unworthy of one with the title "*Messiah!*" Jesus seems to grow in size as he turns back onto his path and attends to his disciples. His rebuking Peter is not a parental scolding. He means just what he says. At that pivotal moment, when Peter seems to have gotten it right, that this one before him is greater than John the Baptist or Elijah or any of the other prophets, it becomes manifest that he, like the demons who would put the Messiah in his place, has drawn a conceptual boundary line around Jesus, has enlisted him, has named his name: "But turning and looking at his disciples, he rebuked Peter and said, 'Get behind me, [Adversary]! For you are setting your mind not on divine things but on human things'" (8:33). It appears that it is not for anyone to determine who this Jesus is, that a designation for him is not to be slapped down on the table like a winning hand, that everything depends on what is *done* as he is spoken of, on *how witness* to him is *born*, i.e., on *how* he is *believed*. Nothing about him settles down upon those determinations that rise to avail themselves, not even upon the most deeply embedded first principles, the most primal *archai*. On the contrary, everything about him depends on the wildly free determination of God. Jesus is commanding Peter and all the disciples: "You, too, are with me to meet this very end, the end to which this path points!" And so, the very next verses make an announcement: "He called the crowd with his disciples, and said to them, 'If any want to become my followers, let them deny themselves and take up their cross and follow me. For those who want to save their life will lose it, and those who lose their life for my sake, and for the sake of the gospel, will save it" (8:34–35). Thus, believing in *this* Messiah does not come easily, say, by carefully measuring his demeanor or character or personality or moral rigor or power or nobility or virtue or spirituality against extant categories—as becomes increasingly clear, as Jesus and those gathered around him move relentlessly south from the site of Peter's botched confession, from Caesarea Philippi in the far north, to Jerusalem, where Jesus on Good Friday is castrated, lynched, and burned.³³

The rest of the book is a telling of this tale, of Jesus' journey to great suffering, rejection, and death, and of the gift of resurrection—the odd commandeering of crucifixion, i.e., of death, by a life that has room even for the dead, those whom death would hold fast, a life that will not exit this hard world, this world that would keep the peace in the face of malefactors, miscreants, and malcontents by crucifying them; resurrection, the odd commandeering of death by a life that in the end travels ahead of anyone who would follow him to oppressed and systematically impoverished Galilee. And it is a telling of the tale of the disciples' *refusal* to follow him, of their fleeing from what must have struck them as the most insanely tragic of all damnations; the tale, that is, of their desperate attempt to save their lives, and their concomitant shameless *loss* of life, loss in fact of everything.

In a world poised to haul them away to councils, to governors and kings, to beat them in synagogues (13:9–13), and to slaughter them in arenas, Mark's attendants, those with ears to hear, understand quickly that the word of Jesus is hard to believe. It is hard to believe, not because only the gullible would believe it, but because it is a word for those as fearlessly devoid of property and propriety as is a little child (10:13–22; cf. 12:41–44).³⁴ In this

---

33. Cone, *Cross and the Lynching Tree*, xv: "Until we can see the cross and the lynching tree together, until we can identify Christ with a 'recrucified' black body hanging from a lynching tree, there can be no genuine understanding of Christian identity in America, and no deliverance from the brutal legacy of slavery and white supremacy." Cf. Myers, *Binding the Strong Man*, 118: "In the second prologue three major plot developments are suddenly brought into focus.... First, the incipient conflict between Jesus and his own followers erupts into full-scale confrontation (8:29ff.), a complication that will continue to escalate until its tragic conclusion. Secondly the mystery surrounding the identity of Jesus deepens when he rejects Peter's 'confession' (8:29). As readers we are now off balance, for we had been led from the beginning of the story to believe Jesus *was* in fact Messiah (1:1). Finally, the real consequences of Jesus' conflict with the authorities is revealed, and he demands that his followers be prepared to embrace the cross (8:34ff.). This new direction in the story is subsequently confirmed by the divine voice in the second apocalyptic moment of the transfiguration (9:2ff.)." Cf. xviii.

34. Myers, *Binding the Strong Man*, 175: "If we 'listen but do not hear' it is not because of the obscurity of the word, but because of our loyalty to the prevailing ideology." Whitfield, *Pilgrim Holiness*, 91: "The martyrs say just what their persecutors saw, yet they spoke differently—from hope."

story it is Jesus himself, the *particularly* vulnerable Galilean, who carries the coming of the Reign of God, who performs it, who is its face and voice, who "undergo[es] great suffering, and . . . [is] rejected by the elders, the chief priests, and the scribes, and [is] killed" (8:31; cf. ch 15). Those who with their bodies believe in him are pointed down this very road. Of course, this is an affront to any social order that valorizes resourcefulness. It is a call to a different sociality; one in which covetousness—the lust to grasp and own and be—has been "condemned in the flesh."[35] When one is resourceful, such a call must always carry a weight beyond what one can bear. The unrestrained possibility of God (Mark 10:23–27) may yet be thrust away by those especially good at economic forecasts. "Jesus, looking at him, loved him and said, 'You lack one thing; go, sell what you own, and give the money to the poor, and you will have treasure in heaven; then come, follow me.' When he heard this, he was shocked and went away grieving, for he had many possessions" (10:21–22; cf. Gen 3:4–6).[36]

The people listening in a village assembly or in somebody else's house to a performance of this Gospel know all too well that, though among these people they have been gifted with "brothers and sisters, mothers and children" (Mark 10:30), they are also to undergo great suffering, indeed to be betrayed by those they love, to be rejected and killed (Mark 13:12). They are no doubt afraid, in large part because they have brought or might yet bring children into such a world.[37] Yet as they stay with the story and imagine as they remember what they hear, there may well be moments in which a marked silence falls upon that room, as if with Moses and Elijah the beloved Son were glorified in *their* midst (9:2–6). Yet they are reminded that the beloved Son is to be heeded not as a truth-spectacular that compels both assent and an awards ceremony, but as this no longer "dazzling" peasant, Jesus. The beloved Son is one among many abased peasants who work alongside one another (7–8) under the shadow of an occupying army. That is, where others would find in this narrative reasons to fear, those who listen well to the end would hear hope in it.

This would be for them no ordinary story. As they let in the spoken words that fill their ears, they must feel as if worlds were rising up against

---

35. If I might use the language of Rom 7:7–8, 8:3.

36. When Jesus lists the commandments of which this man says, "Teacher, I have kept all these since my youth" (10:19–20), he leaves out the one prohibiting covetousness and all the commandments concerned with one's more direct devotion to God.

37. Cf. Dylan, "Masters of War."

"*The Cup That I Drink You Will Drink . . .*"

each other outside their little village or their locked doors, as if the earth quaked, as if the sun darkened (13:8). They understand the admonition, "And what I say to you I say to all: Keep awake" (13:3–37; cf. 14:37).

They know what it is like to be Judas or Peter or a Roman guard or Barabbas or a thief of Golgotha. When they think of him into whom even *they* have been baptized, they may be imagined to be stirred, opened, recklessly grateful, perhaps some among them yearning to pour out to him *whatever* they can lay their hands on, to excess, all they own (Mark 12:42–44; 14:3–9).[38]

In the story's shattering end, when Jesus enters into an irrevocable solidarity with the most lost, with the *damned*, from his pounding chest and open throat a wail of dereliction stands: "My God, my God, why have you forsaken me?" With a cry too deep for words, his asphyxiated heart and lungs growing still, his last breath is squeezed through his blue lips, and his body's muscles, giving up their vital tension, succumbing to gravity, let the weight of what was his body[39] hang limp from the executioner's iron spikes (15:34, 37). When they hear that "the curtain of the temple [is] torn in two, from top to bottom," these people in a village assembly or in a room of somebody else's house remember the heavens above Jesus' baptismal waters, as would anyone who knows how to listen to a story. The room would perhaps grow still, as they hear the unlikely words from an unlikely source, "Now when the centurion, who stood facing him, saw that in this way he breathed his last, he said, 'Truly this man was God's Son!'" (15:39; cf. 3:11). The stillness of the moment would be due in part to the posture of the centurion; as long as he "stood facing him," this Roman functionary would remain an adversary, a manager, not a follower who by definition would always move close *behind* the Messiah.[40] And when they hear in the end of this story, as an almost anticlimax, that the crucified one has been raised from the dead,[41] shaken as they are, they do not have to be told that they stand at a crossroads, facing two antithetical courses of action: They could withdraw from this tale and out of fear say nothing to anyone, or they may

---

38. And yet, cf. Myers, *Binding the Strong Man*, 322: "The temple has robbed this woman of her very means of livelihood (12:44). Like the scribal class, it no longer protects widows, but exploits them. As in disgust, Jesus 'exits' the temple—for the final time (13:1a)."

39. See Wolff, *Anthropology of the Old Testament*, 28–29.

40. Hovey, *To Share in the Body*, 68, 125, cf. 67; and Whitfield, *Pilgrim Holiness*, 103–4.

41. See Kierkegaard [Anti-Climacus], *Practice in Christianity*, 174–79.

remain in it, go ahead to that place where are assembled those who may yet be faithful, and there bear witness to the crucified resurrected one, i.e., follow after him—"who is going ahead of you" (16:6–8).

We are the children of Gutenberg. We *read* our texts. We sit alone, heads down, taking note of verses or pericopes, and we construct in our working memories and on our computer screens how it is that this block of text is to be explained, how it is that a particular reading of it is to be defended. It is a time-honored and respectable way of dealing with a passage of scripture, a text of any sort, really. It is also, however, a visual course of action that privileges the eyes and the rather disembodied mind of the solitary reader. Even if such interpretive work is on its way to publication, it has privacy about it, as does reading or even hearing it.[42]

Thus when we people of the book read the interchange between Jesus and his disciples, say, in Mark 8, we find ourselves considering what such words might mean in a reserved library carrel to the lonely doer who would not be a reader only of this word. Everything changes, however, when it is not with silent eyes that one comes to be engaged by this tale. Everything changes when engagement occurs among those who *do* not, indeed, *cannot* read or write—say, a handful of peasants with richly textured cultural memories and long attention spans, people for whom stories are never private events, people who have no use for verses and pericopes, but whose bodies rise and fall *together* with the dramatic crescendos and decrescendos of the story, especially if it is animated, vivid, ear-ringingly well-performed—say, among a little social body of friends about to break bread in a fringe village assembly or in somebody else's house.[43] For those of us who have been

---

42. Rather like a "communion service" in which, regardless of the size of the crowd, the prepackaged elements are distributed like *Lunchables©* for the private devotional consumption of individual "communicants."

43. Horsley, *Hearing the Whole Story*, 75–77: "The original hearers would have been members of a community of a relatively new movement, people who had recently come to common commitments in similar life circumstances.... New life-giving and 'empowering' forces are at work through Jesus. Oppressive rulers and institutions stand under God's condemnation. 'The kingdom of God is at hand.' Suffering and death are not the end of life.... The Gospel ... continues in the experience of the hearers past the end of any given performance.... In contrast to a modern individualistic reader finding a call to 'discipleship' in response to the disciples' failure after the story itself has ended, the participatory hearing in a community evokes a collective cooperative response by

trained to imagine things in close-up stills, the possibly offensive question concerns what the call of Jesus might signify not only for Peter, not only for all of the disciples, but also for "the crowd" (34),[44] what it might signify for this call to be social all the way through; what it might signify for it to take shape not in a loose affiliation of solitary individuals, nor, for that matter, in a hive, but rather in, with, and under a particular body of people made roomy enough for "that one," the malefactor, the miscreant, or the malcontent. What might it signify, that is, not only for Peter, but even more for a *village assembly* or *house church*[45] to hear the call of Mark 8 to take up its cross and follow Jesus?

This is an apocalyptic question. It is a question of the relationship between a little local body—a statistically insignificant body, a body without status in the world, a body past which the good, the true, and the beautiful would drive with no more acknowledgment than they would give on a wet, dark night to the drunk clothed in bed upstairs dying among strangers in a one-night cheap hotel—it is the question of the relationship between a little local body and the revolutionary coming of the Reign of God.[46] It is a question of the depth of the wound that tears through the heavens, the temple, the body of Jesus, and his grave, a question of the depth of the reach of the two rough hands of the Age to Come into (the) infertile earth, a question of the emptiness of the tomb at the "(e)x" of an end of Mark 16, in the silence after the echo of its last word fills to capacity the little place where illiterate peasants meet. It is a question—in the end—of the extremity of a life that does not need to fix the body of the dead Christ in the tomb in order to shine in the darkness. It is a question, that is, of what it signifies for the

---

that community. . . . Not only are the boundaries between the performed story and everyday reality blurred; the Gospel story (and history) continues in the ongoing work of the movement, which in turn is motivated by the continuing performance of the story."

44. See Myers, *Binding the Strong Man*, 245.

45. Perhaps one in some sense built upon him (as the Matthean account of this story puts it).

46. Myers, *Binding the Strong Man*, 247: "The argument of this second call to discipleship can be summarized as follows. Jesus has revealed that his messiahship means political confrontation with, not rehabilitation of, the imperial state. Those who wish to "come after him" will have to identify themselves with his subversive program. The stated risk is that the disciple will face the test of loyalty under interrogation by state authorities. If "self" is denied, the cross will be taken up, a metaphor for capital punishment on grounds of insurgency. Through *these* definitive choices . . . the disciple will 'follow Jesus.'"

future of every little gathering that the Jesus whom you crucified—by commission or omission—is "going ahead of you to Galilee" (16:7).

If the journey of Jesus in Mark from far northern Caesarea Philippi south to Jerusalem is a journey carved determinedly toward the coming of the salvation of the flesh, a salvation that does not have to suppress death in order to come, a salvation that does not stand in binary opposition to death, but splits open the sky, the curtain, a Galilean body, and his grave, i.e., a salvation that comes even where death might be mistakenly presumed to reign, then the question of the survival of a little local village assembly or house-church is not a question about what might progress with the slow and easy advance of an unfolding process. It is rather a question of what is freely to come, the unsettling arrival of a revolutionary new day, the arrival of wonder.

If the salvation toward which Jesus journeys is to come by having developed—by having broken through the soil, ramified its roots, stretched out its branches, and squeezed out its leaves and fruit—by the inherent potency of its extant processes, coagulated, say, as village assemblies and house-churches, then those gatherings would need to proceed warily, to gain ground with circumspection, to cut their losses, if need be, in order to retain resources adequate to the exigencies of an always dangerously uncertain tomorrow (cf. 11:11–24). The salvation that comes in Mark's gospel, however, does not call for caution. It calls for thoughtful immodesty (cf. 10:50–52), flagrantly extravagant gentleness (cf. 14:3–9); for it arrives precisely where all potency is drained from the body of the Galilean, a body rigid and cold, as cold as the stone crypt in which it is dumped. That this body might be the site of a capacious, vigorous future signals the most transgressive of extravagances.

Especially as it moves out into its second half and to its open end, Mark's glad tidings would have danced before rough workers' bodies, bodies gathered in tight resonant sympathy, bodies abased and exalted to the beat of its performance. The "I believe" of faithful response to this call of Jesus, "If any want to become my followers, let them deny themselves and take up their cross and follow me," is the "I believe" of many throats and bellies, the "I believe" neither of the individual, nor of the group mind, but of a complex body of people not in every respect unlike the one loaf of rough brown bread made of many grains, the one cup of thick red wine made of many grapes.[47] The "I believe" of faithful response is spoken by the

---

47. Cf. "The Didache," 175 (9:1–5).

little village assembly or house-church, by every little village assembly or house-church that has come to see and hear that it does not have to survive in order for the Reign of God to open an airway in the throat of this choking world.[48] The "I believe" of faithful response to the call of Jesus is that of the martyr-church.[49]

It is no mean task in our time to think "martyr" without succumbing to the point/counterpoint logic of heroes and villains. If the term is understood apocalyptically, however, a different logic may be found to be at play in it. A martyr then might be imagined to be a witness to the resurrection of the crucified, but not with analytically calculative eyes. The apocalyptic witness to the resurrection of the crucified is that body that *bears* it witness with hands and feet and backs and faces that work and that wait, a corporeal/corporate witness to the coming of a *potentia*, better, a *dunamis*, not installed already in what is within easy reach.[50] To take up your cross and follow Jesus to Golgotha is for a little local gathering to remember that its future is to come—as a gift. It is not to pursue crucifixion as a *telos*, as a goal that may be completed by a kind of agonistic unfolding, i.e., by a kind

---

48. Hauerwas and Pinches, *Christians Among the Virtues*, 162: "Martyrs . . . have to be ready to lose to their persecutors, dying ingloriously. They can do so only because they recognize that neither their life nor their death carries its own (or anyone else's) weight of meaning; rather that is carried by the God who supplies it."

49. I stumbled upon Hovey's *To Share in the Body* early on as I was thinking through and otherwise working on this chapter. I had already decided to focus on the Gospel of Mark and I had already decided that the phrase for what I wanted to point toward is "martyr-church." I was very happy to find that he had landed on this very phrase and that he was working on the ideas he associated with it by working through Mark. I read the book with much joy, learned a great deal from it, and have recommended the book to my friends. I might note, however, that although I'd want to say much of what Hovey says in this book, I'd use terms like "virtues," "courage," "enable," "identity," "obligated," "intrinsic good," and some others (see, e.g., 60–61, 66, 122–24) either not at all or rather more critically than he has. Further, I'd want to talk about the martyrdom of the *church*, of a locally gathered body of people, parallel to and perhaps more significant than that of those of its members who here and there are martyred. Of course, I would also want to talk about those members who here and there are martyred and I would want to do so with wonder and gratitude, but as a way of saying that it is toward its own martyrdom that the church—as a locally gathered body of people—is to live out into a future it does not have the power to yield. (Hovey comes very close to saying this, however, on 92–93.)

50. Aristotle uses the word *dunamis*, which is later translated as *potentia*, for the latent power that may under the right circumstance be actualized. Thus there is a *dunamis* native to an acorn, which may be actualized as a mature oak tree. See Hope, "Index of Technical Terms," 326. In Mark it is used for the miraculous coming of God. See, e.g., Mark 6:5; 9:1, 39; 13:26.

of seasoned hunter's good aim. That is suicide. Martyrdom is to live toward crucifixion, toward it and through it, out into the coming of a life that does not settle neatly into extant categories, a life, that is, without closure. "Tell no one!" Jesus says. The martyr bears witness to the resurrection of the crucified not by explanation, not by extrapolation, not by giving it a place in a world view, not by settling the matter, but by working and waiting, by turning new eyes to a new dawn, by turning new ears to the pounding hoof beats of an approaching new world, by walking out into what is not-yet with a hope that need not avert defeat in order to overcome.

It is not just that a little village assembly or house-church must be careful to train its members to face life's hardships and to be willing to pay the supreme price, if need be. Certainly, training of that kind is both honorable and difficult, by no means to be despised. Life *is* hard, as hard as nails. Facing it sometimes takes the kind of determination that will not blink even in the face of devils and kings. Yet a little local assembly or house church is not a training camp for heroes. There are no heroes in any such gathering—just as there are no villains. There is just the little body, a body that happens inseparably from the bodies who travel to assemble together, who assemble in intercession to lament, petition, give thanks, and praise; to eat, drink, laugh, and weep; to work . . . and to wait. The little local church happens only where those bodies mingle in their gathering and scattering. For it to be a martyr-church is for it—a social body—to live without fear of extinction, however elusively, even if its extinction looms at the horizon with an incontrovertible inevitability. Even if its extinction will indeed have ended the measurable advance of its good work, the witness of that body need not fall silent, its faithful work need not evaporate. That is the confidence born from the waters of baptism, fed on loaves and fishes, fed on the body and blood of "that [resurrected/crucified] one." And if this little local body is indeed to get behind *that* Messiah and follow him where *he* goes, it will find itself suffering as well. For to follow *this* Messiah is to move into intimate solidarity with those who have no standing before imperial powers and their functionaries, solidarity with those who are most threatened by extinction, those who are most despised and rejected, most targeted for arrest and expulsion. It is to follow the Messiah who goes ahead of us into Galilee.

It is a long and winding road that leads to Galilee, however. Nonetheless, to follow *this* Messiah is to be among pilgrims on this road. A little village assembly or house-church assembles precisely on the *road* to Galilee, for it is to Galilee that the Reign of God travels. And yet there is no telling who will be encountered on that road. Even if we find no readable sign that we are in the vicinity of Galilee, an interruption of our progress may give a kind of signal, an ambiguous signal, like an empty tomb, from which faint echoes of the passage of Jesus are to be heard. These pilgrims look for *ways* of heading out again and they are not simply blind to the way the path leads—because the performance of the good news has so unsparingly marked their line of sight. And so, they look not only for those kindred to them, but above all for strangers; not only for people with comparable world views, but above all for those with alien ones; not only for people with goods for the journey, but above all for those whose deficiencies are likely to drain the goods already on hand; not only for people with plenty of time available for travel, but above all for those whose advanced years, infancy, emotional vulnerability, institutional confinement, illness, scrambled patterns of behavior, or negligible social/political/economic standing makes traveling uncertain—for it is this very wound that tears through the heavens, the Temple, the body of Jesus, and his grave that tears through the borders and prison walls that by exclusion would reserve the future for those who have learned to play to their advantage the world as it now stands. It is perhaps to those whose future has been systematically foreclosed, rather the way a dead body in a tomb has had its future foreclosed, it is perhaps to and through them that the road to Galilee passes, it is perhaps to and through them that the resurrected body of Jesus has already traveled.

We are children of Aristotle, the children of Plato, the children of Socrates. It comes naturally for us in the world-domination of Western Civilization to be adept at categorization: e.g., in terms of kingdom, class, family, genus, and species. It is normal, when one categorizes, typically and habitually to think first of some encompassing domain within the boundaries of which some subject under examination is to be included; then to think of those essential qualities or accidents of history that make the subject different from others included in the same domain. This procedure is sometimes called definition by genus and difference, *genus proximum et differentia specifica*. In following it, one privileges the more abstract of the two terms and thus makes even what differs in, with, under, and about the subject before one a matter of abstraction. This holds perhaps even if one begins by setting the boundaries of the genus by interning and probing a large collection of subjects that one later has branded by it. It is by abstracting differences that a genus comes to stand over a species, even more so, as a kingdom, say, comes to stand over a family. In this scheme of categorization, the particular subject is secondary to its encompassing domain, is granted meaning by and within it, and would evaporate into oblivion without it, a stranger with no place to lay her head, an outcast, crucified, dead, and buried.

Consequently, the first instinct of those thus educated, thus enlightened, when encountering any noun or noun phrase, is to invoke eminent domain. An abstraction is called for to exercise authority over it or the noun or noun phrase is taken *as* itself already the abstraction, the authority to which certain species under this genus must submit. Thus, I may think of "Catholic Church" (with uppercase letters) as *one of* the Christian churches (even if a particularly high or low one, depending on the chart); or I may think of "catholic church" (without uppercase letters) as the "universal church," the domain within the boundaries of which all churches and kinds of churches are to be kept.[51] This is just the declension one is disciplined to carry out, when one encounters that very phrase in Ignatius' letter of the very early second century, "To the Smyrnaeans." There he writes, "where Jesus Christ is, there is the [*katholikē ekklēsia*]" (8:2).[52] However, Ignatius' usage here is not at all clear. It is, e.g., uncertain where to situate this phrase in a nominative taxonomy. It is unclear *where* we should *look* to find it, to lay hold of it; or *how* we should look for it or lay hold of it; or where we should *put* it once we have it. Will it hover high above the ground or walk, steadfast, upon it? Is it to be capitalized?[53] Is it "taxonomic" at all?[54]

51. The rules of capitalization are especially unstable. Capital letters may also signal the more abstract term, as they do, e.g., in Cyril Richardson's translation, i.e., interpretation, of Ignatius.

52. Ignatius of Antioch, "To the Smyrnaeans," in *Early Christian Fathers*, 115. See Polycarp's usage in "The Martyrdom of Saint Polycarp," 151 (8:1).

53. In Richardson's translation, the phrase is capitalized: "Catholic Church." He has made a decision about the "*katholikē ekklēsia*" of which Ignatius is speaking: "It stands for the universal and transcendent Church in contrast to the local congregation" (his introductory comments to "To the Smyrnaeans," 112). And yet, this prioritization of "the universal and transcendent" seems oddly out of place in a discourse set against Docetism.

54. It might be helpful here to invoke a haunting of the ghost of Kierkegaard's pseudonym, Johannes Climacus, that pseudonym who most maintains the incommensurability of the gospel vis-à-vis the habits of this world, the categories by which we manage what falls under our gaze, the universals by which we distinguish between nobility and ignobility, authenticity and inauthenticity, integrity and brokenness. Climacus is a disillusioned ethicist who laughs at the proprieties of proper society but who in his disillusionment stands paralyzed at the very edge of "religiousness." He strains to take in the

"*The Cup That I Drink You Will Drink . . .*"

This is, by the way, the very first "appearance in Christian literature" of "*katholikē ekklēsia*."[55] Custom, therefore, is not to be assumed. We might ask, therefore, how the phrase takes shape in Ignatius' letter.

The letter, "To the Smyrnaeans," is quite brief, one of a handful written quickly as Ignatius, chained to a small detachment of Roman soldiers, was being transported from Antioch, where he served as bishop, to Rome, where he was to be martyred.[56] Many of the stated concerns in this letter repeat those of the others, but they come together with a particularly illuminating coherence here.

Though it speaks of the importance of heeding the bishop, together with the presbyters and deacons who serve with the bishop, the letter does not read like a directive set down to reinforce institutional power; none of

---

light of the "paradoxical" as it dawns on a distant horizon, both unable and unwilling to venture toward that unknown country. It is not just "the infinite qualitative difference between eternity and time" that makes laughable all our attempts to domesticate God. It is in particular the one history that is named "Jesus," the "human-who-is-God," that brings to ruin even the attempt to find continuity between our own deepest depths and the God who, as spirit, is "spiritually other." Therefore, even the "spiritual" significance of discontinuity between God and the human being is relativized to the particular work of Jesus. Kierkegaard [Johannes Climacus], *Concluding Unscientific Postscript*, 570–86. And so, the gospel tells us we meet God where one human being is born, lives, and dies far away, long ago, outside the purview of our calculative and evaluative scrutiny. Thus Climacus is a "humorist."

55. Richardson's introductory remarks, "To the Smyrnaeans," 112.

56. The Empire was vast. For centuries Rome pervaded very nearly every region into which the church moved. It was in the air and the water, underfoot, in hearth and home. Rome was "tolerant." It left room for local customs and was pleased when its subjects grew strong to keep the "peace." It was convinced that it was carrying out a kind of cosmic mandate, a manifest destiny, to bring the world into conformity with the ways of God. Cosmic law extended to the laws of social interaction, which in turn extended to the laws of the Empire, which extended finally to the office of the Emperor. To follow the Emperor was to follow a godly man, embodying a godly order. Of course, *Pax Romana* was a delicate balance and had to be maintained sometimes by extreme measures. Though lining the Appian Way with bodies bleeding and suffocating on crosses was for Rome a rare form of peacekeeping, the threat of violence was not; indeed, it was as omnipresent as Rome itself. And unless it had not only the machines of death but also the will to use them, a threat could not be sustained. The more its displays of violence took place out in the open before crowds of onlookers the more effective they were. It is not that Rome was sadistic. Such measures were simply an efficient way to secure the conditions favorable for the property rights Roman practicality made proper to its private citizens. Its functionaries, themselves under threat, were charged with keeping the enemies of the Roman peace under surveillance. When it was time for Rome to make its might manifest, those under close watch would be hauled off to arenas to die for the good of all. It is a logic all too easily understood.

his letters do. Bishops, presbyters, and deacons are to be understood here not as fingers in the fist of a multinational conglomerate, but as a kind of locus where the work of a particular body of people converges. That is, though these titles are no longer as ambiguous, even interchangeable, as they had been just a few years earlier, their becoming more determinate seems not to be a rigidification. The bishop is not yet a superintendent of an ecclesiastical territory, but is a kind of "localizing of the teaching, ruling, and prophetic functions of the original missionary ministry of apostles, prophets, and catechists."[57] That is, the bishop is indistinguishable from the local church with which the bishop serves. Together, they are local people, performing local work.[58]

It is *as* local that one such church engages and is engaged by others. They do so *by their work*, i.e., close to the ground, not by the mediation of an abstraction, e.g., by an umbrella organization or a general headquarters. They *are* the work they do. Their work *constitutes* them—i.e., in its performance, not as an accomplished fact. Further, theirs is *eschatological* work, a work the weight of which is born not by what was and is, but by what is to come, a future that even in the most memorable moment is at best anticipated. These are churches, because they are *eucharistic liturgies*, work that remembers and hopes toward a *polis* yet to be, work that will not rest in a serene inner experiential presence, work that repeats the work of the Christ toward whom they are a gesture. They labor outward in expectation of the repetition of Easter Sunday, in which will be raised "in the flesh" like Jesus (3:1–2) the children of the liturgy—among whom are to be counted not only the living, but both the dead and the yet-to-be-born, however widely separated in chronic space and time; local people, every one. Such local bodies concur, with a rhythm as syncopated as the celebration of bread and wine, here and there across the face of the earth, at the hospitable tables of widows and orphans who remember Holy Week. Their work is performed on the first day in order to be performed on every day. So, it is no surprise that churches sent delegates to meet with Ignatius and comfort him, as he was transported to Rome. And it is no surprise that Ignatius calls upon

---

57. Richardson, "Letters of Ignatius," 76; and his "Introduction to Early Christian Literature and Its Setting," 20.

58. In Ign. *Pol.* (2:1–2 [118]), Ignatius indicates what he understands a bishop's work to be about: "It is no credit to you if you are fond of good pupils. Rather by your gentleness subdue those who are annoying. . . . In all circumstances be 'wise as a serpent,' and perpetually 'harmless as a dove.' The reason you have a body as well as a soul is that you may win the favor of the visible world."

those very churches to send envoys to make the difficult journey to Antioch to rejoice in the flesh with the members of the church there that the persecution that had cost Ignatius so dearly had at last come to an end.[59]

"To the Smyrnaeans" is a nostalgia-less eulogy to embodiment. It is largely a response to the harm done to the gospel, i.e., to the work of the church, by Docetism, that christological theory (let's be bold to call it a heresy) which denies the flesh and blood of Jesus Christ. In its denunciation of Docetism's revulsion before the earthiness, the defenselessness, the woundedness, the mortality of "the flesh," the letter comes to situate the whole of the economy of God in embodied human living,[60] the living that is work and food and drink. Ignatius is not interested in delineating a *universal principle* of embodied human living, but in bearing witness to the particular coarseness, density, and hospitality of the body of Christ. As he speaks of the body of Christ, he speaks, of course, of the life, death, and resurrection of Jesus (1:1—3:2); but he also speaks of the eucharist (7:1), of the frailty of widows, orphans, the oppressed, the imprisoned, the hungry, and the thirsty (6:2), of baptisms, love feasts, and marriages, and consequently of the bishop (8:1–9:1) and of the martyr (4:2). It is as if the body of Jesus of Nazareth had on the cross lost its integrity, opened, and drawn into itself all that by the breath of the Spirit might open to it, especially all those who labor and are heavy laden.

Again, the bishop, according to Ignatius, is inseparable from the whole network of life-trajectories that intersect as the liturgy of the local church.[61] Though each of its members is entangled in the others, the bishop is uniquely so. It is the bishop who, as *one body*, performs and authorizes to be performed those deeds that by God's grace *gather together* the *ecclesial body*, e.g., in the face of the assaults of heresy on the economy of the Father, the Son, and the Holy Spirit.[62] It is the bishop, together with those the

---

59. See Ign. *Eph.* 21:1; Ign. *Magn.* 15:1; Ign. *Trall.* 13:1; Ign. *Rom.* 10:1; Ign. *Phld.* 10:1–2, 11:2; Ign. *Smyrn.* 11:2–3, 12:1; Ign. *Pol.* 7:1–8:3.

60. LaCugna, *God For Us*, 25: Generally, in the New Testament "'economy' refers to the plan made known in the coming of Christ.... In the Apostolic Fathers *oikonomia* was used to refer to the whole series of events pertaining to Christ. Ignatius of Antioch, for example, in his letter to the Ephesians [18.2], wrote that 'Jesus Christ was conceived in the womb of Mary according to the economy of God' [Richardson has "in God's plan"].... [B]y the end of the third century, *oikonomia* is more narrowly understood as a synonym for Incarnation."

61. I think of John Wesley's description of the church in his "On Zeal": "the entire connected system of Christianity" (314 [II.6]).

62. Ign. *Eph.* 9:1: "I have heard that some strangers came your way with a wicked

bishop sends, who attend to the eucharist, baptism, the love feast, marriage, protection of widows, care for the poor, for slaves, and for outcasts, and in all things the fostering of humility, love, and devotion to God.[63] In such work the *dunamis* that washes over the bishop is at play.[64]

Of course, such *dunamis* is nobody's private property, any more than a miracle is. It is a gift that never ceases being a gift. *God*, "the Father of Jesus Christ, who is everyone's bishop,"[65] ordains the ephemeral, human bishop, whose *dunamis* remains derivative (Smyrn 11:1).[66] Therefore, though his words are soon to become fuel for the run-away train of ecclesiastical authoritarianism, there is still subtlety and humility at work when Ignatius says: "You should all follow the bishop as Jesus Christ did the Father" (8:1). The bishop attends to the eucharistic celebration; the eucharist is not "valid" *unless* the bishop attends to it[67]—as if the bishop were indistinguishable from the eucharist. "Where the bishop is present, there let the congregation gather" (8:2). Certainly, the bishop is as fallible as anyone. Ignatius goes out of his way to speak of himself, Bishop of Antioch, as "the least among" the people of God there, the one who does not "deserve to be a member of that church," but who is given "the privilege" by God (11:1).[68] Ignatius has not

---

teaching. But you did not let them sow it among you. You stopped up your ears to prevent admitting what they disseminated. Like stones of God's Temple, ready for a building of God the Father, you are being hoisted up by Jesus Christ, as with a crane (that's the cross!), while the rope you use is the Holy Spirit. Your faith is what lifts you up, while love is the way you ascend to God."

63. That the unity of the local church happens with the work of the bishop is a theme running through all of Ignatius' letters. See in particular Ign. *Eph.* 20:2; Ign. *Phld.* 7:2—8:2; Ign. *Smyr.* 6:2—7:2, 8:1–2, 13:2; Ign. *Pol.* 2:1–2 (and n. 25), 4:1, 4:3, 5:2, cf. also the letter's opening.

64. Instead of the Greek *dunamis*, it might be more efficient to say "authority" or "power," but we think we know what those words signify. The task of the bishop is to be a capaciousness where the coming of God occurs. The bishop in that sense, we might say, is an icon.

65. Ign. *Magn.* 3:1. The verse continues: "You ought to respect him as fully as you respect the authority of God the Father [*dunamin theou patros*]."

66. See also Ign. *Pol.* 7:3, and the opening, as well as Ign. *Phld.* 7:1–2, where this is affirmed more directly.

67. Or at least someone the bishop has sent.

68. "It is a fine thing to acknowledge," Ignatius writes, not simply the bishop, but "*God* and the bishop" (9:1, emphasis added). Although Ignatius' words above could be read as polite pseudo-self-deprecation, it might be more interesting to let his remarks bleed into his account of the bishop, that to be a bishop is to be "the least among" the women, men, and children of a local church.

forgotten that he is as carnal[69] as the crucified/resurrected Jesus. Indeed, it is as flesh and blood, as vulnerable and weak, that the bishop, too, is to be faithful to the God of the crucified Jesus Christ. And so, the bishop, together with the people of God among whom the bishop serves, must *train* to persevere to the end, to "get to God," as did Jesus Christ (11:1).[70] It is precisely because the way of Jesus to the Father was the way of the cross that the faithful, too, are to expect to bear witness with their bodies, their flesh and blood, at the hands of the same violent powers that slaughtered his body. "Why, then, have I given myself up completely to death, fire, sword, and wild beasts? For the simple reason that near the sword means near God. To be with wild beasts means to be with God. But it must all be in the name of Jesus Christ. To share in his Passion I go through everything" (4:2). This is not a death wish, a longing for dreamless sleep, for emancipation from this troubled world. Ignatius is praying here that he might be faithful to the way of Christ to the cross, in this way to travel on hard ground.

The bishop is to *love*. In fact it is precisely a failure of love that has yielded Docetism, Ignatius believes. Docetism stands aloof from bodies and blood, neutral, at a safe distance, where there is no danger, where there is no conflict, where no one can interrupt. To love, however, is to place oneself in the midst of bodily life where it is most imperiled. It is for me in all my earthiness to touch and be touched by those as earthy, as carnal as am I, those as easy to wound and kill as am I, those in themselves as inglorious as in myself am I. That is, it is for me in the flesh to acknowledge that Jesus Christ was a letter written in blood to the lost, weak, and forsaken of the world, to the hungry and the despised, that announced that the Reign of God is coming and it is coming for the ones to whom the mutilated body of the crucified opens in invitation.

---

69. Cf. Ign. *Pol.* 2:2.

70. "Share your hard training together—wrestle together, run together, suffer together, go to bed together, get up together, as God's stewards, assessors, and assistants.... Let none of you prove a deserter" (Ign. *Pol.* 6:1-2; cf. *Mart. Pol.* 18:3). This "training" may not simply be metaphorical. See Young, *In Procession Before the World*. Cf. Whitfield, *Pilgrim Holiness*, 51: "[Young] is certainly right to suggest that martyrdom in this period was a quasi-liturgical performance meant to convert the world, but in order to understand martyrdom genuinely as something even beyond the conflict between 'two distinct societies' divergent sacrificial systems,' an even broader theological horizon must be found.... There is something more to the martyrs' actions that understands their suffering and death not as competitive and irresolvable but, more importantly, as redemptive and reconciling." See York, *Purple Crown*, 39.

After Crucifixion

> Pay close attention to those who have wrong notions about the grace of Jesus Christ, which has come to us, and note how at variance they are with God's mind. They care nothing about love: they have no concern for widows or orphans, for the oppressed, for those in prison or released, for the hungry or the thirsty. They hold aloof from the Eucharist and from services of prayer, because they refuse to admit that the Eucharist is the flesh of our Saviour Jesus Christ, which suffered for our sins and which, in his goodness, the Father raised [from the dead]. Consequently those who wrangle and dispute God's gift face death. They would have done better to love and so share in the resurrection. (Smyrn 6:2–7:2)

Insofar as it is a body practiced in the art of death and resurrection, of love and sacrifice, of abasement and exaltation, of bearing and being born by others, of the work of the body and blood of Christ, a local church is where the catholic church—every organ and cell of every church at whatever geographical or historical locus—concurs, for "where Jesus Christ is, there is the [*katholikē ekklēsia*]" (Smyrn 8:2).[71]

Ignatius' journey from Antioch to Rome pointedly performs the liturgy of the eucharist.[72] Eucharist is practice for martyrdom,[73] for the por-

---

71. *Mart. Pol.* speaks of Polycarp as "episkopos tes en Smyne katholikēs ekklēsias," "the bishop of the catholic church in Smyrna" (16:2).

72. It is also to be said, however, that martyrs are not only to be found under the watchful eye of an unambiguously hostile, oppressive government. The shape taken by a martyr-life varies according to the places and times in which providence has situated her. In any case, however, she is a member of a body whose kenotic deeds are an extension of the liturgy of the eucharist in such a way that she with her sisters and brothers bears overt and radical witness above all to the crucifixion/resurrection of Jesus, i.e., to the work of atonement. The martyr of the early church bore witness before disbelieving pagan onlookers that they, too, might enter into the path of righteousness. Martyrs gave themselves to those who broke their bodies. The martyr at some other time and place would perform atoning deeds of a different texture, deeds that in the Spirit through the Son would nonetheless open to become the site of the irruptive advent of the Holy Father. The martyr follows the way of truth and life out into the violence of sin and death, waiting actively for the glorification of God there. Above all this means that the martyr is anointed by the Spirit, as was Jesus, to "bring good news to the poor . . . to proclaim release to the captives and recovery of sight to the blind, to let the oppressed go free, to proclaim the year of the [Sovereign's] favor" (Luke 4:18, from Isa 61:1); and to do so with him as he did, with his "mind": so standing in solidarity with the poor, the captive, the blind, and the oppressed that there is for her as there was for Jesus no "them" to be pitied, say, from a safe "above." Of course, when I say "mind" here I am thinking of Philippians 2, but I am also thinking of Romans 12 and most of all of the way Mark 12:30 and 31 play off of each other, as Jesus enters more and more into solidarity particularly with the outcasts among his neighbors.

73. See Ign. *Rom.* 7:2–3 and Ign. *Pol.* 6:1–7:1. See York, *Purple Crown*, 38–42.

tendant repetition of Christ's work, of the breaking of his body and the shedding of his blood.[74] Again and again Ignatius calls for the prayers of the churches to whom he writes so that he may endure faithfully to the end, that he might bear witness to God's faithfulness to the crucified Christ by being gifted with a death like his.[75] Ignatius is remembering the eucharist when he writes: "I am God's wheat and I am being ground by the teeth of wild beasts to make a pure loaf for Christ" (Rom 4:1).

Certainly, death at the hands of the persecutors of the church does not in itself make a martyr. There are fraudulent, pseudo-martyrs among those murdered for the sake, e.g., of the *Pax Romana*. The story of the martyrdom of the elderly Polycarp, for whom Ignatius specially cared, when Polycarp was the young Bishop of Smyrna, provides insight not only into his martyrdom or Ignatius', but also of the *manner* of martyrdom, of its logic, when it was then understood to be "conformable to the gospel" (Mart Pol 1:1).[76]

The account of Polycarp is briefly contrasted with that of Quintus, a recent arrival to Smyrna and therefore not yet well woven into the liturgical life of the church there. Quintus, anxious to be martyred during a time of persecution against the church in Smyrna, "[forces] himself and some others to come forward voluntarily" (4:1), that is, throws himself (and not himself alone!) into the hands of the proconsul. That he apostatizes follows,

74. York, *Purple Crown*, 56–57: "Discipleship . . . is a mark of the church rooted in the Eucharist. . . . If there is no broken body and no spilled blood of Christ, it is difficult to imagine that there could be a church, for it is the body of Jesus that makes the body of Christ, the church, possible. . . . By feeding on the body of Christ, we are transformed into a different creature, one that remembers the sacrifice of Christ and now pledges to participate in that soteriological reality known as the kingdom of God. Our bodies are reconfigured, because they are now directed toward the redemption and reconciliation that Jesus made possible through the cross."

75. See Ign. *Trall.* 2:1, 13:3; Ign. *Rom.* 3:1–10:3; Ign. *Smyrn.* 4:1–2; and Ign. *Pol.* 2:3. See York, *Purple Crown*, 27. Ignatius goes so far as to say that his hope is that he will be raised from the dead in his bonds (Ign. *Eph.* 11:2). What strikes us as contradictory to a liberated life is thus swallowed up in the glorification of a mutilated body that in resurrection is not made whole.

76. Not surprisingly, Polycarp cared for Ignatius, too, and in Pol. *Phil.* 9:1–2 (135) remembered his martyrdom as a faithful witness: "Now I exhort all of you to be obedient to the word of righteousness and to exercise all patient endurance, such as you have seen with your very eyes, not only in the blessed Ignatius and Zosimus and Rufus, but also in others who were of your membership, and in Paul himself and the rest of the apostles; being persuaded that all these 'did not run in vain,' but in faith and righteousness, and that they are now in their deserved place with the Lord, in whose suffering they also shared. For they 'loved not this present world,' but Him who died on our behalf and was raised by God for our sakes."

After Crucifixion

according to the letter, from his failure to heed the gospel. Martyrdom is not a goal to be pursued. Churches are to train for it, to practice for it, to live toward it and through it, but not to *aim* for it (see 18:3). Therefore, though he knows that the city of Smyrna is shouting for his blood, Polycarp, mindful of the gospel and the grace of God, neither flees from nor runs to the city's officials. He yields to the appeal of "the majority" of the church and withdraws to a farm outside the city, where he stays "with a few friends, doing nothing else night and day but pray for all men and for the churches throughout the world, as was his constant habit" (5:1, cf. 8:1 and 16:2).[77] After moving to another farm, he is discovered by the police.[78] He greets them hospitably, when they arrive, converses with them, and serves them "food and drink" (7:2). They in turn give him time to pray, before they take him into the city.

Upon Polycarp's arrival in town, the story becomes even stranger. It is clear that neither the chief of police nor the proconsul wants to execute him. "What harm is there," Herod asks, "to say 'Lord Caesar,' and to offer incense and all that sort of thing, and save yourself?" The proconsul uses a series of rhetorical tools to get him to change his testimony, from gentle appeal to the threat of torture, from pity to anger. Polycarp remains calm and determined. At last, when he refuses to apostatize, the crowd is enraged, "This is the teacher of Asia, the father of Christians, the destroyer of our gods, who teaches many not to sacrifice nor to worship" (12:2). Contrary to their wishes, wild animals are unavailable to provide the most entertaining spectacle in the arena; consequently, after he strips himself of his clothes,[79] he is set at a stake above a large heap of wood to be burned alive. He prays, "Lord God Almighty, Father of thy beloved and blessed Servant Jesus Christ . . . I bless thee, because thou hast deemed me worthy of this

---

77. Perhaps he also prayed for the emperor. Pol. *Phil.* 12:3: "'Pray also for emperors and magistrates and rulers,' and for 'those who persecute and hate you,' and for 'the enemies of the cross,' that your fruit may be manifest in all, so that you may be perfected in him."

78. That it is noted in the letter that the chief of police is named Herod is only one element of this story that shows how closely the death of Polycarp is connected to the crucifixion of Jesus (6:2).

79. What reads like an aside, but perhaps is not, is a note about the removal of his shoes: "When the fire was ready, and he had divested himself of all his clothes and unfastened his belt, he tried to take off his shoes, though he was not heretofore in the habit of doing this because [each of] the faithful always vied with one another as to which of them would be first to touch his body. For he had always been honored, even before his martyrdom, for his holy life" (*Mart. Pol.* 13:2).

"The Cup That I Drink You Will Drink..."

day and hour, to take my part in the number of the martyrs, *in the cup of thy Christ*, for 'resurrection to eternal life' of soul and body in the immortality of the Holy Spirit" (14:1–3).[80] When the fire is lit, his body is surrounded but not touched by the flames: "And he was in the midst, not as burning flesh, but as *bread baking* . . ." (15:2, emphasis added). When it becomes evident that his body will not burn, the executioner plunges a dagger into it: "And when he did this [a dove and][81] *a great quantity of blood* came forth, so that the fire was quenched" (16:1, emphasis added). The eucharistic imagery here is blatant. What it signifies is not, say, that Polycarp has ascended or might ascend to some lofty plane occupied by Christ, to become a kind of co-redeemer. It signifies rather that the celebration of the eucharist and its outworking in martyrdom are a *testimony to* the work of Christ.

> But the jealous and malicious evil one . . . instigated Nicetas, the father of Herod . . . to plead with the magistrate not to give up [Polycarp's] body, "else," said he, "they will abandon the Crucified and begin worshipping this one" . . . being ignorant that we can never forsake Christ, who suffered for the salvation of the whole world . . . nor can we ever worship any other. For we worship the One as Son of God, but we love the martyrs as disciples and imitators of the Lord, deservedly so, because of their unsurpassable devotion to their own King and Teacher. *May it be also our lot to be their companions and fellow disciples!*[82]

Polycarp "was not only a noble teacher, but also a distinguished martyr, whose martyrdom all desire to imitate as one according to the gospel of Christ" (19:1).

---

80. Emphasis added. Whitfield, *Pilgrim Holiness*, 98: "the speech [of martyrs] is not closed; rather it is open to the later memory of the church and also the judgment of God."

81. A likely interpolated, if nonetheless delightful, phrase (see *Mart. Pol.*, 155, n. 33).

82. *Mart. Pol.* 17:1–3, emphasis added. The passage continues: "The captain of the Jews, when he saw their contentiousness, set it [i.e., his body] in the midst and burned it, as was their custom. So we later took up his bones, more precious than costly stones and more valuable than gold, and laid them away in a suitable place. There the Lord will permit us, so far as possible, to gather together in joy and gladness to celebrate the day of his martyrdom as a birthday, in memory of those athletes who have gone before, and to train and make ready those who are to come hereafter" (*Mart. Pol.* 18:1–3).

After Crucifixion

Of course, to those of us who have learned to spiritualize, who spend our days and nights working up strategies for the care of souls, who have with a sigh of relief outsourced the care of bodies to the ever vigilant coercive nation-state, who have turned Luther's *sola gratia, sola fide* into an excuse for disengaged withdrawal from hazardous work, who float above pain and grief in a perpetually delayed bulimic "willingness," who are more than satisfied to live in the warmth of private religious experience, these tales of early or mid-second-century martyrdom seem so intemperate, so preposterous, so unnecessary, so fanatical. If you ask Ignatius how he knows Jesus Christ lives, his answer is to give himself quietly and gratefully to be taken by those who despise his witness, i.e., to be gifted by martyrdom.[83] If you ask us, we answer, "he lives within my heart."[84]

Of course, we are not the first to screen out Jesus' call to imitate his crucifixion. Mark 10 exhibits the phenomenon with great force. Just days from his betrayal, torture, and crucifixion, after declaring that the Reign of God "belongs" to the most vulnerable in that or this world, among whom the faithful are to be numbered (14–16), after commanding the Rich Young Ruler to "go, sell . . . give . . . ; then come, follow me" (21), after telling his disciples that "persecutions" will accompany all the goods they receive (30) and that the Son of Man "will be handed over to the chief priests and the scribes, and they will condemn him to death; then they will hand him over to the Gentiles; they will mock him, and spit upon him, and flog him, and kill him" (33–34), James and John, the sons of Zebedee, approach Jesus, as if he were a genie fresh from a bottle, and ask him to: "Grant us to sit, one at your right hand and one at your left, in your glory" (37). Jesus replies indirectly with discernment, "You do not know what you are asking. Are you able to drink the cup that I drink, or be baptized with the baptism that I am baptized with?" (38). Stupidly, as if caught up into a horror comedy, they answer, "We are able." So, Jesus makes them a promise: "The cup that I drink you will drink; and with the baptism with which I am baptized, you

---

83. Whitfield, *Pilgrim Holiness*, 98: "For the martyrs to say that Jesus is Lord was to speak explicitly in and to their present world, but it was also to speak in such a way as to open up themselves and the world to further nuances of factual discourse. This is what it means for the martyrs to speak eschatologically. . . . [The] martyrs become those who confess a whole new world for which God waits to reenter its history and show himself face to face." (Cf. Ign. *Eph.* 15:1–2; see also Ign. *Magn.* 8:2; Ign. *Phld.* 1:2).

84. Hauerwas, *In Good Company*, 78: "we will not know how to tell our story well unless we are able to know what martyrdom even today might look like."

will be baptized; but to sit at my right hand or at my left is not mine to grant, but it is for those for whom it has been prepared" (39–40).

Churches far and wide have thrown themselves into the good work of healing the wounded. They pull together the resources needed for various kinds of recovery, for marriage counseling, for personal and more broadly social adjustment, for a great many of the disorders that plague a world fragmented, say, by the individualizing pressures of liberal democracy and global capitalism. And by their programmatic activity good is done. And certainly Jesus and the apostles are shown in the Gospels and in the book of Acts to be very much involved in the good work of healing. However, to be healed here in the tale of Jesus is not to be shown to the exit of this hard world, but to be called back into it, into the jaws of the beast that broke your back in the first place. And this is by no means one calling among others, e.g., a calling during rare moments of social unrest for a few über-saints. Nor is it a calling for *collections* of those individuated configurations of human tissue that are labeled and listed on church rolls. The local church itself is called into the jaws of the beast.

When at Caesarea Philippi the momentarily faithful, confessing Peter stands addressed by Jesus in the Matthean account, attention at first focused on Peter, shifts to what Jesus calls "my church" (*mou ten ekklesian*). Whatever we do with "this rock," the church that is built upon it is to have a surprising relationship to hell: "the *gates* of Hades will not prevail against" the church, we hear Jesus say (Matt 16:18, emphasis added). Inasmuch as getting into hell requires no unusual measures, it seems reasonable to take the gates of hell as locked *against* the dead, i.e., those who upon entering this pit abandon all hope. If the church is to burst through them, it seems, again, reasonable to imagine that it would do so from the inside. That is, from all appearances, the church does its work *there, in hell*. And from all appearances it does its work there precisely because that is where Jesus goes. Peter ceases to be a faithful disciple, when instead of following Jesus to Golgotha, he turns his back to the cross, places the full weight of his body between it and Jesus, and setting his resolve against the one he has just named "the Messiah, the Son of the living God" (16), opposes him to his face.[85] Jesus' reply to Peter, the famous "Get behind me, [Adversary]!" speech (23), is a call to Peter to convert, to cease impeding the way of the cross, to turn around, to put himself—and implicitly the church—*behind* Jesus and together follow him *into hell*. Immediately after his rebuke, Jesus

---

85. Hovey, *To Share in the Body*, 67.

says to his disciples: "If any want to become my followers, let them deny themselves and take up their cross and follow me" (24).

Of course, to follow Jesus into hell is no suicide, any more than the martyrdom of Polycarp was. It is not to fixate upon hell as a goal, as if dying—even dying an especially noble death—were an achievement. It is, however, to understand that the final enemy of the good work done by the children of the earth, the enemy of the doxological work of gathering and offering, the enemy of every expenditure of every eucharistic liturgy, will not have had the last word. It is to work and eat and pray, knowing that all flesh is grass, that rust and moths corrupt and thieves break in and steal, that not only losers, but also winners lose, that the curtain falls and the opera house bursts into flames. It is to work and eat and pray, to give birth, shield, lead, and guide, to act and be acted upon, to rejoice and mourn, all looking to a future that by a good pleasure not within our reach comes to our work, as if our work lacked causative force, but rather became a means of grace, an action ordained by God by which we are given to tarry, to wait, to abide, for God.[86] That every church is to follow Jesus into hell signifies that every church is to train for martyrdom, to train for a death like Jesus', to train as a body of people who do not have to survive, to train as a body of people for a day when every discernable vestige of an ecclesiastical past has been wiped from the face of the earth, to train as a body for the eradication of every readable bar code that would signal the register that another commodity has been conveyed down a broad supermarket belt.[87] For a local church to follow Jesus into hell is for it to abandon its presumption that it is needed, that it offers a unique service to the human race, that it is God's hands and feet, that it can make the world a better place. For a local church to follow Jesus into hell is for it to do its good work—to write through erasures, stutteringly to be taken to task; to sink its hands into the soil; to cut, plane, and set in place; to hold, feed, rock, comfort, and serenade; to release and hope; to let every goal and purpose go to an incoming elusive

---

86. Whitfield, *Pilgrim Holiness*, 102: The martyrs wait; theirs is a "precarious truthfulness," particularly "in the very moment of martyrdom." Wesley, "Means of Grace," 383–84 [II.7, III.1]: "But the main question remains. We know this salvation is the gift and the work of God. But how (may one say, who is convinced he hath it not) may I attain thereto? If you say, 'Believe, and thou shalt be saved,' he answers, 'True; but how am I to wait? In the means of grace, or out of them? Am I to wait for the grace of God which bringeth salvation by using these means, or by laying them aside?' . . . According to . . . Holy Writ . . . in using, not in laying them aside."

87. See Whitfield, *Pilgrim Holiness*, 48.

outside; to abide on the cusp of a nothing before which even nihilism bows its head—in everything remembering that the God whom Jesus addresses as Father is love and even the *nihil* of crucifixion cannot separate us from the *creatio* of God in Christ Jesus. It is to live and die among those most imperiled, most neglected, most despised and rejected, those for whom hell hungrily gapes open day after day, those, i.e., whom we perhaps too casually call "the poor." For "where Jesus Christ is, there is the catholic church."[88]

---

88. See York, *Purple Crown*, 125–44.

Interlude

In the first place, *ruach* is to a large extent the term for a natural power, the wind. . . . It does not mean air as such; it means the moving air. Thus the *ruach* in Genesis 1:2 moves over the waters, like the hovering eagle (Deut 32:11), the trees in Isaiah 7:2 "shake" before the *ruach*. . . . The Yahwist knows the *ruach* above all as the power of the "wind" which proceeds from Yahweh and returns to him that also constitutes the breath of man's life. Job 34:14f.: "If he should take back his *ruach* to himself, and gather to himself his breath, all flesh would perish together, and man would return to dust."[1]

The wind coming down from the snowfields up above sounds for a long time throughout the house. It grows loud and high as if in hope of sweeping the whole house, all of us, away into nothing, leaving the canyon as it once was, but the house stands and the wind dies away again, defeated. Then it comes back, feinting a light blow from the far side, then suddenly a heavy gust from our side. "I keep listening to the wind," I say.[2]

What if I took not only my own views of myself into account but also the other's views of himself and of me? . . . Here is the well-known countenance, the smile, these modulations of voice, whose style is as familiar to me as myself. . . . But should the voice alter, should the unwonted appear in the score of the dialogue, or, on the contrary, should a response respond too well to what I thought without having really said it—and suddenly there breaks forth the evidence that yonder also, minute by minute, life is being lived: somewhere behind those eyes, behind those gestures, or rather before them, or again about them, coming from I know not what double ground of space, another private world shows through, through the fabric of my own, and for a moment I live in it; I am no more than the respondent for the interpellation that is made to me.[3]

---

1. Wolff, *Anthropology of the Old Testament*, 32–33.
2. Pirsig, *Zen and the Art of Motorcycle Maintenance*, 153–54.
3. Merleau-Ponty, *Visible and the Invisible*, 8, 10–11.

Interlude

> Abraham remains silent—but he *cannot* speak. Therein lies the distress and anxiety. Even though I go on talking night and day without interruption, if I cannot make myself understood when I speak, then I am not speaking. This is the case with Abraham. He can say everything, but one thing he cannot say, and if he cannot say that—that is, say it in such a way that the other understands it—then he is not speaking.[4]

SOME TIME AGO, IN what seems now immeasurably past, I chanced upon an opportunity to travel along with Frederick Mund's "Ambassadors" choir to Britain—travelling not as a member of the choir nor even as an attendant,[5] really; more as a hanger on.[6] We crossed to the other side,[7] leaving the Atlantic[8] behind us, arriving, touching down, upon a runway of Heathrow Airport; meeting not a few of the other children of our immemorial ancestral father, those whose English is quite other than what they speak back home[9]—back in Oklahoma, back in what used to be marketed as Indian Territory,[10] back where the survivors of the "Trail of Tears" were cast, back where the "Sooners"[11] staked out their property,[12] property twice stolen

---

4. Kierkegaard [de silentio], *Fear and Trembling*, 113: "The relief provided by speaking is that it translates me into the universal."

5. Foakes-Jackson, *History of the Christian Church*, 579–80: "The lowest class of penitents were known as mourners; after this the sinner was promoted to the second grade, the hearers, who with the heathen might listen to the reading of Scripture in the narthex or porch of the church; next he became a kneeler among the catechumens, but departed before the Canon of the Liturgy began; and finally he was allowed to be present at the Mass but not as a communicant. These divisions did not prevail everywhere, and public penance fell rapidly everywhere into general disuse."

6. Cf. Eliot, *Waste Land*, 38 ["I. The Burial of the Dead," lines 43–56].

7. Cf. Levinas, *Ethics and Infinity*, 56, Gen 12:1; John 11:16; and Mark 5:1–3.

8. *Oxford English Dictionary*, s.v. "Atlantic, *adj.* and *n.*": "< Latin *Atlanticus* . . . see Atlas *n.*1."

9. Cf. Horkheimer and Adorno, *Dialectic of Enlightenment*, 78.

10. *Oxford English Dictionary*, s.v. "territory, *n.*1": "< its etymon classical Latin *territōrium* area of land enclosed within the boundaries of a town, in post-classical Latin also denoting a variety of types of area or district." But this lies in the history of *Oxford English Dictionary* etymologies (2nd ed., 1989): "the original form has suggested derivation from *terrēre* to frighten, whence *territor* frightener, *territōrium* '[perhaps] a place from which people are warned off.'"

11. Cf. *Oxford English Dictionary*, s.v. "soon, *adv.*" and Ps 130:5–6.

12. *Oxford English Dictionary*, s.v. "proper, *adj.*, *n.*, and *adv.*": "< Anglo-Norman *proper, propire* . . . belonging exclusively . . . , rendering a concept exactly . . . , identical . .

from faceless,[13] propertyless, aboriginal[14] nomads[15]—but I digress; where was I?—oh, yes—meeting not a few of those foreigners whose written word has made its mark even in the adopted land of Sequoyah.[16]

The choir, after making their roundabout way to the Scots in the north—caged and protected as they were in their coach—returned to London unruffled, perched upon that capital, and sang.

I left it all to them for a time, taking a different route, following a course laid out not by an expressway,[17] but by a pair of iron tracks[18] that carried me and the train in which I nervously sat to old Oxford.[19] For the whole day I wandered aimlessly over its streets, weaving in and out of the

---

., appropriate. . . . immaculate . . . , correct . . . , meticulously neat . . . and its etymon classical Latin *proprius* one's own, personal, private, peculiar, special, particular, suitable, appropriate, expressed in appropriate terms, literal, . . . denoting a particular person or place. . . . Anglo-Norman and Middle French *propre* private property, wealth. . . ." Taylor, *Erring*, 40: "A proper name, therefore, is peculiar, characteristic, and individual. It is one's own, a private possession or private property that one owns. One who has a proper name is not common but is distinctive, correct, of high quality and good character . . . respectable, never soiled, stained, or blemished, always neat, tidy, and clean. To have a proper name is to be true, real—in short, authentic."

13. Cf. Dostoevsky, *Brothers Karamazov*, 236–37.

14. Cf. *Oxford English Dictionary*, s.v. "ab origine, *adv.*"

15. Cf. Deut 26:4–7.

16. *New Columbia Encyclopedia*, 4th ed., s.v. "Sequoya": "North American Indian leader, creator of the Cherokee syllabary. . . . To most Americans he was known as George Guess."

17. Heidegger, "Memorial Address," 45: "An expressway, where nothing grows, cannot be a fallow field."

18. Cf. Claiborne, *Roots of English*, s.v. "eis-1" and *Oxford English Dictionary*, s.v. "track, *n.*"

19. Cf. Suzuki, "Ten Oxherding Pictures, 1, by Kaku-an," 129–30.

Interlude

doorways of a university[20] to which I did not belong; until I stumbled accidentally[21] into *Aedes Christi*, the House of Christ.[22]

I entered Christ Church College on the New Walk side, avoiding the front, the main point of access; avoiding Christopher Wren's[23] Tom Tower and the Great Tom by which it keeps time.[24]

20. *Oxford English Dictionary*, s.v. "university, *n*.": "community, corporation . . . , totality, universality . . . the whole of creation . . . the whole, entire number, sum of things, universe . . . universality, generalization. . . ."

21. *Oxford English Dictionary*, s.v. "accident, *n*.": "use as noun of present participle of *accidere* to fall, to happen < *ac*- ac- *prefix* + *cadere* to fall (see cadence *n*.). . . . The Greek word had been used in Aristotle (e.g., *Metaphysics* 1052a18, 1052a31) as a philosophical term denoting a contingent attribute, or an attribute necessarily resulting from the notion of something, but not entering into its definition; Christian Latin writers from Tertullian onwards use *accidens* in the former of these philosophical senses (more or less precisely, and with various refinements in scholastic writings), often in contrast with *substantia* substance *n*."

22. Cf. *Oxford English Dictionary*, s.v. "dwell, *v*.": From an "Old English [term signifying] . . . to lead astray, hinder, delay; also . . . to go astray, err; to be delayed, tarry, stay; corresponding to Old High German [term], Old Norse [term signifying] to retard, delay, *intr*. to stop. . . . < Old Germanic . . . repr. by Old High German *gitwelan* to be stunned, benumbed, torpid, also to cease, leave off, give up, . . . Old English past participle [signifying] gone astray, gone wrong, perverted; from an Aryan root . . . appearing in Sanskrit [terms signifying] to mislead, deceive." See also Hall, *Oxford*, 36. The Greek "aedes," with a remarkably different history than the official Latin, certainly has for a long time buzzed annoyingly about the ears in this place.

23. *Brewer's Dictionary of Phrase and Fable*, s.v. "Christopher, St.": "Legend relates that St. Christopher was a giant who one day carried a child over a brook, and said, 'Chylde, thou hast put me in gret peryll. I might bere no greater burden.' To which the child answered, 'Marvel thou nothing, for thou hast borne all the world upon thee, and its sins likewise.' This is an allegory: Christopher means Christbearer; the child was Christ, and the river was the river of death." Further, s.v. "Wrenning Day": "St. Stephen's Day (26 December) used to be so called, because it was a local custom among villagers to stone a wren to death on that day in commemoration of the stoning of St. Stephen."

24. Eliot, "Murder in the Cathedral," 203:

> Thomas [to Priests]: However certain our expectation
> The moment foreseen may be unexpected
> When it arrives. It comes when we are
> Engrossed with matters of other urgency. . . .
> The Four Knights: You are the Archbishop in revolt against the King; in rebellion to the King and the law of the land;
> You are the Archbishop who was made by the King; whom he set in your place to carry out his command.
> You are his servant, his tool, and his jack,
> You wore his favours on your back,
> You had your honours all from his hand; from him you had the power, the seal, and the ring.

After Crucifixion

Just south of the cathedral, still outside Mercury's[25] quadrangle—and so, within and without Christ Church College—I turned and marveled at the simple, sturdy stonework of these long-standing walls[26]—the heavy, time-laden architecture. The portion of the wall at which I now stared made the inner/outer boundary of some (anonymous)[27] student's room.[28] A builder routinely insists that at regular intervals walls be interrupted[29] by windows.[30] And so, here, too, as my way was made, the panes of glass[31] of his or hers stood before me.

> This is the man who was the tradesman's son: the backstairs brat who was born in Cheapside;
> This is the creature that crawled upon the King; swollen with blood and swollen with pride.
> Creeping out of the London dirt,
> Creeping up like a louse on your shirt,
> The man who cheated, swindled, lied; broke his oath and betrayed his King.

Bolt, *Man For All Seasons*, 20–22 (act 1, lines 208–10):

> Wolsey: Then the King needs a son; I repeat, what are you going to do about it?
> More (Steadily): I pray for it daily.
> Wolsey (Softly): God's death, he means it. . . . You'd like that wouldn't you? To govern the country by prayers?
> More: Yes, I should.
> Wolsey: I'd like to be there when you try.

25. *American Heritage Dictionary of Indo-European Roots*, 2nd. ed., s.v. "merk-2": "Italic root, possibly from Etruscan, referring to aspects of commerce. . . . Latin *Mercurius*, the god of (inter alia) commerce." Cf. Bauckham, *Theology of the Book of Revelation*, 18, 36, 66, 89.

26. Cf. Matt 28:2 and Mark 13:1–2.

27. *Oxford English Dictionary*, s.v. "anonymous, *adj*.": "Nameless, having no name; of unknown name. . . . A person whose name is not given, or is unknown. . . . Bearing no author's name; of unknown or unavowed authorship. . . . Unacknowledged, illegitimate. . . . Indistinguishable from others of its kind; unexceptional; bland, generic, nondescript. . . . Of a person: generally unknown, unrecognized, or uncelebrated." Cf. Mark 1:23–26.

28. Claiborne, *Roots of English*, s.v. "(s)teu-": "to push, stick, knock, or beat. . . . The family's Latin branch is . . . diverse; it includes *stupere*, to be stunned . . . , and *studere*, to be diligent ('push forward'), which evolved into study and student." Also, s.v. "reuh-": "to open, hence space, whence the Germanic room which means space ('room enough'); the sense of enclosed space came later."

29. *Oxford English Dictionary*, s.v. "interrupt, *v*.": "< Latin . . . [term signifying] to break asunder, break off . . . , < *inter* between + *rumpĕre* to break."

30. *Oxford English Dictionary*, s.v. "window, *n*.": "< Old Norse *vindauga*, < *vindr* wind *n*.1 + *auga* eye *n*.1"

31. Cf. Heidegger, "Language," 201–2: "But what is pain? Pain rends. It is the rift. . . . Its rending, as a separating that gathers, is at the same time that drawing which, like the

Interlude

There upon the window frame traces[32] of some vandal's[33] graffito were cut. The graffito was scratched in dead stone, in a dead language:[34]

DOMINUS

An odd[35] text. "Dominus"—a word that lexicons declare to mean "master of the house, therefore Lord." Dominus. What might this word signify[36]— here on this window frame—cut into stone? What kind of Lord is this that waits[37]—waits to be read?

What light[38] could so obscure a text ever shed, particularly contiguously with so unselfconsciously forlorn and inexplicably precarious[39] a traveler?

---

pen-drawing of a plan or sketch, draws and joins together what is held apart in separation.... Pain is the joining of the rift. The joining is the threshold. It settles the between, the middle of the two that are separated in it. Pain joins the rift of the difference. Pain is the dif-ference itself." *Cassell's French Dictionary*, s.v. "*Glas* [gla], n.m. Knell, passing-bell, tolling. *Glas funèbre*, funeral-knell, death-bell."

32. *Oxford English Dictionary*, s.v. "trace, *n*.1"

33. *American Heritage Dictionary of Indo-European Roots*, 2nd. ed., s.v. "wendh-": "To turn, wind, weave.... Wander, from Old English *wandrian*[;] ... from Latin *wandljaz*, 'wanderer,' Vandal."

34. Cf. Heidegger, "Language," 189, 192–93.

35. *Oxford English Dictionary*, s.v. "odd, *adj., n.*1, *adv.*": "The senses 'odd,' 'odd number' ... apparently developed by metaphor from 'triangle,' ... and thence by extension from the third or unpaired member of a group of three, ... three as the primary 'odd number.'"

36. *Oxford English Dictionary*, s.v. "sign, *n.*": "< Anglo-Norman ... its etymon classical Latin *signum* mark to indicate position, ... impression of a signet, seal, signet, signet ring, ... visible sign or trace, gesture, signal, password, emblem, symbol, token ... , in post-classical Latin also miraculous sign, miracle (Vetus Latina, Vulgate), sign of the cross (4th cent.), of uncertain origin."

37. Cf. Isa 30:18.

38. How is it that this "Dominus illuminatio mea"?

39. *Oxford English Dictionary*, s.v. "precarious, *adj.*": "< classical Latin *precārius* given as a favour, depending on the favour of another, (of property) held by tenancy at will, uncertain, doubtful, suppliant (< *prec-* , *prex* prayer, entreaty ... + -*ārius* -ary *suffix*1) + -ous *suffix*." Cf. Keen, "*Homo Precarius.*"

After Crucifixion

It is rather like that other word for which it sometimes stands: that word . . . "God":[40] or that other, still more ancient and obscure word . . . "*theos*."[41]

The obscurity of this odd text is so pronounced that it is possible[42] only to interpret it allegorically[43]—as perhaps the ancient Origen[44] might suggest—to read its letters according to the spirit—to read it boldly; not in the spirit of slavery, falling back into fear, but in a different spirit, crying out in a different voice—and thus to read it, this odd text, in context. And what context?

Scratched upon another dead stone, directly above the first, marks of an absurd pattern[45] could be found, found on the edge of this very window

---

40. *Oxford English Dictionary*, s.v. "God, *n*.": "The ulterior etymology is disputed. . . . There are two Aryan roots of the required form . . . : one meaning 'to invoke' (Sanskrit *hū*), the other 'to pour, to offer sacrifice' (Sanskrit *hu*, Greek *chein*, Old English *géotan* yet *v*.). Hence [its ancestry] has been variously interpreted as 'what is invoked' . . . and as 'what is worshipped by sacrifice'. . . . Either of these conjectures is fairly plausible, as they both yield a sense practically coincident with the most obvious definition deducible from the actual use of the word, 'an object of worship.'"

41. Kleinknecht, "*Theos*," 67: "The question of the etymology of *theos* has never been solved. It can thus tell us nothing about the nature of the Greek concept of God. *Theos* is originally a predicative term; hence its use is as broad and varied as the religious interpretation of the world and of life by the Greeks. Homer already uses both the plural (*hoi*) *theoi* and the indefinite singular *theos* (*tis*). In this use he is sometimes thinking of divine being and work in general, sometimes of a particular god, and sometimes specifically of Zeus. There is similar variation between *theos* and *ho theos* with no obvious distinction of sense. We also have variations, often close together, between ' the gods,' 'the god,' 'god,' and 'the godhead,' as though they were all monistic terms referring to a single power."

42. There is not, of course, adequate external or internal evidence for the use of this word at this point in this history.

43. Cf. Heidegger, "Origin of the Work of Art," 19: "The art work is, to be sure, a thing that is made, but it says something other than the mere thing itself is, *allo agoreuei*. The work makes public something other than itself; it manifests something other; it is an allegory. In the work of art something other is brought together with the thing that is made. To bring together is, in Greek, *sumballein*. The work is symbol." Heidegger, "Der Ursprung des Kunstwerkes," 4: "Das Kunstwerk ist zwar ein angefertigtes Ding, aber es sagt noch etwas anderes, als das bloße Ding selbst ist, *allo agoreuei*. Das Werk macht mit Anderem öffentlich bekannt, es offenbart Anderes; es ist Allegorie. Mit dem angefertigten Ding wird im Kunstwerk noch etwas Anderes zusammengebracht. Zusammenbringen heißt griechish *sumballein*. Das Werk ist Symbol."

44. As does his homophone.

45. *Oxford English Dictionary*, s.v. "absurd, *adj*. and *n*.": "< *ab*- ab- *prefix*1 [from, away from] + *surdus* surd *adj*. [< Latin *surdus* . . . deaf, . . . silent, mute, dumb, . . . dull, indistinct]." And, s.v. "pattern, *n*. and *adj*.": "Originally a variant of patron *n*. [< *patr*-, *pater* father . . .]."

Interlude

to this very student's room. Out of context—unoffered and untouched, absolute and sufficient in itself, naked and wordless, residing in no other's space and in no other's time, revealing nothing and promising nothing,[46] a kind of *apatheia*[47]—it was, of course, of a different essence or reality or substance[48] than the graffito in whose context it has become entailed.[49] Without the context it yields no deference, but mere defacement.[50]

Yet even now, entailed as it is, it remains an open place, a nothing, a cipher into which everything poured would be sacrificed, an expenditure without return.[51]

Is there more context?

Below the graffito, upon the window's ledge, out of line with the marks beyond it, lay a cold, lifeless body of refuse.

A pear. (More specifically, a pear core.)[52]

As it lay there out of context, denuded and entombed in the window-frame's recession—forsaken and abandoned, despised and rejected, used up and thrown away, displaced and robbed of its time and vitality, a dead and pathetic[53] emptiness—it was, of course, of a different essence or reality

---

46. Cf. Althaus, *Theology of Martin Luther*, 23.

47. Cf. Moltmann, *Experiment Hope*, 73.

48. *Heteroousios*.

49. *Oxford English Dictionary*, s.v. "entail, *v.*1": "< *in* into + *taleāre* . . . to cut."

50. Derrida, *Adieu*, e.g., 60.

51. See Bataille, "Notion of Expenditure," 366–67.

52. *Oxford English Dictionary*, s.v. "pear, *n.*": "Scientific Latin *Pyrus* is after post-classical Latin *pyrum* (4th cent.), alteration of *pirum* by folk etymology after ancient Greek *pur* fire (Isidore) and *puramís* pyramid *n.*" Taylor, *Altarity*, 79–80: "In an image that recalls Hegel's discussion of the sign, Merleau-Ponty describes existence as 'perched on a pyramid of the past [*pyramide du passé*].' This pyramid points to the chiasmic intertwining of past and future. The past that is never present eternally re-turns as the future that never arrives. The non-present future that bounds life and makes the temporal individual 'dreadfully' edgy in death." Augustine, *Confessions*, 25–27: "What was it then that in my wretched folly I loved in you, O theft of mine, deed wrought in that dark night when I was sixteen? For you were not lovely: you were a theft. . . . The pears that we stole were beautiful but it was not pears that my empty soul desired. For I had any number of better pears of my own, and plucked those only that I might steal. For once I had gathered them I threw them away, tasting only my own sin and savoring that with delight; for if I took so much as a bite of any one of those pears, it was the sin that sweetened it. . . . O rottenness, O monstrousness of life and abyss of death! Could you find pleasure only in what was forbidden, and only because it was forbidden?"

53. Cf. Moltmann, *Crucified God*, 273–74.

After Crucifixion

or substance than the graffito in whose context it has become entailed. Without that context it yields no deference; but mere defacement.[54]

Yet even now, entailed as it is, it remains consumed fruit. As still as death. As silent as a lamb that has been led to the slaughter. A sacrifice. An expenditure without return.[55]

The context of the graffito is therefore trine. The mark "Dominus" cuts two ways: piercing, dividing, disclosing, opening, laying bare; entailing what transcends, what ascends and descends, what is exalted and what is abased. Indeed the mark "Dominus" has no point but the signification of the exalted and the abased.

There is more, however. Signification pours back upon the "Dominus" from what it signifies. The "Dominus" cuts two ways. (1) The "Dominus" signifies the exalted. The exalted reciprocates and signifies the "Dominus." But it does so as only the exalted might—as a kind of accidental[56] reciprocity and absent[57] signification. (2) The "Dominus" signifies the abased. The abased reciprocates and signifies the "Dominus." But it does so as only the abased might—as a kind of accidental reciprocity and absent signification.

The cutting of this signification wounds deeply. In this signification what would otherwise be heteroousios becomes decidedly homoousios. Indeed, so much do these three entail one another that (1) the "Dominus" is what it is only as the "Dominus" of the exalted and the "Dominus" of the abased; (2) the exalted is what it is only as the exalted of the "Dominus"; (3) the abased is what it is only as the abased of the "Dominus."

But more than this the entailment cuts out every mediation. (1) The exalted is now so entailed that it is the exalted of the abased, and it is so precisely as it is the exalted of the "Dominus": indeed the exalted has no

---

54. Cf. Levinas, "Trace of the Other," 352, and Isa 3:15.

55. Luther, "Heidelberg Disputation," 290 [XIX–XX]: "He is not worth calling a theologian who seeks to interpret the invisible things of God on the basis of the things that have been created. But he is worth calling a theologian who understands the visible and hinder parts of God to mean the passion and the cross." Cf. Heidegger, "Origin of the Work of Art," 46.

56. *Oxford English Dictionary*, s.v. "accident, *n.*": "unfortunate occurrence or incident, vicissitude of fortune, indication, exterior sign, symptom . . . , chance occurrence . . . , non-essential quality, . . . chance event, contingency, circumstance, . . . contingent attribute . . . , symptom . . . , to fall, to happen."

57. *Oxford English Dictionary*, s.v. "absent, *adj.* and *n.*": "< *ab-* ab- *prefix*1 [< classical Latin *ab-* (prefix) from, away from < *ab* (preposition) from, away from] + *esse* to be (see be *v.*)." Barth, *Epistle to the Romans*, 318: "Our world is the world within which God is finally and everywhere—outside." Cf. Ps 113.

point but what signifies the "Dominus" and the abased. (2) The abased is now so entailed that it is the abased of the exalted, and it is so precisely as it is the abased of the "Dominus": indeed the abased has no point but what signifies the "Dominus" and the exalted.[58] In this entailment there is neither superordination nor subordination.[59] The trine entailment is in this way a playful, ever-restless, disseminant *ousia*; as if each were substantial only in its relations to the others.[60]

This *ousia*, however, does not constitute a geometric unity whose center lies simply within itself; a kind of circle or sphere that rests in its own adequacy. Rather the movements of the signification of the *ousia* refuse to be fixed. As the abased rests heavily upon the stone ledge of the window, it gathers the earthiness of the stone to itself. The movement of signification that entails the trine *ousia* thus becomes a signification also of the heavy stone. Further as the exalted stands open, it discloses the openness of the window and the room beyond it, and the world beyond the room and beyond the college and beyond the university. The movement of signification of this trine *ousia* spills out into every open space and time; not in such a way that there might be a depletion of the *ousia's* reserves— or that the openness of the world would be filled in and closed down; yet the movement of signification that entails this trine *ousia* thus becomes a signification also of the openness of the world. It is as if it were all a kind of sacrifice: a sacrifice of what is sacrificial through and through, a grace of what is graceful through and through, a giving of what is gifted[61] through and through.

---

58. Barth, *CD* 4/1, 246: "The mystery of this passion, of the torture, crucifixion, and death of this one Jew which took place at that place and time at the hands of the Romans, is to be found in the person and mission of the One who suffered there and was crucified and died. . . . It is a matter of the humiliation and dishonoring of God Himself, of the question which makes any question of a theodicy a complete anticlimax. . . . And it is a matter of the answer . . . : that in this humiliation God is supremely God, that in this death He is supremely alive, that He has maintained and revealed His deity in the passion of this man as His eternal Son." Cf. Rom 1:1–4.

59. Cf. *Quicunque Vult*, 705-6: "Now this is the Catholic faith, that we worship one God in Trinity and Trinity in unity, without either confusing the persons or dividing the substance. For the Father's person is one, the Son's another, the Holy Spirit's another; but the Godhead of the Father, the Son, and the Holy Spirit is one, their glory is equal, their majesty coeternal. . . . And in the trinity there is nothing before or after, nothing greater or less, but all three persons are coeternal with each other and coequal."

60. Cf. Zizioulas, *Being as Communion*, 44.

61. *Oxford English Dictionary*, s.v. "give, *v*.": "The verb seems, from the evidence of Gothic, Old High German, and Old Saxon, to have primarily denoted the placing of a

This entailment is a wound of what is wounded through and through.[62]

Therefore, one cannot leave out of account the fact that this wound is found on the window-frame of a room, a(n anonymous) student's room. The wound is upon the edge of the student's window. The student's window is entailed by this wound. Were there no recession, were there no interruption of the wall, were there no panes of glass, were there no room, were there no other removed to the far side of the curtain, were I not looking away from myself and the quadrangle and the cathedral, were I not turned in the direction of the outside of the *Aedes Christi*, were my gaze not the gaze of a stranger, I would see neither wound nor window. I would see only defacement—the defacement of a wall. To find the trine *ousia* is to find the other upon whose wind-ow its trace is cut.[63]

Although my travels to Britain were only momentary, in the great scheme of things, I have somehow never been able to shake that sojourn. It is as if some child's voice, a boy's or girl's voice, I do not know, had called out to me in a sort of sing-song repeated again and again, "Take and read, take and read." I am afraid that I rather noninferentially interpreted the incident as quite certainly a divine command to open the scripture and read. Upon doing so, in that instant, it was as though a light of utter confidence shone in all my heart, and all darkness of uncertainty vanished away.[64] Yet it must be admitted that the scripture which I read was written less on bound pages than on a human face, across the eyes, where the wind blows.[65]

---

material object in the hands of another person." Also note the associations with "gift, *n*.1," a derivative from the verb: "Old High German *gift* (feminine), gift, poison (Middle High German, modern German *gift* (feminine), gift, neuter, poison), Old Norse *gift* , usually written *gipt* gift . . . , plural *giptar* a wedding."

62. Cf. Moltmann, *Experiment Hope*, 80–81.

63. Cf. Levinas, "Trace of the Other," 359.

64. This bit of plagiarizing is, of course, from the *Confessions of St. Augustine*, 141–42 [8.12].

65. Buber, "Prelude: Report on Two Talks," 7–9: "Some time later I was the guest of a noble old thinker. . . . He lived in another university city situated in the west. . . . He listened [to what I said] in a friendly manner but clearly astonished, indeed with growing amazement. When I was through, he spoke hesitatingly, then, carried away by the importance of his subject, ever more passionately. 'How can you bring yourself to say "God" time after time? . . . What word of human speech is so misused, so defiled, so desecrated as this! . . . When I hear the highest called "God," it sometimes seems almost blasphemous.' The kindly eyes flamed. The voice itself flamed. Then we sat silent for awhile facing each other. The room lay in the flowing brightness of early morning. It seemed to me as if a power from the light entered into me. What I now answered, I cannot today reproduce but only indicate. 'Yes,' I said, 'it is the most heavy-laden of all

Interlude

In revelation God tells man that He is God, and that as such He is Lord. In telling him this, revelation tells him something utterly new, something which apart from revelation he does not know and cannot tell either himself or others.[66]

I regard everything as loss because of the surpassing value of knowing Christ Jesus my Lord. For his sake I have suffered the loss of all things, and I regard them as rubbish, in order that I may gain Christ and be found in him, not having a righteousness of my own that comes from the law, but one that comes through faith in Christ, the righteousness from God based on faith.[67]

---

human words. None has become so soiled, so mutilated. Just for this reason I may not abandon it. Generations of men have laid the burden of their anxious lives upon this word and weighed it to the ground; it lies in the dust and bears their whole burden. The races of man with their religious factions have torn the word to pieces; they have killed for it and died for it, and it bears their finger-marks and their blood. Where might I find a word like it to describe the highest! If I took the purest, most sparkling concept from the inner treasure-chamber of the philosophers, I could only capture thereby an unbinding product of thought. I could not capture the presence of Him whom the generations of men have honored and degraded with their awesome living and dying. I do mean Him whom the hell-tormented and heaven-storming generations of men mean. Certainly, they draw caricatures and write "God" underneath; they murder one another and say "in God's name." But when all madness and delusion fall to dust, when they stand over against Him in the loneliest darkness and no longer say "He, He" but rather sigh "Thou," shout "Thou," all of them the one word, and when they then add "God," is it not the real God whom they all implore, the One Living God, the God of the children of man? Is it not He who *hears* them? And just for this reason is not the word "God," the word of appeal, the word which has become a *name*, consecrated in all human tongues for all times? . . .' It had become very light in the room. It was no longer dawning, it was light. The old man stood up, came over to me, laid his hand on my shoulder and spoke: 'Let us be friends.' The conversation was completed. For where two or three are truly together, they are together in the name of God."

66. Barth, *CD* 1/2, 301.
67. Phil 3:8–9.

6 Teaching the Dead to Praise God

Abiding the Face of Devastation

> *I took the stars from my eyes*
> *And then I made a map*
> *I knew that somehow I could find my way back*
> *Then I heard your heart beating*
> *You were in the darkness, too*
> *So I stayed in the darkness with you*[1]

WHEN THE BISHOP SWAYS—SHIFTING her weight from one sturdy or feeble leg to the other and back again, stepping right to left and left to right over a soft or hard-packed dirt floor covered or uncovered by mats, hardwood, or stone, under a flat or pitched roof or the open sky, raising her eyes from what rises from the surface of a table or the floor or her hands, raising her eyes from a scroll or codex or memory to a statistically insignificant body of children, women, and men, new or longtime friends, or strangers tarrying for the night, without whom she would have nowhere at all to go and nothing to do—she teaches.[2] She teaches bodies; she teaches them to walk and to speak; she points the way and she waits; she waits not subsequently, under the tyranny of chronology, but concurrently, *as* she points, *as* she works.

---

1. Welch and Summers, "Cosmic Love."
2. See *Oxford English Dictionary*, s.v. "teach, *v*."

Teaching the Dead to Praise God

She is no leader. It is not her task to lead.[3] The little gathering to whom she looks—the children, women, and men this present evil age would consign to a festering city dump, once it had used them up, the children, women, men, and their already ravaged world—look to her not for leadership, but faithfulness of voice and time. It is her task *with them*, as *one* body, to work and to wait, i.e., together to follow the one she and they call their one head, the one who, she says, has already gone before them into Galilee. It is her task *with them* to step out into that coming peace that is to be done on *earth* as even now, uncannily, it is done in heaven.

The lesson the bishop teaches with her voice, her eyes, her hands, and her daily work, i.e., is not that she knows where to find the exit, a way to some Department of the Interior sanctuary for endangered species, some refuge floating bodilessly at a safe distance above time and trouble. The lesson she teaches is that no matter how perfectly their one head, their incarnate God, reigns in heaven—not only over heaven, but also over all creation—heaven is not our home. Heavenly ether is simply too rarefied for our wet, spongy lungs and thick blood, its clouds too delicately fragile for our heavy, clumsy bodies. We would not joyfully linger, she teaches, were we to find ourselves there. Jesus is the way we are to follow and that way may well lead through a rent veil into a safe house, she says, but if it is lived life that is to be redeemed, we will have shuffled off neither the *what* nor the *how* of a lifetime of hard work, good food, first loves, and last goodbyes. It is this earthy world that is to be set free, and we with it. The bishop before the broken body and shed blood of Christ teaches this, but she is neither educator nor induction officer. The Spirit leads, she tells us. The Lord and Giver of Life leads us—out of and into this present evil age—leaving us with a taste, perhaps an aftertaste, perhaps a foretaste, of the coming sanctity of all that is earthy, a sanctity, she teaches us, that emboldens us to raise our faces to whomever we meet, remembering, however improbably, that this one, too, has a future in the liberation of the world.

It is no mean task to teach *liberation* of any kind. Just saying the word provokes and confuses. It calls to mind too many storylines, too many campaigns, too many hopes and schemes, too many national mottos. It and its cognates are favored by too many competing factions. The vocabulary

---

3. See *Oxford English Dictionary*, s.v. "educe, *v.*" and s.v. "induce, *v.*"

of liberation has been exported via expeditionary forces and trading companies from nearly every corner of Europe to the ends of the earth, from the jungles of Chiapas to the deep pockets of Wall Street, from the West and North Coasts of Africa to the Western Pacific. Competing voices have taken up a variety of permutations of the word since before the privilege of slave ownership began formally to shape it.[4] Especially and increasingly since the modern age began to mark its territory, the term has come to signify a kind of emancipation from slavery. Modern revolutions from the late eighteenth century forward have taken the word as *theirs*. Their symbols are the guillotine, the Gulag Archipelago, the Killing Fields, the auction block, the lynching tree, and Wounded Knee.

It is no surprise that when Paul's declaration, "For freedom Christ has set us free" (Gal 5:1), was read by medieval and Renaissance theologians in their universities, the home of the liberal arts, they found themselves pulled and pushed in various directions. The liberal arts are about freedom, too.[5] Thus Erasmus wrote his paradigmatically sixteenth century liberal critique of Luther, *De Libero Arbitrio Diatribe Sive Collatio*, to which the Reformer, who punned his own name with the Greek *eleutheros*[6] and wrote the treatise *Von der Freiheit eines Christenmenschen*, responded with explosive, sometimes quite illiberal, caustic brilliance in his *De Servo Arbitrio*, contending with Erasmus, as Erasmus had contended with him, over the theological significance of freedom. Neither would give up the term, and neither found the term in the other.

"Liberty," "liberal," "liberate," "freedom" are all words with abundant equivocal uses. It simply is not wise to assume, when those and related

---

4. See the very helpful etymological note in the *Oxford English Dictionary*, s.v. "free, *adj.*, *n.*, *adv.*" For example: "Whereas the sense 'beloved, dear' is reflected in the Sanskrit and Avestan adjectives as well as in senses of the verbal and nominal derivatives in all the Indo-European branches in which they are attested . . . , the sense 'free, not in servitude' appears to be a peculiarity of Germanic and Celtic."

5. Colish, *Medieval Foundations of the Western Intellectual Tradition*, 5: "Literally, the liberal arts were designed for the aesthetic and intellectual formation of students who were both legally free and male." Cf. 177. Gilmore, *World of Humanism*, 206: "The nature of man [according to Christian humanists], fundamentally good although corrupted by original sin, was capable of improvement by an intellectual discipline. Learning . . . would increase piety. . . . In the minds of many of the humanists a new program of education was not only necessary; it was all that was necessary." *Oxford English Dictionary*, s.v. "liberal, *adj.* and *n.*": The liberal arts are those "suitable for a free or noble person . . . , [an] independent, unconstrained [person] . . . , of noble birth . . . , not servile . . . [they] constitute the studies, education, arts, professions] worthy or typical of a free man."

6. Lohse, *Martin Luther's Theology*, 101.

Teaching the Dead to Praise God

words are used in theological discourse, that the hearer or reader will be poised from the beginning to understand what they will have come in the end to signify. They are simply confusing words. It might seem that the wisest course would be simply to drop them altogether. And yet the language—the vocabulary, the imagery, the stories—of freedom is all over the traditions to which the bishop bears witness, as she gestures before the assembly, the bread, and the wine. "On the night when he was betrayed..." (1 Cor 11:23) evokes the memory of God's election of the children of Israel, their deliverance from Egyptian bondage, God's cutting a way for them on dry ground through deep water, God's defeat of Pharaoh's relentlessly pursuing army in that very Sea, God's provision of manna in the wilderness, and Israel's generation-long sojourne on foot after a pillar of cloud by day and of fire by night that moved always before them—to the Promised Land.

It would be a mistake to disengage the political and military energy from the language of the eucharist. The Pharaoh is an absolute sovereign over a mighty nation, his army does his bidding—by means of slaughter, of course, and the threat of slaughter. Pharaoh and his army stand solidly in power precisely because they are so very good at slaughter. The liberation of the Hebrew children from Egyptian bondage takes place in part as a political contest between Pharaoh, his gods in tow, and Yahweh. Yahweh fights not entirely unlike Pharaoh, but differently as well. Yahweh warns Pharaoh by vivid, but vaguely delimited, displays of might. The miracle of the rod, the hand, and the great plagues of blood, frogs, lice, flies, disease, hail, locusts, and darkness all enact Yahweh's power over Pharaoh and his gods. It is the final plague, however, that softens Pharaoh's resolve and weakens his grip: the massacre of the first born. The language of Moses' predictive warning is stark:

> Moses said, "Thus says the Lord: About midnight I will go out through Egypt. Every firstborn in the land of Egypt shall die, from the firstborn of Pharaoh who sits on his throne to the firstborn of the female slave who is behind the handmill, and all the firstborn of the livestock." (Exod 11:4–5)

The verses that follow promise that this deed will break the hearts and throw open the gates of Egypt:

> "Then there will be a loud cry throughout the whole land of Egypt, such as has never been nor will ever be again. But not a dog shall growl at any of the Israelites—not at people, not at animals—so that you may know that the Lord makes a distinction between

> Egypt and Israel. Then all these officials of yours shall come down to me, and bow low to me, saying, 'Leave us, you and all the people who follow you.' After that I will leave." And in hot anger [Moses] left Pharaoh. (Exod 11:6–8)

This tale is political discourse, but not because it fosters the well being of the *polis*. Indeed this tale recounts a disasterous undoing of the *polis*. The Israelites, whom we are tempted to celebrate as the victors of this battle, are not victors; though they are decidedly undefeated. They depart Egypt as a wandering nation without national boundaries, without a city. It is not Israel, but Yahweh—the God who has gratuitously elected Israel, the God who has fought for Israel, when Israel could not fight for itself—who has vanquished Pharaoh, his army, and his gods. This is political discourse *because* it is the tale of the unsettling of the *polis*, the way the unreported forgiveness of great debt is an economic act even in a world saturated by capitalism. One might tease out of the narrative perhaps an oblique, supplemental allusion to a *polis* (uncharacteristically) not to be built on the backs of slaves, day laborers, or nameless artisans, (uncharacteristically) not to rise tall out of footings embedded deeply in bedrock on reinforced concrete legs, say out of the ashes of one or another Great Fire or the rubble of one or another conquest. One might imagine this city-to-come—were it to come—as *arriving*, arriving certainly with hard work, but no less from beginning to end by apocalyptic adventure, i.e., as a gift, as a promise that does not cease to be a promise.

Isaiah's announcement, which Genesis more famously echoes, is that the stories that move into and out of the Passover—the stories of Abraham and Joseph, of Moses and Cyrus, of Egypt and Babylon—are creation stories, stories of the coming of peace where there otherwise is no peace. They are also war stories, of course. However, they are war stories without heroes. No one in them gets the credit for victories except God. The most that might be said of a combatant, Deborah, say, is that she was "a mother of Israel," one who cared for its peasants (Judg 5:7). Of God it is said,

> Lord, when you went out from Seir, when you marched from the region of Edom, the earth trembled, and the heavens poured, the clouds indeed poured water. The mountains quaked before the Lord, the One of Sinai, before the Lord, the God of Israel. (Judg 5:3–5)

God moves, the faithful follow close at hand as the earth trembles, mountains quake, and rain pours down from the heavens. In this way comes their liberation.

It is not always presumed from the beginning that following God close at hand will result in victory, even if by the end of the story victory has resulted. Job's contrition shows this (Job 42:1–6), as does the "Here I am!" of Abraham on the cusp of the long walk to the mountain in Moriah (Gen 22:1, 11), of Moses before the burning bush (Exod 3:4), and of Isaiah in the Temple (Isa 6:8). The logic of this faith concerns following God, the one who goes before the faithful. Victory, when it comes, is surplus.

> O Nebuchadnezzar, we have no need to present a defense to you in this matter. If our God whom we serve is able to deliver us from the furnace of blazing fire and out of your hand, O king, let him deliver us. But if not, be it known to you, O king, that we will not serve your gods and we will not worship the golden statue that you have set up. (Dan 3:16–18)

Of course, deprivation, suffering, defeat, bondage, exile, and death are in the stories of Israel wrongs that the faithful again and again decry in loud laments and petitions that rise to heaven and to the ears of God. God again and again responds mightily, even if sometimes with an exasperating slowness, to carry out concretely in time and space the hard work of deliverance. And yet, God does not forever forestall the wrongs the faithful endure, not even death. Even the faithful one day die, sometimes as they suffer in chains in a foreign land. The death of the faithful is tragic because the faithful, who would praise God, who would sing praises to God all their life long (Ps 142:2), cannot praise God from the grave (Ps 30:9). Death marks the boundary of life. To cross it is to have fallen lifeless, cut off from God. That is the witness of the elect of God, God's faithful child, Israel. God, the God of the living, the Living God, is the polar opposite of death, the one in whom there is no trace of death and dying. By definition God cannot touch death; God cannot be touched by death. By definition, therefore, to die is to fall away from God, to fail to follow God. The dead have died, God travels on, in precisely the opposite direction.[7]

Everything dies. Everyone dies, every woman, man, and child. Ashes to ashes. We are here for a little while, some not long enough to take a full breath. Like the passenger pigeon and the Barbary lion, families, tribes, and

---

7. Ps 139:8 affirms that God is in "Sheol." The point of this verse is that there is no hiding from God. This psalm is far from affirming the death of God.

nations go extinct. The elect are no exception; they, too, are naked flesh, easy to kill. To care for them, to protect them, to tend to them, to give them time to flourish, God moves for them against Israel's enemies, those world historical powers, those high and lifted up, those mighty kings and empires, whose armies would trample Israel underfoot as they marched to bigger and more challenging conquests. God does so not uncommonly by means familiar to those kings and empires, viz., by slaughter. Of course, God also disciplines Israel, sometimes harshly, sometimes by killing a good number of its people as well, but only for the sake of the longterm good of the national body as a whole, the way a badly infected limb might be hacked off to save a life. God kills, that is, to make alive and God kills justly, even if God's justice cannot be measured mathematically, say, in terms of comparative battlefield casualty figures. It is not for ephemeral human beings, dust from dust as we are, a limb hacked off, say, to stand in judgment against God. We, all of us, live only because of God's good pleasure, i.e., because God gives us time and breath to live. We die when the spirit God has given us is withdrawn (Ps 104:29), or so ancient Israel testifies.

Consequently, when the bishop gestures before a loaf and a cup and we all rehearse the declaration, "on the night when he was betrayed . . . ," we recall the overt, bloody liberation of God's elect from Egyptian and Babylonian bondage, as well as a subsequent, gruellingly long series of military/political threats to its survival. And yet something else is recalled in this moment that in no way moderates the wild, terrifying freedom of the God who broke the hearts and will of the mothers and kings of Egypt, something, however, that takes away every reason for securing the survival of the faithful by means of slaughter, something that takes away every threat of every enemy and opens the arms of the faithful not only to the coming of the protector God, but also to those who would snatch away every victory. That something else is also spoken by the bishop before bread and wine: "This is my body that is for you. . . . This . . . is the new covenant in my blood. Do this . . . in remembrance of me" (1 Cor 11:23–25). "Do not be alarmed; . . . Jesus of Nazareth has been raised; he is not here. . . . But go, . . . he is going ahead of you to Galilee" (Mark 16:6–7). "So if anyone is in Christ, there is a new creation: everything old has passed away; see, everything has become new!" (2 Cor 5:17). "For I am convinced that neither death, nor life, nor angels, nor rulers, nor things present, nor things to come, nor powers, nor height, nor depth, nor anything else in all creation, will be able to separate us from the love of God in Christ Jesus our Lord" (Rom 8:38–39). This is the liberation she teaches as she gestures before a loaf and a cup.

This is the liberation that the bishop teaches as she faces the hungry faces facing her, the men, women, and children who with her would eat and drink. It is liberation in the tradition of Moses, liberation from the grip of powers that would brand the faithful with the character, valor, and social mobility that most resonate with national unity. It is an emancipation that will not return again to the flesh pots of Egypt. "For freedom Christ has set us free. Stand firm, therefore, and do not submit again to a yoke of slavery" (Gal 5:1). And yet a liberation that does not have to win, that does not have to survive, is an odd liberation. Though it does not in the least undo human social, political, or economic goods, it gives to them a unsettling impropriety. "I mean, brothers and sisters, the [remainder of] time [is gathered together]; from now on, let even those who have [*echontes*] wives be as though they had [*echontes*] none, and those who mourn as though they were not mourning, and those who rejoice as though they were not rejoicing, and those who buy as though they had no possessions [*katechontes*], and those who deal with the world as though they had no dealings with it. For the present [*schēma*]⁸ of this world [are] passing away" (1 Cor 7:29–31).⁹ To wed, to own, to mourn, to rejoice, to buy, to deal, in all seriousness, with all that is entailed day in and day out over a lifetime, e.g., in a marriage into which children are born, children who are then loved, cherished, guarded, and taught, but—unsettlingly—as if no one, not even they themselves nor their mother and father, owned a thing.

How can this be?

It is not only doubt that presses this question on us. The bishop, tempted to doubt, of course, as much as the rest of us, is commissioned nonetheless both to ask and to answer this question (even if her answer is more provocative than satisfying) for all of us and with us for her, too, gathered as we are together. She tells us that we are to have no interest in killing and no interest in ownership, because Jesus the Galilean, driven by the Holy Spirit, is the Son of God, because Jesus together with the Spirit

---

8. The Greek is *schēma*. *Oxford English Dictionary*, s.v. "scheme, *n*.1": < medieval Latin *schēma*, < Greek *schēma* form, figure, < root *sch-* < pre-Hellenic *zgh-* . . . whence Greek *ech-ein* to have, hold, be in such or such a condition."

9. All the Greek words set off with brackets in this passage from 1 Corinthians are forms of the word *echein*, "to have, to hold."

who drove him into the wilderness are the hands of God that with Jesus' crucifixion have been thrust deeply into this earth, into death and despair, into the grave, and with Jesus' resurrection have drawn the whole damned world with him into the coming Reign of Peace and Freedom. She tells us that in this event the impossible has happened, that the very God who went before the Hebrew children through the wilderness between slavery and the land of promise has gone before us through the grave, that Jesus Christ, the slaughtered lamb, is for us the pillar of fire by night. To follow him, she tells us, is to follow the *Living God* where no living god could ever go: into *death*—naked, exposed, wounded, contacted, infected, seized, ravaged, and devastated: by death—and *there*, with, after, and in this Son of God whom death could not hold, impossibly to praise God, the God of the living.

This is no cult of dying and rising gods, no *Sein-zum-Tode*, no Platonic "practice for dying and death."[10] Each of the faithful, those who follow Jesus, is a body, a body not to be enthralled by a pious image, not to be totalized in the anticipation of its own demise, certainly never to be sloughed off by a then emancipated soul, but a body whose life is a death sentence that ends with a hard period, a death sentence written into the death sentence that is the earthy history of Jesus whose defeat is swallowed up in victory, and with it the defeat of all God's children, too. The baptized—fed together on the loaf and cup, attending to one another, thinking, working, confessing, recurrently repenting, in everything praying without ceasing—learn both all at once and bit by bit to remember day in and day out that their lives are written into the life of Jesus, to hope rather than fear, to pray not only for those to whom they are most naturally attached, but also for their persecutors, with whom also in Christ they live in hopeful solidarity. The baptized learn to celebrate and mourn and live in peace with their neighbors and strangers, to live humbly with the humble, to acknowledge openly their own foolishness and ignorance, and to forego the balance-justice and vengeance that so decimate this world.[11]

---

10. Plato, *Phaedo*, 100 (64a). See 103 (67): "While we live, we shall be closest to knowledge if we refrain as much as possible from association with the body or join with it more than we must, if we are not infected with its nature but purify ourselves from it until the god himself frees us."

11. Cf. Rom 12:9–21. My guess is that if Bonhoeffer had realized that his joining the plot to assassinate Hitler would for more than half a century have turned him far and wide into the military recruitment poster boy for nationalistic programs of slaughter, especially, but not only, among pious Christians, he would have given himself to the downfall of "the Leader" in a different manner.

A liberation such as this inevitably ignites the ire of the powers, for these are no longer compliant subjects easy to scare. Tomorrow, the faithful say with their eyes and knees, is neither provided nor endangered by the powers, not even where the powers most naturally presume to guarantee both, i.e., where they most freely, judiciously, efficiently, virtuously, and routinely rise to kill. It is not hard to imagine a faithful child (perhaps a young mother) of a little local church or village assembly being led before a huge crowd of excited spectators and up onto a rostrum in order to be dissuaded from her perhaps ill-considered complicity in sedition. It is not hard to imagine her father interrupting the proceedings by pulling her down and begging her to forsake her adherence to this false *religio*. "Offer the sacrifice!" we might imagine him saying; "Take pity on [your] baby!" It is also not hard to imagine some emissary of an absentee landlord or emperor, some proconsul, say, presiding over this miserable theater, appealing to her loves: "Offer the sacrifice! Take pity on the baby! . . . Your father has grey hair. . . . Don't put them through this! Do it! Perform the sacrifice for the emperor's well-being." But (and this alone might give us great pause) it is no harder to imagine this faithful child—this young mother under the gaze of salivating drunken macho voyeurs—raising her eyes to look into her condescending inferior court judge's soul and within a circle of drawn swords (or we could as easily say machetes or automatic rifles) without blinking reply, "No! I will not do it!"[12]

In saying this she gives voice to the odd liberation the bishop would teach, the liberation that plays among those celebrants and congregants who were her teachers and those whom she has taught (from the grave) over the course nearly of two millenia. And yet, hers is not the only death at the hands of one or more self-righteous political functionaries that we are tempted to describe as "noble." Indeed echoes of the voice and comportment of Socrates would no doubt be heard by learned pagans and Christians alike, as martyrs in arenas whispered or shouted their solemn testimonies. The seventy-year-old grand master[13] stood in a courtroom before his accusers and judges in 399 BC and, as we recall, after giving an account of his

---

12. "Passion of Saints Perpetua and Felicity," 17 (6.i–v).

13. Of course, of Plato and less directly of other pensive children of Athens, among them, the Macedonian Aristotle, and their Hellenistic and more remote European, Asian, and African heirs, the great sages especially of Western Civilization.

divinely commissioned, spirit led, uninterrupted lifelong career as Athens's most faithful, unyielding, and persistent educator and friend, vowed, "I would say to you, gentlemen of the jury: 'Whether ... you acquit me or not, do so on the understanding that this is my course of action, even if I am to face death many times.'" And he added, "Neither Miletus nor Anytus can harm me in any way ... ; certainly he might kill me ... which he and maybe others think to be great harm, but I do not think so."[14]

Socrates is the educator par excellence. It is of Socrates that Plato writes, when in the seventh book of the *Republic* he allegorizes the ascent of the ignorant out of darkness. Socrates seems to be such a confidently humble man of integrity, such an elegantly aloof servant of men-who-would-be-kings or at least authentic citizens of "the greatest city with the greatest reputation for both wisdom and power."[15] It is just this that makes his tutelage a temptation, both trying and alluring, for those whom the crucifixion/resurrection of Jesus have laid hold of. Of course, Socrates is a strict educator. He trains his young competitors in all seriousness, if playfully, ironically. They are athletes in the making, wrestlers who learn to wrestle by wrestling with him. And he wrestles like a bear. He wrestles and trains his wrestlers not for profit, but for the love of the game.[16] Therefore, he will train any man he happens to meet wherever he meets him, in the agora, the palaestra, outside or inside a courtroom, on the street, though typically only inside Athen's city walls and with only the right kind of people.[17] His wife, Xanthippe, slaves, even his own unnamed children, hover questioningly in the shadows in these canonical texts, if not accusingly, certainly muted.[18]

14. Plato, *Apology*, 35; cf. 33 (30a–e; cf. 28b–d).

15. Plato, *Apology*, 34 (29d).

16. Cf. *Oxford English Dictionary*, s.v. "game, *n*."

17. *Phaedrus*, 230c–e, *Apology*, 34–35 (29d–30a).

18. Xanthippe is mentioned twice in the *Phaedo*, once by name, both times just prior to Socrates' death. The first time, while holding their baby, she makes a comment ("the sort of thing women usually say"), and Socrates sends her away, while she is "lamenting and beating her breast" (96 [60a–b]). The second time is just moments before Socrates drinks the court-prescribed poison. She is not named this time, on hand with "the women of the household" and their two children, the baby and an older child. "He spoke to them.... Then he sent the women and children away ..." (153 [116b]). In Xenophon's *Symposium*, Socrates praises the skill and courage of a female entertainer (a juggler) and says to his (male) friends that women's nature is not inferior to men's, "except in its lack of judgment and physical strength," and that women, too, should be educated, the same as men. His friends counter that his own wife, Xanthippe, could use Socrates' art as an

Teaching the Dead to Praise God

The liberation of Socrates is unfortunately not odd, not uncanny, enough. The wisdom he teaches certainly provides an oblique rationale for a sort of (tough) kindness to those most kindred to him,[19] but to strangers, too; even if selectively. Yet it is also a wisdom that has its center in the self-identical ascending self, as it rises to those integral truths the sadly corrupted, fractured replicas of which lie scattered across the psyches and landscapes of this disintegrating world. Socrates is after authenticity, integrity, identity, serenity, and a better neighborhood. Subsequent to his conviction and condemnation at the end of the *Apology* Socrates, convinced that death will not harm him, pines for "the extraordinary happiness" of uninterrupted company and conversation with the great heroes of the Hellenic past. "They are happier there than we are here . . . and for the rest of time they are deathless, if indeed what we are told is true."[20] The less vivid and more abstract conceptualization of this image of life-after-death in Plato's later work retains the nostalgic desire for homecoming that characterizes both the touching scene at the end of the *Apology*, the moving, if less touching, scene at the end of the *Phaedo*, and the Socratic method overall.

And yet Socrates faces death unblinking, because his character, so well characterized by the master dialectician, his adoring Plato, could never fail this final test, anymore than Odysseus could fail to defeat Penelope's suitors. He dies, but death does not defeat him. He stands tall every step of the way. His is unquestionably a noble death, the death of an immortal. The tale of his manner of facing it, brushing aside the present order of things as a pale reflection of hidden truth, would be unsurprisingly warmly received among literate Christians, at least as a vague semblance of the stories of the martyrs. It is no wonder that Justin, himself to be martyred, thinks of

---

educator, that she is "a wife who is the hardest to get along with of all the women there are—yes, or all that ever were, I suspect, or ever will be." But Socrates counters that this is precisely the point. He has her as his wife, indeed because she is hard to train, like a "high mettled" horse from which a horse trainer learns the art of training horses of all tempers. And so, "I have got her, well assured that if I can endure her, I shall have no difficulty in my relations with all the rest of human kind" (547 [2.9–10]). The slave in the *Meno* is used even more overtly, even if in the end he has come quite close to true knowledge (70–75 [82b–85d]). Of course, Plato imagines his "Republic" as a city of educated men and women, with women occupying important roles of leadership (see 453b–471d, 563b). However, as Socrates speaks of this city, his discourse remains controlled by androcentric, aristocratic, and thus martial virtues. Plato also remains in the shadows, though his is a position of power.

19. *Apology*, 21a–23b.
20. *Apology*, 43–44 (41b–c).

After Crucifixion

Socrates as an ally.[21] And—as we read of death and dying in martyr stories, told and retold in an era that honored the noble death—we find a similar peace of mind among early and later saints. Jesus, though, is a different story. One is left with the impression that the martyrs, like the Socrates who did his duty to the god for 70 long years, desired to get out of here. Jesus seems not to have.

> They went to a place called Gethsemane; and he said to his disciples, "Sit here while I pray." He took with him Peter and James and John, and began to be distressed and agitated. And he said to them, "I am deeply grieved, even to death; remain here, and keep awake." And going a little farther, he threw himself on the ground and prayed that, if it were possible, the hour might pass from him. He said, "Abba, Father, for you all things are possible; remove this cup from me; yet, not what I want, but what you want." (Mark 14:32–36)
>
> "Eloi, Eloi, lema sabachthani?" (Mark 15:34)

Of course, it is routinely and forcefully argued that the distress of Jesus in Gethsemane and on Golgotha was not at all due to the prospect of his imminent demise. Only a coward, we think, would be so distressed by approaching death, even an especially painful one. The cause of his agony, we are told, was that the immense weight of the sins of the world, lifted off us, was heaped in its entirety onto his strong shoulders, up there on that cross. His heavenly Father, we are told, turned his loving face in disgust from the grotesque horror of a Son laid out, butchered, and gnawed by the freaks and hounds of hell. That, we are told, is the reason for his distress. On Golgatha he becomes *sin* for us and God cannot look upon *sin*, God cannot love *sin*, God cannot, sobbing, take into God's loving embrace God's faithful child who in his faithfulness has become *sin*. It is certainly a vivid image, and it has arrested our imagination. And there may be something to it, however obscured. Still, it has not only arrested us; it has locked us down; and it may be that, until we break out of it some dark night, we "may indeed look, but not perceive, and may indeed listen, but not understand" (Mark 4:12; cf. Isa 6:10) what transpires across the long hours of Good Friday.

---

21. *Second Apology*, 10.

Teaching the Dead to Praise God

Jesus, in whom the whole fullness of deity was pleased to dwell (Col 2:9), was from beginning to end a very earthy man. It is this earthiness that has resisted every docetist and idealist effort to turn him into a ghost (Mark 6:49). The pain of his journey from the pain of Gethsemane to the pain of Golgotha is not a substitute pain. It is his pain, because it is his journey. Nobody heaps anything onto Jesus. He does not carry on his shoulders somebody else's weight, the weight, say, of an alien "world." On Golgotha, *he* descends, *he* moves into that already densely tenanted abyss, *he* is forsaken, *he* dies, *he* is damned, *he* is unqualifiedly at home with those who are unqualifiedly at home in hell, i.e., not as a placeholder, but truly, *bona fide*. He has been traveling here his whole life. That is why the Gospel of Mark begins with his baptism in Judea, i.e., in the shadow of the Jerusalem where he was to be slaughtered. Each time he touches the people he meets and they touch him, the abyss cracks open a little more. Sometimes witnesses to these ruptive moments witness (ephemeral) healings as well, perhaps notice healings alone, but as they touch, his body in every case mingles with theirs, more often than not with their defiled bodies; so much so that Temple legates, on assignment in Galilee, and (eventually) their Jerusalem superiors, seated in power, find in every detail of the course of his life nothing but scandal. They are not wrong about him. He does not merely pretend to be one of the defiled. He and they are not members of different classes (Mark 12:31). And with all of the defiled, the Temple authorities would have him cast out of the Temple precincts, out of Holy Jerusalem, out of God's promise, out of hope.

To Rome he is a pathetic dissident, a would-be insurrectionist, a delusional peasant king, who in his dreams and the dreams of his chroniclers would run its legions into the sea (Mark 5:13). He would upset, they believe, the order of efficiency, property, law, productivity, and extrapolable outcome. He fails to operate according to the divine logic, the logic of nature, of Rome, of the Emperor, of his envoys, the logic that proves itself by the endless propagation of Roman coinage. He is, in short, a bothersome fool who drains away attention from the pressing demands of greatness. They are not wrong about him, any more than are the leaders of the Temple. And Rome knew how to deal with local provocateurs. It knew how to swat pests that buzzed annoyingly about its ears. It responded swiftly, justly, demonstratively, and decisively, with violence, of course, but not too much, just the right number of days of prolonged, humiliating public agony to leave an indelibly deterrent imprint on the memories of its contributing subjects.

After Crucifixion

Jesus (and this, too, must have been a minor irritant) would die too quickly for Rome's purposes. Still, he would die and he would die the death of an insurgent brigand. He would serve that educational purpose at least.

The little peasant, a scandal according to Jerusalem's security surveillance logarithms, and madness according to Rome's, speaks with a voice that is silenced, when the time is right, by the back of Jerusalem's hand, the hammer blow of Rome's fist, and the distracted, deafening idle clamor of the crowds of Judeans who had had enough of him and his inflammatory speech. Cities, Jesus would have them believe, will soon "lie waste without inhabitant, and houses without people, and the land . . . utterly desolate . . . and vast . . . the emptiness in the midst of the land. Even if a tenth part remain in it, it will be burned again, like a terebinth or an oak whose stump remains standing when it is felled" (Isa 6:11–13; cf. Mark 4:12). "Not one stone [of these great buildings of the Temple] will be left here upon another; all will be thrown down . . . ; there will be earthquakes . . . ; there will be famines. . . the sun will be darkened, and the moon will not give its light, and the stars will be falling from heaven, and the powers in the heavens will be shaken" (Mark 13:2, 8, 24–25). And to their narrowed eyes and their "Do you not know what we are capable of?" cross-examination, he replies, "'you will see the Son of Man seated at the right hand of the Power,' and 'coming with the clouds of heaven'" (Mark 14:62).

The horror he agonizes through in Gethsemane and then on Golgotha does not seem to be that meted out habitually by Jerusalem or Rome. He faces "the high priest; and all the chief priests, the elders, and the scribes" (Mark 14:53) and he faces Pilate (15:1). To his "I am" the Judeans howl their shock and dismay (14:63–65); to his "You say so" the Roman is simply struck dumb (15:5). Both condemn him, the former with great knowing satisfaction, the latter with confusion, as if the whole affair made no sense to him at all. Jesus yields without a struggle. There is in him none of the just insolence of Socrates, and yet there is in Jesus' countenance here no distress, nothing of the agony of the garden or the hill. In fact what is most striking is the calm, the silence, of Jesus before these ruthlessly powerful men. Socrates has elegant poise in his courtroom irony; even as he wrestles with his opponents he stands tall, an aloof benefactor, both brusquely and alluringly a sagacious educator to the end. Jesus sees nothing to combat, nothing to defend, no noble apology to be made.

And yet he does agonize in the garden; even moreso on the hill, dying in fact in agony. It is hard for us to take in a savior who dies in agony, unless, of course, we imagine it all as merely secondhand suffering, i.e., as a charade.[22] Further, there is nothing in a good first reading of the Gospel that would lead us to imagine, prior to Gethsemane, that he would die so poorly. Even in the aftermath of the Caesarea Philippi pronouncement, this "Son of Man" who is to suffer and die does not seem like the kind of man who would openly bay in pain, no matter the kind of pain. In immediate retrospect, in the light of the great heroes of the Maccabean and Hellenic pasts his death does not measure up to the standards of nobility. Perhaps especially in later retrospect in the light of the deaths of the martyrs, of Perpetua and Felicitas, say, he fares no better. Though Perpetua and Felicitas are not buoyed by the *apatheia* the Stoics admired in Socrates and it is clear that dying comes hard for them, too, they do not shout at heaven, "My God, my God, why have you forsaken me?" They do not give "a loud cry" as they die (15:34, 37). The centurian, who faces Jesus at the foot of the cross may seem to size up the character of his death approvingly (15:39); but he speaks with the same satanic voice that failed to work its con in the synagogue in the Gospel's first chapter (1:24). His words may in some abstract sense be "true," e.g., may accord with the title verse of the book (1:1), but they are no truer to Jesus' *work* than are Peter's obstructive outbursts at Caesarea Philippi (8:29–33). Jesus' death cry, his pathetic expiration, his giving up the ghost (KJV), the evacuation of the Spirit that descended into (*eis*) him with his baptism, is in itself the kind of detail well adjusted parents would do well to skip during storytime at the bedsides of their well adjusted children.

There is nothing about Jesus' death as an isolated phenomenon, as a thing in itself,[23] that does anyone any good. He dies and he is dead. His heart and lungs and brain stop and he no more (the dead weight of dead tissue) yearningly opens his throat to praise God. But this thing, this corpse, this quantum of hardening muscles and blood and skin and bones, is no device for leveraging a happy outcome, no assayer's bag of weights, no money order. He dies as the thieves hanged with him die, as die peasants and castaways all over Galilee, the Decapolis, and as far as nightmares reach, viz., at the hands or under the calculative gaze of Rome and Jerusalem. He is simply and directly one of (*huper*) them. His life, too, has been poured out

---

22. It is too much to describe Augustine as characterizing the agony of Christ on the cross as a charade; still, he does divest Jesus of the cry of dereliction. See *The Trinity*, 136–137 [4.3.6].

23. This phrase need not be taken in a strictly Kantian sense and, in any case, of course, a Kantian *Ding an sich* is no Kantian phenomenon.

like water (Ps 22:14) and it has drained into the dry ground of Israel's bleak wilderness, mingling with theirs. His *death* mingles with theirs. They are his neighbors in death and he takes them in and is taken in by them; they are he and he is they—even as the "are" and "is," the "they" and "he," fade to black.

And yet, in the telling, the death of Jesus—like all deaths a closure[24]—is not a closure alone. The Spirit enters into him accompanied by the Father's voice in Mark's baptismal overture (1:10) and exits from him accompanied by the Father's silence in Mark's baptismal finale (15:37). There is nothing in this text that compels the reader to believe that the Father, who declared his love for the Son from high above the housetops in the first chapter, has come—in the passage to which the first most directly alludes—to disdain him. Even with the Son's cry of dereliction, one need not take the silence of the Father of the beloved Son as a signal of disinheritance. In the Gospel, Jesus' work is marked not only or chiefly by declaration, but also and above all by silence; a silence again and again commanded of those who with gratitude or malice would seize him with a term.[25] Further, it is not only with Jesus' baptism, but also with his crucifixion that the holiest of veils—the curtain whose long, heavy, wide, tall, and deep fabric would preserve the seclusive integrity of heaven and earth[26]—is ruptured, "torn apart" (1:10; cf. 15:38), with apocalyptic ferocity. The closure of Jesus' death is thus—not erased, but—outbid, by an ineffable revelatory "Nevertheless. . . ."[27]

There is, however, no denying Jesus' outcry from the cross: "'Eloi, Eloi, lema sabachthani?' which means, 'My God, my God, why have you forsaken me?'" (15:34). The forsakenness of the Son is the forsakenness of all who die, especially those who die with the "it is finished" of a lifetime without integrity, authenticity, or identity, i.e., among "the outcasts of Israel," among bloody, slimy, oozing, filthy, creeping, naked, limbless, abject,

---

24. His tomb is sealed, after all.

25. See Lash, *Holiness, Speech, and Silence*, 75–95, especially 75–77, 93.

26. Flavius Josephus, *Jewish War*, 302–4: "There were [in the Temple] golden doors 82 1/2 feet high and 24 wide. In front of these was a curtain of the same length, Babylonian tapestry embroidered with blue, white linen thread, scarlet and purple, a marvelous example of the craftsman's art. The mixture of materials had a clear mystic meaning, typifying all creation: it seemed the scarlet symbolized fire, linen the earth, blue the air, and purple the sea. In two cases the resemblance was use of colour; in the linen and purple it was a question of origin, as the first comes from the earth, the second from the sea. Worked in the tapestry was the whole vista of the heavens except for the signs of the zodiac."

27. Cf. Barth, *Epistle to the Romans*, 93–99; *CD* 1/2, 152, 308.

noxious vermin (Ps 22:6)—an illegal alien, say, or a queer (Isa 56:3–8; cf. Mark 11:15–17), or a bandit (15:27), or perhaps a fatherless, childless, futureless, contemptibly lewd woman (5:25), or any crowd of women, men, and children already as good as dead (5:24–41). Everyone dies, some particularly unhappily. The words of dereliction shouted from the cross voice the horror of the damned, with whom Jesus had been rightly counted his whole adult life. They are not his words alone, just as his life is not his life alone, just as his death is not his death alone.

The death of Jesus does its work certainly because of the way it is set apart from other deaths. The proclamation that it is precisely the *Son of God* who dies between bandits on Golgotha is not based on the extrapolative logic of more or better, the outward ex-pression of a kind of rigorously internal comparative judgment, anymore than it is an empirically grounded hypothesis someday to be verified by data collection and analysis. It is a night different from other nights. It is a *there* you can't get to from *here*.[28] But the death of the Son of God is set apart from other deaths in particular because of the way it is inseparable from them. That is, it is not in the strict sense of the term *sui generis*. This one person in two natures, *homoousion tō patri* and *homoousion hēmin*, is Emmanuel, God so entangled in us—in our bodies, in our histories, in the damage that we have done and the damage that has been done to us—that the only path to him is the one beneath the transient shadow cast in mid-course by any unfinished step. The path that he is on, the path he is, does not transport those who walk it to some alien geographical or metaphysical space, some outland. There is no ascension narrative in Mark. Even if, as in Luke-Acts, the story here had ended with his slipping off into the clouds, the heaven that would welcome him would be an earthy one, the full sweep of the world before God's watchful care, perhaps, i.e., in panorama.

"On earth as it is in heaven," Matthew says (6:10). In life and in death he is (with) us. The difference that occurs where he lives and dies is enhypostatic. He is a human being who abandons all the *what*—all the *physis*, the *natura*, that marks him as *a* human—to the coming of God. And though a theology without a story to tell, may insist otherwise, he is a human being who abandons all the *that*—all the *hypostasis*, the *persona*, that marks him as *this* human—to the coming of God. When God comes, God comes where he lives and dies, without robbing him of anything human. Even his (*anhypostatic*) self-effacement is not forced on him; he offers it with

---

28. Cf. "Cyril of Alexandria's Second Letter to Nestorius," 133–34.

After Crucifixion

gratitude (Mark 8:6, 14:23). He lives the life we live and dies the death we die, without qualification; he does so as an open throat, as open flesh, open eyes, open speech, open arms, open lips, lips through which his last breath is released to the coming of God. He is Emmanuel especially here. When he expires, when he gives up the ghost, his life is finished (John 19:30) and it is finished as our lives are finished when we breathe our last. And yet his death is *in toto* the unarticulated prayer, "Veni, Sancte Spiritus." His mutilated body repeats this prayer long after it is taken down from the cross. It repeats it here, with us, bathed and fed as we are. "He called the crowd with his disciples, and said to them, '... follow me'" (Mark 8:34). To follow him thus is with him, *after* him—here and now—to open ... like mutilated flesh, like yearning eyes, like reticent speech, like suppliant arms, like with hot innocence to be kissed and kiss, i.e., in prayer, in hope, undone, marveling toward the promise of a wind that would so trouble dark waters, the dark Jordan, the dark seas, that they would in spite of themselves give up every ship and sailor they had drowned.

> And he was transfigured before them, and his clothes became dazzling white, such as no one on earth could bleach them. And there appeared to them Elijah with Moses, who were talking with Jesus.... Then a cloud overshadowed them, and from the cloud there came a voice, "This is my Son, the Beloved; listen to him!" Suddenly when [Peter and James and John] looked around, they saw no one with them any more, but only Jesus. (9:2-4, 7-8)

This is what the bishop teaches as she gestures before the loaf and cup. She teaches it and with the gathered body learns it. She learns it, as they learn it, in the never to be presumed fresh literate or illiterate reading of God-breathed texts, that is, again and again, in and out of the room, face to face with faces upturned in the room, or not and never in the room. She declares, as if they were her words, but with deference as anything but her words, the "follow me ... !" As her trailing breath and God's inaudibly proclaim the ellipsis that the "follow me" opens into, her memory and hope stir. She silently confesses with Augustine both her sins and the sovereign forgiveness of God, a forgiveness that hallows, that comes as an insuperable eschatological peace, as a future impinging upon the present and the insistent past to which it is chained. God forgives. "And he took them up in his arms, laid his hands on them, and blessed them" (Mark 10:16). But the gift that ruptures the present, that goes forth into "was" and "is" from what is yet to be, is no less a call and a task. Forgiveness *creates*, as Isaiah, Genesis, and Paul understood. And they and those who have heard them well have also understood that to be created is to set out on a journey. We, the forgiven, are little children, newborns, newly created, "created in Christ Jesus." The incarnate Christ Jesus is the universe in which still wet with amniotic fluid our lungs and eyes have uncannily opened. But the incarnate Christ Jesus is no dead space, no lost time. He worked and works, as all flesh works. He is a whole universe in which to live is to be created "for good works" (Eph 2:10), for the works that mark the story of the Jesus who called the crowd with his disciples to journey after him. "Follow me . . . !"

Where he journeys, where we journey after him, is crucifixion. Crucifixion, however, is after Mark 16 no longer simply the horrifying triumph of martial power, pain, and death. Jesus is laid low, but by the Spirit who descends into him at his baptism he stirs and he stands,[29] i.e., "he is risen." He moves elusively, no trace of him remaining in the tomb, only the word of a young man dressed in white.[30] Like the God whose hand no longer covers Moses in the cleft of the rock, the God whom Moses is simply to follow into promise (Exod 33:14–23), the resurrected Jesus leads anew those who would follow him into Galilee, i.e., again under the heel of Jerusalem and Rome, where his journey to crucifixion began—but with an uncanny difference.

The passion of Jesus is lonely only as all our deaths are lonely. He is with us in the loneliness of death, too. And so, he and we are not alone even there. The same blow that strikes him dead, strikes us all dead, and it strikes us in the same way. To walk after him to crucifixion is with him to walk together. It is to walk the path to where people are especially liable to suffer, where they are most vulnerable, most indefensible, where they are slated to lose at a fixed wheel. It is to move in with them, to assume their bad odds, to touch and be touched by them. That is, to walk the path of Jesus is to give up, as the Rich Young Ruler was called upon to do (Mark 10:17–22), the prospect of securing property gated at a safe distance from

29. This, it seems to me, is what is to be said when Jesus' baptism is no longer understood to precede his crucifixion/resurrection chronologically, but rather to concur with it. That is, his descent into the water in chapter 1 is his crucifixion. The breath that he releases on the cross as he dies, returns to him as he comes out of the water of baptism. The rending of the curtain of the Temple and of the heavens opens the space through which the Spirit of resurrection proceeds.

30. See Hovey, *To Share in the Body*, 118–25.

the woes of the world. It is to give up the delusion of perpetuity. This is where Jesus travels and his call to the crowd with his disciples is not just or especially for rich young rulers. He is among the poorest of the poor when he commands, "follow me . . . !" It may seem that the poor would find the news of such a call to be anything but good. No doubt this is true. The poor have no weaker desire than the rich for securing property. There are bread riots, just as there are riots on the floor of the New York Stock Exchange. The poor also know that it takes money to make money. No one is naturally inclined to expect a life worth living to grow where there is no fertility that might yield it. Nothing grows in the wilderness. The news of the resurrection is that to follow Jesus is to find in the wilderness—where it cannot be—enough life not only for all of Israel (Mark 6:31–44), but also for all of the world (8:1–9).

Even the righteous among the rich and the poor will find that message to be scandalous, too much, extremist. But extremists, too, will shrink from it. To follow Jesus back into Galilee is openly, receptively, hospitably to face every face that you meet. It is to befriend every stranger and, if she will, to move in with her (Mark 6:8–10). And when you move in with a stranger—though she is soon no longer a stranger and in any given day may meet you more often than the sum total of all the others you sometimes also meet[31]—she never stops being a face that you meet on the road to Galilee. If she sends you packing, then on down the road you go; but if she contines to welcome you, you stay. Of course, she, too, may hear the call. She, too, may come with more or less passion than you to stand before a tall, broad, clear window and there to dream of the open road. You and she may together set out differently for Galilee. On the other hand, you may spend a whole lifetime with her in her little house in her little village somewhere through which the way of the cross has cut. There is perhaps a special grace for those who stay, that in staying they may not cease to wander. Perhaps it is here where she is cut and bruised, where she is battered by disease and anxiety and an inhospitable world, where she grows weak and old, that the mutilated body of the glorified Jesus is particularly beheld. Perhaps it is here as her yearning eyes meet yours that the transfigured face of the Crucified particularly shines. Perhaps it is in her reticent speech, entangled as it is in yours, that the failure of the unclean spirit and the Roman centurion to trap Jesus in a formulated phrase is particularly with hope remembered. Perhaps it is in her suppliant arms and in her caress that his caress of the hand of Jairus's daughter is particularly felt. Perhaps it is in her hot, innocent kiss,

---

31. Cf. Derrida, *Gift of Death*, 66–69, 71–72, 77–81.

entangled as it is in yours, that you are again and again reminded without condescension that this is indeed the road to Galilee.

The anguish[32] of Jesus in Gethsemane and on Golgatha is the anguish of Emmanuel, i.e., our anguish. It is his anguish, too, of course; his anguish due not to the threatening might of the High Priest or Pilate, but to the horror of death vis-à-vis God, the living God. Jesus, who travels out into the coming of God his whole life long, is with us thrust into the abyss where by definition God cannot go. He is thrust not into an idea, but into a grave. He who is nothing but an open doxological throat—a throat that proclaims to its last breath the coming of the Reign of Justice and Peace and Life—falls across the boundary that separates his beloved Father, the God of the Living, from the starless darkness of a night without the prospect of a dawn. He who would without end joyfully lift up his face to praise God has been thrown down where no throats gape, where flesh hardens, then softens, melts, and dries to dust. God travels on where the dead simply may not and cannot travel. This is the anguish of death, the faithful tell us, the anguish of death for all; i.e., this is the anguish of Emmanuel.

Jesus has not ceased to give himself to the coming of God's Reign when he gives up his last breath in wordless barren doxology outside the gates of Jerusalem (Mark 15:37; cf. 14:32–42). His prayer cannot but be wordless. One crucified does not know how to pray as she ought (Rom 8:26). How could she? How could he? There are no *logoi* that might yield doxology from the cross. How could there be? Even one hale and hearty, with both feet planted firmly on the ground, prays doxologically—uncannily. One crucified, giving up the ghost, lacks even the paltry strength of the unafflicted. In order for a doxology to be uttered at the moment when Jesus' last breath is let go from the cross, the very *doxa* of the Father to whom the beloved Son has now given everything, given unqualifiedly all that he is, would have to travel not away from, but to this fast dying man, would have to be pleased to dwell *here* when and where he dies. The darkness of this day would have to be pierced as if the mutilated body of the Crucified had grown dazzlingly white (Mark 9:3). Borne by the impossibility of miracle, this *dox*ology would exceed every dox*ology*, the way sometimes a groan or a sigh, evoked, not expressed, outstrips articulate speech. The very dying body of the Crucified would then wordlessly voice the *doxa* of the Father.

---

32. Cf. *Oxford English Dictionary*, s.v. "agon, *n.*"

After Crucifixion

Word would become flesh, flesh would become word, the word we could never speak, the word that could only be spoken to and welcomed by us as every possible barrier to it is transgressed (John 1:14).

When this word is spoken, it is spoken to us, because it is spoken to him; it is welcomed by us, because it is welcomed by him—him whose every line of defense is on the cross breached, breached because relinquished. He and this word concur, because he has relinquished every line of defense that might have presumed to hold it at bay. He and we concur, because he has relinquished every line of defense that might have presumed to hold us at bay. His Passion, however, is not simply passive. He is not only acted upon in his suffering. The agony of the cross is a concurrence of the work of the word spoken and the work of the Galilean, viz., the dyothelite work of rupture, the *enhypostatic*, the *anhypostatic*, work of "nevertheless" (Mark 14:36). The agony of this concurrence is the agony of Emmanuel. It occurs here and now, not as a presence that might serenely *be*, but as a *coming*, a coming that would open a way, a task, a future. Jesus' "Come!" (Mark 1:17; 8:34;10:14, 21) is the "Come!" that Matthew tells us is "easy," "light" (Matt 11:30). And it is here, in the darkness. The roominess of the New Jerusalem opens here where this present evil age does its worst. There is no outside the walls of the New Jerusalem; even if there were, the gates are open and any and every outsider may come in. There is no condition for a roomy place in the New Jerusalem. Even the lame, even the dead, even the damned are set free here and run with abandon. But woe to those who would incarcerate the Holy Spirit, who would throw up new lines of defense, conditions that would exclude, include, conclude, occlude the freedom for which Christ has set us free (Gal 5:1), who would yet claim the property right to judge who is in and who is out.

The bishop teaches as she gestures before the remarkable and unremarkable people who come and go where she is given to do her work—before those standing on their own two feet in the prime of life, before infants held, covered, and warmed in their parent's arms beside a font, before the very old or too young adrift on their death beds, moving among them, in and out of time and space, the betrothed, the contrite, the apostate, the ordinand, the addled, the grieving, the gleeful, the ambitious, the bypassed, the prodigy—i.e., the bishop before the cup and the loaf, which (more than like the one who fares as gratuitous ruptured flesh) are nothing without these people he and the bishop love, these people without whom he and the bishop would have nowhere at all to go and nothing to do, these people in whose lives the Father of the Son and the Spirit is through the Son and in the Spirit freely forever entangled.[33] God, never needy or vulnerable, never alone or lonely, is love, and thus Emmanuel. Therefore, the bishop teaches and she prays the epiclesis, because her voice, her eyes, her hands, and her daily work will not do. They are *only* gestures. They do not and cannot hold and they do not and cannot distribute what the people she so loves desperately are without. Her gestures may only entreat, implore, give thanks, and await. It is the Spirit, who saturated the mutilated body of Jesus, who comes to carry to their eschatological end the fleshy prayers of the bishop.[34]

If the healings of Jesus are acts by which the broken people of oppressed Galilee are restored to "can," there is another, more revolutionary act in his work, an act that carries its own potency, i.e., an act that is free to interrupt the intractable protology of "can." The phrase used for this eschatological work, e.g., in the Gospel of Mark, is much too familiar for us to be struck by it. It is hard for us to hear it as anything but proprietary magnanimity, as a kind of investment firm's savvy customer care representative's "No problem." It is nearly impossible for us to hear it as an upending of all that is proper and authentic, all that is good, true, and beautiful. Nonetheless it is, as the horrified scribes in Jesus' house immediately understood. "Son, your sins are forgiven" (Mark 2:5). The forgiveness of sins is the interruption of "cannot" by "may" and then by "does."[35] When "cannot" fails to provide a barrier to "may" and "does," everything unravels, the sun is darkened, the stars fall from the sky, and the powers in the heavens are shaken. And yet it is precisely here in this "Son, your sins are forgiven," this "Little girl, get up!" that the whole of creation is unmade and made anew, that the Galilean peasant carpenter's son comes with great power and glory to reign, when on the cross he is lifted up from the earth and draws all people to himself (John 12:32). To teach this, calls for the bishop's whole heart, soul, mind, and strength, but it also calls for her neighbor; for without her neighbor she has nowhere at all to go and nothing to do (Mark 12:28–31).

---

33. Cf. Barth, *Humanity of God*, 46.

34. Basil of Caesarea, *On the Holy Spirit*, 62 (16.38): "The Originator of all things is One: He creates through the Son and perfects through the Spirit.... Likewise the Son works as the Father's likeness, and needs no other cooperation, but He chooses to have His work completed through the Spirit."

35. Cf. Barth, *Evangelical Theology*, 200: "But he *may* . . . , and since he may . . . , he does. . . ."

Postlude[1]

"What is it?" (Exodus 16:15)

I followed them: I saw them go down Bucareli to Reforma with a spring in their step and then cross Reforma without waiting for the lights to change, their long hair blowing in the excess wind that funnels down Reforma at that hour of the night, transforming it into a transparent tube or an elongated lung exhaling the city's imaginary breath. Then we walked down the Avenida Guerrero; they weren't stepping so lightly any more, and I wasn't feeling too enthusiastic either. Guerrero, at that time of night, is more like a cemetery than an avenue, not a cemetery in 1974 or in 1968, or 1975, but a cemetery in the year 2666, a forgotten cemetery under the eyelid of a corpse or an unborn child, bathed in the dispassionate fluids of an eye that tried so hard to forget one particular thing that it ended up forgetting everything else.[2]

I don't want to be crucified
Don't want
Thorns on my head
Don't want
Walk among the dead
I don't want to be
Jesus
Jesus
Jesus[3]

We declare to you ... what we have heard, what we have seen with our eyes, what we have looked at and touched with our hands ... (1 John 1:1)

Hundreds of kodaks clicked all morning at the scene of the lynching. People in automobiles and carriages came from miles around to view the corpse dangling from the end of a rope. ... Picture cards photographers installed a portable printing plant at the

---

1. Mark 9:49: "For everyone will be salted with fire."
2. Bolaño, *Amulet*, 86.
3. Taylor, "Resurrection Blues."

Postlude

bridge and reaped a harvest in selling the postcard showing a photograph of the lynched Negro. Women and children were there by the score. At a number of country schools the day's routine was delayed until boy and girl pupils could get back from viewing the lynched man.[4]

There is the silence of shame and the silence of gratitude, the silence of indifference and the silence of love, the silence of satiety and the silence of yearning, the silence of disgust and the silence of joy, the silence of ennui and the silence of wonder, the silence of betrayal and the silence of faithfulness, the silence of propriety and the silence of forgiveness, the silence of despair and the silence of hope.

And very early on the first day of the week, when the sun had risen, they went to the tomb. . . . As they entered the tomb, they saw a young man, dressed in a white robe, sitting on the right side; and they were alarmed. But he said to them, "Do not be alarmed; you are looking for Jesus of Nazareth, who was crucified. He has been raised; he is not here. . . . But go . . . he is going ahead of you to Galilee. . . ." (Mark 16:2, 5–7)

O boundless charity! . . . .
O fire of love! . . .
What drove you?
Nothing but your charity,
mad with love as you are![5]

My life is not worth more than any other—not less not more. Nor am I an innocent child. I have lived long enough to know that I, too, am an accomplice of the evil that seems to prevail in the world around, even that which might lash out blindly at me. If the moment comes, I would hope to have the presence of mind, and the time, to ask for God's pardon and for that of my fellow men, and, at the same time, to pardon in all sincerety he who would attack me. . . .

Obviously my death will justify the opinion of all those who dismissed me as naïve or idealistic: "Let him tell us what he thinks now." But those people should know that my death will satisfy my most burning curiosity. At last I will be able—if God pleases—to

---

4. *The Crisis* 10.2 (June 1915), on the lynching of Thomas Brooks in Fayette County, Tennessee. Cited by Cone, *Cross and the Lynching Tree*, 1.

5. Catherine of Siena, *Prayers of Catherine of Siena*, 78–79.

see the children of Islam as He sees them, illuminated in the glory of Christ, sharing in the gift of God's Passion and of the Spirit, whose secret joy will always be to bring forth our common humanity amidst our differences.

I give thanks to God for this life, completely mine yet completely theirs, too, to God who wanted it for joy against, and inspite of, all odds. In this Thank You—which says everything about my life—I include you my friends, past and present, and those friends who will be here at the side of my mother and father, of my sisters and brothers—thank you a thousandfold.

And to you, too, my friend of the last moment, who will not know what you are doing. Yes, for you, too, I want this thank-you, this "A-Dieu,"... that we may meet in heaven, like happy thieves, if it pleases God, our common Father. Amen! Inshah Allah![6]

Do you have eyes, and fail to see? Do you have ears, and fail to hear? And do you not remember? (Mark 8:18)

The wolf shall live with the lamb, the leopard shall lie down with the kid, the calf and the lion and the fatling together, and a little child shall lead them. The cow and the bear shall graze, their young shall lie down together; and the lion shall eat straw like the ox. The nursing child shall play over the hole of the asp, and the weaned child shall put its hand on the adder's den. They will not hurt or destroy on all my holy mountain; for the earth will be full of the knowledge of the Lord as the waters cover the sea. On that day the root of Jesse shall stand as a signal to the peoples; the nations shall inquire of him, and his dwelling shall be glorious. (Isa 11:6–10)

We live between silences.

Try to make believe this is not just madness because this is not just madness.[7]

---

6. From "The Testament of Christian Chergé," quoted in Kiser, *Monks of Tibhirine*, 245–46. Cf. *Of Gods and Men* [*Des hommes et des dieux*], directed by Xavier Beauvois.

7. Arthur Edens, from *Michael Clayton*.

Bibliography

Abraham, William J. *Canon and Criterion in Christian Theology: From the Fathers to Feminism*. New York: Oxford University Press, 1998.
Agamben, Giorgio. *The Time that Remains: A Commentary on the Letter to the Romans*. Translated by Patricia Dailey. Stanford: Stanford University Press, 2005.
Alameda Corridor Fact Sheet. Online: http://www.acta.org/projects/projects_completed_alameda_factsheet.asp.
Althaus, Paul. *The Theology of Martin Luther*. Translated by Robert C. Schultz. Philadelphia: Fortress, 1966.
Anderson, John R. *Cognitive Psychology and Its Implications*. 6th ed. New York: Worth, 2005.
Apocalypse Now. Directed by Francis Ford Coppola. Paramount Home Video, 1999.
Aquinas, Thomas. *Nature and Grace: Selection from the Summa Theologica of Thomas Aquinas*. Translated and edited by A. M. Fairweather. Philadelphia: Westminster, 1954.
Aristotle. *The Nicomachean Ethics*. Translated by David Ross. Revised by J. L. Ackrill and J. O. Urmson. New York: Oxford University Press, 1980.
Astur, Robert S., et al. "Hippocampus Function Predicts Severity of Post-Traumatic Stress Disorder." *Cyberpsychology and Behavior* 9 (2006) 234–40.
Augustine. *The Confessions of St. Augustine*. Translated by F. J. Sheed. New York: Sheed & Ward, 1944.
———. *The Trinity*. Translated by Stephen McKenna. Washington, DC: Catholic University of America Press, 1963.
Barnabas. Translated by J. B. Lightfoot. Online: http://www.earlychristianwritings.com/text/barnabas-lightfoot.html.
Barth, Karl. "An Answer to Professor Harnack's Open Letter." Translated by Keith R. Crim. In *The Beginnings of Dialectic Theology*, edited by James M. Robinson, 175–85. Richmond: John Knox, 1968.
———. *Church Dogmatics* 1/1: *The Doctrine of the Word of God*. Translated by G. W. Bromiley and T. F. Torrance. Edinburgh: T. & T. Clark, 1975.
———. *Church Dogmatics* 1/2: *The Doctrine of the Word of God*. Translated by G. T. Thomson and Harold Knight. Edinburgh: T. & T. Clark, 1956.
———. *Church Dogmatics* 3/1: *The Doctrine of Creation*. Translated by J. W. Edwards et al. Edinburgh: T. & T. Clark, 1958.
———. *Church Dogmatics* 3/2: *The Doctrine of Creation*. Translated by Harold Knight et al. Edinburgh: T. & T. Clark, 1960.
———. *Church Dogmatics* 3/3: *The Doctrine of Creation*. Translated by G. W. Bromiley and R. J. Ehrlich. Edinburgh: T. & T. Clark, 1960.

Bibliography

———. *Church Dogmatics 4/1: The Doctrine of Reconciliation*. Edinburgh: T. & T. Clark, 1956.
———. *Epistle to the Romans*. Translated by Edwyn C. Hoskyns. New York: Oxford University Press, 1933.
———. *Evangelical Theology: An Introduction*. Translated by Grover Foley. Grand Rapids: Eerdmans, 1963.
———. "Fifteen Answers to Professor von Harnack." Translated by Keith R. Crim. In *The Beginnings of Dialectic Theology*, edited by James M. Robinson, 167–170. Richmond: John Knox, 1968.
———. *The Humanity of God*. Translated by Thomas Wieser and John Newton Thomas. Richmond: John Knox, 1960.
———. *Prayer*. 2nd ed. Translated by Sara F. Terrien. Edited by Don E. Saliers. Philadelphia: Westminster, 1985.
Barton, Stephen C. "Dislocating and Relocating Holiness: A New Testament Study." In *Holiness: Past and Present*, edited by Stephen C. Barton, 193–213. New York: T. & T. Clark, 2003.
Basil of Caesarea. *On the Holy Spirit*. Translated by David Anderson. Crestwood, NY: St. Vladimir's Seminary Press, 1980.
Bataille, Georges. "The Notion of Expenditure." In *Deconstruction in Context*, edited by Mark C. Taylor, 360–74. Chicago: University of Chicago Press, 1986.
Bauckham, Richard. *The Theology of the Book of Revelation*. New York: Cambridge University Press, 1993.
Bauernfeind, Otto. "*aretê*." In *Theological Dictionary of the New Testament*, edited by Gerhard Kittel, translated and edited by Geoffrey W. Bromiley, 1:457–61. Grand Rapids: Eerdmans, 1964.
Beale, G. K. *The Book of Revelation: A Commentary on the Greek Text*. Grand Rapids: Eerdmans, 1999.
Bell, Daniel M., Jr. *Liberation Theology After the End of History: The Refusal to Cease Suffering*. New York: Routledge, 2001.
Belo, Fernando. *A Materialist Reading of the Gospel of Mark*. Translated by Matthew J. O'Connell. Maryknoll, NY: Orbis, 1981.
Berquist, Jon L. *Controlling Corporeality: The Body and the Household in Ancient Israel*. New Brunswick, NJ: Rutgers University Press, 2002.
Berry, Wendell. "Watch with Me." In *That Distant Land: The Collected Stories*, 77–123. Washington, DC: Shoemaker & Hoard, 2004.
Betcher, Sharon V. *Spirit and the Politics of Disablement*. Minneapolis: Fortress, 2007.
Bevans, Stephen. "Mission among Migrants, Mission of Migrants: Mission of the Church." In *A Promised Land, A Perilous Journey: Theological Perspectives on Migration*, edited by Daniel G. Groody and Gioacchino Campese, 89–106. Notre Dame: University of Notre Dame Press, 2008.
Bieler, Andrea, and Luise Schottroff. *The Eucharist: Bodies, Bread, and Resurrection*. Minneapolis: Fortress, 2007.
Blanchot, Maurice. *The Writing of the Disaster*. Translated by Ann Smock. Lincoln: University of Nebraska Press, 1986.
Boehm, Mike. "Theater: Cornerstone Mobilizes the Troupe: The Normally Slow and Steady Theater Company Takes to the Streets Over the South Central Farm Eviction. A New Leaf?" *Los Angeles Times*, June 25, 2006.
Bolaño, Roberto. *Amulet*. Translated by Chris Andrews. New York: New Directions, 2006.

Bolt, Robert. *A Man for All Seasons: A Play in Two Acts*. New York: Vintage, 1990.
Bondi, Roberta. *To Pray and to Love: Conversations on Prayer with the Early Church*. Minneapolis: Fortress, 1991.
Bremner, J. Douglas, et al. "The Neurobiology of Posttraumatic Stress Disorder: An Integration of Animal and Human Research." In *Posttraumatic Stress Disorder: A Comprehensive Text*, edited by Philip A. Saigh and J. Douglas Bremner, 103–43. Boston: Allyn & Bacon, 1999.
Brewer's Dictionary of Phrase and Fabel. Edited by Ivor H. Evans. 15th ed. New York: HarperCollins, 1995.
Brown, Raymond E. *The Gospel According to John*. Vol. 2, *XIII–XXI*. Garden City, NY: Doubleday, 1970.
Brueggemann, Walter. *Theology of the Old Testament: Testimony, Dispute, Advocacy*. Minneapolis: Fortress, 1997.
Buber, Martin. *I and Thou*. Translated by Walter Kaufmann. New York: Scribner's, 1970.
———. "Prelude: Report on Two Talks." In *Eclipse of God: Studies in the Relation between Religion and Philosophy*, 1–10. New York: Harper, 1952.
Bultmann, Rudolf. "Welchen Sinn hat es, von Gott zu reden?" In *Glauben und Verstehen*, 1:26–37. Tübingen: Mohr, 1933.
Busch, Eberhard. *Karl Barth: His Life from Letters and Autobiographical Texts*. Translated by John Bowden. Philadelphia: Fortress, 1976.
Byrne, David, and Chris Frantz. "Stay Hungry." Performed by The Talking Heads. *More Songs About Buildings and Food*. CD. Sire Records, 1978.
Catherine of Siena. *The Prayers of Catherine of Siena*. Edited and translated by Suzanne Noffke. Ramsey, NJ: Paulist, 1983.
Cavanaugh, William T. *Torture and Eucharist: Theology, Politics, and the Body of Christ*. Malden, MA: Blackwell, 1998.
Chawkins, Steve. "A New Setting for Their Plots." *Los Angeles Times*, April 28, 2008.
Claiborne, Robert. *The Roots of English: A Reader's Handbook of Word Origins*. New York: Times Books, 1989.
Coakley, Sarah. *Powers and Submissions: Spirituality, Philosophy and Gender*. Malden, MA: Blackwell, 2002.
———. *Sacrifice Regained: Reconsidering the Rationality of Religious Belief*. New York: Cambridge University Press, 2012.
Colish, Marcia L. *Medieval Foundations of the Western Intellectual Tradition, 400–1400*. New Haven: Yale University Press, 1997.
Collins, John J. *The Apocalyptic Imagination: An Introduction to Jewish Apocalyptic Literature*. 2nd ed. Grand Rapids: Eerdmans, 1998.
Cone, James. *The Cross and the Lynching Tree*. Maryknoll, NY: Orbis, 2011.
———. *God of the Oppressed*. Rev. ed. Maryknoll, NY: Orbis, 1997.
Cool Hand Luke. Directed by Stuart Rosenberg. Warner Brothers, 1967.
Copi, Irving M., and Carl Cohen. *Introduction to Logic*. 10th ed. Upper Saddle River, NJ: Prentice-Hall, 1998.
Cousar, Charles B. *A Theology of the Cross: The Death of Jesus in the Pauline Letters*. Minneapolis: Fortress, 1990.
Cushman, Robert Earl. *Therapeia: Plato's Conception of Philosophy*. New Brunswick, NJ: Transaction, 2002.
———. "Worship as Acknowledgment." In *Faith Seeking Understanding: Essays Theological and Critical*, 181–97. Durham: Duke University Press, 1981.

Bibliography

Cyril of Alexandria. "Cyril of Alexandria's Second Letter to Nestorius." In *The Christological Controversy*, translated and edited by Richard A. Norris, 131–34. Philadelphia: Fortress, 1980.

Derrida, Jacques. *Adieu to Emmanuel Levinas*. Translated by Pascale-Anne Brault and Michael Naas. Stanford: Stanford University Press, 1999.

———. "Différance." Translated by Alan Bass. In *Deconstruction in Context*, edited by Mark C. Taylor, 396–420. Chicago: University of Chicago Press, 1986.

———. *Dissemination*. Translated by Barbara Johnson. Chicago: University of Chicago Press, 1981.

———. *The Gift of Death*. Translated by David Wills. Chicago: University of Chicago Press, 1995.

———. *Margins of Philosophy*. Translated by Alan Bass. Chicago: University of Chicago Press, 1982.

Descartes, René. *Meditations on First Philosophy*. Translated by Donald A. Cress. Indianapolis: Hackett, 1979.

Dewey, John. *A Common Faith*. New Haven: Yale University Press, 1934.

———. *Reconstruction in Philosophy*. Enlarged ed. Boston: Beacon, 1957.

"The Didache." In *Early Christian Fathers*, translated and edited by Cyril C. Richardson, 171–79. Library of Christian Classics 1. Philadelphia: Westminster, 1953.

Dostoevsky, Fyodor. *The Brothers Karamazov*. Translated by Richard Pevear and Larissa Volokhonsky. New York: Farrar, Straus & Giroux, 1990.

———. *The Idiot*. Translated by Henry and Olga Carlisle. New York: New American Library, 1969.

Douglas, J. D., et al. *A Concise Dictionary of the Christian Tradition: Doctrine, Liturgy, History*. Grand Rapids: Zondervan, 1989.

Dunn, James D. G. *Christology in the Making: A New Testament Inquiry into the Origins of the Doctrine of the Incarnation*. 2nd ed. Grand Rapids: Eerdmans, 1989.

———. "Jesus and Holiness: The Challenge of Purity." In *Holiness: Past and Present*, edited by Stephen C. Barton, 168–92. New York: T. & T. Clark, 2003.

Dupré, Louis. *Passage to Modernity: An Essay in the Hermeneutics of Nature and Culture*. New Haven: Yale University Press, 1993.

Dylan, Bob. "Masters of War." Performed by Bob Dylan. *The Freewheelin' Bob Dylan*. Columbia Records, 1963.

———. "Rainy Day Women #12 & 35." Performed by Bob Dylan. *Blonde on Blonde*. Columbia Records, 1966.

Ebeling, Gerhard. *God and Word*. Translated by James W. Leitch. Philadelphia: Fortress, 1967.

———. *Word and Faith*. Translated by James W. Leitch. Philadelphia: Fortress, 1963.

Eliot, T. S. "The Love Song of J. Alfred Prufrock." In *The Complete Poems and Plays: 1909–1950*, 3–7. New York: Harcourt, Brace, 1971.

———. "Murder in the Cathedral." In *The Complete Poems and Plays: 1909–1950*, 173–221. New York: Harcourt, Brace, 1971.

———. "The Waste Land." In *The Complete Poems and Plays: 1909–1950*, 37–59. New York: Harcourt, Brace, 1971.

Eller, Vernard. *Kierkegaard and Radical Discipleship: A New Perspective*. Princeton: Princeton University Press, 1968.

Foakes-Jackson, F. J. *The History of the Christian Church: From the Earliest Times to A.D. 461*. New York: Doran, 1927.

Bibliography

Gammie, John G. *Holiness in Israel*. Minneapolis: Fortress, 1989.
Garrett, Lila. "Who Owns the Farm?" Online: http://www.southcentralfarmers.com/scf/2006/07/who-owns-the-farm-by-lila-garrett/.
Gerrish, B. A. "'To the Unknown God': Luther and Calvin on the Hiddenness of God." *Journal of Religion* 53 (1973) 263-92.
Gibbs, Raymond W., Jr. *Embodiment and Cognitive Science*. New York: Cambridge University Press, 2006.
Gilmore, Myron P. *The World of Humanism, 1453-1517*. New York: Harper, 1952.
Gogarten, Friedrich. "Between the Times." Translated by Louis De Grazia and Keith R. Crim. In *The Beginnings of Dialectic Theology*, edited by James M. Robinson, 277-82. Richmond: John Knox, 1968.
Gonzales, Patrisia. "We Are Farmers, Not Gardeners." *Column of the Americas*, July 3, 2006. Online: http://la.indymedia.org/news/2006/07/167399.php.
Groody, Daniel G. *Border of Death, Valley of Life: An Immigrant Journey of Heart and Spirit*. Lanham, MD: Rowman & Littlefield, 2002.
———, editor. *The Option for the Poor in Christian Theology*. Notre Dame: University of Notre Dame Press, 2007.
Gundry, Robert H. *Matthew: A Commentary on His Literary and Theological Art*. Grand Rapids: Eerdmans, 1982.
Gutiérrez, Gustavo. *On Job: God-Talk and the Suffering of the Innocent*. Translated by Matthew J. O'Connell. Maryknoll, NY: Orbis, 1987.
———. "Option for the Poor." Translated by Robert R. Barr. In *Mysterium Liberationis: Fundamental Concepts of Liberation Theology*, edited by Ignacio Ellacuría and Jon Sobrino, 235-50. Maryknoll, NY: Orbis, 1993.
———. *A Theology of Liberation: History, Politics, and Salvation*. Rev. ed. Translated by Caridad Inda and John Eagleson. Maryknoll, NY: Orbis, 1988.
Hagan, Jacqueline. "Faith for the Journey." In *A Promised Land, A Perilous Journey: Theological Perspectives on Migration*, edited by Daniel G. Groody and Gioacchino Campese, 3-19. Notre Dame: University of Notre Dame Press, 2008.
Hall, Michael. *Oxford*. Englewood Cliffs, NJ: Prentice-Hall, 1983.
Hansard, Glen and Markéta Irglová. "Falling Slowly." Performed by Glen Hansard and Markéta Irglová. *The Swell Season*. Overcoat Recordings. CD. 2006.
Harnack, Adolf von. "Fifteen Questions to Those Among the Theologians Who Are Contemptuous of the Scientific Theology," "An Open Letter to Professor Karl Barth," and "Postscript to My Open Letter to Professor Karl Barth." Translated by Keith R. Crim. In *The Beginnings of Dialectic Theology*, edited by James M. Robinson, 165-66, 171-74, and 186-87. Richmond: John Knox, 1968.
Hauerwas, Stanley. *After Christendom? How the Church Is to Behave if Freedom, Justice, and a Christian Nation Are Bad Ideas*. Nashville: Abingdon, 1999.
———. *In Good Company: The Church as Polis*. Notre Dame: University of Notre Dame Press, 1995.
———. *Sanctify Them in the Truth: Holiness Exemplified*. Nashville: Abingdon, 1998.
Hauerwas, Stanley, and Charles Pinches. *Christians Among the Virtues: Theological Conversations with Ancient and Modern Ethics*. Notre Dame: University of Notre Dame Press, 1997.
Hayasaki, Erika. "Seeds of Dissension Linger: Farmers in the South Central Community Decry the Loss of the Land to a Warehouse Project." *Los Angeles Times*, October 31, 2005.

Bibliography

Hays, Richard B. *The Moral Vision of the New Testament: Community, Cross, New Creation: A Contemporary Introduction to New Testament Ethics.* San Francisco: HarperSanFrancisco, 1996.

Hecht, Jamey. "The Future at War with the Past: While South Central's Urban Farmers Face Eviction, Peak Oil Threatens Global Food Supply." March 22, 2006. Online: http://www.fromthewilderness.com/free/ww3/032206_war_past.shtml.

———. "Twilight in the Corn: The Bulldozing of South Central Farm Begins." June 16, 2006. Online: http://www.fromthewilderness.com/free/ww3/061606_twilight_corn.shtml.

Heidegger, Martin. *Being and Time: A Translation of* Sein und Zeit. Translated by Joan Stambaugh. Albany: State University of New York Press, 1996.

———. "Building Dwelling Thinking." In *Poetry, Language, Thought,* translated by Albert Hofstadter, 141–59. New York: Harper & Row, 1971.

———. *Discourse on Thinking.* Translated by John M. Anderson and E. Hans Freund. New York: Harper & Row, 1966.

———. *Introduction to Metaphysics.* Translated by Gregory Fried and Richard Polt. New Haven: Yale University Press, 2000.

———. "Language." In *Poetry, Language, Thought,* translated by Albert Hofstadter, 185–208. New York: Harper & Row, 1971.

———. "Memorial Address." In *Discourse on Thinking,* translated by John M. Anderson and E. Hans Freund, 43–57. New York: Harper & Row, 1966.

———. "The Origin of the Work of Art." In *Poetry, Language, Thought,* translated by Albert Hofstadter, 15–86. New York: Harper & Row, 1971.

———. "Der Ursprung des Kunstwerkes." In *Holzwege,* 1–74. Frankfurt am Main: Klostermann, 1977.

Heitzenrater, Richard P. *The Elusive Mr. Wesley.* Vol. 2. Nashville: Abingdon, 1984.

Hentrich, Thomas. "Masculinity and Disability in the Bible." In *This Abled Body: Rethinking Disabilities in Biblical Studies,* edited by Hector Avalos et al., 73–90. Atlanta: SBL, 2007.

Hernandez, Daniel. "A Brown Day in L.A.: Mayor V. Faces Global Immigration Issues—and Angry Farmers." *L.A. Weekly,* May 25, 2006.

———. "Bushel of Complaints." *L.A. Weekly,* March 17, 2006.

Hernandez, Daniel, and David Zahniser. "Seeds of Secrecy." *L.A. Weekly,* March 10, 2006.

Herzog, William R. *Parables as Subversive Speech: Jesus as Pedagogue of the Oppressed.* Louisville: Westminster John Knox, 1994.

Hetherman, Bill. "Attorney: City Sold South Central Farm at Major Loss for Taxpayers." *City News Service,* July 13, 2006.

Hock, Ronald F. "Why New Testament Scholars Should Read Ancient Novels." In *Ancient Fiction and Early Christian Narrative,* edited by Ronald F. Hock et al., 121–38. Atlanta: Scholars, 1998.

Höffding, Harold. *A History of Modern Philosophy.* Translated by B. E. Meyer. Vol. 2. New York: Dover, 1955.

Hoffmann, Jessica. "History of the South Central Farm: How the Community Has Used the Land Since 1985." *The New Standard,* April 5, 2006. Online: http://newstandardnews.net/content/index.cfm/items/3028.

Homer. *The Odyssey.* Translated by Robert Fagles. New York: Viking Penguin, 1996.

Hope, Richard. "Index of Technical Terms." In Aristotle's *Metaphysics,* translated by Richard Hope, 319–94. Ann Arbor: University of Michigan Press, 1960.

Hopkins, Brent. "The End for South Central Farm?" *The Daily News of Los Angeles*, June 14, 2006.
———. "Last Gasp in Fight for Farm: 10 Arrested as Activists Attempt to Stop Bulldozer." *The Daily News of Los Angeles*, July 6, 2006.
Horkheimer, Max, and Theodore Adorno. *Dialectic of Enlightenment*. Translated by John Cumming. New York: Continuum, 1972.
Horsley, Richard A. *Hearing the Whole Story: The Politics of Plot in Mark's Gospel*. Louisville: Westminster John Knox, 2001.
Hovey, Craig. *To Share in the Body: A Theology of Martyrdom for Today's Church*. Grand Rapids: Brazos, 2008.
Hume, David. *An Enquiry Concerning Human Understanding; A Letter from a Gentleman to His Friend in Edinburgh; An Abstract of a Treatise of Human Nature*. Edited by Eric Steinberg. Indianapolis: Hackett, 1977.
Husserl, Edmund. *Ideas: General Introduction to Pure Phenomenology*. Translated by W. R. Boyce Gibson. New York: Collier, 1962.
———. "Phenomenology." In *Encyclopedia Britannica*. 14th ed. Vol. 17. New York, 1929.
Ignatius of Antioch. "Letter to the Ephesians," "Letter to the Magnesians," "Letter to the Smyrnaeans," "Letter to the Philadelphians," "Letter to the Romans," and "Letter to Polycarp." In *Early Christian Fathers*, translated and edited by Cyril C. Richardson et al., 87–120. Library of Christian Classics 1. Philadelphia: Westminster, 1953.
Isaac, Claire L., et al. "Is Posttraumatic Stress Disorder Associated with Specific Deficits in Episodic Memory?" *Clinical Psychology Review* 26 (2006) 939–52.
Jaeger, Werner. *Paideia: the Ideals of Greek Culture*. Vol. 1, *Archaic Greece: The Mind of Athens*. Translated by Gilbert Highet. 2nd ed. New York: Oxford University Press, 1945.
———. *Paideia: The Ideals of Greek Culture*. Vol. 2, *In Search of the Divine Centre*. Translated by Gilbert Highet. New York: Oxford University Press, 1943.
Jenkins, Philip. *The New Faces of Christianity: Believing the Bible in the Global South*. New York: Oxford University Press, 2006.
———. *The Next Christendom: The Coming of Global Christianity*. New York: Oxford University Press, 2002.
Jenson, Robert W. *Systematic Theology*. Vol. 1, *The Triune God*. New York: Oxford University Press, 1997.
Jonge, Marinus de. *Christology in Context: The Earliest Christian Response to Jesus*. Philadelphia: Westminster, 1988.
Josephus, Flavius. *The Jewish War*. Translated by G. A. Williamson. Revised by E. Mary Smallwood. New York: Penguin, 1970.
Juarez, Rufina. Interview by Craig Keen. Personal Interview. Los Angeles, California, August 1, 2006.
Jung, Carl. *Memories, Dreams, Reflections*. Recorded and edited by Aniela Jaffé. Translated by Richard and Clara Winston. New York: Vintage, 1963.
Kähler, Martin. *The So-Called Historical Jesus and the Historic Biblical Christ*. Translated and edited by Carl E. Braaten. Philadelphia: Fortress, 1964.
Kamenka, Eugene. *The Philosophy of Ludwig Feuerbach*. New York: Praeger, 1969.
Kandel, Eric R. *In Search of Memory: The Emergence of a New Science of Mind*. New York: Norton, 2006.
Kandel, Eric R., James H. Schwartz, and Thomas M. Jessell, editors. *Essentials of Neural Science and Behavior*. Stamford, CT: Appleton & Lange, 1995.

Bibliography

Kant, Immanuel. *Prolegomena to Any Future Metaphysics that Will Be Able to Come Forward as Science*. Translated by Paul Carus. Revised by James W. Ellington. Indianapolis: Hackett, 1977.

Käsemann, Ernst. *New Testament Questions of Today*. Translated by W. J. Montague. Philadelphia: Fortress, 1969.

Keen, Craig. "*Homo Precarius*: Prayer in the Image and Likeness of God." In *The Transgression of the Integrity of God: Essays and Addresses*, edited by Thomas J. Bridges and Nathan R. Kerr, 123–45. Eugene, OR: Cascade, 2012.

———. *The Transgression of the Integrity of God: Essays and Addresses*. Edited by Thomas J. Bridges and Nathan R. Kerr, Eugene, OR: Cascade, 2012.

Kelly, J. N. D. *Early Christian Doctrines*. 5th ed. San Francisco: HarperSanFrancisco, 1978.

Kierkegaard, Søren [Johannes Climacus]. *Concluding Unscientific Postscript to Philosophical Fragments*. Vol. 1. Edited and translated by Howard V. Hong and Edna H. Hong. Princeton: Princeton University Press, 1992.

———. [Johannes de silentio]. *Fear and Trembling*. In Søren Kierkegaard, *Fear and Trembling; Repetition*, edited and translated by Howard V. Hong and Edna H. Hong, 1–123. Princeton: Princeton University Press, 1983.

———. *For Self-Examination*. In *For Self-Examination; Judge for Yourself!* Edited and translated by Howard V. Hong and Edna H. Hong, 1–87. Princeton: Princeton University Press, 1990.

———. *Judge for Yourself!* In *For Self-Examination; Judge for Yourself!* Edited and translated by Howard V. Hong and Edna H. Hong, 89–215. Princeton: Princeton University Press, 1990.

———. [Johannes Climacus]. *Philosophical Fragments or a Fragment of Philosophy*. In *Philosophical Fragments; Johannes Climacus*. Edited and translated by Howard V. Hong and Edna H. Hong, 1–111. Princeton: Princeton University Press, 1985.

———. [Anti-Climacus]. *Practice in Christianity*. Edited and translated by Howard V. Hong and Edna H. Hong. Princeton: Princeton University Press, 1991.

———. [Anti-Climacus]. *The Sickness Unto Death: A Christian Psychological Exposition for Upbuilding and Awakening*. Edited and translated by Howard V. Hong and Edna H. Hong. Princeton: Princeton University Press, 1980.

———. *Works of Love*. Edited and translated by Howard V. Hong and Edna H. Hong. Princeton: Princeton University Press, 1995.

Kiser, John. *The Monks of Tibhirine: Faith, Love, and Terror in Algeria*. New York: St. Martin's, 2002.

Kleinknecht, Hermann. "*Theos*: The Greek Concept of God." In *Theological Dictionary of the New Testament*, edited by Gerhard Kittel, translated by Geoffrey W. Bromiley, 3:65–79. Grand Rapids: Eerdmans, 1965.

Krieger, Robbie, and Jim Morrison. "People Are Strange." Performed by The Doors. *Strange Days*. Elektra Records, 1967.

Lacoste, Jean-Yves. *Experience and the Absolute: Disputed Questions on the Humanity of Man*. Translated by Mark Raftery-Skehan. New York: Fordham University Press, 2004.

LaCugna, Catherine Mowry. *God For Us: The Trinity and Christian Life*. San Francisco: HarperSanFrancisco, 1991.

Lakoff, George, and Mark Johnson. *Philosophy in the Flesh: The Embodied Mind and Its Challenges to Western Thought*. New York: Basic Books, 1999.

Bibliography

Lash, Nicholas. *Holiness, Speech and Silence: Reflections on the Question of God*. Burlington, VT: Ashgate, 2004.

Leibniz, Gottfried. "The Principles of Nature and Grace, Based on Reason." Edited and translated by Jonathan Bennett. Online: http://www.earlymoderntexts.com/pdf/leibprin.pdf.

Lessing, Gotthold. "On the Proof of the Spirit and of Power." In *Lessing's Theological Writings*, selected and translated by Henry Chadwick, 51–56. Stanford: Stanford University Press, 1956.

Levinas, Emmanuel. "God and Philosophy." In *Of God Who Comes to Mind*, translated by Bettina Bergo, 55–78. Stanford: Stanford University Press, 1998.

———. "The Trace of the Other." Translated by A. Lingis. In *Deconstruction in Context: Literature and Philosophy*, edited by Mark C. Taylor, 345–59. Chicago: University of Chicago Press, 1986.

Liddell, Henry George, et al., editors. *A Greek-English Lexicon*. 9th rev. ed. New York: Oxford University Press, 1996.

Lindbeck, George. *The Nature of Doctrine: Religion and Theology in a Postliberal Age*. Philadelphia: Westminster, 1984.

Litwak, Kenneth Duncan. *Echoes of Scripture in Luke-Acts: Telling the History of God's People Intertextually*. New York: T. & T. Clark, 2005.

Llanos, Connie. "Judge Rules on Urban Garden: Sale to Developer Is Upheld." *The Daily News of Los Angeles*, July 27, 2006.

Lloyd, Genevieve. *The Man of Reason: "Male" and "Female" in Western Philosophy*. Minneapolis: University of Minnesota Press, 1984.

Lohse, Bernhard. *Martin Luther's Theology: Its Historical and Systematic Development*. Translated and edited by Roy A. Harrisville. Minneapolis: Fortress, 1999.

Lossky, Vladimir. *In the Image and Likeness of God*. Translated by Edward Every et al. Crestwood, NY: St. Vladimir's Seminary Press, 1974.

Luther, Martin. *Christian Liberty*. Translated by W. A. Lambert. Revised by Harold J. Grimm. Philadelphia: Fortress, 1957.

———. *De Servo Arbitrio*. Translated and edited by Philip S. Watson. In *Luther and Erasmus: Free Will and Salvation*, edited by E. Gordon Rupp and Philip S. Watson, 101–334. Library of Christian Classics 17. Philadelphia: Westminster, 1969.

———. "The Heidelberg Disputation." In *Luther: Early Theological Works*, translated by James Atkinson, 276–307. Library of Christian Classics 16. Philadelphia: Westminster, 1962.

MacIntyre, Alasdair. *After Virtue: A Study in Moral Theory*. 2nd ed. Notre Dame: University of Notre Dame Press, 1984.

Mantzaridis, Georgios I. *The Deification of Man: St. Gregory Palamas and the Orthodox Tradition*. Translated by Liadain Sherrard. Crestwood, NY: St. Vladimir's Seminary Press, 1984.

Margerie, Bertrand de. *The Christian Trinity in History*. Translated by Edmund J. Fortman. Still River, MA: St. Bede's, 1982.

Marion, Jean-Luc. *The Crossing of the Visible*. Translated by James K. A. Smith. Stanford: Stanford University Press, 2004.

———. *God Without Being: Hors-Texte*. Translated by Thomas A. Carlson. Chicago: University of Chicago Press, 1991.

Marroquin, Art. "Deputies Evict Farmers, Supporters from South Central Farm." *City News Service*, June 13, 2006.

Bibliography

"The Martyrdom of Saint Polycarp, Bishop of Smyrna, as Told in the Letter of the Church of Smyrna to the Church of Philomelium." In *Early Christian Fathers*, translated and edited by Cyril C. Richardson et al., 149–58. Library of Christian Classics 1. Philadelphia: Westminster, 1953.

Marx, Karl. "Theses on Feuerbach." Translated by S. Ryazanskaya. In *Karl Marx: Selected Writings*, edited by David McLellan, 156–58. New York: Oxford University Press, 1977.

Marx, Karl, and Friedrich Engels. *The German Ideology: Part One, With Selections from Parts Two and Three and Supplementary Texts*. Translated by W. Lough et al. New York: International, 1977.

McCarthy, Cormac. *The Road*. New York: Knopf, 2009.

McClintock Fulkerson, Mary. "Contesting the Gendered Subject: A Feminist Account of the *Imago Dei*." In *Horizons in Feminist Theology: Identity, Tradition, and Norms*, edited by Rebecca Chopp and Sheila Greeve Davaney, 99–115. Minneapolis: Fortress, 1997.

McCormack, Bruce L. *Karl Barth's Critically Realistic Dialectical Theology: Its Genesis and Development, 1909–1936*. New York: Oxford University Press, 1995.

Merleau-Ponty, Maurice. *The Visible and the Invisible*. Translated by Alphonso Lingis. Evanston: Northwestern University Press, 1968.

Metzger, Bruce M. *The Canon of the New Testament: Its Origin, Development, and Significance*. New York: Oxford University Press, 1987.

Meyendorff, John. *Christ in Eastern Christian Thought*. Crestwood, NY: St. Vladimir's Seminary Press, 1975.

Michael Clayton. Directed by Tony Gilroy. Warner Home Video, 2008.

Milbank, John. *Being Reconciled: Ontology and Pardon*. New York: Routledge, 2003.

———. *Theology and Social Theory: Beyond Secular Reason*. Malden, MA: Blackwell, 1993.

———. *The Word Made Strange: Theology, Language, Culture*. Malden, MA: Blackwell, 1997.

Miller, Patrick D. *They Cried to the Lord: The Form and Theology of Biblical Prayer*. Minneapolis: Fortress, 1994.

Milton, John. "How Soon Hath Time." In *Complete Poetry and Selected Prose of John Milton*, edited by Bennett A. Cerf et al., 25–26. New York: Modern Library, 1950.

Moltmann, Jürgen. *The Coming of God: Christian Eschatology*. Translated by Margaret Kohl. Minneapolis: Fortress, 1996.

———. *The Crucified God: The Cross of Christ as the Foundation and Criticism of Christian Theology*. Translation by R. A. Wilson and John Bowden. New York: Harper & Row, 1974.

———. *The Experiment Hope*. Translated and edited by M. Douglas Meeks. Philadelphia: Fortress, 1975.

———. *The Future of Creation: Collected Essays*. Translated by Margaret Kohl. Philadelphia: Fortress, 1979.

———. *Jesus Christ for Today's World*. Translated by Margaret Kohl. Minneapolis: Fortress, 1994.

———. *Religion, Revolution, and the Future*. Translated by M. Douglas Meeks. New York: Scribner's, 1969.

Myers, Ched. *Binding the Strong Man: A Political Reading of Mark's Story of Jesus*. Twentieth anniv. ed. Maryknoll, NY: Orbis, 2010.

Bibliography

Nava, Alex. "God in the Desert: Searching for the Divine in the Midst of Death." In *A Promised Land, A Perilous Journey: Theological Perspectives on Migration*, edited by Daniel G. Groody and Gioacchino Campese, 62–75. Notre Dame: University of Notre Dame Press, 2008.

Niebuhr, Reinhold. *Man's Nature and His Communities: Essays On the Dynamics and Enigmas of Man's Personal and Social Existence*. New York: Scribner's, 1965.

Nietzsche, Friedrich. *Thus Spoke Zarathustra*. Translated by Walter Kaufmann. New York: Viking, 1966.

———. *Twilight of the Idols; or How to Philosophize with a Hammer*. In *Twilight of the Idols and The Antichrist*, translated by Thomas Common, 5–57. Mineola, NY: Dover, 2004.

———. *Der Wille Zur Macht: Versuch einer Umwertung aller Werte*. Stuttgart: Kröner, 1964.

———. *The Will to Power*. Translated by Walter Kaufmann and R. J. Hollingdale. Edited by Walter Kaufmann. New York: Random House, 1968.

Norrell, Brenda. "Navajo Says Evictions of Farmers from Urban Farm Sends a Message." *Indian Country Today*, June 21, 2006.

Of Gods and Men [*Des hommes et des dieux*]. Directed by Xavier Beauvois. Sony Pictures Classics [Why Not Productions/Armada Films], 2010.

Olyan, Saul M. *Disability in the Hebrew Bible: Interpreting Mental and Physical Differences*. New York: Cambridge University Press, 2008.

Otto, Rudolf. *The Idea of the Holy: An Inquiry into the Non-rational Factor in the Idea of the Divine and Its Relation to the Rational*. Translated by John W. Harvey. New York: Oxford University Press, 1950.

Ouspensky, Leonid. *Theology of the Icon*. Vol. 1. Translated by Anthony Gythiel. Crestwood, NY: St. Vladimir's Seminary Press, 1978.

Pannenberg, Wolfhart. *Basic Questions in Theology: Collected Essays*. Translated by George H. Kehm. 2 vols. Philadelphia: Fortress, 1970.

———. *Theology and the Kingdom of God*. Edited by Richard John Neuhaus. Philadelphia: Westminster, 1969.

Parker, Emanuel. "Huntington Housing Ex-Farm's Trees." *Pasadena-Star News*, December 15, 2006.

"The Passion of Saints Perpetua and Felicity." Translated by Joseph Farrell and Craig Williams. In *Perpetua's Passions: Multidisciplinary Approaches to the Passio Perpetuae et Felicitatis*, edited by Jan N. Bremmer and Marco Formisano, 14–23. New York: Oxford University Press, 2012.

Pelikan, Jaroslav. *The Christian Tradition: A History of the Development of Doctrine*. Vol. 1, *The Emergence of the Catholic Tradition (100–600)*. Chicago: University of Chicago Press, 1971.

Peña, Devon G. "Farmers Feeding Families: Agroecology in South Central Los Angeles." Lecture Presented to the Environmental Science, Policy, and Management Colloqium, University of California, Berkeley, October 10, 2005.

———. "Putting Knowledge in Its Place: Epistemologies of Place-Making in a Time of Globalization: Plenary Address." Place Matters Conference, Diversity Research Institute, University of Washington, Urban Horticulture Center, October 27, 2006.

Peña, Devon G., and Tezozomoc. "Preliminary List of Botanical Species Grown at South Central Community Garden: Prepared June 2005." Online: http://www.schoolworknotes.com/categories/Botanical/doc/6.

Bibliography

Phan, Peter. "Migration in the Patristic Era." In *A Promised Land, A Perilous Journey: Theological Perspectives on Migration*, edited by Daniel G. Groody and Gioacchino Campese, 35–61. Notre Dame: University of Notre Dame Press, 2008.

Pickstock, Catherine. *After Writing: On the Liturgical Consummation of Philosophy*. Malden, MA: Blackwell, 1998.

Pirsig, Robert M. *Zen and the Art of Motorcycle Maintenance*. New York: Bantam, 1974.

Plato. *Five Dialogues: Euthyphro, Apology, Crito, Meno, Phaedo*. Translated by G. M. A. Grube. Indianapolis: Hackett, 1981.

Polycarp of Smyrna. "Letter to the Philippians." In *Early Christian Fathers*, translated and edited by Cyril C. Richardson et al., 131–37. Library of Christian Classics 1. Philadelphia: Westminster, 1953.

Quicunque Vult. Translated by J. N. D. Kelly. In *Creeds of the Churches*, edited by John H. Leith, 705–6. Atlanta: John Knox, 1982.

Rack, Henry D. *Reasonable Enthusiast: John Wesley and the Rise of Methodism*. 3rd ed. London: Epworth, 2002.

Rad, Gerhard von. "*ouranos*, Old Testament." In *Theological Dictionary of the New Testament*, edited by Gerhard Kittel, translated and edited by Geoffrey W. Bromiley, 5:502–9. Grand Rapids: Eerdmans, 1967.

Raphael, Melissa. "Holiness *in extremis*: Jewish Women's Resistance to the Profane in Auschwitz." In *Holiness: Past and Present*, edited by Stephen C. Barton, 381–401. New York: T. & T. Clark, 2003.

"Request Full CEQA EIR Process on ENV-2008-799-MND." Online: http://www.southcentralfarmers.com/index.php?option=com_philaform&Itemid=54&form_id=7&PHPSESSID=8b6b42ff6b20afbe886507e913bbcb52.

Richardson, Cyril. "Introduction to Early Christian Literature and Its Setting." In *Early Christian Fathers*, translated and edited by Cyril C. Richardson et al., 15–26. Library of Christian Classics 1. Philadelphia: Westminster, 1953.

———. "The Letters of Ignatius, Bishop of Antioch, Introduction." In *Early Christian Fathers*, translated and edited by Cyril C. Richardson et al., 74–80. Library of Christian Classics 1. Philadelphia: Westminster, 1953.

Riley, Gregory J. *The River of God: A New History of Christian Origins*. San Francisco: HarperSanFrancisco, 2001.

Ritschl, Albrecht. *Three Essays: Theology and Metaphysics, "Prolegomena" to The History of Pietism, Instruction in the Christian Religion*. Translated by Philip Hefner. Philadelphia: Fortress, 1972.

Rogers, Eugene F., Jr. *After the Spirit: A Constructive Pneumatology from Resources Outside the Modern West*. Grand Rapids: Eerdmans, 2005.

Rogerson, John. "What Is Holiness?" In *Holiness: Past and Present*, edited by Stephen C. Barton, 3–21. New York: T. & T. Clark, 2003.

Rothschild, Babette. *The Body Remembers: The Psychophysiology of Trauma and Trauma Treatment*. New York: Norton, 2000.

———. *The Body Remembers Casebook: Unifying Methods and Models in the Treatment of Trauma and PTSD*. New York: Norton, 2003.

Ruiz Marrujo, Olivia. "The Gender of Risk." In *A Promised Land, A Perilous Journey: Theological Perspectives on Migration*, edited by Daniel G. Groody and Gioacchino Campese, 225–239. Notre Dame: University of Notre Dame, Press, 2008.

Run Lola Run. Directed by Tom Tykwer. Westdeutscher Rundfunk, 1998.

Bibliography

Runyon, Theodore. *The New Creation: John Wesley's Theology Today*. Nashville: Abingdon, 1998.

Rzeznik, Johnny. "Iris." Performed by The Goo Goo Dolls. *City of Angels: Music from the Motion Picture*. Produced by Danny Bramson. Reprise Records. CD. 1998.

Saliers, Don E. *Worship as Theology: Foretaste of Glory Divine*. Nashville: Abingdon, 1994.

Schmemann, Alexander. *The Eucharist: Sacrament of the Kingdom*. Translated by Paul Kachur. Crestwood, NY: St. Vladimir's Seminary Press, 1988.

———. *For the Life of the World*. Crestwood, NY: St. Vladimir's Seminary Press, 1973.

———. *Introduction to Liturgical Theology*. Translated by Asheleigh E. Moorehouse. Crestwood, NY: St. Vladimir's Seminary Press, 1966.

Schnackenburg, Rudolf. *Jesus in the Gospels: A Biblical Christology*. Translated by O. C. Dean Jr. Louisville: Westminster John Knox, 1995.

Schüssler Fiorenza, Elisabeth. *But She Said: Feminist Practices of Biblical Interpretation*. Boston: Beacon, 1992.

Senior, Donald. "'Beloved Aliens and Exiles': New Testament Perspectives on Migration." In *A Promised Land, A Perilous Journey: Theological Perspectives on Migration*, edited by Daniel G. Groody and Gioacchino Campese, 20–34. Notre Dame: University of Notre Dame Press, 2008.

Shiell, William D. *Delivering from Memory: The Effect of Performance on the Early Christian Audience*. Eugene, OR: Pickwick, 2011.

Slumdog Millionaire. Directed by Danny Boyle and Loveleen Tandan. Fox Searchlight Pictures, 2009.

Song, C. S. *Jesus, the Crucified People*. Minneapolis: Fortress, 1990.

"The South Central Farmers' Report from the United Nations Visit on May 2007." June 7, 2007. Online: http://www.southcentralfarmers.com/index.php?option=com_content&task=view&id=295&PHPSESSID=ea2f3a53b909a54aa35564b1b7816219.

Steinbeck, John. *The Grapes of Wrath*. New York: Viking, 1967.

Stookey, Noel Paul, et al. "Old Coat." Performed by Peter, Paul, and Mary. *Moving*. Warner Brothers Records, 1963.

Suzuki, Daisetz Teitaro. "The Ten Oxherding Pictures, I, by Kaku-an." In *Manual of Zen Buddhism*, 127–38. New York: Grove, 1960.

Tanner, Kathryn. *Jesus, Humanity, and the Trinity: A Brief Systematic Theology*. Minneapolis: Fortress, 2001.

Taylor, Mark C. *Altarity*. Chicago: University of Chicago Press, 1987.

———. *Erring: A Postmodern A/theology*. Chicago: University of Chicago Press, 1984.

Taylor, Otis. "Resurrection Blues." Performed by Otis Taylor. *White African*. CD. Northern Blues, 2001.

Tezozomoc. Interview by Craig Keen. Personal interview. Los Angeles, California, August 1, 2006.

Tillich, Paul. *Systematic Theology*. Vol. 1. Chicago: University of Chicago Press, 1951.

———. *Systematic Theology*. Vol. 3. Chicago: University of Chicago Press, 1963.

Tolstoy, Leo N. *What Is Art?* Translated by Almyer Maude. Indianapolis: Bobbs-Merrill, 1960.

Tracy, David. *Plurality and Ambiguity: Hermeneutics, Religion, Hope*. New York: Harper & Row, 1987.

Traub, Helmut. "*ouranos*, New Testament." In *Theological Dictionary of the New Testament*, edited by Gerhard Kittel, tranlated by Geoffrey W. Bromiley, 5:497–502. Grand Rapids: Eerdmans, 1967.

Bibliography

Travis, Merle. "Sixteen Tons." Performed by Tennessee Ernie Ford. Capital Records. Single vinyl. 1955.

Tyson, Ann Scott. "Woman Gains Silver Star—and Removal from Combat: Case Shows Contradictions of Army Rules." *Washington Post*, May 1, 2008.

"United Nations Permanent Forum on Indigenous Issues, 6th Session: Statement by South Central Farmers and La Red Xicana Indigena." May 18, 2007. Online: http://old.docip.org/Permanent%20Forum/pf07/PF07rufina169.pdf.

"Wade in the Water." In *New Jubilee Songs: As Sung by the Fisk Jubilee Singers of Fisk University*. Collected and harmonized by Frederick J. Work, 8–9. Nashville: Fisk University, 1902. Microfilm.

Waetjen, Herman C. *A Reordering of Power*. Minneapolis: Fortress, 1989.

Wainwright, Geoffrey. *Doxology: The Praise of God in Worship, Doctrine, and Life: A Systematic Theology*. New York: Oxford University Press, 1980.

———. *For Our Salvation: Two Approaches to the Work of Christ*. Grand Rapids: Eerdmans, 1997.

Walz, Jesce. "Redeeming Creation." In her unpublished "Newsletter," July 2007.

Ward, Graham. "The Displaced Body of Jesus Christ." In *Radical Orthodoxy: A New Theology*, edited by John Milbank et al., 163–81. New York: Routledge, 1999.

Ware, Kallistos. *The Orthodox Way*. Crestwood, NY: St. Vladimir's Seminary Press, 1995.

Welch, Florence, and Isabella Summers. "Cosmic Love." Performed by Florence + the Machine. *Lungs*. CD. Universal Republic Records, 2009.

Wesley, John. *Explanatory Notes Upon the New Testament*. London: Charles H. Kelly, n.d.

———. "The Good Steward," Sermon 51. In *The Works of John Wesley*, edited by Albert C. Outler, 2:34–70. Nashville: Abingdon, 1985.

———. "The Great Privilege of Those That Are Born of God," Sermon 19. In *The Works of John Wesley*, edited by Albert C. Outler, 1:431–43. Nashville: Abingdon, 1984.

———. "The Means of Grace," Sermon 16. In *The Works of John Wesley*, edited by Albert C. Outler, 1:376–97. Nashville: Abingdon, 1984.

———. "The New Birth," Sermon 45. In *The Works of John Wesley*, edited by Albert C. Outler, 2:186–201. Nashville: Abingdon, 1985.

———. "On Zeal," Sermon 92. In *The Works of John Wesley*, edited by Albert C. Outler, 3:308–21. Nashville: Abingdon, 1986.

———. "Original Sin," Sermon 44. In *The Works of John Wesley*, edited by Albert C. Outler, 2:170–85. Nashville: Abingdon, 1985.

———. *A Plain Account of Christian Perfection*. Kansas City: Beacon Hill, 1966.

———. "The Repentance of Believers," Sermon 14. In *The Works of John Wesley*, edited by Albert C. Outler, 1:335–52. Nashville: Abingdon, 1984.

Whitehead, Alfred North. *Process and Reality: An Essay in Cosmology*. Edited by David Ray Griffin and Donald W. Sherburne. Corrected ed. New York: Free Press, 1978.

———. *Religion in the Making*. New York: World, 1954.

Whitfield, Joshua J. *Pilgrim Holiness: Martyrdom as Descriptive Witness*. Eugene, OR: Cascade, 2009.

Wire, Antoinette Clark. *The Case for Mark Composed in Performance*. Eugene, OR: Cascade, 2011.

Wittgenstein, Ludwig. *Philosophical Investigations*. Translated by G. E. M. Anscombe. New York: Macmillan, 1953.

Wolff, Hans Walter. *Anthropology of the Old Testament*. Translated by Margaret Kohl. Philadelphia: Fortress, 1974.

Wright, N. T. *The Resurrection of the Son of God*. Minneapolis: Fortress, 2003.
Xenophon. *Symposium*. Translated by O. J. Todd. In *Xenophon IV: Memorabilia; Oeconomicus; Symposium; Apologia.*, edited by G. P. Goold, 527–60. Loeb Classical Library 168. Cambridge: Harvard University Press, 1923.
Yoder, John Howard. *The Politics of Jesus*: Vicit Agnus Noster. 2nd ed. Grand Rapids: Eerdmans, 1994.
York, Tripp. *The Purple Crown: The Politics of Martyrdom*. Scottdale, PA: Herald, 2007.
Young, Robin Darling. *In Procession Before the World: Martyrdom as Public Liturgy in Early Christianity*. Milwaukee: Marquette University Press, 2001.
Zizioulas, John. *Being as Communion*. Translated by John Clark et al. Crestwood, NY: St. Vladimir's Seminary Press, 1985.

Index

Abraham (Abram), 19, 41, 48, 53n42, 57, 124, 128n17, 134–36, 143–45, 197, 212–13
Abraham, William, 58n54
Acts, book of, 24, 43n15, 92n52, 193, 225
Adam, xiv, 15, 24n6, 30, 41, 48–49, 54, 58, 93. *See also* Eve
Adorno, Theodore, 197n9
Agamben, Giorgio, 6n24
Alameda (South Central L.A.), 66, 68n7
alien, 11, 13–14, 22, 87, 122, 136, 140, 142, 156, 181, 225
Althaus, Paul, 203n46
analogy, 7, 59n57, 64n68, 80n16, 93n55
Anderson, John, 112n5
anhypostatic, 225, 230. *See also* enhypostatic; hypostasis
Anti-Climacus. *See under* Kierkegaard
apocalyptic, 25–26, 40, 59, 83, 96, 106, 122–24, 159, 173n33, 177, 179, 212, 224
apophatic theology, 155
Aquinas, Thomas, 7n38
Aristotle, 6n32, 9n50, 30, 179n50, 181, 199n21, 217n13
Astur, Robert, 110n3
Athanasius, 58
atonement, 92, 93n54, 95, 188n72
Augustine, 58, 82n21, 84n29, 96, 203n52, 206n64, 223n22, 246

baptism, 13, 15n73, 18, 28, 34, 44, 49–50, 74–76, 78, 84, 154, 166, 175, 180, 185–86, 192, 221, 223–24, 227
Barnabas, Epistle of, 81n18
Barth, Karl, xn2, 18n87, 26n12, 29n21, 44n19, 47n23, 48n23, 48n26, 50n31, 57n48, 64n68, 85n30, 102n83, 158n97, 204n57, 205n58, 207n66, 224n27, 231n33, 231n35
Barton, Stephen, 35n3, 43n13
Basil of Caesarea, 231n34
Bataille, Georges, 134n35, 203n51
Bauckham, Richard, 123n5, 149n68, 150n71, 150n73, 151n75, 152nn78–79, 153n82, 154n85, 155n88, 156n93, 200n25
Bauernfeind, Otto, 97nn69–70
Beale, G. K., 40n9, 122n5, 150n72, 151n74, 151n76, 152n78, 154n84, 157n95
belief, 2–3, 17, 29, 59n55, 61n63, 178–79
Bell, Daniel, 39n6, 120n30
Belo, Fernando, 134n35
Berquist, Jon, 126n11, 127n12, 128n15, 129n18, 130n21, 130n23, 132n26, 132n28
Berry, Wendell, 3n9
Betcher, Sharon, 138n49, 139n51
Bevans, Stephen, 5n22
Bible. *See* Scripture

251

Index

Bieler, Andrea, 16n78
bishop, 46n20, 183–89, 209, 211, 214–15, 217, 226, 230–31
Blanchot, Maurice, 6n30, 82n23
body, xii, xiv–xv, 5, 14, 28–29, 46, 94, 110–11, 118–21, 126–27, 129–32, 135, 139, 148, 185, 187
body of Christ. *See under* church
Boehm, Mike, 66n3
Bolaño, Roberto, 4n16, 131n25, 232n2
Bolt, Robert, 210n24
Bondi, Roberta, 120n77
Bonhoeffer, Dietrich, 216n11
brain, x, xii, xv, 22, 111, 113n11, 116–17, 223. *See also* thought
Bremner, J. Douglas, 111n3, 112n5
Brown, Raymond, 147n66
Brueggemann, Walter, 133n31, 142n56
Buber, Martin, 206n65
Bultmann, Rudolf, x
Busch, Eberhard, 44n19
Byrne, David, 121n1

capitalism, 31–32, 193, 212
Catherine of Siena, 20n89, 108n101, 233n5
Cavanaugh, William, 15n72, 35n3, 44n19, 47n21, 48n24, 49n30, 55n45, 56n46, 105n87
Chawkins, Steve, 73n12
Christianity, 1, 18n87, 139n51, 185n61
church, xiv, 1, 12–13, 16n77, 18n87, 34, 36, 41–44, 46–47, 50, 52, 54, 56–57, 63, 86, 99–100, 106, 108, 124, 184, 196n63; body of Christ, 5n22, 29, 32, 35, 55, 60, 62, 103–4, 162, 216; catholicity, 42, 46n20, 182, 188, 195; martyr-church, xiv, 179–80, 194

Claiborne, Robert, 10n53, 198n18, 200n28
Climacus, Johannes. *See under* Kierkegaard
Coakley, Sarah, 28n18, 57n49, 125n10
Colish, Marcia, 210n5
Collins, John, 122n3, 123n5, 123n7, 152n81
concept, 4n15, 62n64, 78n7, 80n16, 115–16, 207n65. *See also* thought
Cone, James, 24n5, 51n35, 59n56, 93n55, 173n33, 233n4
cosmos, 10, 12–13, 40, 48, 118, 132n28
Cousar, Charles, 39n6
creation, 12n64, 18n87, 41, 43, 49, 53n42, 76–77, 80–82, 106n91, 106n94, 107, 126n11, 166, 209, 212, 214–15, 231
Creator, 12–13, 18n87, 72, 102n83, 106, 137, 144. *See also* God
creed, 6, 13–14, 24, 34, 57–58, 205n59
cross, crucifixion, 5, 15–17, 27–29, 32, 39n6, 43n16, 47, 51–52, 61, 62n64, 64, 76, 86, 89n44, 92, 99, 140, 179–80, 187, 194–95, 227, 229, 232. *See also under* Jesus Christ
Cushman, Robert Earl, 98n72, 101n78
Cyril of Alexandria, 225n28

David, King, 124, 130n21, 136, 145, 150n72
deification, 100n77, 107
Derrida, Jacques, 3n8, 27n14, 163n1, 203n50, 228n31
Descartes, René, 97
Dewey, John, 7n35, 116n23
Didache, 178n47
disability, 134n36, 138n49, 142n56

Index

Docetism, 46n20, 182n53, 185, 187, 221
Dostoevsky, Fyodor, xiin5, 35n4, 198n13
Douglas, J. D., 155n89
doxology, 80n16, 133, 169n28, 229
dunamis, 179, 186
Dunn, James D. G., 40n7, 44n19, 53n42, 93n57, 94n60
Dupré, Louis, 10n58, 12nn63–64, 13n67, 13n69
Dylan, Bob, 24

Easter, 17, 29, 34, 38–39, 48, 58, 75, 105, 107n99, 124–25, 184. *See also* Holy Week
Ebeling, Gerhard, 83n26
Eliot, T. S., 156n90, 197n6, 199n24
Eller, Vernard, 121n2
embodiment. *See* body
empire, 5n22, 122, 124–25, 128, 138n49, 151–52, 155, 183n56, 214. *See also* Rome
Engles, Friedrich, 79n12
enhypostatic, 18, 92n51, 225, 230. *See also* anhyposatatic; hypostasis
Epiphany, 34n2
epistemology, 58n54, 62n64
eschatology, xiv, 14–15, 17, 30, 41, 45, 49, 51–52, 55n45, 59, 82–85, 122, 143, 149, 156, 158, 184, 192n83, 226, 231. *See also* resurrection
ethics, 7, 62n65, 98n72
eucharist, xv, 14–19, 28, 30, 32, 34n2, 46–50, 55n45, 56n46, 57, 60–61, 64–65, 101n78, 104–7, 147n66, 148n66, 157, 184–86, 188–89, 191, 194, 211. *See also* food; liturgy
Eve, xiv, 24n6, 41, 48–49, 93. *See also* Adam

faith. *See* belief
fall, the, 48–49
Father (in Trinity), 5, 13, 15–18, 23, 27–29, 32, 35, 44, 47, 50, 52, 61, 63, 65, 81n17, 90, 92–95, 96n65, 103–5, 143, 147, 154n84, 185–88, 190, 195, 205n59, 220, 224, 229–30, 231n34, 234. *See also* God; Holy Spirit; Son; Trinity
Feuerbach, Ludwig, 79
Foakes-Jackson, F. J., 197n5
food, 15–17, 30, 47, 79–80, 94–95, 107–8, 148. *See also* eucharist
Frantz, Chris, 121n1
freedom, 3n12, 14, 16n77, 32–33, 62, 106, 109, 114, 138, 142, 210–11, 215–16, 230. *See also* liberation
future. *See* eschatology

Galatians, book of, 62n64
Gammie, John, 94n59
Garrett, Lila, 68n9
Genesis, book of, 34n2, 48–49, 54, 196, 212, 227
Gerrish, B. A., 85n32
Gibbs, Raymond, 113n11, 114n15, 115n17, 115n19, 116n22, 116n24
gift, 16n78, 18, 29–30, 46, 50n34, 80–81, 100, 108
Gilmore, Myron, 210n5
Gnostics, 91n46, 108
God, xv, 6–7, 10n51, 13–14, 16n77, 18–19, 21–26, 27–33, 40, 50–51, 64, 77, 80, 83, 86, 102, 106, 123, 126, 128n17, 132–35, 137, 140–43, 146–47, 149, 159, 186, 195, 202, 207, 211–14, 216, 220, 225, 229, 231, 233–34. *See also* Creator; Father
Gogarten, Friedrich, 57n48

Index

Gonzales, Patrisia, 70n10
Good Friday, 17, 34n2, 38–39, 75, 94, 125, 171, 173, 220. *See also* Holy Week
Gospels, 14, 39n5, 40–41, 85, 90, 146, 193. *See also individual Gospels*
grace, 16n78, 29, 31–32, 50n34, 55, 159
Greeks, 7–13, 17, 40, 97–101, 202n41
Groody, Daniel, 3n9, 52n39
Gundry, Robert, 27n14
Gutiérrez, Gustavo, 47n32, 52nn39–40, 88n38, 89n42

Hagan, Jacqueline, 2n3, 3n11
Hall, Michael, 199n22
Hansard, Glen, 37n1
Harnack, Adolf von, 44n19
Hauerwas, Stanley, 44n19, 52n39, 56n47, 62n65, 88n39, 101n79, 179n48, 192n84
Hayasaki, Erika, 66n3
Hays, Richard, 43n16, 54n44
healing, 2n2, 9, 18–19, 125, 138–39, 143, 167–68, 170, 193, 231
Hebrew Bible, 126n11, 127n11, 128n15, 135n38. *See also* Old Testament
Hebrews, 87n37, 131, 166, 211, 216. *See also* Jews
Hecht, Jamey, 66nn3–4
Hegel, Georg Wilhelm Friedrich, 10n55, 203n52
Heidegger, Martin, 7n36, 10nn54–55, 57n50, 78n8, 80n17, 81n17, 83, 198n17, 200n31, 201n34, 202n43, 204n55
Heitzenrater, Richard, 86n34
Hentrich, Thomas, 132n26, 135n38
Heraclitus, 10
Hernandez, Daniel, 66n3
Herzog, William, 136n43

Hesiod, 10
Hetherman, Bill, 66n3
Hock, Ronald, 171n32
Hoffmann, Jessica, 66n3
Holbein the Younger, xi
holiness, ix, xiv, 19, 36, 40n7, 43n13, 44n19, 46, 50, 53n42, 83, 88n40, 94, 102, 120n77, 133n31, 134, 143–44, 169n27
Holy Saturday, 34n2, 38–39, 49. *See also* Holy Week
Holy Spirit, 15–16, 28–29, 31, 36, 43n15, 44, 47, 51–52, 53n42, 54–58, 59n55, 61–65, 80–81, 84, 85nn32–33, 86, 89n44, 92, 95, 99, 103–4, 107, 125, 143, 145, 149, 156–57, 166, 171, 185, 188n72, 191, 196, 205n59, 209, 215, 223–24, 227, 230–31, 234. *See also* Trinity
Holy Week, 15, 34n2, 38, 43, 46, 54, 56, 105, 184. *See also individual days*
Homer, 8, 10, 135n37, 202n41
hope, 31–32, 35, 45, 47–51, 55–56, 59n55, 60, 64, 67, 69, 76, 89n44, 100, 102, 123, 142, 149
Hope, Richard, 179n50
Hopkins, Brent, 66n3
Horkheimer, Max, 197n9
Horsley, Richard, 164n4, 176n43
Hovey, Craig, 166n13, 175n40, 179n49, 193n85, 227n30
Hume, David, 2n7
Husserl, Edmund, 27
hypostasis, 18nn86–87, 225

icon, 5, 24, 34, 48, 57, 148, 186
idol, 62n64, 133
Ignatius of Antioch, 46n20, 182–89, 192
image of God, 50, 64, 126

254

Index

immigration, migration, x, 1, 2n4, 3n11, 4n17, 5n22, 20n89, 69n9, 87n37, 122, 124, 159
incarnation. *See under* Jesus Christ
intellect. *See* thought
Irglová, Markéta, 37n1
Isaac, 41, 48, 128n17, 136, 143
Isaac, Claire, 111n3
Isaiah, book of, 32, 101, 124, 144–45, 157n96, 169n27, 196, 212–13, 227
Israel, xii, 12–13, 104n86, 127n12, 128n15, 129n18, 129n21, 130n22, 131–37, 141–42, 144, 167n21, 211–14, 224, 228. *See also* Hebrews; Jews

Jacob, 41, 48, 136, 140, 143, 145
Jaeger, Werner, 8n39, 8n41, 8n43, 9n48, 97n71, 98n72
James, book of, 26n11
Jenkins, Philip, xin2
Jenson, Robert, 17n82, 47n23
Jerusalem, 13, 43, 92, 149, 154, 157, 173, 178, 221–23, 227, 229–30
Jesus Christ, 13–15, 18, 25–27, 33, 44–45, 47–49, 51, 60, 63, 74, 90, 92, 131, 145, 166–72, 207, 215; crucifixion and/or resurrection, 19, 28–29, 32, 39–40, 44–46, 49–50, 60, 65, 75, 81n18, 84, 91, 93, 97–99, 105, 107, 124–25, 148, 150, 154, 162, 166, 170, 173–75, 178, 181, 185, 187, 192, 216, 220, 222–27, 230–31, 233; and discipleship, xiv, 54, 148, 168, 173, 176–77, 189n74, 192–93, 228; incarnation, 18n87, 24n6, 44n19, 85n33, 92n51, 96, 101–2, 124–25, 185, 221, 226–27; lamb of God, 38, 65, 105, 107, 124–25, 149–50, 152–53, 154n84, 155–57, 204, 216; Messiah, 104n86, 106n90, 125n9, 131, 136, 152n80, 153–54, 170–72, 173n33, 175, 180, 193–94; as migrant, 4n17; and poor/peasants, 30–31, 42, 53n42, 91, 94, 125, 146, 174, 221–24; story/history of, 17, 48, 75, 78, 93–94, 103, 159; sufferings/passion, 5, 22–23, 28, 39, 41, 148, 174, 220, 222, 227, 229–30; return, 52, 82, 152n80; work of, 35, 94–95, 146, 167–68, 189, 191
Jews, 40, 68, 126, 157n96, 191n82, 205. *See also* Hebrews; Israel
Job, book of, 22–23, 89, 133n32, 213
John the Baptist, 166–67
John, Gospel of, 96
Johnson, Mark, 115n18, 116n21, 116n23
Jonah, book of, 169n28
Jonge, Marinus de, 100n77
Josephus, Flavius, 224n26
Juarez, Rufina, 68n6, 69, 73n12
Jung, Carl, 27–28
justice, 7, 39n6, 43n16, 52n39, 89, 94–95, 98n72, 141, 143, 152, 165, 214, 216, 229
Justin Martyr, 219–20

Kähler, Martin, 40n8
Kamenka, Eugene, 79n11
Kandel, Eric, 111nn4–5, 113n11
Kant, Immanuel, 6n33, 223n23
Käsemann, Ernst, 123
Keen, Craig, 52n38, 201n39
Kelly, J. N. D., 58n51, 65n72
kenosis, 93, 97, 155, 188n72
Kerr, Nathan, 159–62
Kierkegaard, 16n78, 18nn85–86, 24–25, 26n11, 49n28, 49n30, 51n34, 52n41, 54n43, 58,

Index

Kierkegaard (*cont.*)
    61n60, 61n63, 63n66, 76n4, 86n35, 97n68, 121n2, 143n60, 158n99, 182n54, 183n54;
    Anti-Climacus, 6n30, 26n11, 75n2, 175n41; Climacus, Johannes, 4n15, 6n30, 11n61, 25, 26n9, 49n28, 85n31, 86n35, 182n54, 183n54;
    silentio, Johannes de, 143n60, 197n4
kingdom of God. *See* Reign of God
Kiser, John, 234n6
Kleinknecht, Hermann, 202n41
knowledge. *See* thought
Krieger, Robbie, 140n54

labor. *See* work
Lacoste, Jean-Yves, 59n57, 60n59
LaCugna, Catherine Mowry, 16n75, 29n22, 53n42, 65n72, 185n60
Lakoff, George, 115n18, 116n21, 116n23
language, 48n23, 57n48, 64, 82n23, 99–100, 113–19, 123n5, 155n89, 156
Lash, Nicholas, xin4, 155n89, 224n25
law, 44, 82, 91, 98, 132–33, 141, 166n15, 183n56, 207, 221
Lazarus, 19, 97
Leibniz, Gottfried, 83
Lessing, Gotthold, 4n15
Levinas, Emmanuel, 3n12, 48n26, 51n34, 57n48, 97n67, 156n92, 158n98, 197n7, 204n54, 206n63
liberation, xv, 39n6, 43n16, 47n23, 123n5, 172, 209–10, 214–15, 217, 219. *See also* freedom
Liddell, Henry George, 88n45, 99n74, 171n32
Lindbeck, George, 60n58

liturgy, xiv, 5, 14–18, 28, 32, 34, 46, 48–50, 57, 62, 104–7, 184. *See also* eucharist; prayer; work; worship
Litwak, Kenneth Duncan, 145n64
Llanos, Connie, 66n3
Lloyd, Genevieve, 11n60
Logos, 14, 18n87, 64n68, 114. *See also* Word
Lohse, Bernhard, 210n6
Lord's Prayer, 34n2, 106n94, 161–62
Lossky, Vladimir, 65n72
love, 3, 18, 27, 40, 43n16, 50n34, 52, 59n55, 63n66, 77, 187, 233
Luke, Gospel of, 7n36, 25, 82n22, 143, 146n64, 148n66, 225
Luther, Martin, 26nn10–11, 43n14, 52n41, 85n32, 86n34, 204n55, 210
lynching, 93n55, 173, 230, 232–33
Lyons, George, 159–62

MacIntyre, Alasdair, 101n79
Mantzaridis, Georgios, 100n77
Margerie, Bertrand de, 65n72
Marion, Jean-Luc, 7n36, 48n26, 50n34, 62n64, 94n61
Mark, Gospel of, x, xiv, 26, 32, 163–65, 168–71, 173, 176–78, 179nn49–50, 188, 192, 224–25, 227, 231
Marroquin, Art, 66n3
martyrdom, xiv, 12n62, 24, 46, 58, 74, 88, 97, 125, 150, 151nn73–74, 153, 155, 157n96, 173n34, 179–80, 183, 185, 187n70, 188–92, 194, 217, 219–20, 223. *See also* church: martyr-church
Martha, 97, 147
Mary: Magdalene, 147; mother of Jesus, 24n6, 124, 136, 143, 144n61, 145–47, 185n60; sister of Martha, 97

Marx, Karl, 79
Matthew, Gospel of, 225, 230
Maundy Thursday, 34n2, 38–39. *See also* Holy Week
McCarthy, Cormac, 150n70
McClintock Fulkerson, Mary, 50n33
McCormack, Bruce, 64n68
Meier, John, 4n17
memory, 48, 50, 56, 80, 111, 112n5, 113, 115, 116n23, 135, 160, 191n80, 191n82, 208, 211, 226
Mendelssohn, Moses, 4n15
Merleau-Ponty, Maurice, 196n3, 203n52
Messiah. *See under* Jesus Christ
metanoia, 5, 32, 61, 64, 78, 99
metaphysics, x, xv, 10, 22
Metzger, Bruce, 58n52
Mexico, 2n4, 3n11, 67, 69–72
Meyendorff, John, 18n86, 32n26
migration. *See* immigration
Milbank, John, 6n25, 44n19, 50n34
Milton, John, 37
Moltmann, Jürgen, 25n7, 39n6, 49n29, 143n59, 203n47, 203n53, 206n62
Moriah, Mt., 128, 143–44, 213
Morrison, Jim, 140n54
Moses, 19, 44n19, 124, 132n26, 134n33, 135n38, 143–46, 174, 211–13, 215, 226–27
Myers, Ched, 165n10, 165n12, 167nn20–21, 168n23, 168n26, 170n29, 173nn33–34, 175n38, 177n44, 177n46

nature, 10, 11n60, 12, 14, 18, 24n6, 59, 64n70, 94, 136n42, 218, 221, 225. See also *physis*
Nava, Alex, 16n76
New Testament, 7n36, 43n16, 55n19, 53n42, 54n44, 58, 100n77, 136, 185n60

Niebuhr, Reinhold, 86n35
Nietzsche, Friedrich, 38n3, 61nn61–62, 92n49, 142n57, 151
nihilism, 6, 61, 142n57, 195
Norrell, Brenda, 66n3

obedience, 83n27, 133
Old Testament, 53n42, 58, 126n11, 145n64. *See also* Hebrew Bible
Olyan, Saul, 134n36, 141n55
ontology, 7, 10, 80n17, 97, 101n78, 123
Origen, 202
Otto, Rudolf, 25n8
ousia, 7, 205–6
Ouspensky, Leonid, 48n26

Pannenberg, Wolfhart, 25n7, 49n30, 80n16, 84n28
Parker, Emanuel, 66n3
Parmenides, 8n39, 10
particularity, 4, 6, 14, 18, 23, 39n6, 44n19, 45, 95–96
Paul, 6, 27, 29, 43–44, 86n35, 92, 99, 104, 125, 152, 189, 210, 227
peasant, 4, 31, 40, 53n42, 78, 122, 125–28, 131, 136–37, 143, 145–46, 148, 163, 165–66. *See also* poor
Pelikan, Jaroslav, 65n72, 122n4
Peña, Devon, 67n5
Perpetua and Felicity, 217n12, 223
Peter, 28–31, 40, 147–48, 172, 175, 177, 193, 220, 226
Phan, Peter, 4n17
philosophy, 9, 11n60, 57n48, 76n4, 98n72, 124, 157, 199n21, 207n65
physis, 10–14, 225
Pickstock, Catherine, 98n72, 100n77
Pilate, 13, 46n20, 153, 222, 229
Pinches, Charles, 56n47, 101n79, 179n48

Index

Pirsig, Robert, 196n2
Plato, Platonism 2n7, 8, 9n46, 9n48, 10, 58, 93, 96, 98, 140, 181, 216, 217n13, 218–19
Polycarp, 189–91, 194
poor, poverty, 1, 24, 26n7, 27, 30–32, 35, 42, 52, 66–67, 78, 87–88, 90, 128, 195, 228. *See also* Jesus Christ: and poor; peasants
prayer, x–xii, xiv, xvi, 3–4, 6, 9, 10n51, 12, 14–16, 19, 26n12, 29–31, 35–36, 42–43, 48n23, 51n37, 56–57, 61–63, 65, 72, 75–77, 81, 84, 87n36, 93n55; 99–101, 106, 122, 128, 137, 141, 145, 154n85, 187, 189–190, 194, 200n24, 216; of Jesus, 5, 54, 58, 92, 95, 137, 141, 145, 162, 167, 220, 226, 229; in liturgy, ix, 16–17, 34n2, 58, 107, 124, 198, 221. *See also* liturgy; worship
priest, 96n64, 117–18, 126n11, 131–34, 172, 174, 192, 222, 229
PTSD, 110n3, 111n4, 139

Quicunque Vult, 205n59

Rack, Henry, 86n34
Rad, Gerhard von, 27n13
Raphael, Melissa, 51n35
reason, rationality, xvi, 10–11, 16n77, 59n55, 60, 85, 98, 115n18, 116n23, 155n89
redemption, ix, 17, 64, 76–77, 106–7, 150, 151n75, 156, 158, 189n74. *See also* salvation
Reign of God, 18–19, 25, 41, 50n31, 55–56, 58–59, 63, 66n1, 85, 89n40, 92, 99, 106, 123, 145–48, 151, 153, 154n84, 167–68, 174, 176n43, 177, 179, 181, 187, 189n74, 229
resurrection, xiv–xv, 5, 16–17, 19, 28, 32, 39n5, 43n15, 44–46, 52n42, 53n42, 54, 56n46, 61, 62n64, 64–65, 75–76, 96–97, 99, 105–6, 124–25, 147–48, 150n72, 154n84, 156–57, 162, 166, 168n22, 168n25, 169n28, 173, 179–80, 185, 188, 189n75, 191, 216, 218, 227n29, 228. *See also* crucifixion; escatology
Revelation, book of, 25, 58, 122, 151n73, 151nn75–76, 152nn78–79, 153n82, 154n84, 155n88
Rich Young Ruler, 26n11, 28, 30–31, 156, 192, 227–28
Richardson, Cyril, 182n51, 182n53, 183n55, 184n57, 185n60
righteousness, 58n53, 65, 76, 83–85, 86n35, 88–89, 95, 96n64, 98–99, 143, 188n72, 189n76, 207
Riley, Gregory, 136n42
Ritschl, Albrecht, 9n47
Rogers, Eugene, 14n70, 24n6, 31n24, 146n65
Rogerson, John, 53n42
Romanos the Melodist, 45n6
Rome, 13, 150n73, 152nn79–80, 153–54, 170, 183–84, 188, 221–23, 227
Rothschild, Babette, 110n2, 113n8, 113n11, 114n12
Ruiz Marrujo, Olivia, 2n4, 6n29
Runyon, Theodore, 59n55
Rzeznik, Johnny, 74n1

Sabbath, 53, 81n18, 105, 106n90, 124, 141, 168
sacrament, 16n77, 28n17, 35, 56n46, 103–4, 106n91, 107–8

Index

sacrifice, 15, 17, 19, 22, 27–28, 35, 46, 51n37, 62–63, 93–95, 99n73, 101, 103, 117, 133n31, 134, 139, 141, 143n60, 148, 162, 187n70, 188, 189n74, 190, 203–5, 217
Saliers, Don, 47n23, 48n23, 51n36, 56n46, 106n93
salvation, ix, 30, 48, 59n56, 64, 90, 125, 137, 141, 150, 153–54, 178, 191, 194n86. *See also* redemption
Samuel, 124, 144–45
San Diego, xv, 54
Satan, 89, 167n18
Schmemann, Alexander, 15n71, 16n77, 17n80, 30n23, 47n22, 48n25, 51n36, 56n46, 59n57, 104n86, 106nn90–92, 106n94, 107n96, 107nn98–99, 108n100, 140n53
Schnackenburg, Rudolf, 50n32, 102n82
Schottroff, Luise, 16n78
Scripture(s), Holy, 13, 30, 38, 57–58, 59n55, 168n26, 176, 206. *See also* Hebrew Bible; New Testament; Old Testament
Schüssler Fiorenza, Elisabeth, 11n60
Senior, Donald, 1n2
Shiell, William, 164n4
silentio, Johannes de. *See under* Kierkegaard
sin, 49, 53n42, 58n53, 64, 85n31, 85n33, 86, 90–91, 114n14, 144, 146–47, 188n72, 203n52, 210n5, 220
slavery, 13n69, 30, 40, 53n42, 60, 62n64, 87, 93, 124, 128, 136–37, 145n64, 151, 166, 173n33, 186, 202, 210–12, 215–16, 218, 219n18
Socrates, xv, 3, 8, 97, 98n72, 181, 217–20, 222–23

Son (in Trinity), 15–16, 18n87, 28–29, 43, 50, 51n36, 52–53, 55, 92, 93n53, 96nn64–65, 100n76, 107, 145–46, 165–67, 171, 174–75, 185, 188n72, 191–93, 205nn58–59, 215–16, 220, 222–26, 229–31. *See also* Jesus Christ; Trinity
Song, C. S., 5n18, 35n4, 39n6
South Central Los Angeles, xv, 19, 66–67; South Central Farm, 19, 66n2, 67–73, 85, 90–91
Steinbeck, John, 78n10, 109n102
Steiner, George, xin4
Stoicism, 10n51, 126, 151n77, 223
Stookey, Noel Paul, 21n1
Summers, Isabella, 208n1
Suzuki, Daisetz Teitaro, 198n19
symbol, 59n57, 106n91, 123n5

Tanner, Kathryn, 39n5, 49n27, 50n34, 54n43
Taylor, Mark, 198n12, 203n52
Taylor, Otis, 232n3
Techau, Donna, 31n24
telos, 17, 45, 85, 163, 179
Tezozomoc, 67n5, 69, 71n11
theology, x–xiv, xvii, 4n17, 21, 24, 26, 28–29, 31–32, 44n19, 45–46, 47n23, 48, 50–57, 59–63, 65, 80n16, 85n32, 123, 155, 204n55, 210, 225
Thomas, 39n5, 45, 89n40, 96n65, 147
thought, xii, 11, 26–28, 51, 82n64, 63–65. *See also* brain
Tillich, Paul, 9n47
Tolstoy, Leo, 140n52
Tracy, David, 6n31
tradition, 2n3, 12, 22, 56, 59n55, 72, 86, 88, 101n79, 105n88, 165n10
Traub, Helmut, 27n13
Travis, Merle, 5n23

259

Index

Trinity, 15, 18, 29, 32, 51n36, 52n42, 53n42, 205n59. *See also* Father; Son; Holy Spirit
truth, 49n31, 50n31
Tyson, Ann Scott, 112n7

virtue, 7, 97–101, 172, 179n49, 219n18

Waetjen, Herman, 164n4, 165nn11–12, 166n15, 166n17, 167n20
Wainwright, Geoffrey, 47n22
Walz, Jesce, 77n5
Ward, Graham, 64n19
Ware, Kallistos, 84n28
Welch, Florence, 208n1
Wesley, John, 24, 26, 28n19, 29n20, 32n25, 33, 51n37, 58n53, 59n55, 64n69, 86n34, 99n76, 105n88, 185n61, 194n86
Western Civilization, xii, 10–11, 44n19, 45, 101, 116, 128, 140, 181, 217n13
Whitehead, Alfred North, 7n34, 10n55, 101n80
Whitfield, Joshua, 173n34, 175n40, 187n70, 191n80, 192n83, 194nn86–87
wholeness, 11, 19, 98, 129n21, 131–32, 134n36, 138, 139n51, 140, 143, 146, 167n21, 189n75

Wire, Antoinette Clark, 163n3, 164n4, 164n6, 165n10
Wittgenstien, Ludwig, 2n7
Wolff, Hans Walter, 4n14, 175n39, 196n1
Word (in the Trinity), 18n86, 90, 96–98, 101–2, 230. *See also* Logos
work, xiv, 4, 15–17, 26n11, 32, 46, 53, 54n43, 55, 61, 78–83, 87, 89–92, 94–97, 101–4, 116–17, 122, 126, 178. *See also* liturgy
worship, 15, 28, 34, 47–48, 101n78. *See also* liturgy; prayer
Wright, N. T., 125n9, 152n80, 157n96

Xanthippe, 218
Xenophon, 218n18

Yoder, John Howard, 54n44, 64n70, 91n48, 105n89, 154n84
York, Tripp, 187n70, 188n73, 189nn74–75, 195n88
Young, Robin Darling, 155n87, 187n70

Zahniser, David, 66n3
Zizioulas, John, 205n60

www.ingramcontent.com/pod-product-compliance
Lightning Source LLC
Chambersburg PA
CBHW030612230426
43661CB00053B/1957